THE UNEASY
ALLIANCE

THE UNEASY ALLIANCE

Religion, Refugee Work, and U.S. Foreign Policy

J. Bruce Nichols

New York   Oxford
OXFORD UNIVERSITY PRESS
1988

Oxford University Press

Oxford   New York   Toronto
Delhi   Bombay   Calcutta   Madras   Karachi
Petaling   Jaya   Singapore   Hong Kong   Tokyo
Nairobi   Dar es Salaam   Cape Town
Melbourne   Auckland

and associated companies in
Berlin   Ibadan

Library of Congress Cataloging-in-Publication Data

Nichols, J. Bruce.
The uneasy alliance.

Bibliography: p.
Includes index.
1. United States—Foreign relations—1945–
2. Ecclesiastical law—United States. 3. Freedom of
religion—United States. 4. War victims—Legal status,
laws, etc. 5. Church and state—United States.
6. Humanitarianism. I. Title.
JX1417.N52 1988   327.73   87-17179
ISBN 0-19-504274-3

2 4 6 8 9 7 5 3 1

Printed in the United States of America
on acid-free paper

This book is dedicated to
BEATRICE
—and to Carissima, if she wants it

Acknowledgments

In the early stages of this research, one of the country's foremost experts in church/state questions said quite bluntly that despite his own manifest commitment to understanding their significance in the United States, he "wouldn't touch issues raised in U.S. church/state contacts abroad with a ten-foot pole." Having passed well beyond his proposed limit, I now understand what he meant.

This is one of those books that could never have been written or conceived by a single individual. The unfolding story of the role of religious institutions in U.S. foreign policy sprawls in dozens of directions at once, many of them highly sensitive, often only dimly visible. The selection of refugee matters as a case study grew from a two-day meeting of thirty religious, governmental, and legal experts held at the Carnegie Council (then known as the Council on Religion and International Affairs) in October 1981. From that point forward, it has been a collaborative process, involving an advisory committee, codirectors, project staff, and literally hundreds of people who have been active in refugee matters over the last forty-five years.

First things first. The Lilly Endowment, whose generous financial assistance made this book possible, deserves pride of place for creating the circumstances under which it was researched and written. Bob Lynn, Lilly's senior vice-president in charge of religion grants, knew full well that church/state issues in the context of foreign policy were potentially explosive, yet his commitment to a serious inquiry remained firm. Along with Lilly's financial assistance came the guidance of three scholars with their own interests in related fields: Jay Demerath, professor and chair of the Department of Sociology, University of Massachusetts, Amherst; John Mansfield of the Harvard Law School; and John Demos, professor of American history at Yale. At our initial planning conference sponsored by Lilly, papers were given by Ben Armstrong, National Religious Broadcasters; Eileen Egan, Catholic Relief Services; Duane Friesen, Bethel College; Paul McCleary, Church World Service; and James Scherer, Lutheran School of Theology at Chicago.

Two individuals served as codirectors of the research, suggesting contacts and lines of approach when my own resources ran dry. Fr. Tom Stransky, novice master of the Paulist Fathers and himself an expert on global Christian mission, unfailingly offered sage advice. Sharon Worthing Vaino, a New York attorney, consistently demonstrated a knowledge of church/state law that only a dedicated scholar could hope to approach. Both were available to steady my grasp when I needed help. An advisory committee met yearly for three years in order to prod and question our progress. The committee included Jerald C. Brauer, F. Marian Chambers, Wade Coggins, Eileen Egan, Philip M. Klutznick, Gene Stockwell, and Marilyn Zak.

In my actual research and writing, a host of people provided special assistance. Their contributions varied widely: whether in correspondence, archival assistance, scholarly pointers, brief but pointed interviews, sharing their own historical experience, or other means, each was invaluable. They included Leyda Barbieri, Cliff Benzel, Walt Bogdanich, Landrum Bolling, Jake Buhler, Bernard C. Confer, John Contier, Lawrence M. Dawson, Dale DeHaan, Arthur E. Dewey, Eugene Douglas, Naomi de Espinosa, Susan Forbes, Tom Fox, Edward McG. Gaffney, Dennis Gallagher, Keith Gingrich, Ken Hackett, Julia Hausermann, Tom Hawk, Dean Kelley, Paul Kittlaus, Anthony Koslowski, Susan Reid Lewis, Shep Lowman, Debbie Mace, Mark Malloch-Brown, Peg Mangum, Leon Marion, James Mac-Cracken, Jan Miller, Richard John Neuhaus, Stephen Nasitir, Edward M. O'Connor, Jim Pines, Margaret Potee, Robert Quinlan, Dean Francis M. Sayre, Arthur Simon, William M. Snyder, Mary Solberg, Bishop Edward E. Swanstrom, Clyde Taylor, Cyrus Vance, Gordon Walker, Ingrid Walter, Jerry Weaver, John F. Wilson, and Elliott Wright. A special mention must be made of the interest and support I received from Elizabeth Clark Reiss, historian, archivist, and former acting director of the American Council of Voluntary Agencies for Foreign Service. I would like also to acknowledge the assistance of many who asked that their assistance not be acknowledged. These included not only officials in governmental, intergovernmental, and religious bodies, but many refugees and foreign nationals who placed themselves at some risk by participating in this research. The final version of the events chronicled here is of course my own, and none of the people listed here should be held responsible.

Within the Carnegie Council itself I received constant encouragement and assistance. Robert J. Myers, President of the Carnegie Council, gave the project his support from beginning to end and insisted on a spirit of open inquiry and evaluation. Ulrike Klopfer and Eva Becker provided logistical and bookkeeping assistance. Several graduate students put in long hours as project interns or legal researchers. They included Paul Ellis, Dirk Forrister, Jack A. Jenkins, Sister Bernadette Kenney, Karen Knie, Lauren Lou, and David Schiedemantle, whose analysis of establishment clause issues was particularly helpful.

From their first knowledge of this project, staff at the New York offices of Oxford University Press have been committed to seeing it through as a book. First credit here goes to senior editor Cynthia Read, whose support and interest have been constant. As the book progressed, associate editor Susan Meigs helpfully rooted out excess in various guises, and Adrienne Mayor offered highly competent copy editing from distant Montana. Laura Brown and her trade marketing staff were equally professional in their contributions. It has been a pleasure to work with them all. Legal librarian Tamar Raum compiled the thorough index.

This book would never have appeared without the dedication of Linda Griffin Kean, my research associate at the Carnegie Council throughout the course of the project. Without her initiative at many critical points we could not have assembled the collection of archival materials necessary for this book. She shared with me from the beginning a sense of the importance of the topic, and her studied commitment and sense of humor combined to make her invaluable.

Finally, I offer my grateful thanks to my wife Beatrice, who persevered at the difficult points and was always there for the joyous and amusing ones as well. This book is affectionately dedicated to her.

B. N.

Contents

Acronyms

The following acronyms are used for organizations and institutions that appear in the text.

AAEJ   American Association for Ethiopian Jews
ACVA   American Council of Voluntary Agencies [for Foreign Service]
AFSC   American Friends Service Committee
AID   Agency for International Development
AJC   American Jewish Committee
AJDC   American Jewish Joint Distribution Committee
ARA   American Relief Administration
BRC   British Refugee Council
CAMA   Christian and Missionary Alliance
CARE   originally Cooperative American Remittances to Europe
CCSDPT   Committee for the Coordination of Services to Displaced Persons
              in Thailand
CEDEN   National Evangelical Committee for Emergencies and
              Development [Honduras]
CRALOG   Council of Relief Agencies Licensed for Operation in Germany
CRIA   Council on Religion and International Affairs [now the Carnegie
              Council on Ethics and International Affairs]
CRS   Catholic Relief Services
CVAV   Council of Voluntary Agencies in Vietnam
HIAS   Hebrew Immigration Aid Society
ICEM   (later ICM) Intergovernmental Committee for [European]
              Migration
ICMC   International Catholic Migration Commission
IGC   Intergovernmental Committee for Political Refugees
INS   Immigration and Naturalization Service
IRC   International Rescue Committee
IRO   International Refugee Organization
IVS   International Voluntary Services

NCWC	National Catholic War Council (later National Catholic Welfare Commission)
OFRRO	Office of Foreign Relief and Rehabilitation Operations
ORT	Organization for Relief and Training
PACPR	President's Advisory Committee on Political Refugees
PWRCB	President's War Relief Control Board
SAWSO	Seventh-Day Adventist World Service Organization
SSRAP	Southern Sudan Refugee Assistance Project
UNBRO	United Nations Border Relief Operation
UNHCR	United Nations High Commissioner for Refugees
UNRRA	United Nations Relief and Rehabilitation Administration
UNRWA	United Nations Relief and Works Agency
USO	United Service Organization
WRB	War Refugee Board
WRS	War Relief Services (later Catholic Relief Services)

THE UNEASY
ALLIANCE

Introduction

When the subject of this research ("When Church and State Go Abroad") was announced in 1981, a friend not much interested in the role of religion in public life today commented dryly, "How abstract." In the years that followed I have had many occasions to reflect on the implied judgment that religion and religious institutions have precious little to do with the intricacies of American foreign policy. Her comment may reflect a majority view, both then and now, that religion has taken a back seat to more powerful political, economic, and military interests which today mold America's relations with the rest of the world. In a world of power politics and vast economic struggles, casting the American church/state issue in an international framework seemed to her a somewhat academic issue.

I have no desire in this book to challenge the importance of such competing interests in the formation of U.S. foreign policy. What I do hope to demonstrate, however, is that institutions representing explicitly religious goals and communities play an active and expanding role in determining America's ties with the rest of the world. This role has been obvious in many times and places, most recently in famine and drought crises in Africa. The topic examined here, overseas assistance to refugee populations, is one of the most active areas of joint effort between the U.S. government and U.S.-based religious institutions. Under the broad banner of humanitarian assistance, religious voluntary agencies and other private organizations have carried the major burden of providing assistance to the growing population of refugees around the world. The purpose of this book is to place the post-World War II history of this cooperative humanitarianism in the context of American church/state traditions, to understand the impact of the postwar political climate on religious participation in government-sanctioned humanitarianism, and to examine the role of church/state law in these evolving relationships.

I will return again and again to the evolution of relations between the institutions of religion and the institution of government. Domestically, these relations are governed by a long legal and cultural tradition embodied in the First Amendment's religion clauses, which state that "Congress shall make no law respecting an establishment of religion, nor prohibiting the free exercise thereof." Often loosely translated as the "separation of church and state," this tradition has come under increasing strain in the pluralistic development of modern welfare societies. The American public has periodically praised and damned the courts for its church/state decisions, many of which puzzle experts. To the average citizen in the 1980s, church/state law appears to arise from a welter of inconsequential matters (the right to display a Christmas crèche on public land), or overly technical issues (categories of permissible government aid to religious schools), all of limited scope. However, the courts have not directly altered their highly permissive stance on the participation of religious institutions in state welfare programs—the area of greatest growth in church/state cooperation—since 1899. To a large degree, welfare institutions (such as hospitals) have escaped strong pressures toward church/state separation; the mutually overlapping interests of religion and government in meeting human need have been too great. The very language of "humanitarianism" grows from the common efforts of private and public officials to meet needs common to all.

The irony of this apparent trivializing and overcodifying of church/state law is that the larger questions of political engagement of religion and religious involvement in government—the matters of greatest concern to the framers of the Constitution—have been lost in a forest of small timber. As with the increase of religious involvement in domestic social welfare, the courts have paid virtually no attention to the growth and significance of church/state issues overseas.[1] This book attempts to bring this broad and early function of the Constitution's religion clauses—assuring the independence of the institutions of government and religion—back into focus in the context of America's international foreign policy goals. By concentrating on one area in which church and state have actively cooperated overseas, we will examine the meaning of domestic church/state traditions abroad in an era in which America finds itself self-consciously cast as a great power. In the words of Hans Morgenthau, both the United States and the Soviet Union are today promoting their versions of a new nationalistic universalism, a "secular religion, universal in its interpretation of the nature and destiny of man." Traditional religions (chiefly Protestant, Catholic, and Jewish) at times support and at times oppose the manifestations of this secular religion in foreign policy. In the field of refugee work since World War II, the institutions of church and state have been found in both intimate affairs and unrequited loves.

Refugees are by definition at home in a no-man's-land, an observation made by career American diplomat George McGhee as he saw hundreds of thousands of Palestinians left homeless following the formation of Israel in 1948. This notion of being at home in a no-man's-land captures first of all the dilemma of refugees fleeing from their homes; of children, families, even entire peoples cut off from their roots and forced to adapt to temporary homes where they are frequently unwanted strangers. Whether the population in question is Palestinian or Afghan, Salvadoran or Nicaraguan, the sober judgment of a prominent Episcopal priest active in postwar refugee affairs applies: "These people have become the pawns of international political tensions." Indeed, refugees inhabit a no-man's-land in more than the literal sense. Politically, they are not an independent problem requiring independent solutions. In addressing their homelessness, except in the increasingly difficult solution of third country resettlement, the political problems that caused them to flee must first be solved.

McGhee's identification of a no-man's-land might also refer specifically to the new status of refugees in the world after the upheavals of World War II. In many ways refugees today are singled out for special humanitarian assistance, ranging from medical care, food, and housing to skills training, development activity and global resettlement. All of this is delivered virtually cost-free to the refugees, but the cost to governments, particularly the U.S. government, is substantial, reaching the half-billion dollar per year mark in the early 1980s. For all of these acts of globally based (though largely Euro-American) welfare, the lives of the majority of today's roughly 10 million political refugees are confined to an archipelago of camps removed from the broader community of nations. They have in recent years included a million Ethiopians and Eritreans in camps dotting eastern Sudan; 3 million Afghan refugees camped along the northwest border of Afghanistan in Pakistan; 15,000 to 20,000 Salvadorans in Honduras. Within a two-week period in 1985, 250,000 Cambodians crowded across the border in Thailand, yet such movements today are so frequent that the exodus drew little attention in the press. Yearning for their own homes, these refugees are trapped, victims of political instabilities in a no-man's-land of agony, insurgency, and interminable waiting.

Much of the concern and care for refugees that has been marshaled by governments in the modern era has its roots in religious traditions that embody commitment to the stranger and the oppressed. This commitment has not always led to the incorporation of refugees into secure social and political surroundings, as millions would readily attest. In fleeing persecution, refugees have found themselves stranded in a realm of conflicting jurisdictions, politics, tribes, and nations. Acting on theological commandments within the Judeo-Christian tradition, religious bodies have consistently stepped forward as logical sources of care and assistance for these homeless poor. Yet the search for durable solutions remains dependent on the interest and goodwill of governments.

Through this involvement with refugees, churches and the U.S. government have discovered another perpetual no-man's-land, that political arena in which religious and governmental claims to final authority joust their way to public legitimacy. Humanitarian work abroad with refugees after World War II was conceived of as an obvious zone of cooperation between the government and private religious interests. The refugee cause fused the best of religious emotion and patriotic fervor, reminding Americans that their ideals still lived within the great institutions of government and voluntary religious service. The refugee camps of Europe and the Far East became the crucible for America's postwar conscience; to abandon the refugees would have been tantamount to abandoning America's moral patrimony. Thus in the ruins of Europe, home of all the forms of church/state alliance that the Founding Fathers had sought to avoid, began one of the more adventurous church/state affairs in the history of the republic.

It has not been an easy road. As hopes for addressing the "root causes" of postwar refugee movements fade under the current global political stalemate, there is less and less room for idealized versions of refugee aid. The refugees are today's international victims, made homeless by regional and proxy conflicts often aggravated by the wider struggle between democracy and communism. Often, as was true of hundreds of thousands of Ugandans living outside their country in the early 1980s, they are the victims of their own nation's internal inability to govern itself. Tribal and racial disputes that have endured for centuries—one thinks again of the Palestinians caught between the Israelis and the Arab states—generate new political wrinkles today when victims of such disputes cross internationally recognized boundaries, often placing themselves under the jurisdiction of hostile governments. Such long-term root causes will not be settled by international humanitarian assistance, however, well-meaning.

I treat refugee work overseas as a case study of a need that has drawn modern American institutions of religion and government together beyond the borders of the nation. The United States' response to overseas refugee populations became the focus of our study on the recommendation of religious, governmental, and legal specialists who assembled at the New York headquarters of the Carnegie Council on Ethics and International Affairs (then known as the Council on Religion and International Affairs or CRIA) in October 1981. For two days, we met and discussed activities that bring religious bodies and the U.S. government into contact in the field of foreign policy. The majority of some thirty participants chose the refugee field as the best focus, and the wisdom of this choice will, I hope, be borne out in the body of this work. In the 1940s refugee work became emblematic of American commitments to international humanitarianism. It was also at that time the primary means by which religious bodies began to build a role for their own institutions within the realm of postwar U.S. foreign policy. Once the refugee relief agencies had a track record of voluntary action and fund raising, they could make their case for using direct government assistance in their overseas work.

At the Carnegie Council's 1981 conference, religious leaders explored the full range of overseas activities that today engage church and state, including missionary work, refugees and hunger relief, development, telecommunications, policy formation, and related lobbying activities. While it was clear that no single study could adequately cover all of these activities, it was also obvious that any one activity sponsored by religious agencies might easily include some or all of the others. Refugee work, for instance, increasingly overlaps with development concerns and with efforts by religious bodies to have their goals incorporated in legislation passed by Congress. Individual agencies such as the American Friends Service Committee or Catholic Relief Services commonly provide services to refugees and undertake broader disaster relief and development projects. Therefore, while our inquiries concentrate on overseas refugee work, additional material relevant to a broad understanding of church/state relations abroad has been included.[2]

Even as the focus on refugee work emerged in the planning of this study, it was clear that it would not be possible to write an exhaustive analysis of church/state matters in even this limited field. Merle Curti, the eminent historian of overseas American philanthropy, noted for instance that from 1939 to 1945 nearly 600 private voluntary organizations—many of them religiously based—operated overseas.[3] This book necessarily presents a representative picture of church/state concerns that have arisen since World War II. I draw on a variety of sources: agency and governmental files and archives, personal collections, interviews, memoirs, and other period materials.

The book addresses the major refugee efforts of Protestants, Catholics, and Jews during World War II and in the postwar period. In choosing church/state dimensions of contemporary refugee situations abroad, I attempted to give an accurate sense of the development of refugee work from the European setting of the 1940s to the global scale of the 1980s. Since the book concentrates on the evolution of church/state relations, it should not be seen as an effort to provide an exhaustive history of the institutions involved or of the refugee problem itself. In some cases—such as the struggle of Jewish agencies to move the U.S. government to act to save the lives of European Jews during World War II—exhaustive documentation has already been assembled and analyzed.[4]

The Project on Church and State Abroad has gathered three basic types of material for analyzing current church/state relations. The first consists of historical research. While the book concentrates on refugee assistance after World War II, earlier precedents for cooperation between church and state abroad are also considered. It is in examining this history that any sense of the abstractness of church/state ties abroad fades. The project examined available material from the archives of both governmental and private agencies and enjoyed a particularly fruitful relationship with the American Council of Voluntary Agencies in Foreign Service, which served as a coordinator of private voluntary foreign aid from 1943 to 1984. During the early 1980s, numerous private and public officials whose careers paralleled the growth of postwar international humanitarianism provided personal recollections and judgments, a number of which have been included.

Second, Honduras, Sudan, and Thailand were selected for special case studies. These three countries reflect the geographical, political, and cultural diversity in which Americans who serve refugees abroad today find themselves. In each of these countries, interviews were conducted with refugees, voluntary agency workers, and embassy, governmental, and intergovernmental officials to determine the nature and purpose of church/state cooperation. Every effort was made to explore different sides of particular questions. Despite the limitations on research of this type, it was our belief that an adequate understanding of the problem of refugees and the institutions of religion and government that serve them could not emerge without some representative picture of the current state of affairs. The bulk of documentation in this book on current refugee problems comes from this research, but I have also included occasional examples from other countries which may help clarify contemporary church/state relations abroad.

It is these ties between religion, the state, and foreign policy with which the third area of research, church/state legal issues, was concerned. Refugee specialists may be surprised to find that the standard matters of refugee and humanitarian law—international conventions, immigration statutes, United Nations mandates and the like—are not at the heart of the legal questions posed here. Instead, refugee matters are treated as the prism through which we examine how church/state relations in foreign affairs have progressed. Refugee law, while it does play a role in setting ground rules for cooperation between private and public officials, answers none of the institutional or civil liberty questions that arise in relations between church bodies and the U.S. government abroad. Our question is not what role do foreign governments have in restricting the religious activities of Americans living under their jurisdiction, nor do we attempt to compare U.S. church/state traditions with those of other countries. It is much more direct: what is the role of U.S. law in regulating the overseas contacts between U.S. government officials, programs, and policies and U.S. citizens and agencies with religious affiliations?

This question is approached from three perspectives, two of which stem from the application of the religion clauses of the First Amendment. The first clause, originally written to prevent the establishment of a state church, prohibits laws that "establish" religion. In the modern era, there has been increasing concern about various forms of governmental assistance to religion. Though the courts have not directly addressed funding matters of refugee assistance from a church/state perspective, the levels of such assistance are substantial; by the early 1980s the Agency for International Development was annually allocating some $600 million in various forms to private agencies, most of which had religious origins and purposes. Hundreds of millions more were spent at home and abroad through religious agencies serving refugees.

Domestically the free exercise of religion has been both protected and limited; U.S. citizens may rightly wonder whether similar boundaries apply overseas. Many refugee workers interviewed abroad found such questions abstract in the face of the needs of the refugees they served. Others who suddenly had their visas revoked, religious material banned, or programs curtailed by unexpected U.S. government directives felt otherwise.

Do such protections and restrictions of religious liberty apply abroad? Though I reach specific conclusions concerning the value of the First Amendment's religion clauses, this third fundamental question about the role of the law abroad is in many ways the most troubling of all. In the modern era, reasons of state such as "national security," "compelling state interests," and the like are invoked to protect and guide the foreign policies of various U.S. administrations. The refugee problem itself, and hence cooperation in refugee assistance between church and state, has often followed the contours of the U.S.-Soviet stalemate. Sometimes the civil liberties of U.S. citizens have been swept aside to pursue broad national interests. In these settings domestic and international law have proven to be of limited value. Moral and political leaders have found themselves face to face in a no-man's-land somewhere beyond the rule of law, yet it is still a land in which the moral content of decisions looms large. In refugee work all parties try to act in the name of humanitarianism, which provides a common framework for cooperative efforts, but this is a fragile framework indeed. This book explores the evolving efforts of all such parties, and evaluates the contributions of American church/state traditions beyond the nation's borders.

1

Overseas Is Different

The mingling of morality and political calculation has been a standard aspect of American foreign policy from its early days. Whatever the content of that morality at any given time, political leaders have always needed to resort to religious values and language to build public support for U.S. policy. Before World War II most foreign policy bore the imprimatur of the dominant Protestant culture: righteous, somehow separated from the world and its values, yet still willing to assert a connection between virtue, hard work, and success. The agents of government and organized, largely Protestant, religion carried on their labors abroad in relative independence, secure that they were after all members of the same family.

With World War II this equation dissipated. Catholics began to use the political clout that went with being the largest religious body in the nation; in no field did they become so quickly dominant as in private foreign aid and refugee work. Jews pressed their new preoccupation with Israel, adding a major new item at the intersection of religion and foreign policy. Before we begin examining these and other important factors in detail, we need to plot a path through the complex issues that intersect when church and state go abroad.

From Indian Nations to Captive Nations

When the United States' ties to the rest of the world are examined by historians, it is often in the context of the "special mission" of America. Thomas Paine wrote that the Revolution "was not made for America alone, but for all mankind." John Quincy Adams, drawing on the early Puritan vision of the American covenant as "a city on a hill," said that it was not America's job to impose its form of government on others, but to attract them by the force of our example. Abraham Lincoln revered the Declaration of Independence for "giving liberty, not alone to the people of this country, but hope to the world for all future time."[1] The immense enthusiasm for foreign missions that appeared among Protestants in the nineteenth century drew on this belief in America's special missionary role.

Such factors, combined with various degrees of colonial religious establishment before and immediately after independence, produced an early mingling of the missions of church and state beyond the boundaries of the colonies. From its first days, the Continental Congress employed missionaries to conduct governmental business under treaties with the Indian Nations. The missionaries' state tasks continued after the ratification of the Constitution and the Bill of Rights, and were not thought to violate the establishment clause. When church and state shared common interests outside the United States—in this instance, civilizing and Christianizing the North American Indian Nations—it made sense for the government to work with, even to fund religious missions. This cooperative spirit between church and state in Indian affairs extended well into the twentieth century and provides a historical precedent for contemporary church/state ties abroad. To the modern eye schooled in the post-World War II understanding of church/state law, such efforts to fulfill America's mission to the wider world have always involved stronger ties between religion and government than the religion clauses of the Constitution appear to sanction.

Before 1939, religious institutions were relatively free to carry on independent mission and service activities abroad. To government officials, adventurism within the American voluntary community overseas during the Spanish Civil War meant that more control over the actions of Americans abroad would be necessary. Already faced with an existing refugee problem and the prospect of massive wartime relief needs, officials of the Roosevelt administration realized they had to support religious agencies to achieve U.S. objectives in Europe. In 1939, Franklin Roosevelt announced to aides that he believed that the refugee problem in particular could be solved "on a broad religious basis."

Cooperation with the U.S. government during World War II formed the basis for subsequent postwar agreements between church groups and government agencies abroad. Using the concept of the "three faiths of America"—Protestantism, Catholicism, and Judaism—government and religious authorities built firm cooperative ties. These included religious participation in intergovernmental humanitarian projects and distribution of the nation's surpluses and goods. Some of the government institutions that came into existence then to regulate the activities of private humanitarian agencies still function today. Their main purpose is to assure that private agencies maintain coordination with government programs and policies.

Thus began a period of some twenty-five years of close bonds between the government and relief societies established by the various churches and religious groups. While many church/state ties from the World War II era still exist, others have been lost along the way. Some religious bodies drew back from the politicizing of refugee programs in the 1950s; others enthusiastically participated in early efforts to encourage refugees to flee the Soviet Union's "captive nations" of Eastern Europe. The Vietnam War raised new concerns in many religious circles over the value of continued participation in programs identified with U.S. foreign policy. Agencies that formerly approved of government aid to religiously sponsored relief have withdrawn, and groups formerly wary of government aid now clamor to show that they too are eligible.

To speak of "eligibility," however, is to get ahead of our story. When during the world wars the international magnitude of human needs began to outstrip the capabilities of either the civil or religious authorities working alone, men and women of goodwill began to establish institutions and pursue methods of cooperation that would respect the integrity of all parties involved. This has not been an easy task and the issues, despite my friend who found them "abstract," are concrete. They concern the continued allegiance of organized religion to America's global strategies and purposes, which, since World War II, have regularly been given over to countering the Soviet Union's nationalistic universalism with our own.

Humanitarianism and National Security

Examining this allegiance between political and moral authorities from a church/ state perspective has not meant simply applying domestic church/state law to interactions with refugees. To begin with, religious involvement with refugees has regularly been classified by government (and by many religious bodies themselves) as "humanitarian" rather than "religious." This has come about for a variety of reasons, not the least of which is the government's disinterest in funding religious activities or churches. There are also abundant historical reasons for this use of terms. In its earliest stages refugee work was dominated by religious bodies; today these groups have been joined by numerous secular organizations; humanitarian language helped meet a need for describing shared objectives among different parties. To avoid conflicts extraneous to actual care for refugees, and because of the church/state concerns just mentioned, the work of the private sector has come to be called "humanitarian," a term that has broader currency in a pluralistic society than the vaguely sectarian adjective "religious."

In the mid-1940s humanitarianism was redefined; there was a clear need to describe the activity in which both private and public authorities engaged. First, humanitarian activity, whether directed at flood victims, refugees, or other groups, means meeting the immediate needs of the victims. Further, the aid must remain politically neutral, and its distribution must not be discriminatory.[2]

This matter of terminology is not inconsequential; in the international political arena pressure is constantly exerted on care-givers to compromise their commitment to these principles. The national security rationale first developed by the Truman administration placed most refugee matters squarely within the framework of the rivalry between the West and the Soviet Union. The years since World War II have demonstrated that the ground rules for humanitarian work are no stronger than the governments that enforce them, and no weaker than the principles of the individuals who carry out the work.

At times the U.S. government has responded favorably to theological and political arguments for aiding refugees which were not directly tied to U.S. policy toward the Soviet Union. On balance, however, national security concerns rather than humanitarian or theological objectives have charted the course of government policy since World War II. In practice this has meant a government whose commitment could hardly be called "politically neutral."

A current example will indicate how far the balance has tilted away from strict humanitarianism toward security concerns. By the mid-1980s 2 million to 3 million Afghan refugees crossed into northern and western Pakistan, forming the largest concentration of refugees in the world. The United States and Pakistani governments have restricted the traditional presence of voluntary agencies and at the same time heavily armed the refugees to resist the Soviet presence in Kabul. The crisis facing religious agencies and others helping refugees today springs in large part from strategic geopolitical game plans centered within areas of refugee concentrations, areas that were once considered centers of a more neutral humanitarian assistance.

The postwar history of church/state involvement with refugees demonstrates that the imbalance between security and humanitarian objectives did not occur overnight. Church/state involvement abroad has been determined more by administrative decisions in government and in religious bodies than by a formal application of judicial decisions regarding church/state relations. Those administrative decisions usually are determined on the basis of the relative power of contending parties. Thus, it is no surprise that government priorities—usually based on national security—have come to dominate. "The moral limitations upon the struggle for power on the international scene," said Morgenthau, "are weaker today than they have been at any time in the history of the modern state system."[3] Yet, humanitarian needs have not disappeared, they have expanded, and they are renegotiated between private relief and the government with every new refugee crisis.

Into the Field

The field studies of church/state involvement abroad were selected to illustrate the significant post-Vietnam difficulties that face those who seek to aid refugees: the cold war security issues; the flight of thousands of people across national boundaries and subsequent debates over what constitutes proper care; and the new predominance of refugees from impoverished regions of the so-called Third World. Refugee problems created decades ago persist today in the form of the 2 million to 3 million Jews living in the Soviet Union or the 2 million Palestinians living in foreign camps or Israeli-occupied territories. In the 1980s, however, attention has shifted to refugee populations of Central America, Africa, and Asia. Thus we will look at American involvement in Honduras, the Sudan, and Thailand. In each country, refugee assistance (whether it came bilaterally or indirectly through the office of the UN High Commissioner for Refugees) expressed a strong U.S. strategic commitment to these countries of first asylum.

The fall of South Vietnam brought a new term into use among refugee workers: "mass exodus." Tens or hundreds of thousands of people fleeing their homes became a common sight for television viewers in America during the Vietnam War. During this period it was common for the populations of entire regions to cross national boundaries to avoid civil disturbances. When countries of first asylum are unable to feed and care for their own native population, refugees are an added burden. In Asia and Central America, there were new pressures on the United States to resettle refugees.

This often meant diff.cult judgments by U.S. officials. Which individuals actually qualify as refugees? Which standards should be applied: domestic provisions, UN definitions, or some combination of the two? Could individuals qualify as political refugees, or were they only economic migrants (and hence not entitled to special treatment from the U.S. government)? How would the relations between the U.S. government and political leaders in the countries generating mass exodus affect decisions on the status of the asylum seekers as refugees? Well before governments can answer such questions, religious agencies step in to care for the basic and immediate needs of the homeless refugees.

The arrangements between religious agencies and the U.S. government to help refugees after World War II were intended as a temporary expedient. Under extraordinary circumstances, church and state made common cause abroad. Today, that alliance has become established. Specialized religious agencies handle the emergencies of mass exodus on short notice and are now among the world's largest private relief efforts. For those who work abroad with refugees, their assignment invariably includes caring for the human wreckage stranded by political miscalculations. When there is no relief agency in a specific trouble spot, the United States has in recent years often worked with traditional missionary agencies. Though they may lack the secular approach deemed appropriate for receiving government assistance, such agencies often bring detailed and invaluable experience of local conditions and populations.

Protestant, Catholic, and Jewish Approaches

Judeo-Christian religion, while united on the broad goals of humanitarian assistance to refugees, has developed a variety of distinctive styles relating to U.S foreign policies. Protestants have been the most reluctant of the three religious traditions to accept government funds for refugees and relief abroad, an attitude that often stems from fidelity to their understanding of the religion clauses of the Constitution. The Protestant vision of the postwar world emphasized gradual expansion toward internationalism and universalism in politics and religion, and initially took little notice of the military and political questions posed by Stalinism and the cold war.

To help this new era emerge, the mainline Protestant churches took an independent, prophetic, and frequently critical stance toward American foreign policy, even though many were caught up in the anticommunism of the early 1950s. In much Protestant thought, freedom to take an independent stance toward the government is best maintained by the separation of church and state. Short-term cooperative ventures, such as the wartime refugee problem, were permissible exceptions since they were carried out in the spirit of emergency humanitarianism. As short-term cooperation gradually shifted to regular government assistance, Protestants and others found themselves in difficult waters.

For many reasons Catholic and Jewish agencies have taken a much more aggressive approach toward securing government aid than Protestant groups. Protestant leaders who favor government aid often have been discouraged from accepting it by fellow Protestants skittish over church/state questions. The modern forms of state response to refugee problems—including large-scale facilities and international movement of populations—originated in the early lobbying of Jews and their supporters. This role was thrust upon the Jewish community by events in the 1920s and 1930s in Europe and Russia. The Catholic church, with broad experience in caring for immigrants to the United States in the early part of the century, quickly adapted their social skills during World War II to techniques of refugee aid developed by those serving Jewish refugees in care and resettlement work.

Such enthusiasm for government aid among Catholics and Jews did not go unnoticed in Protestant circles. The late 1940s brought Protestant indignation over Catholic efforts to take advantage of government assistance in overseas work. At home Paul Blanshard, founder of Protestants and Other Americans United for the Separation of Church and State, called attention to the disproportionate benefits flowing to Catholic health and welfare institutions domestically through such legislation as the Hill-Burton hospital bill of 1946. More Catholics than Protestants qualified for resettlement in the U.S. under postwar legislation—a victory for Catholic lobbying in Washington. Jewish religious and political leaders in the United States sought to avoid undue emphasis on direct government assistance to Jewish refugees abroad, fearing a backlash of anti-Semitism. In the rough-and-tumble free market of private and governmental assistance to refugees, all agencies, religious or otherwise, worried constantly that their place in the field might be usurped. The potential for religiously based political divisions growing from such quarrels lies as close to the surface today as it did in the 1940s.

Evangelism and Political Advocacy

Also troubling to exponents of refugee humanitarianism has been the explicit evangelism and political advocacy on the part of many delivering assistance. Evangelism, defined as direct witness to religious faith, has long been central to international missionary efforts. It remains an element in many Christian relief efforts today. Throughout the late 1970s in Thailand, for example, the presence of missionary societies among the private sector agencies raised the question of the role of missionary activity among refugee populations. Many UN officials in the country recalled the efforts of a Catholic missionary order in the mid-1970s to baptize Laotian refugees in northern Thailand before they were issued food ration cards. Again and again, religiously motivated workers in Protestant and Catholic agencies were reminded by UN and U.S. officials that religion per se—specifically evangelism and forms of direct religious witness such as Bible classes—were not welcome in the Thai refugee camps. Yet in most cases it was religious motivation that had inspired relief workers to travel halfway around the earth to serve their fellow human beings.

One UN official who had worked in Thailand for a secular relief agency described the dilemma in personal terms:

> Think of a young nurse who has come to Thailand to help refugees, and finds herself on the night shift. Alone in a ward in the camp hospital, she is met by a Cambodian woman crying hysterically over the loss of her entire family under Pol Pot. She is not physically ill, but mentally she has no reason to go on living. Facing this wrenching human need, who am I to say that this nurse has no right to tell her Cambodian friend that Jesus Christ is the only reality she has ever met capable of responding fully to her suffering?[4]

This view is hardly shared by all government and intergovernment authorities. Far more common is the view that the mass exodus of human beings from their homes and livelihoods creates a situation far too complex to be further confused with foreign religious elements, particularly Christian evangelism. Religious leaders counter by pointing to the presence of indigenous Christians among the refugees, but on the whole public officials and some relief agency workers believe that humanitarian care-givers should be free to practice their religion as long as efforts to communicate its content to others are officially controlled.

Immediately after World War II the European character of the refugee problem called forth Protestant, Catholic, and Jewish participation. Adherents of these three faiths in Europe experienced the tragic effects of the war; activating their fellow believers in the United States to care for them was an obvious and effective strategy. But in the years that followed, America's religious relief agencies found themselves involved in areas of the world where different religious traditions predominated. American Mennonites and Quakers served Palestinians in the Middle East; the National Council of Churches aided Hindu and Muslim refugees during the partition of India in 1947; and by 1949 Catholic Relief Services had become active in the French colonies in Indo-China, particularly Vietnam, just when Western governments were seeking to prevent communists from taking advantage of the power vacuum created by the French exodus. With Jewish relief activities concentrating on the establishment of Israel, American Christian agencies continued to expand their services beyond the range of needy European Christians. This expansion was largely based on the humanitarian doctrine of nondiscrimination in the provision of care.

The question of religion and national security was remarkably joined in refugee matters in the Sudan in the 1980s. Most U.S. voluntary agencies were initially wary of involvement in Sudan, despite the desperate conditions of its 1 to 1.3 million refugees, including Ugandans in the south, Chadians in the west, and Eritreans and Ethiopians in the east. Some Sudanese officials, themselves influenced by the Islamic fundamentalism of Iran, believed that the religious relief agencies were only the latest version of a sort of religious invasion. The Muslim Khartoum government in 1983 and 1984 was in no mood to encourage the participation of religious outsiders in the Sudan. With the imposition of Islamic law in August 1983, Christians in the southern part of Sudan feared for their own safety under their Islamic authorities. It was a period in which the effects of U.S. support for the Khartoum government were having unforeseen impacts in the Christian south, where U.S. religious groups—most funded directly or indirectly by the U.S. government—were taking an active part in the care of Ugandan refugees.

That summer Mr. R, a provincial executive of the Anglican church, sat in his office in Juba, the major city in southern Sudan. His church was involved in a refugee project funded by the State Department. "I am just one humble man in the middle of Africa," he said, "but I want you to tell the people in Washington that it is in their interest to learn to listen to people other than themselves. It seems that as a part of the policy of separation of church and state you have in your democracy, Christians separate their Christianity from their politics. This gives us a foreign policy from the United States that is not affected by Christian values. This is puzzling to us, as we very proudly think of America as a Christian nation."

Of course, religion is not always separated from politics in the United States, and Mr. R's church was benefiting from a U.S. government project. His point, however, was that the refugee project apparently had been conceived without reference to the local religious and political setting. Disputes between Khartoum and Washington over the proper church/state ties (Muslim authorities in Khartoum objected to local church involvement in the refugee project) had aggravated tensions between Sudanese Christians and Muslims. "People in the refugee camps will not be helped by people in Washington," he said. "They will not be helped by people in Khartoum, or by people in Juba. They will be helped by local people in the camps. And they are there because as Christians, they are committed to helping the poor. . . . America should be thinking about the embarrassment it is causing here in Juba."[5]

Experience of the postwar years shows that religious agencies cannot simply be transformed into neutral instruments of utilitarian social engineering. The role of religious commitments among refugees and relief workers aiding them in a sense was invisible because European refugees of the 1940s were largely Jewish and Christian. Today this "three faiths" domain no longer holds. Although the three countries studied in this book exemplify particular Third World issues, Sudan is in many ways the most complicated, because the refugee problems often carried overtones of interreligious conflict. Mr. R's inability to understand "Christian" America's support for Islamization in largely Christian southern Sudan is a good case in point. Christian evangelism was forbidden by the U.S. government in its refugee project; it was doubly jeopardized by Khartoum's official support for Islamic evangelization in the Christian south. American officials protested to Sudanese Christians that their hands were tied; Khartoum's policies were those of a sovereign government, and while U.S. officials could express sympathy for the Christians privately, there was little more to be done.

Religious commitments have also led believers to incorporate a strong concern for justice in their international activities. The U.S. government frequently champions the cause of particular refugee populations and ignores others. This has led private refugee agencies to political advocacy, occasionally designed to compensate for the perceived injustices of official governmental policies. Broadly defined, political advocacy refers in this book to the efforts of governmental and private relief workers to champion the cause of particular refugee groups to the tacit or explicit detriment of others equally in need of humanitarian assistance.

Even when religious groups and the U.S. government supported the same refugee population the results could be controversial. The world was surprised by the December 1984 news of the airlift of Ethiopian Jews (known as Falasha) from eastern Sudan to Israel. As press notices revealed the heretofore secret operation, little attention was paid to the U.S. government's role in promoting the Falasha operation. The airlift (known as Operation Moses) was treated in the press as a great humanitarian success story. Most of those working to transfer Falasha to Israel were from the world of international Jewish charity, some in the United States, others in Israel. Yet despite intense interest in the question of Ethiopian Jews among some American Jewish leaders, the Sudanese portion of the operation would have only been possible with the support of the U.S. government, communicated to President Nimeiry's government in Khartoum. Officially, holders of Israeli passports are not welcome in Sudan. In the eastern region, where the Falasha mingled among other Ethiopian refugees, members of the Muslim Brotherhood were known to attack people of cultures and religions other than their own. Knowledge that the Khartoum government was quietly supporting Operation Moses could have started riots among the Sudanese population.

Once the full dimensions of the airlift were made public, it became imperative to bring those Falasha still in Sudan to Israel. At this point, the U.S. government moved from a position of quiet support to semipublic cooperation with interested Jewish agencies. American government-sponsored planes flew some 2,000 Falasha to Israel. In essence, the Reagan administration agreed to help the Israelis and their American Jewish supporters out of a tight spot. It was not the first time in the postwar period that the U.S. government has taken special efforts on behalf of Jews wishing to emigrate to Israel. The Falasha operation, which focused on the needs of about 15,000 refugees out of a total population of some 600,000 in the region, hardly met humanitarian standards of neutrality and nondiscrimination. Indeed, it raised questions over the neutrality of the U.S. government policy toward Ethiopian refugees.

Concern in Washington over Soviet involvement in armed revolution in Central America in the early 1980s resulted in new polarities among groups advocating the needs of different refugee populations. Following a pattern familiar since the 1940s, U.S. care and resettlement policies favored those refugees fleeing Soviet-dominated governments, in this case Nicaragua. Refugees fleeing countries supported by the U.S. government find less sympathetic treatment awaiting them outside their own homelands. In Honduras, Salvadoran and Guatemalan asylum seekers are tolerated, but those from Nicaragua are warmly embraced.[6] It is impossible for U.S. religious agencies to avoid the messy politics of this open favoritism practiced by U.S. policymakers; many counter by advocating the cause of the Salvadorans and Guatemalans.

We will return to these and similar matters as we examine the evolution of church/state relations abroad today. Examples from Honduras, Sudan, Thailand, and other countries will be used extensively in the final half of this book as we scrutinize the role of the U.S. Constitution and courts in church/state activities abroad. Here we may simply note the increasing complexity of handling mass exodus, the shifting of refugee populations to the Third World, and the ever-present U.S.-Soviet tensions politicizing the humanitarian work of refugee care.

What common threads run through today's church/state encounters in refugee work abroad? First, church structures have altered substantially to assume responsibility for refugee problems. Religious agencies must routinely interact with governments and the specialized intergovernmental agencies, including the UN High Commissioner for Refugees and the World Food Program. This requires not only bureaucratic dexterity, but a willingness to do business in the way government does business. Often, both government and religious officials prefer to keep the details of such matters out of public view.

Second, government has become dependent upon the services of private agencies, both religious and secular, in humanitarian assistance. While cooperation of U.S. religious and secular authorities in foreign territories is a long-standing tradition, such cooperation for refugee aid at the time of World War II was seen as purely temporary. It met U.S. moral obligations as well as conformed to the demands of the Geneva Convention that "an occupation army has the responsibility of preventing disease and unrest in an occupied area."[7] Once the European displaced person problem was met, it was believed that church groups could return to prewar patterns of service. Instead, refugee problems have steadily grown, deepened in political complexity, and in many instances, become permanent fixtures on the international agenda. The Palestinian refugees, roughly 700,000 at the time of the establishment of Israel, now number nearly 2 million. A comparable number of Eritreans and Ethiopians have at some time lived in refugee camps in eastern Sudan since 1965. All parties providing assistance to these refugees, from UN agencies to their donor governments to the voluntary organizations, are increasingly subject to charges of merely running a stopgap operation no longer capable of durable solutions.

Third, church/state cooperation with today's refugees frequently strains the concept of humanitarian assistance as a category of aid separable from wider social and political struggles. William Shawcross aptly titled his 1984 book on humanitarian assistance in Cambodia *The Quality of Mercy*. He argues that international political problems have severely limited the ability of private organizations and governments to deliver aid to those in need. Such concerns cannot be limited to or summarized by church/state tensions. Shawcross makes it clear that competition between humanitarian relief bodies, both religious and secular, is one of the major difficulties facing those who wish to aid refugees in need. Any effort to measure church/state cooperation abroad by domestic church/state standards must begin with some comprehension of the complications that arise in such cooperation overseas.[8]

What about Church/State Law?

Government officials (and the courts) have been equivocal over the role of U.S. law abroad in the postwar period. This ambivalence is evident in the church/state field. As the European nations extended their power in foreign lands, it was common for the cross to follow the flag. Spanish conquistadors and Roman Catholic priests worked together in colonizing Latin America in the sixteenth century, and close ties often existed between nineteenth-century European powers and Christian missionaries in colonizing parts of Africa and Asia. Is there a new link between U.S. political power and religion abroad? If the answer is yes—as it arguably is—what relation does this link have with domestic church/state traditions?

The expression "church and state" encompasses historical, political, and legal realities. Once a decision is made to pursue church/state matters beyond the level of sloganeering (the "separation of church and state" being the chief obstacle here), it becomes clear that the courts have not followed a direct line of interpretation from the First Amendment's religion clauses to the present. Another way of explaining modern confusion over U.S. church/state traditions is to acknowledge that relevant laws and court decisions may capture a given historical reality, but they cannot predict or control it. Outside national boundaries, the separatist tradition in church/state law has never controlled contacts between religion and government.

Later chapters of this book therefore enter cautiously into the role of law, specifically church/state law, in the postwar history of the U.S. government and religious institutions overseas. Our goal is to set forth the historical outline of a cooperative movement between U.S. institutions of church and state in serving refugees. As a movement, it is still unfolding outside the reach of many domestic legal constraints. The contours of the church/state ties are often more responsive to immediate circumstances and needs than to formal doctrines and interpretations of the separation of church and state. Church/state law is at present largely irrelevant to the cooperative practices of religion and government outside the United States, but this is far from saying that it has no role.

Church/state law overseas functions more like an echo of our national conscience. To Americans who work abroad as part of religious organizations, that echo is sometimes faint, sometimes loud, often troubling. "Church and state? Oh God!" exclaimed one field worker with an evangelical agency serving refugees in Thailand. To him, church/state matters were just another hopelessly tangled aspect of the efforts of Americans and others to help the region's refugees. To others the echo is stronger, occasionally providing government officials with the rationale for restricting religious activities of private citizens. In neither of these instances, however, do church/state domestic laws regulate contact between religion and government in any strict, authoritative sense. Such laws project an echo that may be attended or dismissed.

With this caution in mind, we will look at three broad legal themes that have emerged in the historical and contemporary involvements of church and state abroad. Each theme has a parallel either in domestic U.S. church/state legal traditions and/or in international law concerning the rights of humanitarian agencies. (Religious bodies active in humanitarian service are granted no distinctive rights in modern international law; their protection has been subsumed under the category of humanitarian organizations.) The three themes are the growth of political and theological conflicts in refugee work that can be traced to religious freedom, the role of government support for and funding of private religious agencies, and an assessment of the realities of and prospects for the application of U.S. protections of religious freedom and other civil liberties to U.S. citizens working abroad.

In the United States today, talk about "religious freedom" is almost as common as reference to "separation of church and state." There have always been limits to religious freedom, as the Mormons discovered in the last quarter of the nineteenth century or as public school teachers who want students to pray in class discover today. In today's political climate, limitations on religious freedom are multiplying. Later chapters examine conflicts inherent in theological and political approaches to the refugee dilemma. Such contemporary developments as the sanctuary movement for Central Americans within the United States highlight the increasing strains on postwar compromises between religious and governmental authorities.

There is very little jurisprudence in the field of religious freedom abroad. Obviously, the U.S. government cannot control the actions of other sovereign nations toward U.S. citizens who act on religious motivations within their boundaries. But surely issues can and must be raised concerning limitations placed on religiously motivated individuals by U.S. officials, programs, and policies, namely, the freedom to directly proclaim religious beliefs and the freedom to pursue advocacy positions based on religious concepts of justice.

Should such disputes reach the court system, religiously motivated groups and individuals face an almost insurmountable array of administrative and legislative provisions defending the government's right to pursue its definitions of national security and the president's foreign affairs power. The modern grounding of foreign policy on the basis of national security, itself grounded in the war power assigned to the government by the Constitution, is the single most fundmamental power in defense of national sovereignty. Historians and political philosophers have long struggled with the contradictions between democracy and the protection of national sovereignty. The question facing religious agencies active in refugee relief, therefore, is how best to defend international humanitarian service from short-term political expedients. The U.S. tradition of religious freedom may make significant contributions to the debate at this point.

The second legal theme, direct and indirect government support for religious agencies abroad, has been persistently, though quietly, debated in the postwar period. Federal funding has become something of a humanitarian "catch 22." Very few overseas relief agencies can compete without the size and scale made possible by government assistance. This need for government funds to compete with other private voluntary agencies was insured by legislation of the late 1940s which incorporated private voluntarism into overseas relief, development, and refugee programs. The presence of such funding inevitably undercuts the independence and freedom of the private agency in pursuing the goals for which it was originally founded. Accepting federal funds both allows agencies to compete on a significant scale and requires that they trim the very features that distinguished the voluntary, often explicitly religious character of their service.

A success ethic defined by the size of an agency's operations and its ability to draw lucrative government contracts and grants affects nearly all serious voluntary relief efforts overseas today. In the competitive field of contracts with the U.S. government and with various international agencies such as the UN High Commissioner for Refugees, religious agencies face the same demands of the marketplace as their secular counterparts such as Save the Children, CARE, and Africare. Here there is no artificial emphasis on a "wall of separation" between church and state; the churches do not desire it and the government could not impose it. (Any effort of the government to deny funds to religiously based relief agencies active abroad, on the grounds that it violated the establishment clause of the First Amendment, would immediately be met with a challenge that such a denial specifically discriminated against religious institutions and constituted an unacceptable violation of the agencies' religious freedom.)

Justice William O. Douglas once wrote that the most effective way to establish an institution is to fund it. Since the 1960s the courts have elaborated on this fundamental suspicion of the effects of direct government assistance on organized religion. Yet any attempt to apply such standards would destroy the current system of church/state cooperation in refugee work abroad. The fact that these domestic standards have not been evenly or aggressively applied in the matter of federal funding of religious relief may carry with it some important clues about the future of the separationist tradition in overseas church/state ties.

The applicability of U.S. law to U.S. citizens overseas—its "extraterritoriality," in the language of lawyers and diplomats—is another legal question. As America's influence abroad expands and contracts, the private activities of U.S. citizens overseas are inevitably affected, whether they be economic, political, religious, or humanitarian. What happens when an American feels that U.S. government policies are hindering his or her actions? With the demise of an earlier system of extraterritoriality (which often featured consular courts abroad for Americans seeking to resolve disputes under U.S. law), it has become open to question whether or not U.S. law is applicable in the dealings that citizens have with U.S. officials, policies, and programs overseas. While the State Department prefers to assert that "the Constitution stops at the water's edge," this is often more a rationale for pursuing the government's chosen policies than proof that U.S. civil liberties are irrelevant to such policies.

Religious institutions in the United States today normally have ties and inter-ests that carry them beyond strictly defined national interests. Jews are bound to Israel and to other Jewish communities facing oppression overseas. Catholics and Protestants each in their own ways and communities are drawn into new expres-sions of the universality of Christianity. Yet when these interests run counter to definitions of the national interest, individuals and groups may find their missions jeopardized and the law functioning in only a limited fashion. Given the substantial nature of many disputes over refugees we will examine here, religious and govern-mental leaders may be forced to search out a new definition of national security that incorporates genuine humanitarianism as a means of addressing latent church/state conflict.

Today, more than 50,000 American citizens work abroad for Protestant and Catholic agencies at any given time. Roughly 85,000 U.S. citizens work in Israel. When these figures are contrasted with the 15,000 employees of the State Depart-ment and the Agency for International Development—roughly a third of whom are in Washington at any given time—the potential of religiously motivated workers for carrying out foreign policy goals is thrown into sharp relief. Our inquiry suggests that extralegal factors may be far more critical in building and sustaining interna-tional refugee assistance than a strict reliance on assumed protections under U.S. or international law.

This book is not written with a utopian ideal in mind. My primary concern is to reach a realistic understanding of the complex issues that have arisen out of coopera-tive relations between the U.S. government and U.S. religion abroad in the postwar era. If it focuses unduly on the problems of church/state relations overseas, it is because these are the points of contact, of friction, and we can expect them to recur. Lacking the historian's long-term perspective, we would be foolish to claim that this account is exhaustive. It is selective, drawn from records that are still shielded in part from the public, so its limitations must be acknowledged.

It may be argued that an equally important but very different book, highlight-ing only the successes of church/state cooperation since World War II, could have been drawn from the available materials. The story of refugees is indeed full of luminous details of human triumph, and I trust that enough of these moments emerge in these pages to give a balanced portrayal. Many books chronicling such details have already been published. Three that come immediately to mind are *For More Than Bread,* by Clarence Pickett, longtime director of the American Friends Service Committee; *Transfigured Night,* the story of American relief agencies co-operating in Germany after World War II by Eileen Egan and Elizabeth Reiss; and *Life Line to a Promised Land,* Ira Hirschmann's story of rescuing Eastern Euro-pean Jews during the war. Each of these accounts demonstrates the value of private relief as well as the emerging necessity of its coordination with White House foreign policy.

None of these or similar accounts, however, stress the long-term development of relations between religious institutions and the U.S. government in foreign affairs. And in this framework, it will become clear that the ideal of separating church and state has distinct limits. Thus my friend who remarked on the "abstract" nature of the topic is particularly mistaken. Religious institutions and the govern-ment agreed nearly a half-century ago that they could and should cooperate in assisting refugees, much as they have made similar decisions in the area of relief and development. And operations go smoothly when, as after World War II, the religious community and the government agree on what is to be done.

When agreement among participating parties is harder to come by, the notion of cooperation, not only of institutions but of power and morality, becomes difficult; the quality of mercy is indeed strained. Such circumstances will try the best efforts of pluralistic American civilization. Hans Morgenthau wrote that

> from the beginning of American history there has always existed an intimate and organic relationship between the moral stature of America—as conceived by itself and by the outside world—and its position among the nations of the world. . . . It is this ethos which has been the source of America's strength at home; it was one of the main sources of its prestige and influence abroad.[9]

Care of the world's refugees has been one of the great postwar tests of America's moral stature; it has also been a great testing ground for the cooperation of church and state abroad. Out of this cooperation have emerged millions of success stories, if we judge by lives saved and enhanced. The larger story, that of the slowly fraying bonds between religious institutions and the government in foreign policy, is still being told. It began in the eighteenth century as Americans were forced to negotiate peaceful relations with the Indian Nations.

2

Humanitarian Cooperation through World War I

Religion and Refugees in Early America

When the Bill of Rights was written in 1789 there were two issues concerning religion before the Congress: the maintenance of religious freedom, and the barring of a national religious establishment. That the two issues were intimately related is reflected in the final version of the First Amendment's religion clauses: "Congress shall make no law regarding the establishment of religion, or prohibiting the free exercise thereof." According to existing records, the relationship between religious and governmental authorities beyond the boundaries of the United States was at no time part of the official debate.

Some, however, believed that the religion clauses in their final form were responsive both to domestic tensions over religion and to international reasons of state. There was undeniable concern on the part of many that the Anglican church—particularly if established as a state church—could promote an undesirable tie between Great Britain and its former colonies. Such "reasons of state" arguments were also directed at the role of Catholicism in the young nation. The Roman Catholic bishop of Baltimore, John Carroll, wrote in a document left unpublished at his death in 1830 that any hint of disfavor toward Roman Catholicism in the new nation would have damaged potential ties with France. "Nothing," wrote Bishop Carroll, "could have retarded the progress of that alliance more effectually, than the demonstration of any ill will against the religion which France professed."[1]

Such matters would certainly have been part of prudent statecraft in a young nation chiefly populated by refugees from European religious persecution and their descendants. From the seventeenth century onward, the record of the colonies toward religious refugees was uneven. Quakers seeking asylum from persecution in England were turned away from the Anglican colony of Virginia in the 1650s and 1660s. Roger Williams, forerunner of today's Baptists, was expelled from the Massachusetts Bay Colony. Proponents of the religion clauses sought to eliminate such domestic strife by assuring religious freedom and limiting the institutional ties of any one church to the state. But these provisions, as discussed at the time of the ratification of the Bill of Rights, were concerned with foreign affairs only secondarily, and not at all with the religious freedom of refugees from abroad.

One of the earliest recorded refugee flows to the young republic was the movement of several thousand people seeking asylum from turmoil the French Revolution had brought to the island of Santo Domingo. When charity subscriptions in several large cities proved insufficient, Congress authorized an appropriation of $15,000 in 1794. Madison, with an eye toward relations with the young French republic as well as the novel and perhaps unconstitutional use of government funds for such charity, warned that such an act "might hereafter be perverted to the countenance of purposes very different from those of charity."[2] It was a prophetic warning.

The common notion of the "separation of church and state" was not formulated until 1802, in a personal letter written by Jefferson. The early foreign policies of the colonists assumed basic ties between Christian belief and the proper conduct of affairs of state. Benjamin Franklin had proposed that the Great Seal of the new nation show the Israelites crossing the Red Sea, God's chosen people seeking asylum from oppression in their true home, where they would dwell with him. Such visions of America as God's new Israel were common, and when America began exploring its ties with the world beyond its boundaries, the symbolism and substance of religious institutions were important to national authorities.

Missionaries as Ambassadors to the Indian Nations

In no area was this particular church/state bond expressed more fully than in relations with the Indian Nations. From the time of the Continental Congress, missionaries were placed on government salary to secure friendly relations with Indian tribes. During the Revolutionary War the support of the Indians was considered critical to American success against the British. At the time, many missionaries were employed by mission societies based in England and Scotland. John Adams and other members of the Continental Congress accurately believed that the missionaries' allegiance to the American cause was worth securing. The government's use of church workers to help build diplomatic, cultural, and religious ties with the Indian Nations continued unbroken from before the Revolution at least through 1912, constituting a historical basis for arguing that church/state ties in foreign affairs have never been ultimately controlled by the separatist reading of the religion clauses of the Constitution.

When Indian affairs were structured into the new federal government, they fell under the Department of War, whose first secretary, Henry Knox, was a friend of the Indians. In 1789 he proposed to President Washington that missionaries be stationed near Indian reservations as "friends and fathers." One of their responsibilities would be to give the Indians gifts from the government, which were "intended to attach them to the United States." The plan was adopted by the government and by its local Indian commissioners. As R. Pierce Beaver has noted:

> The President and the Secretary of War directed the commissioners who were making treaties with the southern tribes to include in the treaties stipulations that missionaries reside in each tribe and "the object of this . . . be the happiness of the

Indians, teaching them the great duties of religion and morality, and to inculcate a friendship and attachment to the United States." Henceforth for a hundred years this would be basic federal government policy.[3]

Knox's early formulation of a joint approach to the Indians only slowly took hold, largely because of the stipulation that "no attempt should be made to teach the peculiar doctrines of revealed religion except to those Indians to whom any of its mysteries have aready been unfolded." This "no evangelism" policy did not draw the support of the missionary forces of the day.[4]

Madison and Jefferson, the principal supporters of the independence of church and state, were notably reluctant to apply their principles in cases that touched on securing the national interest. (More accurately, perhaps, neither saw the church's use of government funds for the Indians' social welfare and education as a violation of the no-establishment clause.) During their terms as president both supported the use of government funds for missionaries in service in the Indian Nations. In a treaty he signed with the Kaskaskia Indians in 1803, Jefferson acknowledged that most of the tribe had converted to Roman Catholicism, and he authorized the government to provide $300 for a church building and $100 a year for the support of a Catholic priest.[5] James Madison, as president, was an eager advocate of "full partnership" between the federal government and church groups in Indian matters. In 1816 cooperation between the church (namely, the American Board of Commissioners for Foreign Missions) and the government was inaugurated in order to serve the Cherokee and Choctaw tribes. Two years later President Madison requested that Congress approve a "Civilization Fund," and in 1819 a bill was passed, authorizing an initial $10,000 for the use of "capable persons of good moral character" to work with the Indians.[6]

Church missions were the only agencies capable of running Indian schools. For more than fifty years, from 1819 until the act was repealed in 1873, church agencies and the government cooperated to evangelize and civilize the Indians. Baptists, Jesuits, Presbyterians, Moravians, Congregationalists, and others combined their private resources with resources of the Civilization Fund. By 1826 there were thirty-eight such government-subsidized schools. Working under frontier conditions, local mission installations often appeared as islands of civilization; one board sent mission "families," including "a superintendent and assistant, both ordained ministers, a schoolmaster, a farmer, a blacksmith, a carpenter, other necessary mechanics, and a physician."[7] Such an effort approximates what specialists now refer to as "development"; it is certainly closer to the broad social concerns of contemporary development efforts than to stereotypes of strictly pious and otherworldly religion.

Although both church and governmental officials acknowledged the beneficial results of this partnership in mission to the Indians, the government sought from the beginning to limit the nature and the extent of any mission which it funded in whole or in part. We have already noted the effort of Secretary Knox to restrict evangelistic activities. The precariousness of the partnership was dramatically illustrated in a series of events that should be examined by all students of religious freedom overseas. Though the resulting court cases did not directly address the question of religious freedom, they demonstrated that the will of the president and Congress could effectively override decisions of the judicial branch designed to protect what we would today call prophetic religious actions.

In the 1820s the presence of Native Americans east of the Mississippi caused political difficulty for the federal government. With the white population in the region growing rapidly, the government was unable to guarantee the security of the Indians. In 1824 and 1825 President James Monroe sent removal messages to Congress, but not until 1830 did Congress pass the Removal Act. The question went to the Supreme Court, where the Indian case was energetically argued by Jeremiah Evarts of the American Board of Commissioners for Foreign Missions. Evarts sought to hold the United States to the treaties it had signed with the Cherokees of Georgia allowing them to remain on their tribal lands. While the case was pending before the Supreme Court, the Removal Act passed Congress, and President Andrew Jackson began the process of forcing the Indians out. Serving the Cherokee at the time were several members of the board who had originally come under the partial sponsorship of the federal government's Civilization Fund. These missionaries actively resisted the removal and were imprisoned by the state of Georgia. In this case the laws in question, passed in 1829 and 1830, allowed the state of Georgia legal jurisdiction over Indian lands and made provision for removing the Indians. The American Board of Commissioners once again turned to the Supreme Court for relief, testing (in what can surely be called an early instance of advocacy within religious bodies) not only the right of Georgia to imprison the board's missionaries but also the basic right of the Cherokees to remain on their own land.

The Supreme Court sided with the missionaries and the Cherokees; Chief Justice John Marshall wrote the Court's opinion in the case of *Samuel Worcester* v. *State of Georgia*. Noting that the defendant Samuel Worcester, a missionary, was in the Cherokee Nation "in accordance with the humane policy of the government of the United States for the civilization and improvement of the Indians," Marshall recalled the history of treaties with the Indians, stating that "one of their objects [was] the civilization of the Indians, and their conversion to Christianity—objects to be accomplished by conciliatory conduct and good example; not by extermination." Marshall argued that the intercourse between the United States and the Cherokee nation was the responsibility of the federal government, and that Georgia had acted illegally in legislating an extraterritorial extension of its authority into Cherokee lands. He ordered Worcester freed, since he had been performing "under the sanction of the chief magistrate of the Union, those duties which the humane policy adopted by congress had recommended."[8]

Unfortunately for the American Board of Commissioners and the Cherokee tribe, President Jackson bypassed the Supreme Court's decision in *Worcester* v. *Georgia* and ordered the U.S. Army to continue the Cherokee's removal. Thus, members of an American religious society serving Indians under a U.S. government mandate were prevented by executive action from fulfilling a task to which they deemed themselves called. The fact that the Supreme Court sided with them against the federal government was simply ignored. In as many words, the executive branch had anticipated the Supreme Court's verdict in the Mormon polygamy cases of the 1890s: religiously motivated individuals were free to believe anything they chose, but the government—through the courts or through the president—had tremendous leeway to limit their "free exercise of religion" if it was subversive of what the government considered to be "good social order."

Debates over the selection of church groups to work with the Indians became heated by the late nineteenth century, when the Catholic church challenged the

Protestant sympathies of the government's Bureau of Indian Affairs. Catholics alleged that government agents frequently tried to undermine the authority of Catholic priests among the Indians, and that priests serving on reservations or in administrative posts were barely tolerated within the system administered by government.[9] Other signs of government partiality had been plain to see when President Ulysses S. Grant first announced the government's new "Peace Policy" toward the Indians in 1869. His appointment of ten Protestants to a new Board of Indian Commissioners earned it the nickname of "the Church Board," but many Catholics were outraged over such discrimination. Other Catholic leaders proceeded to address the practical question of government subsidies by forming in 1873 the first religious lobby in the history of the country, the Washington-based Catholic Bureau of Indian Missions.

Some Protestant church leaders began to see the implications of democratic logic: if the government aided Protestants, it would also be obliged to aid Catholics. Protestants who wanted Catholics off the government payroll believed that they would have to set the example by withdrawing first, but this strategy backfired. The Catholics had no intention of withdrawing from their Indian schools. The Catholic use of public funds, seen by Catholics as a right they could claim on the same grounds as Protestants, prompted Baptists to agitate for a constitutional amendment to protect the United States from the "meddlesomeness of ecclesiasticism" springing from those "bred in state-church and church-state ideas of Europe."[10] The Missionary Council of the Protestant Episcopal Church supported such an amendment to make such "misappropriations in the future impossible."[11] Yet no such amendment was in sight. To the contrary, by 1890 the Catholic church was receiving nearly 75 percent of all government contract expenditures for Indian schools.[12]

There is good evidence that the question of access to government funds exacerbated tensions between Protestants and Catholics in the late nineteenth and early twentieth centuries. Indian rights advocates caught in the interreligious bickering eventually came out against all government funding of sectarian schools because it was "manifestly contrary to the American idea to aid religious bodies in the propagation of their faith, and the dangers and entanglements growing out of such a policy are evident and prove in practice serious."[13] Protestant churches were praised (by Protestant idealists) for voluntarily withdrawing from the program. Eventually, as domestic interreligious tension grew, the connection between government funding for schools in the Indian Nations and the establishment of religion came to the Supreme Court in a 1908 case, *Quick Bear* v. *Leupp*.[14]*

One final church/state dispute over missions to the Indian Nations, over Catholics' right to wear religious garb and insignia in mission schools, erupted in 1912. At a Washington hearing on the matter the government acknowledged publicly what it preferred to say quietly and with little fanfare, namely, that compromise was needed in order to continue to serve the Indians. President William Taft ruled that Catholics who were currently wearing religious insignia and garb could continue, but that no new employees in federal schools would be allowed to do so.[15] It was a decision that made few parties to the dispute happy, in part because the president had dodged the separation issue by not clearly deciding what constituted forbidden mingling of religion and government.

*See discussion of this case, pp. 000–000.

The ecumenical spirit between Protestants and Catholics that has flourished since the 1950s makes these early squabbles sound petty. Yet nothing is capable of dividing otherwise friendly religious bodies as severely as the matter of their respective relationships with temporal powers. The establishment question arose in these early debates primarily because of the Protestants' fear that the Catholic church, by expanding its funding relationships and political contact with the federal government, was encroaching on the unofficial Protestant establishment. Calling for renewed attention to the separation of church and state was a (not entirely successful) Protestant strategy for keeping the Catholic church "in its place." The dispute has survived in altered forms into the present era, and the matter of religious garb and insignia reappeared during the Second World War.

Religious Welfare and the State

This early history of church/state ties in dealing with the Indian Nations also bears on the broad question of how the government should best care for people who for various reasons become wards of the state. Whether the population in question has been Native Americans, the nation's poor, or refugees from other countries, state and national governments have traditionally appealed to religious societies for help. This remedy, the only one available before the 1930s, was, in the coolly pragmatic language of the 1868 New York State Constitutional Convention, "a mere matter of expediency and economy."[16] A church/state case decided by the Supreme Court in 1899, *Bradfield* v. *Roberts,*[17] was the first to address the question of whether religious institutions performing welfare services were eligible for government assistance. The case tested whether the District of Columbia could legally transfer $30,000 to a Catholic hospital for the purpose of constructing isolation wards to combat contagious diseases.

The action was challenged as a violation of the establishment clause, but the Supreme Court held that the government was within its rights since the hospital clearly served a secular purpose, whatever its sectarian origins. As long as it held a separate corporate identity from the parent church, government support violated no law:

> Whether the individuals who compose the corporation under its charter happen to be all Roman Catholics, or all Methodists, or Presbyterians, or Unitarians, or members of any other religious organization, or of no organization at all, is of not the slightest consequence with reference to the law of its incorporation.[18]

Here was the beginning of legal reasoning on the role of religious welfare in modern society. Religiously based services were welcomed on the basis of their ability to provide a service with clear secular purpose. "The Court reasoned that the hospital was a separate legal entity with a secular purpose and that its ownership and management by Catholic sisters did not make it a religious organization." We will return to this question of whether welfare bodies organized by churches—particularly those active abroad—are "religious" institutions. Certainly early church mission to the Indian Nations was primarily religious. But by 1899, the courts implied, the religious motivation of religiously grounded agencies was "of not the slightest consequence" to their secular function.

The interreligious and political disputes resolved in the *Quick Bear* and *Bradfield* cases have been echoed in establishment questions of the modern era, particularly those involving the role of religion and religious practices in institutions funded entirely or in part by government. Much as some of the early fathers of the republic had seen the "establishment of religion" as having broader application than merely preventing the establishment a national church, some Americans at the turn of the century attempted to apply the establishment clause to the use of government funds by sectarian welfare agencies.

In *Bradfield,* the Court held that a hospital run by Catholic sisters was a public and secular institution, and therefore eligible for government assistance. In *Quick Bear,* the Court held that the use of Indian treaty and trust funds for the provision of sectarian education was also legal. Such government assistance, even though not designed to grant special privilege to particular churches, inevitably generated disputes among parties contending for the funding. These decisions could not have anticipated today's struggles over government policy toward the global refugee problem, but they must be kept in mind as we turn to the development of religiously based welfare abroad in the early twentieth century. Many of the same problems remain. The Indian mission disputes from 1870 to 1912 also demonstrated that government entanglement with religious bodies in politically sensitive areas of social welfare was capable of dividing the population along religious lines. We will soon see that this potential is also present today in the fields of refugee and relief work abroad.

Protestant and Catholic Efforts at the Time of World War I

By the end of the nineteenth century, missions, immigration, and emergency relief overseas rather than refugee matters dominated the welfare activities of religious agencies and committees.[19] For the government's part, the institutions it formed for cooperating with private voluntarism abroad were (with the exception of the American Red Cross, established by congressional charter) temporary panels or emergency administrations assembled in response to specific needs. Though neither the government nor religious bodies had a tradition of forming joint foreign operations, it appeared increasingly necessary as the government found its services ever more in demand abroad, and American religion discovered new fields of overlapping interests with government.

Public expression of the shared interests of religion and government overseas was common by the end of the last century. Missionaries in China were Americans' greatest source of information about that nation before the advent of radio; many missionaries eventually joined the State Department. Under extraterritorial treaties with the Chinese, missionaries and other Americans worked from compounds within which U.S. law prevailed. The interests of the missionaries went hand in hand with those of U.S. seamen, entrepreneurs, and diplomats. At the time of William McKinley's invasion of the Philippines in 1898, Protestantism was a heady partner with government in setting the tone of U.S. foreign policy. Mrs. McKinley was a keen supporter of Protestant missions to the Philippines, and the president himself acknowledged publicly that he had spent the night in prayer before finally reaching the conclusion to proceed with an invasion of the islands. Throughout the

Spanish-American War, American religious groups sent humanitarian assistance to the war zones, particularly to refugees held in camps in Cuba.

Protestants, while strong on the odd disaster or war relief efforts overseas, were not (by comparison with newly expanding efforts by Jews and Catholics) overly concerned with refugees in the early part of the century. Refugees were not of great interest to the Protestant missionary societies of 1910; indeed, the world missionary conference that year in Edinburgh concentrated on the extension of the phenomenal growth of the overseas missionary endeavor in the previous fifty years. To acknowledge the presence of refugees is to draw attention to political disorder; such was not the purpose of the Protestant mission movement of the day. The assembled Protestants in Edinburgh, still overwhelmingly English and American, stood ready to disseminate the Gospel to every land. Refugee problems did not coincide with their foremost purpose, "the evangelization of the world in this generation."

The year 1910 was a high-water mark for the Pax Britannia, and delegates to Edinburgh looked forward to the uninterrupted extension of Anglo-Saxon dominance and order. At home, American Protestants overseas were acknowledged as pillars of this emerging world order. Yet if refugees were absent from the agenda of Protestant mission work, they were also absent from the political agenda of the leaders of the English-speaking world. The eleventh edition of the *Encyclopaedia Britannica* (1911), perhaps the last great attempt to gather together all human knowledge into a unified field, contained no entry for "refugee." Focusing rather on scientific and economic concerns, the encyclopedia explained "migration" and "coolie" at length. The Protestants had had some success with abolishing slavery, but they had not yet eliminated the need for servile labor in many parts of the world; mass economic migrations were accepted facts engineered by governments eager to turn a profit from colonial holdings. In 1904 England contracted with China for over 50,000 indentured laborers, who were then shipped halfway around the globe to serve in the Witwatersrand gold mines of South Africa.[20] Such movements were common; Indians and Chinese were by governmental agreements shipped to Africa, East Asia, Australia, the Pacific, and Central and South America.[21] Church leaders for the most part looked the other way.

With little direct involvement of governments in humanitarian assistance, Protestant mission agencies gradually came to accept some responsibilities for material assistance to refugees and other victims abroad. This included providing direct aid as well as applying diplomatic pressure on American and other governmental authorities. In 1915, a major refugee problem caused by the genocidal persecution of Armenians in Turkey stirred the conscience of Americans. Ambassador Henry Morgenthau, Sr. alerted his fellow countrymen to the persecution in Turkey, and a coalition of missionary societies and other charities formed the American Committee for Relief in the Near East, later shortened to Near East Relief. Ambassador Morgenthau invited the committee to coordinate its efforts through the American embassy. Joined by other Canadian and British groups, in 1919 Near East Relief raised nearly $20 million that went toward refugee problems in Armenia; by the end of the year the committee was feeding over 300,000 people a day.[22]

No codified international definition of a refugee existed at the time; for Americans the issue was immigration. Once Congress took steps to limit Chinese immigration in 1882, 1888, and 1892—on grounds that they refused to assimilate—the practical outcome was favored status for European migrants, a population which by the end of the nineteenth century was largely Jewish and Catholic. Political refugees were undifferentiated from economic migrants; both fell under the Statue of Liberty's emotive concept of "huddled masses." Their reception (barring anarchists, prostitutes, paupers, and the diseased) was the extension of America's traditional hospitality to those in need. Aside from practical concerns—notably the availability of land and the new needs of industry—aiding these early immigrant and refugees was the American, the Christian, thing to do. Protestants, led by Jane Addams and others, encouraged the settlement house movement, which served immigrants living in large cities. Catholic and Jewish leaders, absorbing the spirit of American voluntarism that had so entranced Alexis de Tocqueville in the early days of the republic, formed societies specifically devoted to caring for their own people once they reached Ellis Island. One order, the Missionaries of St. Charles Borromeo (known as the Scalabrinis), grew from the concerns of Bishop Giovanni Scalabrini, who saw 28,000 members of his diocese of Piacenza migrate to the United States in his first ten years as bishop. The order still works closely with Italians and other immigrants. Their research center, the Center for Migration Studies on Staten Island, is one of the most complete migration research facilities available today.

Before World War I the Catholic Colonization Society encouraged Catholics to settle in rural areas near a Catholic church and a parochial school. Such colonies usually followed ethnic lines. The Raphael Society established a branch in New York in 1883 in order to care for German immigrants to the United States. Societies serving Irish, Dutch, Polish, and other nationalities also emerged. The Society of St. Vincent De Paul, founded in France and active in the United States since 1845, was perhaps the most effective of all the Catholic immigrant organizations. Most societies operated independently of government assistance, and church/state struggles were rare, occurring only in occasional governmental allegations of fraud.[23] Local Catholic charities as well as national efforts such as the Knights of Columbus proliferated, and were not united at the national level until the church faced the pressures and needs of World War I.

Jewish Humanitarian and Relief Efforts

One of the first Jewish agencies, the Hebrew Sheltering and Immigration Aid Society (which later adopted the acronym HIAS), began in 1908. HIAS was the result of a merger of different organizations, some financed by wealthy "uptown" New York Jews and others supported by poorer Jews living on Manhattan's Lower East Side. These earlier efforts dated back to 1880. For Jewish immigrants and refugees, HIAS offered relief, intercession with the authorities in special cases, and other help in adjusting to America. Within its first ten years, supported only by the contributions of concerned Jews, HIAS assisted nearly 83,000 immigrants.[24]

Even though Zionism was by 1908 an established political ideology in some Jewish circles, HIAS publicly avoided the question of Jewish emigration to Palestine. It was not until Germany imposed an official boycott on Jewish businesses in 1933 that HIAS began formal cooperation with the Jewish Agency, the international humanitarian organization begun in 1922 (now an integral part of the Israeli government) which played a decisive role in the movement of Jews to Palestine.

Through its contributions to the Jewish Agency and to the Youth Aliyah, HIAS helped bring young Poles and Germans to Palestine, beginning a policy that would offer emigrants or refugees a choice of moving either to the United States or to Israel. Originally supported entirely by private contributions, HIAS would later partially adapt its program to the availability of U.S. government assistance in the international movement of refugees.

While HIAS would through the years specialize in bringing immigrants and refugees to the United States, Israel, and elsewhere, another Jewish institution, the American Jewish Committee (AJC), helped create a movement that would work closely with Jewish refugees and other needy people in distress overseas. The AJC itself had emerged from a 1906 article in the *American Hebrew* by the conservative Jewish scholar Cyrus Adler. Adler called for "a national Jewish organization in the United States which can, in cases of necessity, cooperate with similar bodies in other countries for the welfare of Jews elsewhere."[25] Pogroms against Jews in Russia had stirred new interest in the fate of Jews around the world, and Adler and his colleagues sought to raise a powerful Jewish voice in national and international political circles. Adler's concerns were taken up by wealthy Jews who sought to centralize Jewish opinion and political clout in a single organization. This group included Jacob Schiff, philanthropist and investment banker; Cyrus L. Sulzberger of the *New York Times;* and constitutional lawyer Louis I. Marshall.

Controversy surrounded the AJC from its earliest meetings, and the controversies frequently turned on questions of the relation between religion and politics, often specifically on the ways Jews could exercise influence on the national government. A perennial question in the Jewish community, whether it should be treated as a religious or an ethnic bloc, arose in the earliest proposals for framing the purpose of the AJC. An initial report in meetings of February 1906 suggested that the purpose of the new group would be to "promote the cause of Judaism." This simple statement appeared to accept a religious definition of the interests of the Jewish community; it was rejected in favor of a compromise offered by Adler which blandly proposed that "it was desirable to form a body to be known as the American Jewish Committee." A statement of purpose favoring "the cause of Judaism" called to mind "ecclesiastical pretensions."[26] Given the minority status of the Jewish community, and the interest of the committee's founders in marshaling political power, the ethnic/cultural vision of the Jewish community prevailed, and it consistently dominated Jewish humanitarianism until a new interest in religious roots began to take hold in the mid-1970s.

In what remains one of the most successful applications of pressure on the U.S. government's foreign policy by any religious constituency, the American Jewish Committee in 1911 dramatically altered relations between the United States and Russia over the question of treatment of American Jews traveling in Russia. Since the 1880s native Russian Jews had been singled out for persecution by successive czarist regimes. Despite American diplomatic protests, by the 1890s Russian consular officials were inquiring into the religious backgrounds of Americans seeking to travel to Russia in order to deny visas to Jews.[27] In 1907 Secretary of State Elihu Root issued a statement on the subject, formally announcing that the government could not assure the safety of former Russian Jews who visited Russia under an American passport. Members of the AJC protested that this amounted to the segregation of Jews from the broad protections of the U.S. government. Subsequent adjustment of Root's policies (largely through pressure from the AJC) did nothing to change the attitude of the Russians, who continued to detain and humiliate visiting American Jews. When the failure of normal diplomatic channels was obvious to all parties in the dispute, the AJC took a momentous decision "to cut the tangled Gordian knot at its most vital point . . . the ancient treaty of commerce and navigation between the two countries."[28]

Almost singlehandedly, the American Jewish Committee brought Jewish concerns into the political and economic mainstream by forcing the Congress to terminate the nearly eighty-year-old treaty regulating U.S. commercial ties with Russia. The struggle was one of the first to use open, public strategies instead of diplomacy in cases of human rights abuses, marking the dimensions of a debate over strategy which still continues in church/state controversies about refugee policy. The campaign to alert the public was an overwhelming success. By December, when the move to terminate the treaty finally came to a vote in Congress, it passed by a lopsided majority of 300 to 1. The AJC had demonstrated that religiously based concerns were interrelated not only with human rights, but also with economic issues, and that on occasion such concerns could be imposed on political and economic matters. The vote in effect marked the end of U.S. trade relations with czarist Russia and firmly established the AJC as a force in the conduct of the nation's foreign affairs. It also set a precedent that would be forcefully recalled in the 1970s when the American Jewish community turned to the needs of Soviet Jews.

This early success of the American Jewish Committee in affecting U.S. foreign policy prefigured the committee's subsequent involvement with the government over refugee matters. Just before World War I, the AJC undertook the relief of refugees in Palestine following an urgent telegram from Ambassador Morgenthau in Turkey. Morgenthau received $50,000 and appointed a committee in Palestine to administer the funds.[29] It was an early and straightforward instance of governmental assistance to particular religious constituencies in meeting overseas needs.

Uniting American Jews for overseas relief was not an easy task. Zionists, wealthy German Jews, labor-oriented secularists, and independent Orthodox Jews all had distinct and occasionally contradictory goals. A compromise organization, the American Jewish Joint Distribution Committee (AJDC), emerged under AJC leadership in 1914. Under the compromise, distribution of relief funds and goods would be made jointly, but individual groups would retain their own fund-raising capabilities and constituencies.

The success of the AJDC—known as "the Joint" by generations of grateful Jews around the world—was remarkable. In its first months it pioneered the development of arrangements that would become a commonplace of church/state cooperation abroad—government aid in shipping relief goods abroad. When Turkey expelled 1,200 Russian Jews from Palestine in December 1914, several U.S. Navy ships were used to transport them to safety in Alexandria, Egypt. In March 1915 the U.S. Navy shipped 900 tons of AJDC relief supplies to Palestine; a second shipment courtesy of the government followed the next year.

By the end of World War I, the AJDC had operations in Palestine, Russia, and several European countries, each of which would continue to be recipients of its benevolence. When Jewish displaced persons became a central focus of Europe's World War II refugee problems, new relief bodies would appear, but the AJDC would remain intimately involved with Jewish refugee relief abroad. In World War I, however, European refugees seemed beyond American assistance. The *American Jewish Year Book* of 1917–18 estimated that there were some 55,000 Jewish refugees in Poland "whose condition is even more wretched than that of the rest of the population," yet "these victims of the war are constantly moving from place to place, which makes it more than ordinarily difficult to relieve them."[30] In Russia, however, where by mid-1917 roughly a million Jewish refugees had sought asylum, American Jews supplied food, money, clothing, housing, and employment.

Palestine remained another question. According to a report filed in July 1916 by the U.S. consul in Jerusalem, only 18,000 of the 82,000 Jews in Palestine were self-supporting; the rest depended on American charity. "Jerusalem has been, even in normal times, rich in its poor population, living upon the charity of our brethren abroad," according to the report.[31] Relief for Jews in Palestine, and the effort to bring more refugees to the region, would continue as a central endeavor of the American Jewish community, one that would bring its leaders into ever-closer contact with governmental strategists in addressing the refugee problem.

World War I: Early Church/State Coordination

The entry of the United States into World War I provided the first occasion for the government to join international humanitarian efforts with foreign policy concerns. Nearly all the religious leaders of the day, even many who had espoused pacifism, viewed participation in the war as a solemn necessity. Significant new religious initiatives emerged, and at the suggestion of President Woodrow Wilson's secretary of war, Protestants, Catholics, and Jews worked together in fund raising.

The war gave American Catholics the impetus to unite their social service activities under a single organization. Within four months of America's entry into the conflict the National Catholic War Council (NCWC) came into being. Its formation was necessitated by the appalling disunity of American Catholicism. When the Council was formed in 1917, the American bishops had not met in formal assembly since 1884; there was almost no communication, coordination, or cooperation among the existing 15,000 Catholic societies.[32]

Every bishop was asked to send a cleric and a layperson to a national meeting at Catholic University in August 1917. The largest of the Catholic organizations, the Knights of Columbus, was soon operating hundreds of centers for military personnel without reference to creed. Sixty dioceses were represented at the meeting, which gave birth to the NCWC. After the war, the NCWC was transformed into a permanent coordinating body, the National Catholic Welfare Conference.

When in 1918 the War Department decided to conduct a joint fund appeal to the American public for wartime needs, participants included the NCWC, the YMCA, the YWCA, the Salvation Army, and the Jewish Welfare Board. President Wilson urged that they "unite their forthcoming appeals for funds, in order that the spirit of this country . . . may be expressed without distinction of race or religious opinion."[33] The joint goal of $170 million was exceeded by $18 million.

Government efforts at "merging" international religious humanitarianism were varied and often successful, but the process was not without political rancor. Behind-the-scenes negotiations assured that Protestants would receive preferential treatment, conducting their fund-raising several months ahead of Catholics and Jews. The Knights of Columbus protested publicly, stating that the separation "would be drawing a religious line in a time of war that cannot fail to cause great criticism and disturbance throughout the country."[34] President Wilson's appeal for cooperation disguised the debate in the public eye. James Cardinal Gibbon, the senior Catholic prelate of the day, stressed the positive, stating that "while it remains true, that there will be a merging of forces, and no mention made of Catholic, non-Catholic or Hebrew activity, a magnificent opportunity is here presented of adding glory to the church."[35]

In April 1917, representatives of three branches of another American religious group, the Quakers, met in Philadelphia to discuss some common form of humanitarian service that could be performed for the soldiers and the destitute along the Western Front in Europe. Out of that meeting grew the American Friends Service Committee (AFSC). Its function was "rooted in the conviction that each human life is sacred, each man a child of God, and that love, expressed through creative action, is the only power that can overcome hatred, prejudice and fear."[36] The Quakers had already established a reputation for nonpartisan humanitarianism. President Grant had named them as his choice to implement the government's "Peace Policy" toward the Indian Nations in 1869; they now sought a new expansion of their international ministry.

Three years later, another religious agency springing from a similar Anabaptist tradition, the Mennonite Central Committee, was formed to bring humanitarian service abroad. Over the years, both would provide incalculable service to i ifugees and displaced persons, and both would break new ground in defining the nature of Christian mission and of humanitarian service and its relationship to the civil authorities. Each sought to expand earlier, church-based notions of service toward universalism and human brotherhood. Reinhold Niebuhr suggested some years later that the AFSC exemplified belief in natural progress in the course of human affairs. Happily, this perspective coincided with that of contemporary government officials seeking to develop new forms of humanitarian assistance overseas.

The Quakers had long been active in overseas missions; now during World War I they joined in a new commitment to pragmatic Christian service. When the first unit of sixty-one young Quakers arrived in France to provide relief among the troops, one of their leaders evoked a characteristic Quaker combination of the religious "inner light" and service to a higher patriotism:

> We are here because we feel that we must do something, not expecting an easier life than the millions of men who are following their light in other ways, and we are ready to do the hardest and lowliest kind of work. It is not that our blood is any less red or our patriotism any less real; it is that we are conscious that we are servants of a King who is above all nations—the King of Love—and that we must live out his gospel of love.[37]

With such high-minded religious ideals, it was perhaps inevitable that the differences (rather than the similarities) of purpose between religious agencies and the government in providing relief would emerge. The U.S. military officer in charge of the quasi-governmental American Red Cross in Belgium in 1917 made the following observations:

The same reasons which impel us to clean up slums in peacetime impel us to deal effectively with refugees in wartime. Leaving aside all motives of brotherhood and humanity . . . refugees have to be cared for or they will get in the way of armies, block roads, create city slums, breed contagion which spreads to troops, and if maddened by hunger, start riots and take troops needed elsewhere to put them down.[38]

While such a view could hardly be said to typify a "government perspective" on refugees, it does suggest that pure humanitarian motivation is not the only thing on the minds of government officials facing refugee problems.

In little over a hundred years, Madison's misgivings about the nature of governmental involvement in charity were already giving way to the crushing realities of modern political and humanitarian necessities. Early efforts at cooperation between religious and governmental authorities were mostly informal, but a global war demanded greater coordination. Refugee issues may serve as a potent public reminder of American humanitarian commitments, but the First World War brought forth the essential reality, namely, that refugee and humanitarian affairs were continually subject to broader political currents.

Despite constant pressure from religious and other private sector leaders, the cause of refugees has rarely progressed beyond that of a second- or third-rate political issue. As religious and governmental leaders explored their common interests in refugee and relief work abroad, the talk of partnership in humanitarian work often obscured the realities of religious engagement with the power and interests of the state. In the modern era, private religious relief—when not agressively pursuing its own ends—increasingly would be relegated to "mopping up" after governmental errors of judgment, wars, or other catastrophic events.

3

The Gathering Storm
(1919–1939)

Religious and governmental leaders emerged from their wartime cooperation to find not peace, but new crises abroad. Amid cries for universal disarmament and an end to war, religious leaders, aware of the existing human need, knew that in the meantime there was more than enough work to go around. The twenty years before World War II saw the continuation of a variety of ad hoc cooperative efforts abroad between U.S. authorities and religious relief groups, but no major expansion of long-term arrangements.

Three developments of the period stand out for their significance in later church/state ties. The anti-Semitism in Europe, particularly Germany, exerted continual pressures and demands on Jewish refugee advocates. In their search for allies, they turned to Congress, the White House, and a small circle of Protestant and Catholic leaders committed to refugee problems. Though Jewish efforts were less than successful before World War II, they helped convince Franklin Roosevelt that the humanitarian impulses of the nation's religious communities, if harnessed to the war effort, could be an important resource in U.S. foreign policy.

However, the efforts of American private humanitarianism during the Spanish Civil War alarmed many government officials who were fearful of being drawn into a foreign conflict. From this concern arose the second significant trend for future church/state relations abroad: the first legislation and administrative procedures designed to impose governmental controls on private foreign assistance. Because it was not a member of the League of Nations, the United States was somewhat of an outsider in organized international diplomacy. This meant that humanitarian assistance from the United States was subject first of all to American rather than multilateral control. This was evident in a third development of the period, the fumbling efforts at organizing international assistance to refugees. In short, the government held back from serious consideration of the problems of the Jews, avoided multilateral refugee efforts until it was assured its own interests were met, and imposed new controls over private voluntary assistance abroad.

Postwar Efforts: Quakers and Jews Take the Lead

Fear of political problems hardly daunted the American Friends Service Committee. "In this period of rapid change we must find our way into patterns of life which are creative and rooted in a commitment to the preservation of spiritual values," wrote longtime AFSC director Clarence Pickett.[1] It was the pursuit of such resolutely Quaker goals that led the AFSC to extend its cooperation with the federal government after the Armistice. Based on its desire to transcend the divisions of war, the AFSC resolved to undertake programs to feed the estimated 1 million starving children in Germany. Many people were displaced from their homes in Germany, forerunners of the millions of "displaced persons" whose care called forth massive U.S. church/state cooperation following World War II.[2] But the AFSC's plan to aid German children flew in the face of American public opinion, which opposed aid for the belligerent government of Germany. An AFSC appeal for funds in the summer of 1919 brought only $30,000.

Fellow Quaker Herbert Hoover, who had been responsible for coordinating food supplies to Europe during the war, saw that it might be possible to use the AFSC's aspirations to further the national interest; in the words of one observer of the period, Hoover believed that "America's mission lay in countering the threats of war, disease, starvation and bolshevism, using food as an instrument." Hoover's approach was a political compromise that linked a huge national farm surplus with the somewhat delicate private efforts of German Americans to provide assistance to Germany. According to Hoover, if the German Americans dominated relief efforts, the country might face a situation in which it would be "so easy to slip over the line from charity to [anti-American] propaganda." Hoover believed that the AFSC could blend the right kind of charity and the right kind of politics. His solution was ingenious: based on the agency's reputation for fairness and impartiality, he offered the AFSC the job of distributing $100 million of government-purchased food in Europe. In exchange, the AFSC would direct its public fund-raising campaign at German Americans, blunting that group's independent efforts to provide relief. An agreement was reached with the Friends in November 1919. The *New York Times* quoted Hoover as saying that "to prevent such a [relief] campaign having political import, I have asked the Quakers to take charge." In essence, the Friends' image as a neutral agent helped position them to assist the federal government in addressing politically sensitive refugee and relief problems both at home and abroad.[3]

The truth was clear to those who followed the political debate over the government's appropriation of the funds. As one senator said, "Food and politics have had an inevitable and inseparable connection ever since the beginning of the war; and they have it still."[4] When the primacy of the law was pitted against the accomplishment of ends deemed morally or politically necessary by the government, the latter frequently carried the day. For instance, the initial response to the AFSC's request for funds from German Americans (who were reluctant to give up control to the new Quaker agency) was disappointing. Facing a major shortfall, Hoover quietly ignored legislation banning the use of government funds for "enemy children" and transferred $4 million in government assistance to the Quakers.

As Hoover had looked ahead to a stable Europe, questions of U.S. church/state relations overseas appeared entirely secondary; Hoover felt that the government could benefit from association with the Quakers' reputation for nonpartisanship. For their part, the Quakers were eager to help starving children; the use of government food surpluses also freed the AFSC's work from suspicion under the 1917 Trading with the Enemy Act, which remains one of the government's chief means of restricting refugee and relief assistance to populations or governments it deems hostile. Hoover authorized AFSC workers in Germany to include the following message on the cards that permitted individual Germans to receive government-funded assistance: "To those who suffer in Germany, with a message of good will from the American Society of Friends (Quakers) who for 250 years, and also all through this great war, have believed that those who were called enemies were really friends separated by a great wall of misunderstanding."[5]

The Russian famine operation introduced the idea of government regulation into the peacetime relief and refugee operations administered by private U.S. citizens abroad, a pattern that would be expanded in the mid-1930s. Domestic political objections to foreign assistance had become commonplace by 1921 when calls arose for aid to refugees from the Russian Revolution and to Russian victims of yet another bitter famine. This relief campaign of the early 1920s opened a new stage of peacetime church/state partnership abroad. Jewish agencies were joined by church groups, the Red Cross, labor unions, and a variety of leftist and radical committees that openly supported the goals of Lenin's government. Once a representative of the U.S. government signed an agreement with the Russians to provide assistance, Hoover demanded that all participating private agencies affiliate with the American Relief Administration (ARA) in Russia, which would coordinate the efforts of private groups and insure that supplies reached their intended destinations. Such a unified approach, administered by the U.S. government, would, in Hoover's view, bring the full authority of the president to bear on the task of keeping the relief operation a healthy distance from the Bolshevik authorities, whom Hoover later denounced as "malignant."[6]

Some of the agencies working in Russia in the 1920s considered the ARA's attitude toward controlling relief to be highly political. While most church agencies (including the AFSC, the Mennonite Central Committee, the Joint Distribution Committee, the relief arms of the Federal Council of Churches, the National Catholic Welfare Conference, the National Lutheran Council, the YMCA and YWCA, and the Southern Baptist Convention) affiliated with the ARA, others did not. Leftist committees and the liberal Russian Famine Fund, which boasted the support of politicians such as Alfred E. Smith and Norman Thomas, never affiliated with the ARA, giving rise to charges and countercharges that the government's relief program was essentially counterrevolutionary. The AFSC, still seen as the most impartial of agencies, was allowed to distribute relief gathered by the Russian Famine Fund. Perhaps the most remarkable aspect of the operation, which over three years distributed tens of millions of dollars worth of assistance, was the fact that Americans, without even the formality of diplomatic relations, were aiding Russians. Despite the cool relations between the governments of the two nations, the people-to-people nature of the operation was evident. In 1922, the exiled Maxim Gorky wrote to Hoover: "I know of no accomplishment which in terms of magnitude and generosity can be compared to the relief that you have actually accomplished. . . . The generosity of the American people resuscitates the dream of fraternity among people at a time when humanity greatly needs charity and compassion."[7]

The Jewish Joint Distribution Committee, while participating in the ARA's operations, also continued its own independent efforts. In particular, the committee aided refugees and needy Jews affected by the Russian-Polish war of 1920, feeding more than 300,000 children and sheltering refugees displaced by the hostilities. That same year the AJDC organized a special committee on refugees, which at that time concentrated on assisting Jews stranded in ports of call. So successful were the fund-raising efforts of the AJDC that unlike several religiously based agencies that eventually became dependent upon government assistance, the AJDC to this day has always received the bulk of its support from the Jewish community. This fact has at times encouraged an almost brash sense of independence of Jewish philanthropy from the aims of government. Two years later the AJDC was joined in Poland by an American branch of an international Jewish agency formed in Russia in 1880, the Society for the Promotion of Trade and Industry among Jews (known as ORT after the initials of its name in Russian). The American ORT, using AJDC funds as well as its own, began a program of educational and vocational training for Jews that would extend eventually to the rest of Europe, North Africa, and Palestine.

Of all the agencies providing refugee aid and relief in this early period, only those of the Jewish community, Catholic Church, the peace churches (Quakers, Mennonites and Brethren), and the Protestant Near East Relief have survived. From the mid-1920s to 1939, very few permanent new agencies would emerge from the religious community.[8] Committees for aiding various refugee populations continued to emerge, but there is little evidence that most Protestant or Catholic leaders in the 1920s considered the refugee problem a permanent issue.

Refugee Needs and Traditional Missionary Goals

Besides ad hoc arrangements, religiously based agencies working with refugees routinely sought more frequent cooperative ventures with government than the more traditional missionary societies ever had. In the words of later court decisions, refugee work had an "identifiable secular purpose," thus forming a legitimate area of overlapping concern for both religion and government. This had not been the case with the overtly evangelistic goals of much traditional missionary work. Despite the sizable influence of supporters of overseas mission work, such overtly religious agencies came under increasingly critical scrutiny in the years before World War II.

In the midst of postwar political isolationism and the rising national affluence of the 1920s, overseas religious benevolence of all kinds began a steady decline. Robert T. Handy, a careful student of the period, has even suggested that a "religious depression" settled over Protestant America for a decade beginning around 1925. Americans appeared to be ready for a break from overseas giving. Missionary societies went begging for funds as the missionary motive itself began to decay within the church. An Episcopal writer in 1934 suggested that the missionary spirit "in these our times is completely outmoded. The very words which by connotation are associated with it—rally, drive and revival—smack of adolescent immaturity, and are infinitely distressing to the refined and sophisticated ears of our generation."[9] Liberal Protestant leaders were turning to social issues as a means of acting on the Gospel.

Evangelical Protestants, led by conservative Presbyterians, found such liberal theological arguments abhorrent. To them, "social work" seemed a too facile identification of the world's needs with God's call. When John D. Rockefeller in 1932 sponsored an inquiry by laymen into the role of foreign missions, the resulting report urged abandonment of an exclusive focus on the religious, evangelistic character of foreign church work in favor of the models emerging in the newer service agencies. The conservative *Presbyterian Magazine* called the inquiry's conclusions "as comforting as a dentist's drill":

> It has been privately stated for some time that this Layman's Inquiry [is] the beginning of a great movement to rip to pieces foreign missionary work as it has been carried on, to take away much of its distinctively evangelical character, and generally to revamp it along modernistic lines. Wealth, worldly learning, social prestige, all are enlisted behind this effort. . . . It is a proposal to the Church to let the world run its missions.[10]

This stand, despite support within church missionary circles, remained distinctly a minority view in the church at large.

The Protestant missionary movement, the proudest incarnation of America's religious hopes for the rest of the world in 1910, found itself crowded to the side by the efforts of organized religion to keep pace with the sheer sufferings of humanity. Modern governments and methods of waging war were creating political refugees in Europe more quickly than they could be aided. The Balkan states were awash with displaced persons after the Great War; continuing hostilities between Turkey and Greece did not begin to reach a settlement before 1923. Displaced Russians flooded Eastern Europe from Poland to Constantinople. By 1927 some 9 million Italians lived outside fascist Italy.[11]

Furthermore, the religious pluralism of America, increasingly tied to the growing numbers and influence of Catholics and Jews, made it politically more difficult to identify firmly America's foreign policy interests with the interests of Protestant missionary activity. Protestant missionary societies, their primary efforts still directed at church building and evangelization, were nonetheless accustomed to praise of their educational and civilizing work. More frequently now they faced public criticism of their religious goals and methods. Though some leaders were willing to speak out about the growing refugee crises in Europe and the Middle East, the Protestant rank and file was still almost as remote from the issues as they were in 1910. International Protestant relief was still on the whole far too disorganized to mount unified efforts. Perhaps equally important, few of the refugees of the 1920s and 1930s were Protestants.

The Rise of Hitler and European Refugees

Growing Jewish alarm in America and elsewhere over Hitler's plans for the Jews had a marked effect in bringing religiously based groups in contact with U.S. government policy toward refugees. The contact was frequently hostile on both sides. There was a difference between the Jewish refugee problem and the other refugee problems created by World War I. Most of the wartime refugees were repatriated to their homelands once hostilities ceased. But the Jews of Eastern Europe and Germany were becoming an "unwanted element" in their homelands. Solving the problem meant resettling them elsewhere. Immigration legislation in 1922 had reaffirmed that American authorities intended to keep a tight rein on who was admitted to the United States. Since there was at the time no legislative definition differentiating refugees from economic migrants, immigration and naturalization laws formed the legal basis for governmental actions. A political problem of specific concern to a segment of the American public was therefore left with no direct legal remedy.

Refugees had become fixed in the public mind as a European, largely Jewish problem. Christian leaders who worked throughout the 1930s to involve churches in refugee assistance encountered widespread apathy in the churches. Jewish leaders, however, with years of experience in overseas relief as well as in domestic lobbying, began involving the government in the plight of German Jews. Their limited success was due in part to growing internal dissension within the Jewish community.

The State Department and the British Foreign Office (itself well aware of the depth of the problem due to its colonial mandate for Palestine) realized in the early 1930s that special treatment for the Jews of Germany could set a precedent capable of generating international chaos. Only 700,000 to 800,000 Jews lived within Germany itself; the overwhelming majority of the *Ostjuden* (Eastern Jews), some 7 million to 8 million in 1914, were spread across Poland, the Baltic states, Hungary, Czechoslovakia, and other nations of Eastern Europe. Poland and other East European regimes hinted that favored treatment for Jews seeking emigration from Germany to the West would encourage mass expulsions of Jews in their own territories. This possibility in itself was enough to give pause in diplomatic circles.[12]

Non-Zionist Jews, led by the American Jewish Committee and others, pressed for liberal immigration policies to the United States. They continually fought the Zionist American Jewish Congress over virtually every facet of Jewish public life. The refugee problem often figured prominently in such debates; Zionists clearly preferred more liberal immigration quotas for Palestine. The State Department and other government branches discovered that they could often buy time by playing one faction against another and by pointing to high domestic unemployment during the Depression.

The government sought cooperation with U.S. religious interests, but it was nervous about spotlighting programs primarily geared to assisting Jews. Indeed, the emergence of Nazi persecution of the Jews in the early 1930s created a climate of confusion and anxiety that disrupted the tranquillity of post–World War I religious involvement in refugee programs. Reinhold Niebuhr's characterization of the American Friends Service Committee's ethos of commitment to natural progress in human affairs was light-years away from the anxiety the Jewish community was now exhibiting over the fate of their fellow Jews. Furthermore, the government had come to recognize that private American voluntarism overseas could not always be counted on to support government policies. This had been true in Russia in the early 1920s, and it would prove true again among church agencies providing refugee and relief services during the Spanish Civil War.

The economic depression that began in 1929 placed new pressures on American immigration policy and on those private and public agencies that implemented the policies at home and abroad. With rising unemployment, immigration had once again become a politically volatile issue. Facing the increased persecution of Jews abroad, American Jewish leaders looked with dismay at the inequities of the immigration quota system, but feared public debates on the matter. About half of the 150,000 places in immigration quotas of the later 1920s were for the English and Irish, and most of them went unfilled. To make matters worse, President Hoover in 1930 sent regulations to U.S. consuls charging them to withhold visas from those persons "likely to become a public charge," a restrictive clause that appeared in the Immigration Act of 1917. This broad category could be stretched to include much of the Jewish refugee population of Germany and Central Europe.[13] Visa applications to travel to the United States quickly fell by 75 percent.[14] Shortly after his election, Franklin D. Roosevelt extended this "public charge" policy, which according to some analysts had the effect of "severely limit[ing] the number of refugees admitted as immigrants."[15]

To Jewish agencies working in Russia and Central Europe, the strict enforcement of the "public charge" clause by immigration officials meant a heavier burden in refugee camps; the same was true later for agencies such as the AFSC which served refugees from the Spanish Civil War. With no option for voluntary repatriation or third country resettlement, private agencies had to either help refugees establish themselves locally or face long-term maintenance of camps, a costly and difficult task. The Jewish press emphasized the importance of charity to support overseas work and downplayed the immigration issue to avoid stirring up anti-Semitism.[16] Jewish leaders continued nevertheless to work privately through church, governmental, and League of Nations channels to open up Jewish emigration possibilities. Leaders in the American Jewish Committee and the Joint Distribution Committee actively promoted a reorganization of the refugee mechanisms of the League of Nations.

Even though the League of Nations had established an office for refugees under Fridtjof Nansen in 1921, the office had remained independent of the League and made little concrete progress in finding durable solutions for refugee problems. By 1933, Jewish leaders were still hopeful that a reorganization would provide the basis for effective action on the German refugee problem. In October, at the urging of Henry Morgenthau, Sr. and Felix Warburg, President Roosevelt nominated James G. McDonald, a Quaker and president of New York's Foreign Policy Association, as "high commissioner for refugees (Jewish and other) coming from Germany." Though elected by vote of the League of Nations, the new high commissioner was also independent of the League, leaving his efforts without a firm constituency. Even more important, the new high commissioner would receive no funding from governments. The bulk of the financial support McDonald received came from private Jewish relief societies. Of his advisory council of twenty voluntary agencies, ten were Jewish, and Felix Warburg was personally obliged to supplement McDonald's meager salary so that he could remain financially independent.

As the doors of Western European nations began closing to German refugees, available solutions to the refugee problem dwindled. McDonald pursued alternative resettlement schemes with Jewish leaders, looking at Russia, Latin America, and (to the occasional discomfort of some of his supporters at the American Jewish Committee) Palestine. These were only minimally successful; McDonald realized that any long-term solution would require the participation of the U.S. government. However, the United States was not a member of the League, nor did it wish to intervene unnecessarily in what was clearly an internal matter of the German government. While the United States was rhetorically supportive of the high commissioner, it was not inclined to act.

When McDonald protested the strict enforcement of the "public charge" clause against refugees, Roosevelt responded that the government would not substantially change its immigration quotas to address the situation of German Jews; his letter included a vague promise that refugees would henceforth receive the most considerate attention and the most generous and favorable treatment possible under the laws of this country. There was not a word about raising the quotas or abandoning the "public charge" clause.

McDonald grew increasingly frustrated with what he saw as apathy among governmental, Jewish, and Christian agencies concerned with the German refugee problem. Among government officials, McDonald discerned sympathetic rhetoric but limited interest in attacking the refugee problem. Christians formed new organizations in the mid-1930s, notably the Federal Council of Churches' American Christian Committee for Refugees and the Catholic Committee for Refugees. Both proved to be precursors of permanent refugee organizations, the Protestant Church World Service and the Migration and Refugee Services of the U.S. Catholic Conference, but neither came close to matching the fund-raising capabilities of similar Jewish organizations in the 1930s.[17]

This cooperation in the nongovernmental realm was not enough to salvage the operations of the high commissioner's office. McDonald was not taken in by the lack of substantial progress on the problem. Indeed he saved his strongest criticism for Christian and Jewish leaders; he felt they were so preoccupied with the potential impact of the refugee problem on domestic politics that they came close to abandoning their duty. "I am shocked at the apparent lack of concern on the part of many Christian leaders for the victims of persecution conducted by those who call themselves Christians," he wrote to an official of the Federal Council of Churches. McDonald, though a lifelong supporter of Jewish causes and eventually America's first ambassador to Israel, was also frustrated by the constant infighting among Jewish factions, which he felt siphoned valuable energies away from a solution to the refugee problem. To a leader of the Jewish Joint Distribution Committee, he complained about "the failure of the Jewish world to respond adequately. . . . except for a few individuals here and there, and except for the leaders of the Zionists, who . . . you must admit have the courage of their convictions—there has been no response anywhere proportionate to the need."[18] Distraught over what appeared to him as indifference to the plight of refugees, McDonald abruptly resigned his post on January 1, 1936. It was clear to him that efforts to establish an effective multinational response to refugee problems had reached a dead end. In consultation with leaders of the American Jewish Committee and the American Jewish Joint Distribution Committee, McDonald decided to write a public letter of resignation that would further focus attention on the seriousness of the problem and the inadequacy of the response.

Jewish leaders were concerned about the effects of a public debate over the admission of expanded numbers of Jewish refugees to the United States. In 1938 Representatives Emmanuel Celler and Samuel Dickstein sought to break the logjam in refugee admissions to the United States by organizing hearings for new legislation. The Celler/Dickstein proposals involved circumventing the immigration quota system by a concept known as "mortgaging." Under quota mortgaging, future quotas for Germany, say from 1939 to 1945, would become available immediately to refugees who faced pressing needs at the moment. The congressmen also wanted any new legislation to liberalize interpretations of the "likely to become a public charge" clause.

A coalition of Christian and Jewish groups including the Federal Council of Churches' American Christian Committee for Refugees, HIAS, the Joint Distribution Committee, and the National Catholic Welfare Conference's Catholic Committee for Refugees met to discuss the situation. It was difficult to assess the impact of such public debates in a country unsympathetic to immigration in the midst of its own economic depression. The assembled Christian and Jewish leaders shared the opinion that "efforts to secure such legislation at the present time will be distinctly unwise."[19] The agencies realized that they faced a restrictionist policy in the government that would not be improved by controversial public hearings. The hearings were postponed.

The situation unearthed elements of religion's involvement in the government's foreign policy apparatus. The refugee issue had reactivated, largely on Jewish initiatives, the World War I era "three faiths" alliance of Protestants, Catholics, and Jews. Support for this alliance in the Christian world rarely extended below the upper levels of church leadership of the day. Church funding of refugee causes in the late 1930s and early 1940s rarely reached 20 percent of the total raised by the Jewish community, but the concept of commingling funds and working together on common concerns all the groups faced in their relations with the government had been firmly planted. The National Refugee Committee established under joint Christian and Jewish leadership in 1939, though mainly the result of Jewish initiative, was another instance of such "three faiths" cooperation.

A more complex issue in the church/state realm was Washington's unwillingness to pursue the interests of one of the nation's own religious minorities. In contrast to the success of the Jewish community in overturning the trade treaty with Russia in 1911 over the issue of human rights, the government was notably unresponsive on the question of German Jews. As Jews and many Christians saw the situation, it was all the more reason for America's religious communities to band together to guard their common interests in overseas activities. Yet the government had a precedent for avoiding involvement in welfare activities focused on a particular religious group. Had a State Department counsel sought legal precedent for limiting government involvement in private welfare restricted by race or creed, it could have been found in the 1899 *Bradfield* decision. However, the situation of Jews of Germany was a political problem, not primarily a legal problem of providing welfare in a settled domestic context. Political expedience rather than legal efforts to instill evenhandedness would prevail.

The Spanish Civil War and New German Aggression

Besides the problem of German Jewish refugees, another crisis of the 1930s drew the attention of Christian agencies that had worked abroad since World War I:

relief for victims of the Spanish Civil War. The magnitude of this refugee problem temporarily dwarfed that of Germans facing persecution by Hitler; observers estimated that between 1 and 3 million refugees were displaced within Spain during the war.

The AFSC representative in Spain in 1937 sent this plea to the Friends' headquarters in Philadelphia: "Shall we send food to these undernourished orphans and refugee children and mothers who stretch out their hands in hunger to us? . . . Shall we mediate a love that will reach those who suffer in the dark shadows of this modern crucifixion?"[20] Clarence Pickett, then director of the American Friends Service Committee, believed that the Spanish Civil War was an opportunity for the AFSC to provide neutral humanitarian service in the midst of the "climate of doom" that was enveloping Spain and all Europe.[21] This capacity, so critical in placing the Friends in the front rank of religious relief in earlier years, again made them the leading private agency in refugee relief. They were joined in a special committee on Spain by representatives of the Federal Council of Churches, the Mennonite Central Committee, and the Brethren Service Committee. The American Red Cross decided not to intervene in the conflict, but encouraged the AFSC and donated hundreds of thousands of dollars worth of gifts in kind.

But the reputation of the Friends for neutrality was not strong enough to quell growing suspicions in the Roosevelt White House that relief agencies were playing a partisan role. It was well known that the Spanish War had revived old divisions among American religious groups. Protestants (and the umbrella secular relief group, the Medical Aid Committee) were notably partial to the Republicans; Catholics generally supported Franco's Nationalist movement. The AFSC had to tread carefully through this minefield; even though staff sympathies were with the Republicans, the Friends alternately found themselves in territory held by Nationalists and Republicans, and maintained that they offered services to noncombatant refugees on an evenhanded basis. However, in 1939 the Friends and other American agencies serving in Spain followed the defeated Republican refugees across the Pyrenees into France "in the bitter cold and snow, with defeat and despair in their hearts."[22] They remained with the 250,000 to 300,000 refugees in camps in western France until the rupture of diplomatic relations between the United States and Vichy France forced the Friends' removal in 1942.

Assurances of AFSC neutrality were not enough for legislators debating the U.S. position on the European conflict in 1939. Under pressure from the Nye Committee in the Senate to reduce arms shipments, the Congress in 1935 had passed the Neutrality Act designed to keep American economic and military interests from becoming embroiled in the growing hostilities. During the Spanish Civil War, Secretary of State Cordell Hull used this legislation as the basis to withhold passports for members of several private voluntary medical units, arguing that such controls were necessary to preserve U.S. neutrality. Tighter regulation of all private American relief abroad followed from congressional debates in 1939, when new provisions of the Neutrality Act established a registration system under the Commerce Department for all relief agencies shipping goods abroad. In all, twenty-six voluntary agencies responded to the government's request that they register and submit monthly statements of contributions. Thus, according to Merle Curti, "was begun an official supervision of voluntary giving for overseas relief, which was to become a continuing aspect of American policy."[23]

The Watered Down Hopes of Evian

Facing the desperate situation of Jews in Europe, American Jews welcomed any expansion of the role of the government in the Jewish refugee problem. Nothing short of the full authority of the U.S. government, in concert with its European allies, could bring assistance at needed levels. A new ray of hope appeared in March 1938, when President Roosevelt announced that the United States would call a world conference on refugees in Evian, France.[24]

In mid-April, representatives of the voluntary agencies met at the White House to discuss the Evian Conference; in addition to Bernard Baruch, Henry Morgenthau, Jr., James G. McDonald, and Joseph Chamberlain, other participants represented Protestant, Catholic, and Jewish organizations. Baruch was a longtime confidant of the president; Morgenthau was the secretary of the treasury. Chamberlain, professor of law at Columbia University, had served as chairman of the National Coordinating Committee, which had been established in 1935 by the State Department to regulate all private refugee relief.[25] From this meeting arose the President's Advisory Committee on Political Refugees (PACPR). McDonald, ineffective in his previous role as high commissioner for German refugees, was named chairman of the committee, a move that augured poorly for the seriousness with which its recommendations would be taken by the Roosevelt administration. After a second meeting, Roosevelt had no contact with the committee. Given other political pressures of the day, the refugee problem continued to be given low priority by the government. The PACPR itself continued for several years, engaging the State Department in various battles over visa restrictions, but it never exercised a formative role in America's refugee policy.

Myron C. Taylor, president of U.S. Steel and soon to be named Roosevelt's envoy to the Vatican, headed the U.S. delegation to Evian. One reporter noted that the nine days of proceedings resembled a poker game, with suspicions of U.S. motives running high. Why, wondered Britain, France, and other allies, had the United States called such a conference rather than working through existing refugee structures of the League of Nations? And what was its purpose, given U.S. assurances that it had no intention of raising its immigration quota, and would not call on other participants to do so?

Such misgivings were not resolved by the formation of a new, non-League of Nations agency, the Intergovernmental Committee on Political Refugees (IGC). Most observers felt the committee was mere window dressing, since its mandate did not include raised immigration quotas and it specifically excluded the possibility of more immigration to Palestine, the solution favored by most private Jewish groups. When it became clear that the United States was not only refusing to expand its resettlement activities, but also failing to admit the full existing quota from Germany, it was obvious that Evian would solve nothing for the refugees. One observer left in disgust, calling the conference "a facade behind which the civilized governments could hide their inability to act."[26] Among the Jews of

America and elsewhere, a chilling message of the indifference of others to their fate was beginning to emerge.

Avoiding a "Jewish Problem"

Whatever governments had said at Evian, nothing concrete came of the gathering; none of the Western democracies wanted to be directly involved with Berlin on the subject. Indeed, it was said in those days that no one spoke of Jews except in Berlin. The State Department had advanced the "neutral" term "political refugees," which both masked the essentially racial nature of the problem and lent the cause a sense of implied urgency. The president had loaded his committee of advisors earlier in the year with Christian representatives in part because of their interest, but administration officials were sure that such broad representation would aid in camouflaging the specifically Jewish character of the problem.[27]

Thus, when Hjalmar Schacht, the moderate head of the German Reichsbank arrived quietly in London to negotiate a Western "buy off" of German Jews in December 1938, members of the IGC listened eagerly, but kept the offer out of the public eye. George Rublee, newly appointed American head of the IGC, knew that the Germans' cooperation would be essential in saving the lives of—and eventually resettling—the German Jews. But with American public opinion increasingly in favor of restricting immigration, the hands of diplomats were tied.

The proposal involved moving 150,000 wage-earning Jews outside Germany over a three-year period. Schacht's plan, inspired in part by Germany's growing foreign trade deficit, called for the German government to impound 25 percent of all assets belonging to departing Jews. This fund would be held in trust by the Germans as collateral for an international bond issue arranged through a corporation formed by "international Jewry." Theoretically, according to arguments advanced by Schacht, the refugees would repay the expense of resettlement through the proceeds of resettlement projects, in which they would work. This represented one of the earliest efforts at capitalizing the refugee problem, an idea that would emerge again in the 1980s among some Third World officials frustrated with ineffective methods of refugee assistance from the West.

In the stony silence of the London conference room, Schacht insisted that the morality of the Reich's Jewish policies was not under discussion; he had come to do business. After he left, the IGC representatives divided into two committees, one of government representatives, the other of leaders of the private voluntary community. The members of each realized that they were being asked to participate in a ransom demand based on German theories of international Jewish organization. Despite the efforts of Rublee and others, no agreement was ever made. Years later Schacht was acquitted in the Nuremberg trials on the strength of the argument that had his plan been accepted, no German Jew would have died during the war.

Negotiations surrounding the Schacht proposals reflected the reluctance of government officials to admit private voluntary representatives as partners at this bottom-line level of addressing the refugee problem. Though the agencies had participated in initial responses to Schacht, the IGC had proceeded with negotiations on a German agreement without consulting either the agencies or the international Jewish leadership. As work on this agreement progressed, private efforts necessarily slowed. Every option presented difficulties.

No private agency—no group of private agencies—was capable of funding alternative resettlement schemes, let alone administering them. Internationally, Jews threatened to boycott any direct agreement with the Reich. American Jews wondered whether they could safely entrust their fellow Jews to non-Jews; Paul Baerwald, head of the Jewish Joint Distribution Committee, confided to Rabbi Stephen Wise that he was reluctant to take responsibility for a venture that would involve non-Jewish funding. Baerwald was told that there was no way that Congress could legally appropriate funds for the resettlement of refugees, and that this would have to be borne by private voluntary organizations. Resettlement schemes arose from England (British Guiana) and the United States (the Virgin Islands, Alaska, and the Philippine province of Mindanao).

The strongest proponent of such resettlement schemes was President Roosevelt himself, though Roosevelt's solutions to the refugee problem often produced fanciful schemes that never materialized. In 1938, he wrote to the president of Johns Hopkins University, Isaiah Bowman: "Frankly what I am looking for is the possibility of uninhabited or sparsely inhabited good agricultural lands to which Jewish colonies might be sent . . . , all this is merely for my own information because there are no specific plans."[28] Roosevelt eventually had resettlement options investigated in Africa and Latin America. In 1939, speaking to the officers of Evian's Intergovernmental Committee assembled in Washington, FDR encouraged them to consider the feasibility of massive resettlement projects somewhere in the "many vacant spaces of the earth's surface." In a striking adaptation of the words of Emma Lazarus inscribed on the Statue of Liberty, Roosevelt told the delegates that America was ready to help the refugees, as long as they moved elsewhere. "Let us," he said, "lift a lamp beside *new* golden doors and build *new* refuges for the tired, the poor, the huddled masses yearning to breathe free."[29] (emphasis added)

"Seekers of Peace" and "Seekers of Light"

Roosevelt believed that the entire religious community should participate in solving refugee problems. Roosevelt was one of the few public officials who realized that the refugee crisis would not only remain after the war but would probably expand. Given this perception, he moved personally to assure a continued partnership between the government and America's religious communities in providing relief and resettlement services. In a confidential memorandum to Secretary of State Hull in October 1939, Roosevelt set forth a plan to achieve the necessary public support: a solution to the "whole refugee problem," he reasoned, could be promoted "on a broad religious basis, thereby making it possible to gain the kind of world-wide support that a mere Jewish relief set-up would not evoke."[30] To him, the obvious first step was to send an "Ambassador on Special Mission to the Vatican" to assure participation of the Roman Catholic church. Accordingly, in December Myron Taylor was sent to Rome, instructed to stress the administration's particular concern for Catholic refugees and to encourage the active participation of the Vatican in meeting refugee needs.

In the bleak Christmas season of 1939, Roosevelt composed a telegram to leaders of the Federal Council of Churches, the Joint Distribution Committee, and to his Vatican envoy Myron Taylor, outlining what he hoped would be an attitude of cooperation between religious groups active overseas and the U.S. government. An excerpt from this message to the "three faiths" of America shows Roosevelt's skill at invoking the parallel responsibilities of the nation's religious leaders (the "seekers of light") and its political authorities (the "seekers of peace"):

> Again, during the several centuries which we refer to as the Dark Ages, the flame and sword of barbarians swept over Western civilization; and, again, through a rekindling of the inherent spiritual spark in mankind, another rebirth brought back order and culture and religion.
>
> I believe that the travail of today is a new form of these old conflicts. . .[yet] in their hearts men decline to accept, for long, the law of destruction forced upon them by wielders of brute force.
>
> Always they seek, sometimes in silence, to find again the faith without which the welfare of nations and the peace of the world cannot be rebuilt. . . .
>
> I believe that while statesmen are considering a new order of things, the new order may well be at hand. I believe that it is even now being built, silently but inevitably, in the hearts of masses whose voices are not heard, but whose common faith will write the final history of our time. They know that unless there is belief in some guiding principle and some trust in a divine plan, nations are without light, and peoples perish. They know that the civilization handed down to us by our fathers was built by men and women who knew in their hearts that all were brothers because they were children of God. They believe that by His will enmities can be healed; that in his mercy the weak can find deliverance, and the strong can find grace in helping the weak. . . .
>
> Because the people of this nation have come to a realization that time and distance no longer exist in the older sense, they understand that that which harms one segment of humanity harms all the rest. They know that only by friendly association between the seekers of light and the seekers of peace everywhere can the forces of evil be overcome. . . .
>
> It is, therefore, my thought that though no given action or given time may now be prophesied, *it is well that we encourage a closer association between those in every part of the world—those in religion and those in government—who have a common purpose.* I, therefore, suggest that it would give me great satisfaction if you would from time to time come to Washington to discuss the problem which all of us have on our minds, in order that parallel endeavors for peace and the alleviation of suffering may be assisted.[31] (emphasis added)

No clearer bid for cooperation between the government and America's religious institutions could be expected or offered. Unfortunately in 1939 the moral, legal, and logistical problems involved in such cooperation were far from being solved.

No credible international organization had been formed to coordinate governmental efforts; the Roosevelt administration spoke eloquently of the plight of European Jews, but its actions indicated a desire to distance itself from politically unpopular efforts to liberalize immigration law or otherwise to increase the number of Jews reaching America. International diplomats considered schemes to purchase the lives of refugees; political leaders dreamed of impractical colonization plans; religious leaders argued for their favored approaches; and the public was left divided between the appeals of refugee advocates and the shrill denunciations of immigration restrictionists and America Firsters. No one power, no collection of private and public authorities, was capable of addressing the root causes of the burgeoning problem of political refugees, and now Europe itself was submerged in war.

Those who followed events in Washington knew that the situation was about to undergo significant alteration. The issue was not one of simply maintaining continuity with America's traditions of providing safe haven to the oppressed. The issues would focus on the size, scale, and efficiency of the particular relief organization, be it Protestant, Catholic, Jewish, or secular. The spiritual and religious aspects of the work became entirely secondary to the government; for the moment the government welcomed a pragmatic alliance with America's religious bodies.

Roosevelt's rhetoric about "trust in a divine plan" aside, the U.S. government had a serious, unsolved, and growing refugee problem on its hands, and it needed all the help it could get. Religious groups had done their part in meeting human needs associated with the nation's foreign policy, stretching back to before the constitutional foundations of the republic. They would do so again, and in the process of aiding new waves of refugees, they would usher in an era of church/state cooperation beyond the nation's borders. By casting wide their humanitarian net, religious agencies would find themselves caught up in new political dilemmas, but they believed it was worth the struggle. Most shared the hope that their efforts might ameliorate the tragedy of the cataclysms shaking the world and that it might be possible, in a world dominated by constant struggle and conflict, to do something for the victims.

4

The World War II Alliance (1939–1945)

It is a truism that World War II changed the political and economic shape of the world. The war's effect on subsequent U.S. church/state relations abroad is no exception. Over little more than a decade the efforts of U.S. religious communities to serve those in need overseas were rapidly annexed and adapted by Washington's foreign policymakers. The needs of the coming era dictated that church and state learn to go abroad *together,* and no endeavor demonstrated that necessity better than refugee work. World War II was the decisive turning point in the humanitarian alliance between church and state in refugee work abroad.

In the brief interlude between the political aggressions of Hitler and Stalin, Americans confronted the shock of Auschwitz and Dachau, unlocking powerful religious feelings in both the Jewish and Christian communities. The holocaust drew Jews to a renewed Zionism and hope for a Jewish state. Facing an overwhelming sense of abandonment by God and by their fellow human beings, they built new organizations to help their surviving brethren and strengthened traditional structures. Before the decade was out, Jews would shed tears of joy over the accomplishment of the Zionist dream, 'Heretz Israel.

Among Christians, there was a sense that a new work of religious restitution was at hand, an era of service for the greater good of humanity. Horror at the fate of the Jews of Europe and the numbing effects of the wider conflict demanded a concerted response from church and state. Herbert Hoover, called from retirement once again in 1945 to survey humanitarian needs in Europe, approached the U.S. military occupation of Germany from a theological perspective. "We can carry on the Military Government of Germany by the tenets of the Old Testament of 'a tooth for a tooth and an eye for an eye,' or we can inaugurate the precepts of the New Testament. The difference in result will be the loss of millions of lives, the damage of all Europe, and the destruction of any hope of peace in the world. I recommend the New Testament method."[1]

What exactly Hoover had in mind in suggesting that the occupying forces adopt the "New Testament method" is unclear. Were such a proposal made in the 1980s, those who follow Supreme Court rulings on church/state relations doubtless would find it highly suspect. What is clear is that refugee work in the 1940s saw a new integration of government policy and the efforts of religious agencies, an integration that took place largely without reference to constitutional questions of church and state. The patterns set in this period still determine the basic framework of the government's alliance with religious bodies and other private groups active in international relief work.

A clear pattern was established. The expansion of the foreign affairs power of the executive branch became increasingly dominant and virtually irreversible. One of the greatest wartime tasks of the Roosevelt White House was planning ways in which the United States could manage a postwar coalition of victor nations. This meant administrative tasks, regulatory groups, and structures of oversight on a scale previously unknown. Such expanded executive power, including military strategy on a global scale, placed new strains on the delicate constitutional balance of powers between Congress, the president, and the courts. No segment of society was left a fully autonomous role, as the private voluntary world soon discovered. As in most wartime situations, the autonomy and freedom of religious institutions were curtailed. Law under these circumstances became more of an administrative tool and less an independent beacon of objective justice, thus bearing out the view of the nineteenth-century legal scholar Gierke, who said law "is the result not of a common will that a thing shall be, but of a common conviction that it is."[2] Under a series of executive orders, laws of Congress, and administrative decisions, public and private forces joined with common conviction to help the world's needy.

Europe's war-torn refugees were the chief beneficiaries of the ensuing partnership between church and state. Few quarreled at the time with religion's entry into the political arena or bothered to look deeply at long-term institutional ramifications. Even fewer noticed that traditional notions of the separation of church and state were less than adequate for describing the new levels of moral, financial, and administrative cooperation between church and state begun in the 1940s. Before the decade ended, new domestic church/state rulings and disputes would further clarify the extent to which this cooperation abroad lay beyond the framework that the Supreme Court was developing at home.

Neutrality Legislation of 1939

As official Washington struggled to avoid involvement in the European conflicts, the voluntary sector abroad became a political orphan. There was no international strategy for refugees, only promises and schemes ranging from incarceration to some form of migration to safety, an option that could not be undertaken without the active participation of the U.S. government. Once the war came, however, U.S. officials shelved all such efforts. Religious agencies were preoccupied by the horror of refugees' innocent suffering, and they pursued this theme before Congress as well as in Europe and Palestine. They sought strategies for maintaining their services in Europe and elsewhere, arguing that they provided the desperately needed humanitarian component of the American presence in the war.[3]

Experienced overseas voluntary agencies understood that the United States government's relief and refugee commitments would be determined by international security concerns as well as domestic political pressures. Acknowledging the legitimacy of the war goals was an assumed requirement for any private agency that hoped to be taken seriously as a legitimate political voice. By September 1939 Secretary of State Cordell Hull called attention to existing neutrality legislation that made "all solicitations and collections of funds. . .subject to the approval of the President. . .under such rules and regulations as he shall prescribe."[4] The Neutrality Act of 1939, signed into law on November 4, extended the neutrality provisions governing the conduct of American relief activities in Spain, and now covered Poland, Germany, the United Kingdom, and France. In addition to governing the collection of funds, the act controlled certain forms of relief to nations the president considered belligerent.

The neutrality legislation might have limited American liability, but it did nothing to address the suffering in Europe. The words of Quaker representatives still active in France reflected a growing sense of desperation. "You get an average of 37,000 refugees pouring through a town each day. . . . Practically none of them have any clothing but what they stand up in," said a Quaker broadcasting to America from Paris in June 1940. The following month, a report came from Toulouse:

> One of the great problems is the condition of 40,000 Belgian boys between the ages of 15 and 22, who were evacuated by their government as they had not yet been mobilized. . . . They are housed in camps, garages, barns. . . .They are hungry all the time. . . .They are becoming a social menace. . . . The army is all over the place, being demobilized.

From Marseille, in September:

> It is heartbreaking to be charged with the responsibilities of deciding who shall eat and who shall go hungry, who shall have clothing and who shall have none. Dispensing charity in France today means exercising the power of life or death over one's fellows. How does one do it and retain his sanity?

In the fall of 1941, the curtailment of feeding programs for refugee children forced workers to select which children would be fed, often in view of the others:

> While this sad little choice is being made, the other children come forward and ask eagerly, "May we not have milk also?" And looking down on what is often a small thin face, the answer is made as cheerfully as possible, "*no! You* are *well!* The doctor has ordered it for the sick ones. You must be thankful that you don't need it!"[5]

Despite official restrictions, American voluntarism surged with new life. The Quakers spent nearly $1 million on war relief in 1940; donations to all agencies the year before was $2.5 million. In 1941, the total donations from private sources jumped to $28.5 million. While this record was the pride of the agencies and their constituencies, government officials realized that relief work was being conducted on far too small a scale to meet the needs that lay ahead. Not only would relief services need to be expanded, but the government would also have to standardize private efforts and insure that they did not overlap.

Organizing Wartime Relief

The government, following President Roosevelt's lead in asking religious leaders for closer cooperation in fending off a fundamental threat to American society, encouraged church groups to form relief societies that would both raise funds and, with fellow believers abroad, operate relief programs where needed. Before the United States entered the war, there was general agreement within the State Department that the relief agencies' activities abroad should not embroil the United States in the conflict. Once America entered the war, religious groups were expected to conform to Allied military policy. For the most part, refugee care would rely on the same Jewish and Christian organizations whose help would later be needed in the wartime and postwar humanitarian assistance. Roosevelt also knew that close Jewish and Catholic involvement with government initiatives carried the potential for political divisiveness at home, something he was eager to avoid during wartime. Far from anticipating mass slaughter of European Jews, Roosevelt foresaw a massive influx of millions of refugees to other Western nations. At once the most visionary and disinterested of migrationists, he was all for helping refugees so long as the attending political complications could be avoided.

Who would organize the effort? The head of the New York-based Foreign Policy Association, when asked to lead Roosevelt's 1938 advisory committee on political refugees, declined with the rejoinder that his interests were "after all [more] international relations than relief or philanthropy."[6] The government's early responses were cautious, quiet, and largely ineffective. It wanted the help of America's religious institutions, but it wanted to avoid the interreligious squabbles of World War I. When the neutrality controls were strengthened in 1939, State Department officials called a meeting to discuss relief coordination; only the American Red Cross was brought in as a partner to these discussions. After the meetings, a memo to Roosevelt suggested the formation of a "small, self-appointed committee" to coordinate, supervise, and consolidate relief "by endorsing certain organizations and refusing to endorse others." It was three years before the the final version of this plan materialized.[7]

While publicly stating its intention to keep America neutral in the European conflict, the State Department was also in the early months of 1941 quietly planning a new role for America in the postwar world. In early March, Secretary of State Cordell Hull sent a letter to President Roosevelt in which he discussed the supervision of overseas relief societies. Of these groups, only the American Red Cross carried explicit congressional authority. The other agencies were essentially free agents, existing on private funds and accepting government assistance at times of emergency. Their help would be needed to maintain peace in the postwar world.

The time had come, according to Hull, to strengthen the connection between voluntary foreign aid and official American policy. A first step had been taken with the Neutrality Act of 1939. Agencies would be officially "licensed" for operations abroad only if they registered with the State Department. Export of relief goods, already limited by the 1917 Trading with the Enemy Act, would be reported to the Commerce Department. The task, Secretary Hull advised the president, was to regulate agencies so that they could serve as conduits of government-funded assistance. Despite cautions from such journals as the Catholic *Commonweal* that such direct government involvement would undermine "that personal element which imparts to charity its true nature and its characteristic graces," many agency and government officials were ready to proceed with new arrangements.[8]

Hull offered two basic arguments for a closer link between private and public activities overseas, both of which made perfect sense at the time and are still essential elements of State Department doctrine in working with private groups. First, a strengthened public authority in this field would help assure that the goals of the agencies were actually met, and that the public would be protected from fraudulent groups. Second, without greater coordination, the best of human efforts would end up in duplication, inefficiency, and failure to meet the situation in an even-handed way. While it may not have been stated publicly, officials anticipated that any relief activities after the war would be supervised by the Allied military governments and a good working relationship with American civilians in the field would be essential. Hull's rationales covered the territory of church/state cooperation without unnecessarily drawing attention to anticipated conflicts over direct involvement with Catholics and Jews.[9]

It took a crisis to move the government to act. Military reverses in Europe and in the Pacific in the first half of 1942 left the White House no choice but to request even stronger relief efforts. In radio broadcasts in June of that year, Roosevelt forcefully called for national unity in winning the war:

> We Americans have been compelled to yield ground, and we will regain it. We and the other United Nations are committed to the destruction of the militarism of Japan and Germany. We are daily increasing our strength. Soon we, and not our enemies, will have the offensive; we, not they, will win the final battles; and we not they, will make the final peace.

That same month, at a national meeting of war-related charities, Winthrop W. Aldrich, chairman of New York's Chase National Bank, suggested that overseas relief efforts should be federated. Given America's difficult military position overseas, the suggestion was greeted with enthusiasm.[10]

The President's War Relief Control Board

Frustrated with the inability of his own State Department to move quickly on such problems, Roosevelt named a civilian committee to investigate possible arrangements between the nation's private relief activities and the government's strategy for victory. Accepting the committee's conclusion that "the establishment of a single authority with adequate regulatory and supervisory powers" was needed, on July 25, 1942, Roosevelt issued Executive Order 9205 creating the President's War Relief Control Board (PWRCB). Its function of formalizing relations between private and public humanitarian efforts, in altered form, remained part of government bureaucracy through the mid-1980s. Its beginnings as a presidential advisory group lifted the sights of the private relief community. In a single executive order they achieved access to the president which circumvented the various cabinet departments.

As the government liaison with the world of voluntarism, the board had wartime powers, including authority over all solicitations, sales, collections, distribution, disposal of funds, and contributions in kind for overseas relief and refugee work. In exchange for government protection and access to federal assistance, whether administered directly or through the emerging intergovernmental structures of relief such as the United Nations Relief and Rehabilitation Administration (UNRRA), certain conditions applied. For instance, the PWRCB asked many agencies to rename themselves to include the word "American." All agencies that participated in government-sponsored fund raising were required to have governing boards consisting of American citizens only; their programs overseas were to be conducted "purely in the American interest."[11] Decisions on the disbursement of government assistance would be made by executive and budget committees that did not include representatives of the agencies themselves. The PWRCB was given police powers to crack down on overseas relief agencies that violated political and administrative regulations. The use of such powers, however, was generally limited to agencies that served as fronts for shipments of munitions or supplies to political factions, most of which were ethnic rather than religious in origin. The new regulations also gave the board control over the timing of agency fund-raising appeals and the authority to consolidate agencies that shared similar objectives.

The National War Fund

The PWRCB's major effort at coordinating overseas relief was the establishment of the National War Fund, the centralized, government-supported fund-raising machine that regulated appeals and divided donations among selected private agencies based in the United States. The fund emerged from a December 1942, meeting at the New York headquarters of the Chase National Bank, where Winthrop W. Aldrich gathered five other appointees to manage the War Fund at the request of the PWRCB. Rather than invite representatives from religious and other agencies, the government had appointed prominent academics, business leaders, and bankers who could preside without partisanship. The resulting plan consolidated fund-raising drives through local and state community chests, a wartime United Fund that would then be disbursed by the government to areas of greatest need overseas, using the voluntary agencies that qualified as members.

In a lively memoir detailing his service as general manager of the War Fund, Harold J. Seymour observes that one of the touchiest problems was deciding on who qualified as recipient agencies. Nearly 600 agencies registered with the board, but only 23 participated in the National War Fund. What principles, then, governed inclusion?

Registration with the President's War Relief Control Board quickly became essential in establishing an agency's credibility and trustworthiness. Second, in the interests of efficiency only one agency would be included for a particular operation or function—agencies were consolidated around service to prisoners of war, to refugees, or to specific countries.[12] The third principle was a nondiscrimination clause, stating that all funds had to be disbursed "without regard to color, creed, race or political affiliation." Seymour spells this out: "Specifically, it meant that labor-sponsored projects could not be designed for the relief of labor groups alone, and that no denominational relief program, to the extent that it was financed by the National War Fund, could confine its work to the adherents of its own faith." This principle of nondiscrimination had been accepted in government funding at home and it seemed logical to extend it abroad, where in fact it was already emerging as a common law principle of international humanitarianism. The problem was that it did not meet the reality of humanitarianism as practiced in 1942.[13]

Accommodating the Catholic Church

The question of direct participation of religious agencies was itself a political, if not legal, question. Questions of church and state prior to World War II were often connected with anti-Catholicism; controversy still existed over the Catholic role in the War Fund. According to Seymour, to list the newly formed War Relief Services (WRS) of the National Catholic Welfare Conference "without policy explanation. . .would be to invite question and confusion." Despite such difficulties, "everyone wanted to include the Catholic agency, both in the interest of unity and for the practical reason that the world-wide organization of the Roman Catholic Church. . .provided a ready channel for speedy, effective, and economical relief."[14]

In fact, negotiations were already under way in 1942 between the White House and NCWC leaders to explore a closer relationship with the Catholic hierarchy in the United States and their superiors in the Vatican. One participant in these negotiations recalled that they were conducted in an atmosphere that verged on desperation. "No one knew where the world was going," he said. "It seemed to all to be a moment of supreme crisis."[15]

Roosevelt already had appointed Myron Taylor to the Vatican, but the organized services of American Catholics were now required. The goals of the president were twofold. First, he wanted the NCWC to organize a national agency devoted to overseas relief. The Bishop's War Emergency and Relief Committee, in existence since 1939, was raising comparatively small amounts of private funding and providing limited overseas services. In late 1942, Roosevelt's representatives met with leaders of the NCWC; it was noted that in planning the new War Fund it might be advantageous to organize a "super agency" that would supercede the bishop's committee and preclude applications to the War Fund by the sixty or so Catholic charities actively related to service institutions in the war zones. He also wanted to open more extensive intelligence contacts with the Vatican on situations inside Germany.

Exactly one month after Winthrop Aldrich announced plans for a National War Fund, a special meeting of the National Catholic Welfare Conference's administrative board responded to the government's request for a new overseas agency. Government guarantees of funding to supplement private resources were assured. The new agency, the War Relief Services of the NCWC, was admitted to the National War Fund on April 28; two days later eleven projects budgeted at nearly $2.4 million were submitted to the budget committee of the War Fund. Projects included work with Polish refugees in Mexico and Palestine, Catholic refugees in England and Portugal, prisoners of war, and services to seamen. Also included was an initial request to cover the expenses of the Catholic Committee for Refugees, which since 1936 had been assisting refugees coming to the United States.

From late May through most of June, representatives of the new War Relief Services negotiated acceptable conditions under which they would work with government funds. On June 25, Aldrich and WRS announced the signing of a memorandum of agreement. The agreement stipulated that government funds would cover "health and welfare projects. . .as distinct from church and religious activities," and gave the National War Fund responsibility for negotiating with any foreign agencies that were affiliated with the new agency. After the successful completion of these negotiations the incorporation papers for War Relief Services were filed on

June 28.[16] As a matter of wartime pragmatism, WRS was raised to favored status among the voluntary agencies. By September of 1944, the fledgling agency was active in thirty-three countries.

Roosevelt's goal of more sophisticated intelligence in Germany through improved links with the Vatican was also accomplished in part through WRS, whose personnel maintained contact with the largely Catholic opposition Centrist party in Germany, which had been forced underground by the Nazis. This intelligence network complemented formal channels of information passed on to the United States through Myron Taylor and two assistants at the Vatican.[17] Thus the Catholic War Relief Services—today as CRS the largest voluntary agency in the world—included intelligence links with the U.S. government from its earliest days. Participants clearly felt that rendering assistance to the Allies was the only sane route, an act of religious and patriotic duty. Though agreements for cooperation in intelligence were not part of the formal agreements between WRS and the government, the Roosevelt administration expected and received cooperation.

Administrative arrangements rather than congressional or court decisions governed the formation of cooperative church/state ties during the war. Indeed, the hair-splitting church/state legal decisions of recent years would have had little place in the administration of government contracts with religious bodies through the National War Fund. Seymour emphasizes that mutual understanding and goodwill were the true moving forces within the War Fund, "rather than. . .a legalistic basis of binding contracts. . .[which] in themselves were scarcely worth their ink and paper." (This flexibility over the significance of legal issues should be kept in mind when we explore legal matters of church and state in greater depth.) Private and public forces were working together not because of financial contracts, but in a national covenant for survival and victory in the midst of war. "Dynamic federation" and "maximum decentralization" were concepts common to all. The fund sought to dispense, along with its funds, "authoritative advice" rather than "authoritarian control" over the way funds were spent. Such fine distinctions may be lost when agencies see their responsibilities abroad in conflict with governmental "advice." This was the case with the refugee problem, which was becoming far worse than had been expected. By 1943 refugee advocates in religious and other agencies knew that the Roosevelt administration, for all of its sympathetic rhetoric, had little intention of taking decisive action in the midst of the war.[18]

The Refusal to Rescue Jews

The resettlement of refugees in the United States was never in favor during the war. The State Department's assistant secretary for special problems, Breckinridge Long, was charged with responding to the pleas of advocacy groups. Refugee advocates were to him "communists, extreme radicals, Jewish professional agitators, refugee enthusiasts." Alluding to the frequent intervention of Supreme Court Justice Felix Frankfurter in behalf of Jewish refugees, Long called Jewish refugee workers "Frankfurter's boys." Long represented an unabashedly nationalist point of view: "As usual, they (the radicals) espouse some foreign cause. . .rather than advocate the AMERICAN point of view or propose some practice in our own interests. . . . There is a constant pressure from Congressional and organized groups in this country to have us proceed on behalf of non-Americans; so far I have been able to resist the pressure."[19]

Long determined he would use his post to emphasize the security problems involved in bringing refugees to the United States. He resented the liberal interventions of the President's Advisory Committee on Political Refugees and opposed them throughout the war. There was little doubt that powerful conservative members of Congress, as well as the overwhelming majority of the public, favored the restrictionist policies Long advocated. The importance of security questions in public debate over immigration affairs at this time cannot be overestimated. In 1940, for instance, the Immigration and Naturalization Service (INS) was transferred from the Department of Labor to the Justice Department, where it remains to this day. According to Secretary of Labor Frances Perkins, this was done because the administration had decided that immigration was primarily a security rather than an economic issue.

The record testifies to the unpleasantness that arose early in the war between the government and privately organized efforts of citizens committed to helping refugees overseas and at home. Quite unlike the "three faiths" world of refugee assistance that emerged after the World War I, the bulk of the refugee aid from the United States at the beginning of the 1940s came from Jewish sources. The National Refugee Commitee (the existing coordinating structure for voluntary agencies prior to 1943) was headed by a Protestant, Joseph Chamberlain, and contained Protestant, Catholic, and Jewish agencies. However, Jewish agencies and funding predominated. Most of the existing Protestant and Catholic groups found that they could not raise funds from their constituencies in large amounts, and quietly accepted subsidies from Jewish groups. Long's observation that refugee advocates were largely Jewish was true; he also discerned that Catholic and Protestant support was limited at best, and he acted accordingly.

The most bitterly disappointing of all the battles for the agencies assisting refugees came in the State Department's reaction to the news that Hitler had begun the mass extermination of the Jews. Acting on reliable information obtained through informants at the World Jewish Congress in Bern, Switzerland, Stephen Wise notified the State Department by telegram on September 2, 1942, that Jews were being murdered. Wise also informed Justice Frankfurter, whom refugee advocates did indeed use as a channel to the president. Roosevelt assured Frankfurter that reports of deportations from France and elsewhere only represented the movement of Jews to the Eastern Front for forced labor.

Such explanations could not effectively counter the reports from Poland of mass murder. Someone in the State Department—Feingold speculates it was Long himself—suppressed additional information coming from the American embassy in Bern in January 1943. Early requests for relief supplies for the Jews were refused by the State Department on the grounds that such aid would be diverted to the German war effort; in 1943 even the liberal Unitarian Service Committee agreed with the bleak logic of this position. Yet as accounts of exterminations of the Jews became widespread, the withholding of relief was transformed into a public tableau of political morality.

In March 1943 a public rally was held in Madison Square Garden, sponsored by Jewish groups, the American Federation of Labor, the Congress of Industrial Organizations, the Church Peace Union, and others. The large turnout and attendant press coverage indicated the depth of public concern for the European Jews. In difficult situations involving public pressure, governments often call conferences to mollify opposition and buy time. It was this course that the authorities chose: the State Department and the British Foreign Office decided to call an Anglo-American conference to assess the situation. From the beginning, it was clear that little of substance would happen. The conference would be held in Bermuda, and no representatives of the press or private refugee agencies would be invited. Long's idea was to revive the totally ineffective Intergovernmental Committee while American negotiators pressed the goal of military victory as the only feasible solution. Rescue of refugees from Axis territories was not considered.

Two suggestions that had emerged from the Madison Square Garden rally, negotiating with Berlin through neutral intermediaries and forming an intergovernmental agency that could effectively provide relief and safety, were ignored. As one British delegate recalled years later, the Bermuda conference was simply "self-justification, a facade for inaction. We said the results of the conference were confidential, but in fact there were no results that I can recall."[20]

Washington's fragmented response to the situation in Europe cannot be blamed entirely on the State Department. The welter of conflicting claims and private interests in the refugee problem has always kept official policy between a rock and a hard place. As soon as one attempt at forming a national coalition of refugee advocates was in place, groups that felt they were not getting a fair hearing would separate and start a new coalition. Each faction could then invoke the cause of the refugee, making consensus even more unlikely. No effort to organize private efforts had yet taken hold in the turbulent period of the Bermuda conference; there were no clear established lines of authority between the voluntary community and the government. Voluntary agencies had virtually no role in formulating a plan of action. Looking at the confusing efforts put forth by various Jewish factions in Washington at the time, the *American Hebrew* said, "The spectacle is enough to make the angels weep. . .many people cannot but come to the conclusions that some of the groups are exploiting the situation for reasons of their own."[21]

Complementarity and the American Council of Voluntary Agencies

In 1942 the field of private voluntary relief was still dominated by religious agencies. The government had the President's War Relief Control Board to officially oversee arrangements, but it was clear that coordination at the agency level was needed. Therefore, in the words of a participant, "the government gathered the so-called 'three faiths'—Protestant, Catholic, and Jewish—and drew a roof over them, and that was the beginning of interfaith ecumenism."[22] That "roof" became the New York-based American Council of Voluntary Agencies in Foreign Service (ACVA).[23]

Small groups of leaders from various voluntary service agencies had been discussing the question of their relationships with the government and each other since November 1942. The guiding force who eventually brought the agencies together and coordinated them with the government was Joseph Chamberlain. By the end of 1942, Chamberlain had circulated drafts of a memorandum entitled "Private International Service Organizations in Post-War Relief." Approved by leaders of a core of half a dozen agencies, the memorandum addressed several issues, including relationships between private agencies and the government. The American-run agencies were praised for their ability to maintain direct contact with the government while serving nonpolitical and objective ends. It also noted, however, that they would be most effective if they were allowed to remain independent agencies. Chamberlain's memorandum circulated in Washington and among agency officials.

Planning for cooperation in relief and rehabilitation (including the postwar care of refugees—ACVA was not actively involved in the rescue efforts during the war) proceeded in Washington and New York. By August 1943, when agency executives met in New York, many were worried that uncertainty over the forms of government regulation of private relief might mean that agencies would have to accept military or other government proposals. All private funds sent abroad during the war required a license from the Foreign Funds Control Division of the Treasury Department. The executives were concerned to maintain their independence "with the least possible interference by the Government. . .private agencies can be effective in building morale only if they are independent and allowed to carry on their work in their own way." At the end of the meeting, it was agreed that planning for an association of private agencies should begin.[24]

On October 7, 1943, agreement was reached to form a coordinating council, eventually named the American Council of Voluntary Agencies for Foreign Service. Joseph Hyman of the American Jewish Joint Distribution Committee stated at the meeting, "As I see it, the whole reason for this council is that, wherever we can cooperate in planning and thinking and in common action we should do so." Chamberlain was elected chairman; representatives of Jewish and Catholic agencies were elected to the two vice-presidential posts and the head of a Protestant agency was named secretary-treasurer. The first committee of the new ACVA was formed to address the question of displaced persons.

Chamberlain reminded the group that one of their immediate functions as a council would be to consider the role of the private voluntary sector in international relief efforts, a topic on the agenda at the upcoming planning meeting of the United Nations Relief and Rehabilitation Administration (UNRRA) in Atlantic City the following month. The *Memorial* ACVA eventually submitted to UNRRA constituted the first public act of the young council, in which it set forth its own views on the proper relationship between private and public efforts at international relief.

From the beginning of the government's direct involvement with voluntary agencies abroad, officials promoted the idea of complementarity: "volagencies," in the new slang, would work alongside government, complementing and assisting federal services. The notion of complementarity seemed appropriate for the situation in which religious and secular authorities found themselves. It certainly captured the hierarchical flow of power from the state to the citizens involved in voluntary service. The remarkable partnership of church and state abroad in the late 1940s grew in part because the religious agencies came to acknowledge their dependence upon government. The agencies and their sponsoring religious bodies gathered around national policymakers, offering partnership, but the focus of their activities—refugees—left them perpetual stepchildren in the distribution of power. As we have noted, President Roosevelt, and Truman after him, saw the refugee question as a political cul-de-sac. Roosevelt was receptive to religious leaders and others, particularly Rabbi Stephen Wise, but unwilling to become personally involved with the problem. Truman believed that once the Displaced Persons Act passed and Israel was established (both in 1948) the refugee problem had been solved.

It is not surprising that the long-term ramifications of church/state cooperation were not a major concern. The war was indeed a moment of supreme crisis; lives and nations were at stake. Saving lives involved a complex operation with many instrumentalities, and religious bodies were the key element in the voluntary sector, performing tasks and extending mercy to individuals in ways the government rightly recognized as beyond its capabilities. Once the semiofficial "three faiths" policy was publicly advanced by ACVA and government officials after the war, the central role of American religious philanthropy abroad—as a complement to official policies—was firmly fixed. In 1945, less than one third of all private philanthropy abroad was channeled through sectarian religious sources. Many Americans gave to the Red Cross and national or ethnic funds during the war. Only two years later, over 75 percent of private philanthropy overseas was flowing through Protestant, Catholic, and Jewish agencies, a ratio that would remain fixed through the 1950s.[25]

Belated Rescue Efforts

In 1943 Secretary of the Treasury Henry Morgenthau, Jr. (whose father had encouraged private humanitarianism in the Middle East during World War I) came to believe Treasury staff reports suggesting that the State Department was actively blocking ransom and relief efforts to help European refugees. Enraged at what he perceived as callous indifference, Morgenthau personally directed the preparation of a report to President Roosevelt alleging that the State Department "was neither psychologically nor administratively suited to carry out an operation which required commitment and compassion to succeed."[26] The report was presented to Roosevelt on January 17, 1944; five days later an executive order established the War Refugee Board, the most serious effort to date of the administration to counter the procrastination of the State Department. Yet even this new step forward carried a barb: the government would provide only $1 million in financing; the rest would be supplied by the preponderantly Jewish rescue groups, most specifically by the Joint Distribution Committee and the World Jewish Congress. However tentative and politically self-protective the move, the government had allowed the moral compassion of the Joint Distribution Committee and associated groups to rise above the mechanisms of government, and a flurry of rescue activity resulted from Eastern Europe to North Africa.

This was a turning point, particularly for the efforts of agencies directed toward saving the lives of Jews. It had the effect of freeing the issue of aid to victims of Nazi concentration camps from the bureaucracies of the State Department, the PWRCB, UNRRA, and other regulatory agencies. The War Refugee Board embodied a new "pro-rescue" attitude in the administration. The War Refugee Board in 1944 implemented the only domestic resettlement colony of the war, a camp in Oswego, New York, for 1,000 refugees.

Oswego was to be considered similar to a shipper's "free port" where, according to a New York *Post* columnist who originated the idea, "you can put things down for a while without having to make a final decision about them."[27] A congressional debate ensued on the subject; Secretary of War Henry Stimson, no friend to refugee agencies, advised Roosevelt that such a plan would need to be approved by Congress. Foreseeing a long debate, Roosevelt ignored Stimson and simply issued another executive order authorizing the War Refugee Board to proceed with the plan. Reflecting Stimson's hostility, the army administered the camp as if the refugees were prisoners, causing (according to voluntary personnel at Oswego) many cases of mental breakdown.[28] Yet many thousands of refugees were saved by the actions of the War Refugee Board. Free of much governmental red tape, it paid ransoms, organized clandestine movement of people across European borders, and supplied relief. In Portugal, its agents distributed false baptismal and birth certificates.

One of the board's methods of simplifying the diversity of opinion among refugee advocates was to follow the tactics of the State Department and deny licenses to agencies it considered disruptive of a smooth relationship between the government and cooperative agencies. Orthodox Jews were singled out as troublemakers, in part due to their claims for special treatment. An executive of one Orthodox agency noted that "the interest of religious Jews [is] always menaced by the preponderance of the wealthy and privileged Jewish organizations, especially the [Jewish] Agency [an international Zionist body that would eventually form the government of Israel in 1948] and the Joint [Distribution Committee]."[29] There was little recourse for such agencies. The War Refugee Board had no public consultative board, through which private agencies could express their views; most operations were conducted in secrecy. Feingold offers an explanation of the complexity of the arrangements:

> In 1944 it was not only necessary to vitalize the American government's effort but to mobilize and coordinate at least a half-dozen nations and agencies which composed the rescue forces. Included was Britain, the neutrals, the Vatican, the [International Committee of the Red Cross], the private rescue organizations, the people of the occupied areas, and the victims themselves.[30]

Opposition to rescue efforts continued from Secretary Stimson and military field commanders in Europe; American military leaders specifically blocked efforts to liberate Auschwitz before the Nazis surrendered.[31]

Arrangements at War's End

With the conclusion of the war, pressure began to mount for President Truman to address the question of resettlement; many Jewish refugees were understandably unwilling to return to their former homes. The British government had not relaxed its restrictions on immigration to Palestine. Non-Jewish refugees also sought resettlement far from their former homes. On December 22, 1945, Truman took the first of many postwar emergency measures, issuing a directive allowing the admission of refugees above and beyond existing U.S. quotas. The measure was limited, given the millions of refugees stranded throughout Europe, yet it was a significant victory.

Truman's directive covered those who had been forced laborers in Germany, who had fled their homes during invasions, were interned in concentration camps, had escaped political or religious persecution, or were family members of such persons. Over the next three years more than 41,000 of these people emigrated to the United States. Fear of charges of discrimination prevented U.S. immigration authorities from officially asking displaced persons their religious affiliation.

Long experience with migration—and the emergency response following the disclosure of the Nazi concentration camps in 1942—had given Jewish agencies the strongest position to respond to the terms of the directive. In addition to HIAS and the Joint Distribution Committee, two other agencies were ready to assist with the increased migration flow: the International Rescue and Relief Committee (later the International Rescue Committee), which had been serving Jews and other victims of Nazism since 1933, and the Vaad Hatzala Emergency Committee, which concentrated on Orthodox rabbis, scholars, and their dependents. Yet another umbrella grouping for Jewish migration services was formed in the first year of expanded migration, the United Service to New Americans. In 1946–47, approximately 65 percent of the new immigrants admitted under the directive were Jewish: the Jewish agencies were the most efficient in moving people.[32] Another contemporary study estimated that under the full term of Truman's directive from 1946 through 1948, 10 percent of the refugees accepted in the United States were Roman Catholic, the rest primarily Jews and Protestants.[33]

A key provision of the Truman directive allowed private agencies to expand their migration work by presenting corporate rather than individual affidavits to the Immigration and Naturalization Service in behalf of refugees seeking admission to the United States. Under this provision, agencies themselves could guarantee that adequate housing and employment would be provided for a given number of refugees; previous systems had depended upon the individual support of American sponsors for each refugee. This corporate system had been pioneered in an experimental arrangement in 1934 between the State Department, the INS, and European-Jewish Children's Aid, Inc.[34] The corporate affidavit system allowed for the establishment of a large-scale "pipeline" of refugees moving through the various phases of official registration and paperwork under the patronage of a centralized agency, relieving the government of the time-consuming responsibility of checking the claims of individual Americans willing to sponsor newcomers.

Many protested that the directive was too limited. In September 1946, *Life* magazine stated editorially that "the most shocking fact about the plight of these displaced persons is not that they are interned. It is that the United States Government and people have the means to open the door for many of them but have not done so. . . . If we are to remain the leading nation of Our World, we also have a deep moral obligation not to be too exclusive."[35] The postwar refugee needs of Europe were no longer shielded by government concerns of "enemy-controlled territory." America was administering German territory under a military government and actively sought civilian help in aiding new floods of refugees that appeared after the war. While the private agencies had insisted that the least possible interference by the government was the preferred situation, the pattern of complementarity to government objectives was firmly set when private efforts had been restrained and redirected during the war. After all, in the course of a few months in wartime a government license and review board (the PWRCB), a government authority for channeling funds (the National War Fund), a national relief agency, the Office of Foreign Relief and Rehabilitation Operations (OFRRO), and an international relief agency (UNRRA) had all been superimposed upon their activi-

ties. In early 1943 officials from these agencies and the American Red Cross had
issued the following statement:

> While the resources and services of Government will be drawn upon to furnish the
> primary supplies for mass emergency relief of civilian populations, voluntary orga-
> nizations rendering essential services will also need to be maintained. . . . Contin-
> uation of such voluntary relief work is essential not only as an expression of the
> generous sympathies of the American people but also as a distinctive service that
> quasi-public and voluntary societies can render to *complement* public resources
> and services.[emphasis added][36]

This critical concept of complementarity would be developed further in coming
years, but at the conclusion of the war, it seemed self-evident to public and private
officials and was the heart of the remarkable and growing partnership between
church and state abroad. In its assumption of a hierarchical relationship between
the "primary" responsibility of the government and the supportive role of religious
and other voluntary agencies, it closely followed the Catholic political philosophy of
subsidiarity. But it was not the law, certainly not church/state law, that sustained
the operation. It was the need of all parties, in response to political and military
challenges, to coordinate a single effort that preserved something of the moral
dimension of American ties to the outside world.

5

The Remarkable Partnership
(1945–1952)

Refugee problems began anew with the end of the war. No sooner had the war with Germany and Japan ended than American leaders confronted a hostile Soviet state that thought nothing of expelling unwanted populations from its occupied territories or of murdering Soviet refugees returned to the Soviet Union by the Allies. Some 10 million refugees, known collectively after the war as "displaced persons," required assistance in Europe. For nearly a decade, religious agencies extended their wartime service into resettling, repatriating, and caring for these unwanted and homeless people. In addition, the agencies moved aggressively into the legislative arena and began accepting new forms of regular government assistance. In one form or another, all the private agencies were forced to ask new questions about the relationship between peacetime national security goals and their central humanitarian and religious purposes.

From Wartime Controls to Peacetime Coordination

Centralized coordination of relief and refugee services under the United States Military Administration of Germany was the goal of the officer in charge, General Lucius Clay. Clay favored straightforward military control without civilian involvement. Before and immediately after the liberation of Germany, however, the agencies had earned a hearing in Congress and the executive branch; Clay agreed to their participation provided that they organized one central agency with which military officials could relay needs and coordinate activities. This agency, known as the Council of Relief Agencies Licensed for Operation in Germany (CRALOG), was formed with President Truman's approval in late 1945 after the survey team of ACVA visited Europe.[1] Seventeen of CRALOG's twenty-five member agencies represented Protestant, Catholic, or Jewish constituencies in the United States (Jewish participation began in the 1950s). The formation of CRALOG at the insistence of military authorities provided new training in agency cooperation abroad.

On December 16, 1945, a joint refugee survey team, involving representatives of ACVA agencies, the PWRCB, UNRRA, the War Fund and other concerned groups, met for the first of a six-month series of meetings under the aegis of ACVA's Displaced Persons Committee. Refugee needs cataloged when the survey team's report was published in June 1946 overwhelmed the $20 million in private resources then at the agencies' disposal. Two principles emerged from this reality. First, the survey report concluded, "The principle of Governmental responsibility recognizes the primary justice of spreading the burden of cost equitably among all its citizens. It recognizes also that only government has resources adequate to discharge the responsibility."[2] Implicit was the assumption that the government would continue to turn to the services of the voluntary community. The voluntary community in turn, led by the strong interest on the part of Catholics in government subsidies in refugee and relief work, had long been anticipating increased government resources. As early as 1944, Catholic War Relief Services acknowledged that such funds were "imperative" in order to render "a more complete welfare job."[3] The agencies believed that their funds should not go for the purchase of food and medicine. If for some reason agencies were required to use their own resources for food or medicine, any check writing was to be accompanied by "strenuous efforts to persuade the proper governmental authorities to assume their rightful responsibility at the earliest date."[4] The survey authors realized that the refugee situation far outstripped their private resources; government cooperation was not merely invited, it was assumed.

Second, the report argued that given their limited resources, the agencies should provide specialized services to displaced persons. These included individual case work, informal educational activities, religious needs, vocational training, and resettlement and international migration. In the confusion following the war, such divisions of responsibility were not at all self-evident. One worker from ACVA at the time noted that the survey team had found in Europe "disrupted communications and transport, [logistical problems] of every kind, and above all, an unclear picture of who among the military, the governmental and intergovernmental agencies was doing what, and the place of the volags [voluntary agencies] in the overall effort. It was clear that their efforts should be supplemental in nature, this had been agreed by all concerned. But the spelling out of this principle in practice was another matter."[5]

The ACVA survey noted that among fourteen religiously based agencies, an average of 7 percent of their budgets went toward "religious services and supplies."[6] From its earliest days Catholic War Relief Services had routinely included missals, mass cards, rosaries, and other religious items in its overseas shipments.[7] It is clear from the efforts made to unite agencies with their coreligionists among the refugees that governmental authorities expected a certain level of religious activity, much as military chaplains met the religious needs of military personnel. American volunteers were working side by side with representatives of sister organizations from Europe and elsewhere who knew little of U.S. church/state traditions; extreme notions of separation of church and state were not pressed in the refugee camps. Since the agencies were mainly dealing with their fellow believers, Lutheran World Relief was, for instance, free to conduct theological education and diaconal training programs among Lutheran refugees. For the most part, authorities in Germany and elsewhere pragmatically accepted religious activities as part of the work of the religious voluntary agencies after the war: according to one analysis in 1953, fully 90 percent of postwar relief was provided by religious agencies.[8]

The ACVA survey was a major step in a new lobbying drive in Washington on behalf of the displaced persons. According to Eileen Egan, who supervised Catholic WRS aid to Polish refugees in Mexico, religious leaders were exercising the right of a sovereign people to petition their government, asking that the floodgates of people-to-people help be opened. Using a clause of the Trading with the Enemy Act that allowed assistance to a "mortally wounded enemy," Catholic leaders in Washington recalled the command of Jesus: "If your enemy be hungry, give him to eat; if he thirst, give him to drink."[9]

Administration and coordination of refugee aid remained in the White House. The experience of the President's War Relief Control Board during the war indicated that it would be useful for the president to retain control over private foreign relief. Thus on May 14, 1946, President Truman terminated the PWRCB and established in its stead the Advisory Committee on Voluntary Foreign Aid to, in his words, "tie together the governmental and private programs in the field of foreign relief."[10] Wartime relief agencies were invited to submit nominations to the new Advisory Committee. As a liaison between the private and public sectors, the Advisory Committee began its life as an independent governmental body, mediating differences and working toward common solutions. Within four years, it would be integrated directly into the State Department, much to the dismay of the voluntary agencies that recalled its original purposes as a presidential go-between for the agencies and the State Department. The Advisory Committee's original function, registration of voluntary agencies, remained under the committee's control until 1979, when registration was placed directly within the State Department's Agency for International Development (AID), a direct descendant of the original aid mechanisms established for the Marshall Plan in the 1940s.[11]

Accepting the invitation to register entailed certain obligations; the executive director of the Advisory Committee explained that they were "voluntary." They included

> the obligation to record with the Committee, for public inspection, a quarterly financial statement, a monthly report of foreign money transfers and commodity exports, a periodic budget and public audit, and current operations at home and abroad. [The agencies] undertook to record voluntarily with the Advisory Committee the information that they had been required to provide under license during wartime.[12]

Thus, the postwar years saw a variety of efforts to cement the cooperative relationships between religious bodies and the government. Cooperation with federal and multinational authorities was now almost second nature for U.S. religious groups involved with refugee care. From the 1945–46 survey of European refugee needs, it was understood that the voluntary societies, religious and secular, were there to assist in and augment governmental programs.

Agencies, Ecumenism, and New Pressures

Wartime disputes with the State Department and others had taught the agencies that the government would probably continue to use the refugee problem to bargain politically. But it was not uncommon for agency leaders to express the political as well as humanitarian motives of their overseas activities. Clashes over the legitimacy of government policy decisions were inevitable. For example, CRALOG members successfully fought the premature closing of refugee camps in the American Zone of Germany.[13] Other political protests were less successful: Countess Alexandra Tolstoy of the Russian Orthodox Tolstoy Foundation spoke out repeatedly against the settlement of the Yalta agreement which consigned 2 million Russians to involuntary repatriation, where many faced forced labor or death under Stalin's regime. Fundamentally, however, all the ACVA agencies defended the U.S. government's military occupation as the chief means of bringing order and assistance to the lives of millions of needy persons. In 1946, Catholic War Relief Service officials explicitly pointed out that overseas aid was a valuable method of fighting communist activities.[14] Under such circumstances, and lacking the immediacy of the pressures of war, church/state questions were bound to arise.

One of the first public airings of church/state questions after the war came with the founding of CARE. Spurred by the availability of surplus army rations, government planners approached leaders of the voluntary community with the idea of a cooperative agency that would channel packages of food and supplies, paid for by individual American donors and directed to their friends and relatives in Europe, many of whom were refugees and displaced persons. The resulting agency, CARE, grew out of three weeks of negotiations and planning in the fall of 1945 at ACVA offices in New York and represented the collective efforts of twenty-two different agencies. Some of the religious members of the CARE coalition began to object to the way the agency was taking form. Rather than restrict its services to distributing designated packages sent to friends and relatives of Americans, CARE soon began to accept coal, mass shipments of blankets, and undesignated CARE packages. With undesignated giving, the people-to-people nature of CARE seemed to be threatened, prey to priorities other than those of the agencies, which still frequently concentrated their work in communities of their own faith. Agencies argued that by using undesignated packages, state priorities would replace those of religious bodies, damaging the concept of religious autonomy in such decision-making areas.[15]

With no compromise in sight, religious agencies began withdrawing from CARE; the last remaining religious agency, the American Friends Service Committee, withdrew in the 1950s. But CARE went on to become one of the great organizational triumphs of the postwar world of voluntary foreign aid. Any American who watched television or was on the CARE mailing lists in the 1950s might have assumed from the agency's promotions that CARE was the principal organization through which Americans sent voluntary contributions abroad. Along with CRS (Catholic Relief Services, the peacetime name given to War Relief Services), it eventually became the principal agent for the U.S. government's overseas food programs.

The war itself had inured the agencies to the necessity of accommodating government priorities. With the liberation of various European countries in 1944, all agencies active in the National War Fund were asked to "reduce dramatically or eliminate completely their budget request for services other than direct assistance to liberated countries of the world." On the battlefield, indeed across the entire face of postwar Europe, representatives of governmental agencies and executives from the private voluntary world were exploring the interlocking nature of their responsibilities. In response to persistent efforts within the government to examine all resettlement possibilities, War Relief Services began scouting its Catholic contacts for assistance in locating refugee settlement options in South and Central America.[16]

The most immediate concern was the administration of Germany, whose people faced mass starvation in the winter of 1945–1946. A potential conflict arose as the war ended and relief supplies were needed inside the country. The 1917 Trading with the Enemy Act prohibited private citizens from shipping relief to Germany; agencies had been informed by the PWRCB that the statute would be enforced. It was NCWC's War Relief Services that broke the impasse by returning to the fund-raising solution that had been pioneered by the American Friends Service Committee after World War I. The WRS applied to the War Fund for permission to solicit donations in those dioceses "within the confines of which live large numbers of Americans of German extraction."[17]

Even for the agencies that were involved in Europe, it was difficult to predict the specific issues the postwar period would bring. No one expected that many of their leaders would head vastly expanded agencies, administer government foreign aid, or learn the art of lobbying Congress. There was a job to be done; it would end with the settlement of war-related problems. As (then Monsignor) Edward E. Swanstrom described the future to his board of trustees in 1945, there would be no War Relief Services after the war, after the job was done.[18]

Less sanguine were the Jewish agencies, who faced the incomprehensible savagery of Dachau and Auschwitz and new waves of expulsions from the Soviet-dominated territories of Eastern Europe. Observers of Jewish relief during the war often carried away two dominant impressions: the remarkable growth of Zionism as a political force and the hold it had in the hearts of many Jewish refugees.[19] To many, open immigration to Palestine appeared to be the only humane course to follow after the war. Questions remained about the nature of political governance in Palestine, but Jewish agencies were not waiting for an answer; by 1945 the Joint Distribution Committee was receiving more private donations than any other private agency. Jewish workers in Europe and the Middle East were quietly shipping Jews to Palestine illegally, boosting Jewish population in a place of relative quiet and safety. The success of the Jewish agencies in providing migration services did not go unnoticed in the voluntary community. Late in the war, Catholic War Relief Services sent a senior executive to Geneva to meet with officials of the International Committee of the Red Cross. His purpose was to learn from Red Cross officials the methods used by Jewish agencies and individuals in establishing migration services, so that similar efforts could be built in Catholic circles.

Less secure in the field of overseas relief were the Protestants. Adept in the politics of public protest, Protestants were the key public voice in the "three faiths" appeal for aid to refugees; they also proved to be the least skillful of the three at securing financial and political support from the government for their own refugee work abroad. While the new World Council of Churches fielded a strong team in refugee assistance, and were rewarded with U.S. government aid, Protestant ecumenical efforts in the United States were still undermined by dissension.

UN Relief and Rehabilitation Administration

Even though religious agencies carried the bulk of the responsibility for the actual care of refugees in camps in Europe and the Far East, this was only a limited part of government foreign aid. In 1945 and 1946, the civilian supply programs of the U.S.

armed forces abroad distributed more than $2 billion in emergency assistance; the government channeled another $3 billion through UNRRA, the United Nations Relief and Rehabilitation Agency, from 1943 to 1947.[20] All such programs, whether private, governmental, or intergovernmental, were considered temporary, to be discontinued within roughly five years. Never before had any government or governmental alliance gone so far in anticipating and planning for postwar relief needs; the planning of CARE, for instance, began in 1943.[21] More than one analyst of the period has noted that it is remarkable that so many needs were actually foreseen by authorities during the war.[22]

UNRRA was a formidable presence in the field of refugee work, supervising care and repatriation. Its strength did not come from its organizational efficiency or its political power, both of which were limited; it came from the size of its budget. The United States supplied over 70 percent of UNRRA's budget; much of this went toward the purchase of U.S. foodstuffs and other supplies, which were then administered by UNRRA or by private agencies under contract for the provision of services. UNRRA also represented the last phase of cooperation between the United States and the Soviet Union in humanitarian aid. Formed at meetings of Allied leaders in Atlantic City in November 1943, UNRRA dissolved as part of the growing estrangement of the Soviet Union and the United States in 1947. American leaders, including Herbert Hoover, denounced the continuation of relief supplies to Yugoslavia when that country attacked U.S. planes in the summer of 1946. In Hoover's view, the Soviet-backed communist leadership had ceased to speak for the people; the aid sent to Yugoslavia could no longer be called humanitarian assistance, it was manifestly political. He linked attacks on U.S. planes with the known facts of Soviet behavior at home: "They are setting up concentration camps in each of those [satellite] countries and deporting many to Siberia," charged Hoover. UNRRA itself was, in Soviet-dominated territories, supervising forced repatriations to Russia; Stalin was also encouraging Eastern European allies to expel persons of German ethnic origin; millions poured into Austria and the American, British, and French zones of occupied Germany.[23]

UNRRA offers a case study of the rapid breakdown of the wartime alliance. Italy, France, Holland, and Belgium all protested the role of Soviet employees of UNRRA; each nation eventually refused to allow UNRRA to operate within its territory. American military authorities eventually refused to allow UNRRA in territory under U.S. control when it was clear that Soviet workers manipulated eligibility criteria for displaced persons, assuring that Soviet sympathizers had first access to food and other services.

Western officials were determined that any international body dealing with refugees and displaced persons would embody a nondiscriminatory protection function for refugees threatened within their country of asylum or by forced repatriation. The Soviets denied that their presence in UNRRA resulted in discriminatory treatment of displaced persons, but it was disagreement over the centrality of voluntary repatriation as the official international standard that caused the major political rift.[24] In the Soviet view, support for anything other than general repatriation, voluntary or otherwise, constituted an unacceptable infringement of national sovereignty of nations eager to have their refugees back. Similarly, international oversight designed to protect refugees who had returned home was not to be permitted. At the end of the war, 7 million of the estimated 11 million displaced

Europeans were repatriated; some 2 million forcibly returned to the Soviet Union perished.[25] Testifying in 1947 in behalf of new legislation for displaced persons, General George Marshall stated that most still awaiting a solution were from territories that had come under communist control since the war.[26]

Resettlement and the Displaced Persons Act

Private agencies were powerless to achieve a durable solution to the refugee problem without governmental support for resettlement outside of Europe. Most displaced persons were able to repatriate themselves after the war; but millions of "expellees" of German descent were exiled from countries that fell under Soviet domination after the war. Many were reintegrated into German society, but thousands of others remained interned in refugee camps, their future bleak without resettlement possibilities abroad.

One might have expected that the ACVA survey report would have stressed questions of resettlement and repatriation, but this was not the case. Rather, the 1946 report noted that immediate problems of food and housing were more important; only "limited efforts" had been made on the basic problem of what would happen to the displaced persons. Aside from the 41,000 refugees resettled under Truman's 1945 directive, most major legal and political questions remained unsolved as the wartime relief model prevailed well into 1948 in Europe and elsewhere.

Every analysis of the displaced persons problem in Europe pointed to the need for new legislation that would bypass Congress's restrictive quota system and the Immigration and Naturalization Service. The religious agencies, by now with some years of experience, undertook to lead the charge in Congress. Again ACVA provided a critical forum for advancing the "three faiths" ecumenism, acting as a kind of national conscience. This pragmatic (rather than strictly religious) ecumenism proved a powerful force in Congress, offering as it did a unified voice in support of humanitarian aid to the 800,000 persons still in camps in Europe.

In the first eighteen months after the war, more than one hundred programs of immigration reform had been introduced in the Congress.[27] Domestic political pressures were building to do more for the homeless of Europe. President Truman referred to the problem specifically in his 1947 State of the Union Message, asking Congress to help "find ways whereby we can fulfill our responsibilities to these thousands of homeless and suffering refugees of all faiths."[28] Like Roosevelt before him, Truman emphasized that the problem concerned all of America's religious communities.

Though Truman praised the religious communities' work in meeting the challenge, the problem would be addressed primarily by the Western governments through the new International Refugee Organization (IRO) and possibly a revived Intergovernmental Committee on Political Refugees, dating from the prewar era. A month after his State of the Union Message, Truman sent another message to Congress recommending "firm and prompt leadership of the United States" in the organization of the IRO. Even as the religious agencies and other private groups were again cast as supporting players rather than as full partners in this new political reordering of refugee assistance, they had by word, deed, and force of presence in Washington achieved a moral victory in having established two key elements—third country resettlement and prohibition of forced repatriation—as cornerstones of the emerging Western approach to refugee problems.

In April 1947, Congressman William G. Stratton of Illinois introduced a bill that would allow 100,000 displaced persons per year to enter the United States for four years. Public support for the measure was strong. On May 20, the Washington *Post* editorialized: "The enactment of the Stratton bill is the very least we can do to help solve a problem whose existence is a blot on our vaunted civilization. Failure to take constructive action on the displaced persons problem will subject the United States to the charge that our professions of democracy and humanitarianism are the veriest mockery." Leaders of the religious voluntary community agreed and urged members of Congress to support the legislation. With a government-backed plan for resettlement coming into view, many of the larger agencies began administrative shifts separating resettlement activities from overseas relief work.[29]

Debate on the legislation continued for over a year in the House and Senate; refugee workers abroad continued to extend what assistance they could. The problem was not going away, it was getting worse. Polish refugees could be found in over two dozen countries, including India and England, where a standing army of 250,000 Polish refugees had been gathered to defend Poland against both the Nazis and the Soviets.[30] The Russians continued to create "expellee" populations of ethnic Germans forced into Western territory from their homes in Soviet-controlled sectors of Eastern Europe. Ever since the war ended, it had been common to see destitute people walking along the roads in the liberated countries, some heading home, others still in flight. Still others were moved secretly in trucks and vans; refugee work for some inevitably involved open advocacy for the interests of the refugees themselves. In particular, Jewish displaced persons, aware that the United States would be more likely to pursue liberal policies for refugees in its occupied territories than would England or France, streamed into the American Zones with the aid of efficient Jewish rescue efforts. To a lesser degree, the same was true of some Catholic refugees; many still found themselves without official protection or provision, and understandably migrated to where assistance was the most widespread.

The Senate eventually reported out a bill that arbitrarily took the date of President Truman's directive of December 22, 1945—the directive the legislation was designed to supplant—as a cut-off date for eligibility for resettlement in the United States. Anyone who had arrived in refugee camps after that date would not be considered eligible. Catholic and Jewish agencies, many of whose "clients" had fled to American camps well after this proposed cut-off date, strenuously protested.

The Senate version of the Displaced Persons Act also specified territorial and occupational preferences that, some opponents contended, unduly favored Protestant refugees. An alternative cut-off date of April 21, 1947, was proposed. This was the date that General Clay, who certainly knew of the illegal flow of refugees into the American camps, closed the camps to all newcomers. Conservatives in the U.S. claimed that this later date would inevitably mean that more communists would eventually be admitted to the United States. They were referring to the ongoing flow of expellees from Soviet-dominated areas, which they assumed would contain some intelligence personnel. In the final version of the bill the 1945 date was used.

Two years later, with more pressure from the agencies and the support of President Truman, some of the discriminatory measures of the first bill were amended for the last two years of its mandate. The discriminatory clauses of the original version had forced government representatives into admissions operations that, politely analyzed, were "so intricate . . . as often to obscure the humanitarian character of the effort."[31] Remarkably, struggles over these matters did not disrupt the essential unity of the voluntary community expressed through the American Council of Voluntary Agencies. The whole refugee question was merely temporary, they reasoned; better to move ahead with an imperfect compromise, so that some might be saved. "In those days," recalled Bishop Swanstrom, "all the agencies, Protestant, Catholic and Jewish, were interested in the same thing. . . . Within the Executive Committee of the [American] Council, we saw eye to eye on many things and moved in the right direction together."[32]

To carry out the bill's provisions, the Displaced Persons Commission was established outside the regular bureaucracy of the executive branch. Despite the political controversy that raged around the work of the commission, the commissioners saw themselves continuing the official American sympathy for refugees. In their final report, they quote approvingly George Washington's Thanksgiving Day Proclamation of 1795, which asks Americans to pray that God might "render this country more and more a safe and propitious asylum for the unfortunate of other countries"; similarly, Thomas Jefferson's questions of 1801 ("Shall we refuse . . . hospitality . . . to the unhappy fugitives from distress? . . . Shall oppressed humanity find no asylum on this globe?") gave proof to the commissioners that "the great American tradition" of refugee aid still existed.[33]

At the suggestion of one of its members, the Displaced Persons Commission agreed that the best way to maintain a pool of reliable agencies, both for overseas work and for resettlement in the United States, was to continue to rely on the registration standards established by the State Department's Advisory Committee. With no more than two dozen employees at a given time, the commission was very successful in supervising an effort that ultimately included thousands of public and private employees.[34] Though the commission was formed specifically to carry out the will of Congress, there was room for much administrative flexibility. In the commission's legal services division, for example, law was a means to an end. Law would be treated "like all other staff services, an instrument to help rather than to hinder."[35]

This observation on the function of law in refugee matters is of no small interest. It parallels the comments by Harold Seymour of the National War Fund on the secondary significance of contracts in cooperation between public and private authorities in wartime. While governmental and religious authorities were cooperating fully on refugee matters in Europe, a different sort of storm was brewing in church/state law at home. Efforts to interpret the "wall of separation" between church and state were suddenly raising sharp questions about the use of government funds by religious groups.

Interest in these developments in church/state law was intense. In a year overflowing with events of significance for Jews, the lead article in the *American Jewish Yearbook* of 1948 was not about Israel or even the displaced persons of Europe: it was about a Supreme Court case in Illinois that set forth in notably strong language the centrality of separation of church and state. The case, *Everson* v. *Board of Education,* strictly limited the state's role in funding the transportation of Catholic students to and from their schools. "This is not . . . just a little case over bus fares," argued Justice Rutledge. "In paraphrase of Madison, distant as it may be in its present form from a complete establishment of religion, it [funding student transportation to parochial schools] differs from it only in degree; and is the first step in that direction."[36]

Although the *Everson* case did indeed mark a new era of efforts to define the significance of the religion clauses of the Constitution, it was hardly considered applicable to foreign affairs in the immediate postwar era. Religiously based agencies of all backgrounds were clearly eager to obtain the political and financial assistance of the U.S. government in their work with refugees, and the government was eager to have the help of the agencies. The role of the law was limited to supporting administrative decisions required by unsettled political and social conditions abroad.

At Work in Europe

In Europe the United States assumed growing responsibility for binding the wounds of a world war and setting the continent back on its feet. The celebrated $12 billion Marshall Plan, and the forms of economic and development aid (then called "technical assistance") administered through the Point Four Program, resulted in the creation of the Economic Cooperation Administration to administer and distribute the aid. Church agencies created for war relief and refugee aid faced a new set of options for expanded work with government programs; when the Point Four Program was augmented by the early temporary feeding programs for countries allied with the United States, many of the largest church agencies began negotiating for a role in the distribution abroad.

New legislation incorporating the work of the agencies into official foreign aid was needed. In 1947 Congress passed a bill that assured that the private agencies would receive reimbursement from the government for ocean freight expenses incurred in shipping relief to Europe.[37] This was the first piece of legislation that guaranteed the agencies continued federal assistance; clearly the government wanted their help in supplying foreign aid, and this seemed a popular and apolitical means of encouraging cooperation. The following year Congress began the process which eventually developed into the multimillion dollar "pass-through" arrangements under which agricultural surplus was distributed through the religious agencies and other private concerns.[38]

After the collapse of UNRRA, international coordination of refugee work was placed under the authority of the new International Refugee Organization. Representatives of several of the voluntary agencies participated in discussions in London in which formal agreements between participating governments were reached. The IRO was not a UN organization; it was formed without the participation of the Soviet Union. Despite efforts to exclude UNRRA staff considered to be communist sympathizers, some U.S. officials continued to object that the IRO was in this regard little better than its predecessor.[39] By 1949, the IRO was being publicly discussed as a holding operation that had long outlived its usefulness. American officials began pushing for yet another organization that would focus on winding down international attention to refugee problems.

The agencies made their own internal adjustments to the postwar changes. The

Displaced Persons Act caused an unprecedented admission of refugees to the United States, which in turn required increased capabilities within the private sector. While the religious agencies lobbied in Washington for an improved system of resettlement, many began separating their resettlement services from relief activities abroad. The National Council of Jewish Women and the National Refugee Service combined to form the United Service for New Americans in 1946, eventually merging in 1954 with HIAS. In 1947 the National Catholic Resettlement Council was separated from Catholic Relief Services, the descendant of NCWC's War Relief Services. Lutheran Resettlement Service took over migration concerns from Lutheran World Relief, and the newly formed Refugee Commission of the World Council of Churches began administering European relief, with Church World Service concentrating on Protestant resettlement in the United States.

Under Truman's earlier directive, the majority of refugees admitted were Jewish. In the four years of the Displaced Persons Act, Catholics made up 47 percent, Protestant and Orthodox Christians 35 percent, and Jews 16 percent. The notion that religious agencies should primarily serve their fellow believers among refugee populations estabished, for all effective purposes, a hegemony in refugee relief and migration services among four major religious traditions: Roman Catholics, Lutherans, Jews, and mainline Protestants. In terms of future church/state ties this was the distinctive innovation of the Displaced Persons Act.

Confusion in the administrative arrangements of resettlement to the United States ignited old interreligious rivalries. Just days before the first ship of refugees sailed for America—60 percent of whom were Catholic—a Protestant field administrator wrote to his New York headquarters protesting the activities of the CRS representative stationed at the dock. The letter gives a valuable picture of the multicentered, publicity-conscious world of administrative structures in which the agency workers lived:

> The [NCWC] Munich worker [Miss Ryan] . . . had the brilliant idea that it would be nice for her to go home on the first emigrants' ship, thus giving the NCWC a nice piece of publicity. She apparently sold this idea to her New York office and Monsignor Swanstrom officially made the request. IRO refused to have any individual agency represented on the boat unless all the agencies were so represented. All the other agencies felt that their staff were too busy here to take time off for a boat ride. When it was put up to the Council by IRO, the Executive Committee of the Council felt that it would be unwise for us to sponsor anybody on this boat as our representative. Miss Ryan then proceeded to make herself rather unpleasant about the whole matter and cabled New York saying that she was being blocked by other agencies. Monsignor Swanstrom . . . [demanded] that she be permitted to accompany the ship. IRO is being put into a rather embarrassing position, since they did not want to offend NCWC. . . . The matter was passed back and forth between IRO Geneva and, at the moment I don't know what the result is. . . . Personally, I couldn't think of a worse representative for the voluntary agencies than Miss Ryan, nor one who speaks less for [the agencies].[40]

Such complaints were not unusual, nor were they limited to the early, frequently confused stages of the resettlement operation. In 1950 several Protestant agencies responded with shock to the news that CRS had forwarded 200,000 pounds of U.S. government surplus butter to CARITAS (the international Vatican-sponsored Catholic relief agency) for distribution among the German populace; no Protestant official had a clue how such an arrangement could have been made unilaterally between the U.S. government and CRS, and several angrily demanded their fair share.[41]

As had been the case during the war, Protestants struggled to pull together a unitary structure that would combine private donations and government funding in a broad international network. It was nearly impossible; by 1948 Catholic and Jewish agencies had the jump. The Protestant world was unable to organize resettlement and care structures on anything like the scale of its religious competitors. The Church World Service director of Displaced Persons Operations wrote to his home office some weeks after the passage of the Displaced Persons Act for specific instructions on how to organize the resettlement program. He had already been visited by representatives of the Catholic and Jewish agencies involved in resettlement and noted that they seemed organized and ready to begin as soon as the word came from government authorities. He reported he had "found it very difficult, when asked point blank by Army, State Department or IRO officials what our agency plans to do in terms of the new Bill, to give any intelligent answer."[42] Church World Service, Lutheran World Federation (an international voluntary agency, based in Geneva), and the new Refugee Division of the fledgling World Council of Churches worked hard in the early months of 1948 to forge a joint program. Arguments over administrative arrangements and personality differences slowed cooperation; the World Council of Churches nonetheless began accepting resettlement contracts with the U.S. government, an arrangement that continued into the 1980s.

Under the 1950 revisions of the Displaced Persons Act, security procedures tightened. The roles of the agencies in the refugee "pipeline," as the process of moving them from the camps to resettlement destinations abroad was known was secondary to a rigorous governmental screening process.[43] Administrative struggles with the new international bureaucracies often served to sharpen the goals of the Displaced Persons Commission. Even though the IRO was headed by an American, its officials did not accept the complex eligibility requirements established under the act, and frequently challenged resettlement decisions made by the commission. This created situations in which the IRO, as an international organization, asserted the priority of international arrangements over the national laws of the United States. Under such challenges, U.S. law ceased to be a tool of administrative flexibility for the Displaced Persons Commission; it became instead a guardian of "the best interests of the United States."[44] No measure of international cooperation would be permitted to infringe on the best interests of national security, as defined by the government. This struggle between international ideals and national purpose remains a difficult and recurring issue in international refugee problems today, and affects church/state conflicts over the global role of the United States. It is worth remembering that at this early stage of modern refugee work, national security interests easily overpowered international agreements and structures.

In the case of the IRO there was never any formal agreement of divisions of responsibility between the governmental and intergovernmental partners; IRO and Western officials worked out administrative arrangements at a series of conferences, leaving the daily administrative questions to be debated between Washington and IRO's head office in Geneva. This meant that "complaints and counter-complaints, with and without explanations, were the order of the day. . . . In fairness, it must be noted, this was only the natural pattern among agencies equally desirous of accomplishing a common humanitarian goal."[45] Furthermore, the Displaced Persons Commission insisted on direct relationships with the agencies "without the intermediations of any other body," including the IRO.[46]

Under the new 1950 legislative provisions giving the Commission responsibility for the German expellees, voluntary agency personnel were not allowed to see classified security information in the files of resettlement applicants.[47] They protested, stating that they could not adequately counsel applicants without knowledge of the charges against them. A compromise was reached, permitting the religious agencies to discuss the contents of the security files with the local representative of the Displaced Persons Commission. This no doubt helped, but it also underscored the limitations on private cooperation in solving the refugee problem. Agencies had not been asked to participate in the wartime organization of overseas relief at the governmental level. They had always understood the supplementary nature of their work in relation to government, but now they discovered this included restricted access to government files on individuals. Again, the Commission saw such steps as necessary for the protection of the rule of law, and insisted they were in the best interests of the applicant:

> Even when parts [of a file] could not be publicly discussed because of security restrictions, it became a guarantee to the alien, to the American voluntary agencies, and to the American sponsor, that consideration of the applicant's case would be on an objective, non-discriminatory, and strictly legal basis, since once a matter of record it would be subject to the review of other Government agencies.[48]

The government's concern for security was so strong that the opinions and assistance of the religious agencies in this area were considered entirely secondary. They were ruled out of court with the assertion (made by government appointees) that the government could be depended upon to act in an objective, nondiscriminatory, and strictly legal manner. Even though the agencies demonstrably had their own interests to protect, this assertion in the midst of the most complex and politically dangerous foreign humanitarian operation the U.S. government had ever attempted left many wondering how serious a "partnership" officials really wanted with the private sector.[49]

Cooperation beyond Europe

The U.S. church/state relationship in the Far East after the war was beneficial for all parties. The missionaries received government help in reestablishing missions in China; sisters of the Catholic Missionary Society of America (the Maryknoll Sisters), among others, were transported to inland mission stations on U.S. Navy vessels. The government relied heavily on the cartographic skills of mission societies in Asia and on islands in the Pacific. In northern Thailand, a critical region for Japanese activity in and around Burma during the war, U.S. Baptist missionaries were patriotic supporters of agents of the Office of Strategic Services, the early forerunner of the CIA. By 1949 CRS was already exploring food programs and assistance to the wounded and dislocated in Vietnam, where French colonialists were abandoning resistance to communist revolutionaries in the north under Ho Chi Minh.

It was only natural, given such extensive involvement of private U.S. citizens in the region, that the services provided refugees in Europe would be extended in the Far East through active cooperation with church agencies. Though personnel were often recruited from among the mission agencies active in Shanghai, Hong Kong, Singapore, Manila, and other centers of missionary activity, the new World War II agencies, Lutheran World Relief, Church World Service, CRS, and others, were all active in the field, aiding refugees in camps and in migration services, and exploring the new field of technical assistance.

Refugee work in the Far East was not, in its early stages, limited to Christian agencies. For several years during and after the war, the Joint Distribution Committee assisted a community of 12,500 Jewish refugees—mostly Russians—who had made their way to Shanghai, eventually helping many to migrate to the United States, Israel, and elsewhere. Thus, the "three faiths" theme of private assistance complementing governmental initiative was extended beyond Europe (secular agencies such as the International Rescue Committee were also active in Asia). Jewish agencies would show relatively little interest in developments in the Far East after 1950. Jewish donors were primarily interested in aiding stranded Jews, just as Lutherans or Catholics had been mainly concerned with their coreligionists in Europe.

In their operations in the Far East, Christian agencies worked with Asians of different faiths than their own, or of no faith at all. To many people, such humanitarian services, devoid of reference to specific creed, epitomized a new Christian engagement in the world. The emergence of this humanitarian ethic dovetailed with the notions of neutral government involvement and international brotherhood that transcended old boundaries. Lacking the coreligionist theme of their European activities, the agencies addressed the question of their proper role in Asia from the perspective of human need, so evident in the sordid detention camps of Hong Kong.

Even as the victorious Allies were searching for solutions for their "temporary" refugee problem in Europe and the Far East, the first of the postwar refugee flows associated with the breakdown of European colonial empires engulfed India and Pakistan. Several of the agencies active in Europe and the Middle East sent assistance teams to the scene, calling on the services of missionaries in the region. Refugee services here never developed on the scale that existed in Europe. The political pressures on Western governments were not as intense—and the thought of helping nearly 20 million displaced persons was overwhelming to agencies that already had their hands full.

The difference between voluntary agency involvement in refugee problems created by the India-Pakistan partition and those resulting from the Korean War illustrated the same pattern that had emerged during the two world wars: the agencies concentrated on humanitarian needs that were of direct interest to the public and governmental authorities of the United States. In Korea the voluntary agencies set up coordination mechanisms similar to CRALOG in Europe; once again they were channels of material and medical assistance under the authority of

U.S. military officials. In 1952 the National Council of Churches issued the following description of the role of the churches in meeting the refugee needs:

> The plight of the world's uprooted peoples creates for the United States, as for other liberty-loving nations, a moral as well as an economic and political problem of vast proportions. Among these peoples are those displaced by war, and its aftermath; the refugees made homeless by reason of Nazi, Fascist, and Communist tyranny and more recently, by military hostilities in Korea, the Middle East, and elsewhere; the expellees forcibly ejected from the lands of their fathers; and the escapees whom every day break through the Iron Curtain in search of freedom.[50]

The cold war tone of this report is unmistakable.

Church authorities of the day continued to assume the complementarity of religiously based programs to broader government initiatives. The same National Council of Churches document stated that the administration of refugee programs "should be on a humanitarian and nonsectarian basis operated by the government with complementary services provided by voluntary agencies." Areas in which the agencies could play a role overseas included the selection and processing of people to be resettled in the United States, complementary religious and welfare services in the camps, maintaining family structures, and planning for placement in the United States.

Responding to Israel

By recognizing the sovereign State of Israel on May 15, 1948, President Truman provided the political weight that Zionists had long hoped for in the struggle for a Jewish state. In the midst of a brief war with Arab and native Palestinian forces, the private international Jewish Agency, which had moved Jews to Palestine since 1922, formed a government. This action abolished the category of a homeless Jewish refugee. Henceforth, all Jews who fled or were cast out of their native land had an automatic promise of asylum in Israel. Yet many questions remained concerning the Jews still in Europe's refugee camps and the millions of other Jews living in North and South Africa, western Soviet territories, and southern China.

More immediate in the minds of international observers was the fate of the Palestinians. Without international assistance, their condition was similar to that of refugees in Europe during World War I: destitute and helpless, they were considered a nuisance and threat to military authorities attempting to restore order. According to an observer from the British Foreign Office, the British officers in the region "may be hated now but that is nothing like the hatred which the Jews are laying up for themselves in the future if they don't allow these people back."[51] But Jewish control of Israel depended on establishing a strong Jewish majority; there was no way the Palestinians could be allowed to return to their homes.

The result was anarchy. Initial hope that Arab states might provide the needed assistance did not materialize. The British opposed involvement of the IRO, arguing that the IRO had no mandate to deal with persons internally displaced in their own countries. Count Folke Bernadotte, the UN mediator for Palestine, proposed interim relief that culminated in a "long-range" plan—but the plan only ran through September 1949! In December 1948 the U.S. ambassador to Egypt was appointed the first director of UN Relief for Palestinian Refugees in the Near East. He brought the International Committee of the Red Cross, the League of Red Cross Societies, and the American Friends Service Committee into the relief efforts, but they were poorly funded. Within a year the agency was replaced with a separate relief body, the United Nations Relief and Works Agency (UNRWA), which still coordinates international Palestinian relief today. The AFSC remained, and was eventually joined in its work with Palestinians by the Mennonite Central Committee and others.

An old hand at refugee problems and longtime friend of Jewish causes, James G. MacDonald, former League of Nations High Commissioner for Refugees, was the U.S. special representative (and eventually the first U.S. ambassador) to Israel. He informed Washington that the UN efforts were "both inappropriate and inadequate" and suggested that the Red Cross be given ultimate responsibility. Before any further resolution was reached, some 150,000–200,000 additional Palestinians were expelled from Israel at the end of 1948 and the first month of 1949. The refusal of the Israeli government to allow repatriation of the Palestinians then and in succeeding years has created an apparently intractable problem. American officials at the time warned that Arab governments were likely to avoid direct solutions (such as absorption of the refugees in neighboring Arab countries) in order to make political use of the Palestinians against Israel. This has also proven to be the case. International response to the situation, separated from UN efforts at international coordination and lacking the broad protection function that the UN Office of High Commissioner for Refugees extends to other refugees, has been hampered by the inability of the immediate participants to reach settlement on the root causes.

Jewish agencies and the U.S. government developed close ties designed to facilitate the movement of Jews to Israel. Jewish agencies such as the American Joint Distribution Committee had long assisted the same populations of Jews as the Jewish Agency, whose leading figures now dominated the government of Israel. The resulting mixture of private and governmental efforts aiding Jewish refugees and immigrants typified the complex issues raised by the founding of Israel, none of which were easily contained within U.S. church/state traditions.[52] In the following years, Israel and the leaders of the American Jewish community lobbied their causes before the Congress and the president in Washington; moving Jews to Israel has persistently been near the top of the list. Aid to Jewish refugees is *sui generis* in the postwar world. For the most part Jewish refugees are not handled under the auspices of the UN Office of High Commissioner for Refugees. In most refugee situations resettlement is a matter of life and death for the refugee; Jewish refugees are moved to Israel for these reasons as well as for the security of Israel. The claims of Zionism create what is essentially a continual religious and political "pull factor" that lays a claim on all Jews living outside Israel.

From the beginning the Congress (if not the State Department) has been sympathetic to these claims, a sympathy that has been reflected in U.S. refugee policy and appropriations. In its first three years Israel added 600,000 new Jewish citizens, bringing the Jewish population of Israel to 1.25 million in 1951. The young nation could not handle the costs of absorption and turned directly to the U.S. Congress through the predecessor of the Israeli lobby today known as the American Israel Public Affairs Committee. The battle in Congress over refugee-related appropriations under the Mutual Security Act offers a useful framework for understanding the pressures the refugee problems surrounding Israel have brought to bear on the U.S. government and the "three faiths" coalition.[53] This drive was spearheaded by a coalition of Jewish leaders who met in Washington in 1950 to formulate a plan whereby increased Jewish charity and private investment would be added to new U.S. foreign aid, with refugee resettlement in Israel a specific goal.

American involvement in Israeli resettlement matters was hardly visible to the public in the early 1950s; attention was instead focused on the strident anticommunism that accompanied the Korean War. The refugee problem appeared to be a largely European one, and Americans believed that it was only temporary, and would be solved by their generosity in resettling the displaced persons of Europe. Much of the material issued by the private agencies celebrated their success in eliminating the hardships of camp life for hundreds of thousands of refugees.

The same period, however, saw the collapse of a truly international humanitarianism. With the demise of UNRRA and the IRO, refugee work came under the control of the Western allies. Refugee aid could now be used to demonstrate the superiority of Western values. It also meant that humanitarian aid now had a political base, on the front line of ongoing conflict between the Soviet Union and the United States. This grated on many religious officials in the voluntary sector and many began to speak out in the hope that private humanitarians would be given a more neutral role in international politics. But because they were essentially powerless without their political base in Western democracy, there was little they could do but continue their efforts to build a strong refugee program into U.S. foreign policy.

It was this overall commitment in the late 1940s that prompted observers and participants alike to speak of a "remarkable partnership" between church and state in refugee assistance abroad. The major religious agencies that came of age during the war found that their success in legislative efforts for refugees had been achieved at the price of accommodating their international efforts to U.S. policies. There was never a question of absolute governmental control; the agencies generally were free to pursue situations of interest to them. But with reimbursement of ocean freight charges by the government and the possibilities of vastly expanded use of food subsidies, certain limits were emerging for those who used these options. The "three faiths" of Europe had been the perfect setting to build an international humanitarianism grounded in the religious commitments of American citizens. Even as the agencies were attempting to bring the European problems to an end, however, urgent new refugee and disaster relief problems arose in the Middle East and Asia.

6

"The United States Must Run this Show" (1950–1964)

In the years immediately following the displaced persons operation, the religious agencies that had survived the pressures of the war realized it was possible that their efforts could form a permanent supplement to U.S. foreign policy initiatives. With American responsibilities abroad constantly expanding, the future for private agencies eager to demonstrate goodwill looked promising. Yet it was also a time for sober assessment of the postwar political realities. New legislation strengthened the military buildup that began with the Korean War, further diminishing relative levels of economic and humanitarian assistance. A new structure of international refugee assistance emerged in the United Nations, but the United States replaced the displaced persons legislation not with a national refugee program but with a series of ad hoc bills and executive actions that never went beyond response to specific crises. As the agencies expanded their base of operations beyond Europe, new tensions in the wartime coalition of religious voluntarism began to appear.

By the time John Kennedy was elected president, government assistance to private foreign aid was at record levels and growing. The turning point had come with the passage in 1954 of the Food for Peace legislation, P.L. 480. In a striking act of pragmatism Congress helped to alleviate domestic farm surpluses and at the same time strengthened humanitarian assistance to needy allies. The agencies, particularly Catholic Relief Services and CARE, were willing participants in this distribution of surplus commodities which appeared to cost them next to nothing. Overseas services to refugees and others were expanded by the joint involvement of the agencies in the Cuban refugee resettlement of the early 1960s—their last cooperative venture before the trauma of Vietnam.

The Cold War and New International Initiatives

The Mutual Security Act of 1951 affected all the relief agencies. On the positive side, the act extended previous cooperative arrangements by which the private agencies were reimbursed by the federal government for ocean freight expenses in transporting material abroad.[1] Under the new act's authorizations, defense spending jumped sharply from $17.7 billion in fiscal year (FY) 1950 to $44 billion in 1953. The agencies of the American Council of Voluntary Agencies were "horrified" to read that the act's preamble described foreign aid not as "economic assistance" (as had been the case in the 1948 legislation) but as furthering the "mutual security . . . of the free world."[32] With this brief change in wording, any hope that humanitarian activities could be distinguished from military and national security concerns appeared to have been eliminated. The Friends, the Lutherans, and the Catholics all objected to the changes, and in February 1952 ACVA debated the issue in executive session. Although the changes they desired were eventually embodied in the legislation, they were, judged from subsequent events, largely cosmetic. From the perspective of refugee assistance, the act only forged further links between U.S. refugee policy and national security concerns.

Officials realized that the refugee problem could be of continuing propaganda value in the struggle with the Soviet Union, and looked for ways for the United States both to act unilaterally and to impose stronger controls on existing international arrangements. Thus in 1949, changes in the Displaced Persons Act proposed by the Truman administration authorized the government to admit up to 15,000 recent "escapees" from Soviet-dominated territories that were not covered under the IRO constitution.[3] (Congress eventually cut this figure to 500, though several thousand "escapees" entered the country each year through 1956.) Technical assistance under the Point Four Program and the Marshall Plan was moved out of the State Department to the Economic Cooperation Administration, but refugee matters remained under the direct control of the secretary of state.

While the church and relief agencies worked to obtain changes in the law that would produce more equitable refugee assistance, their criteria often stemmed from particular ethnic or religious perspectives. In 1949, for instance, Church World Service circulated a working paper setting forth its concerns for revisions in the Displaced Persons Act. Along with expressing the basic theological and humanitarian rationales for Church World Service involvement with refugees, the paper pinpointed several concerns that had more to do with church/state and interreligious relations, for example,

> That a proper proportion of Protestant and [Eastern] Orthodox people be admitted to this country.
>
> [The existing bill] establishes an unhealthy pattern of sectarian competition, rivalry and misplaced responsibility for the effectiveness of the law.
>
> It shifts a large part of the financial responsibility from the treasury of the nation to the treasuries of the several Church groups.[4]

When it became clear in 1951 that the pending McCarran-Walter Immigration Act would institutionalize the antiquated immigration quota system of 1924 with only minor reforms, church agencies were quick to testify against the bill in hearings. If the agencies had accepted the anticommunism of the State Department as a fact of life, they were not about to surrender their role as guardians of the world's homeless. Yet as this Church World Service document makes clear, the agencies necessarily had to fight together on the Washington stage for independent humanitarianism, while they grounded their individual rationales in particular religious concerns. They were looking for ways to unite and compete at the same time.

Escapee Politics and Government Contracts

The Refugee Relief Act of 1953 (occasionally known as the "Church Bill" due to the active support it received in Congress from religious refugee agencies) essentially continued (though on a smaller scale) many of the programs authorized through 1952 under the expired Displaced Persons Act. The previous year, under the Mutual Security Act, President Truman made an initial allocation of $4.3 million to a new State Department program to be known as the United States Escapee Program. Manifestly political, the Escapee Program was designed to combine anti-communist Voice of America and Radio Free Europe broadcasting with refugee reception camps placed conveniently close to the borders of Eastern European nations under Soviet domination. Voluntary agencies assisting in this work could help individuals while at the same time discrediting Stalin's regime.

It was the Escapee Program that initiated the system of direct government contracts with the voluntary agencies for refugee services abroad. Church World Service, Lutheran World Relief, the Joint Distribution Committee, and CRS were all again on the scene, among the first to obtain service contracts with the U.S. government for overseas reception, care, and resettlement work. The State Department, recognizing the political significance of the refugee issue in demonstrating the superiority of Western values, also used appropriations of the act to attach refugee reception units to the U.S. missions in Germany, Austria, Italy, Trieste, Greece, and Turkey. Representatives of the four agencies met with State Department representatives in Geneva and Frankfurt to learn their responsibilities under the new contractual arrangements. At the initial meeting the Lutherans announced that their understanding of the separation of church and state made it impossible to accept a direct contract. Several weeks later, they announced that a review of the matter suggested that their initial judgment had been wrong, and that they would participate in the Escapee Program.[5]

Critics of deeper religious involvement in government-sponsored programs dogged the efforts of the voluntary agencies to assure the public that their humanitarian efforts were above partisan concerns and criticisms. As late as 1953, one professional observer still spoke of the work of the State Department and the INS with religious and ethnic societies as a "new departure in United States administration abroad," referring to unnamed "difficulties."[6] International refugee agencies such as the IRO had explained its policy of using religious agencies pragmatically: faced with the need to care for a culturally and religiously diverse Europeans without "overlapping or omission," the fact remained that "in practice the only such group [of agencies] comprised the religious agencies."[7]

Whether voluntary agency officials were aware of it or not, the Central Intelligence Agency and the Psychological Strategy Board of the National Security Council had been active in exploiting refugee and escapee flows for at least three years before the establishment of the official Escapee Program. Members of Congress, the Departments of State and Justice, and military and CIA officials debated whether migration policies should be generous (aiding virtually all who responded to radio offers of asylum in the West) or limited to leaders who could aid resistance, provide intelligence, or otherwise discredit the Soviet government. Congressman Kersten of Illinois, whose amendment to the Mutual Security Act established the Escapee Program, favored a plan that would have incorporated escapees into the military forces of NATO. The U.S. ambassadors to Austria and Czechoslovakia argued strongly that rather than forming an army (this approach had already been tested with disastrous results among Polish refugees in England), the West should make good on its radio promises and resettle as many as possible in the United States.[8] Almost all government officials active in refugee problems counted on the propaganda value of the escapees at some level.

The voluntary agency that offered the strongest support for Escapee Program was the International Rescue Committee (IRC), formed in 1933 to help prominent refugees to escape from Hitler's Germany. With several CIA officials on its board or directing escapee programs, the IRC was for a time considered a candidate for taking over all escapee work, but a National Security Council investigation disclosed that "the present Executive Director of IRC has not been reliable in dealing with the U.S. Government and is not fully supported by the State Department." Protestant theologian Reinhold Niebuhr, at the time a member of IRC's board of directors, was also not considered "pro-American enough" to be involved in oversight of an official program, so the plan was dropped.[9]

There was yet another side effect of the Mutual Security Act for agencies that contracted with the government. Under the act's provisions employees of agencies that "worked for the government" in this sense were subject to security clearances by the Federal Bureau of Investigation. This meant that the FBI could question ACVA or the individual agencies about any employee. For example, the appointment of ACVA's director of a technical assistance information project was held up for several months while the FBI investigated his background.[10]

The American Friends Service Committee eventually withdrew from government contracts after employees of an assistance project it sponsored in India were asked to sign loyalty oaths (the AFSC never accepted contracts to work in the Escapee Program). The relationship between the Friends and the U.S. government had worked well as long as government officials were supportive of the Friends' desire to (in the words of their founder, George Fox) "be valiant for the truth upon earth; tread and trample all that is contrary under. . . . [and] Be patterns, be examples in all countries." This spirit inevitably came into conflict with the military buildup, arms shipments, and anticommunism of the late 1940s and early 1950s. "As Friends . . . we have felt that our first line of responsibility in the political field is to our own American leaders," said Clarence Pickett in the early 1950s, but the loyalty oath requirements tested the limits of that commitment.[11] Despite the protest inherent in the Friends' withdrawal, the security clearance authority remained in place until the Kennedy administration, when it was discarded.[12]

The New International Refugee System

By the beginning of the 1950s, the United Nations was already dead as a meeting ground between East and West on the refugee issue: refugees were simply too volatile, too subject to political misuse on both sides. It had long been clear that the Soviet Union would not provide financial support to any new UN body charged with the care of refugees, and that the United States sought to minimize all contact with the Russians in this field. As one assistant secretary of state said, commenting on U.S. involvement in postwar Germany, "We must avoid getting into another UNRRA. The United States must run this show."[13]

The result was, under the circumstances, both more and less than might have been hoped. The United Nations Office of High Commissioner for Refugees (UNHCR), created by the General Assembly on December 14, 1950, was given jurisdiction over refugees that met the qualifications under previous arrangements of the League of Nations and the IRO, producing what was essentially a Europe-centered description of a refugee. But the broad definition that appeared in the Convention Relating to the Status of Refugees, signed in July the following year, has remained at the heart of subsequent development of international law concerning who is and is not a refugee. The convention stated that a refugee is anyone who

> owing to a well-founded fear of being persecuted for reasons of race, religion, nationality, membership of a particular social group or political opinion, is outside the country of his nationality and is unable or, owing to such fear, is unwilling to avail himself of the protection of that country; or who, not having a nationality and being outside the country of his former habitual residence as a result of such events, is unable or, owing to such fear, is unwilling to return to it.[14]

This definition remains in effect today.

The limitations on the High Commissioner for Refugees grew from the limited participation of nations in establishing and supporting the convention. Only twenty-six states participated in the writing of the convention in 1951, none except Yugoslavia aligned with the Soviet Union. The UNHCR was charged with material assistance and protection for refugees under its mandate, but not with resettlement; that would be the function of another body still in formation. But once the formalities were in place, it was obvious that there would be no appropriations with which the UNHCR could carry out its responsibilities. If the Ford Foundation had not produced a $3 million grant to cover expenses in the early years, it is doubtful that the agency would have survived.

Though the United States was politically in control of the new agency, it became traditional to elect a European as high commissioner, with the position of deputy high commissioner reserved for an American. van Hoeven Goodhardt, the Dutchman elected as the first high commissioner, and Myron Taylor, Roosevelt's original representative to the Vatican, discussed the the selection of the deputy. Taylor noted that since religious voluntary agencies would be playing a key role, the perfect choice would be a Quaker who worked for the State Department. "I think I was the only Quaker in the foreign service," said James M. Read, who came to his job as the first deputy high commissioner from a foreign service position on the staff of the U.S. Military High Command in Germany. In an interview some years later Read recalled that the government had made the fledgling UNHCR as nonoperational as possible, and that State Department officials frequently let UNHCR officials know where the power really lay. They "could make the UNHCR feel like they were a lot of little boys," said Read.[15] Though receipt of the 1954 Nobel Peace Prize added prestige to the UNHCR's role, the agency was undeniably under the thumb of the United States and its Western allies; the United States did not want an independent UN agency telling it how to run refugee programs.

The United States insisted that an international resettlement agency be established outside the United Nations system, a decision that again caused concern among voluntary agencies eager to support truly international objectives. Thus, along with the new Escapee Program, the Mutual Security Act of 1951 included appropriations of $10 million to finance a new Western, non-UN resettlement agency, eventually known as the Intergovernmental Committee for European Migration (ICEM, later shortened to ICM). The U.S. contribution was contingent on two factors: that the IRO be abolished, and that the new ICEM have absolutely no Soviet participation. Both conditions were met. Resettlement to this day is not a UN responsibility; this international method of "durable solutions" is still implemented largely through two organizations created in the early 1950s, ICM and the International Catholic Migration Commission (ICMC). This "division of labor" in refugee assistance arose from security concerns of the early cold war, and (like the U.S. Escapee Program) remains in effect today.[16]

In addition to assisting Europeans to move to the United States, both IRO and ICEM became involved with the new task of moving Jewish immigrants and refugees to Israel. Large Jewish populations in North Africa and Arab countries were, after the founding of Israel, religious and political candidates for resettlement in the new nation. Since such movements were not always popular with the nations the immigrants and refugees were leaving, it did not hurt to have an intergovernmental authority behind the actual movement of persons; HIAS and other private agencies could not control them on their own authority. Among the famous movements in which the IRO played a role in moving Jews to Israel was Operation Magic Carpet (1948–49), during which almost 50,000 Yemeni Jews were flown to Israel, and Operation Ezra, which brought thousands of Iraqi Jews to Israel in 1950. In all, more than 700,000 Jews from Libya, Morocco, Syria, Egypt, Iraq, and Yemen arrived in Israel between May 15, 1948, and the end of 1952.[17]

Crises in the Middle East and Hungary

In 1955 Israel reemerged at the center of a new foreign policy debate. After a large Soviet arms sale to Egypt, Israel pressed the United States for security assurances for Israel's borders with Arab countries, then for arms that would match the Soviet-financed Arab arms buildup.[18] The Soviet move undeniably pressured Americans to become militarily involved in the Israeli-Arab conflict, a course that had been studiously avoided ever since Truman's original reluctance to commit military personnel on the ground. The subsequent war over the Suez Canal involving British, French, Israeli, and Egyptian forces added a new layer of political difficulties to the already complicated issue of the Palestinian refugees.

The matter was hopelessly stalemated. In December 1955, the United States, Great Britain, and Turkey introduced a resolution in the General Assembly urging Arab governments in the region to take a more active role in the search for a solution to the refugee problem; James Wadsworth, U.S. representative to the United Nations, publicly criticized the Arabs for failing to "let us help them help themselves." Of the $62 million dollars the United States appropriated for UNRWA for the Palestinians in FY 1956, all but $16.7 million went unspent, in part due to the uncooperative attitude of many Arab leaders who sought to use the issue to undermine support for Israel.[19] In addition to the effects of long-standing intra-Arab quarrels, which often had the effect of holding the Palestinians hostage, Arab governments were reluctant to accede to international solutions that were predicated on the long-term existence of Israel. The Palestinian refugee problem was more visible to the public than the movement of Jews to Israel from other countries in the region. Christian agencies and others who had worked among the Palestinian refugees since 1948 helped to keep the claims of the refugees in the public eye.

Throughout this period—indeed, until the Refugee Act of 1980—the Congress and the president continued to handle new refugee emergencies on a piecemeal basis. The Palestinian problem was, due to pressures from Jewish groups, administratively segregated from other refugee matters within the State Department. This followed the UN pattern that placed Palestinian issues under UNRWA rather than the UNHCR.[20] Palestinian issues were handled directly by the Middle East and International Organization desks in the State Department rather than through the Bureau of Refugees and Migration.

The Refugee Relief Act of 1953 was to expire at the end of 1956, but in early November of that year, a new refugee crisis erupted in Hungary as Soviet troops moved in to put down a revolt. A special meeting was called by the American Council of Voluntary Agencies headquarters in New York the following day, where a representative of President Dwight Eisenhower was present to discuss the government's emergency plans. Openings along the Austrian-Hungarian border made it possible for thousands of Hungarians to flee in the first weeks of the confrontation; through contracts with the Escapee Program many of the larger agencies already had personnel in Austria. The president authorized the use of the nearly 6,000 unused places in the expiring Refugee Relief Act, as well as an additional 32,000 under the emergency "parole" status first authorized by the attorney general under 1917 immigration legislation.

The voluntary agencies moved into action. Not only were they called on to feed and clothe the refugees, but also to decide which refugees would be resettled to the United States. The government asked the agencies to agree on religious "quotas," which were set at 62 percent Catholic, 25 percent Protestant, 9 percent Jewish, and 4 percent "other." Roland Elliott of Church World Service offered the following picture of the situation they faced:

> Last night I was at the Hungarian frontier. Some 2,800 crossed over to Austria and safety. The total at that time was approximately 15,000. Approximate because there is no way to keep count of all who struggle through the marshes, across the rivers and canals and the open fields. I saw some of these people as they rose out of the mist and darkness to find that at last they had reached this goal of safety after hours or even days on foot. . . . Gaunt, weary, wet to their waists, their eyes shone with courage and hope. "Why have you come?" I asked. Their answer was one word, "FREEDOM"!! I was ashamed to ask more. . . .
>
> But more truly than anything I already have described, I have seen the face of Jesus Christ, as His Church together is struggling to meet this tragic and heroic situation . . . we have the privileged responsibility of opening our homes to those who come to the U.S.A.[21]

The religious agencies' handling of the resettlement selections, on short notice and pressed by reasons of state clearly beyond their control, was quickly doused with cold water in the U.S. press. The religious quotas raised church/state questions for some:

It has paid to be a member of a church in good standing during the rush of Hungarian refugees to find refuge in the United States. No matter how decent or deserving they may be, people who don't profess any particular faith or who have gotten in trouble with church authorities because of divorce or similar transgressions from church law, have been relegated to the back seat in seeking admission to the United States. You must be sponsored religiously, they are told.[22]

The selection process in Austria dovetailed with the resettlement process in the United States, where refugees were normally resettled by local congregations. After the INS took over the selection process in response to criticism of the voluntary agencies, it resettled refugees in congregational settings that often had no relation to the religious commitments of the refugees.

To expedite the movement of refugees out of Austria they were held temporarily at Camp Kilmer, an army base in New Jersey. This arrangement was protested by the agencies and in December President Eisenhower established the President's Committee for Hungarian Refugee Relief. Its function was "to assist in every way possible the various religious and other voluntary agencies engaged in work for Hungarian refugees, and coordinating their efforts." At Camp Kilmer, the religious agencies were joined by government officials from the Department of Health, Education and Welfare, the army, the INS, the State Department, the Escapee Program, and Radio Free Europe, all trying to bring the crisis to a humane end. With resettlement efforts encouraged by a letter from Eisenhower to state governors, Camp Kilmer was closed as a refugee way station by April 1957; by the end of the year the president declared that the Hungarian refugee crisis itself was finished, despite the fact that some 170,000 refugees remained in Europe.[23]

New Pressures on "Three Faiths" Ecumenism

The expansion of the community of voluntary agencies working internationally was changing the face of the wartime "three faiths" pattern of service. Throughout the 1950s the private agencies favored with the greatest cooperation from the U.S. government in their work abroad were the major Protestant, Catholic, and Jewish bodies operational before and during World War II. Other religious agencies whose work also dated from the wartime era remained in the field, such as the World Relief Commission of the National Association of Evangelicals, Hadassah, the Brethren Service Committee, the YMCA and YWCA, the Salvation Army, the Seventh Day Adventist Welfare Service, and others.

Not all the agencies were religious, and some had fallen on hard times. Many of the wartime ethnic aid societies were restructured or politically redirected. The wartime relief efforts of the Christian Science Church were refused reregistration with the Advisory Committee in 1952. The Boston-based Unitarian Service Committee ran afoul of government authorities when one of its workers operating in the American Zone of Germany was denounced as a Soviet agent. Prominent among the growing secular agencies were CARE and the Save the Children Federation. Save the Children had first joined ACVA in 1944 after more than a decade of work with children in poverty-stricken Appalachian communities, and CARE, originally a hybrid of the major postwar religious groups, had taken a purely secular course.

Government contracts, grants, and food aid flowed not to the agencies with the best or most traditional motives, but to the ones that could get the job done. Save the Children with its international affiliates became one of the major players in the post-Vietnam world of voluntarism.

The Middle East problems arising from the formation of Israel continued to bring new participants as well as new issues to the world of voluntary agency cooperation with the U.S. government. Long-term participants such as Hadassah, the Jewish women's charity group, expanded their programs and their use of government assistance. In 1959 an Islamic agency, Ja'miat 'al Islam, applied for the first time for membership in the American Council of Voluntary Agencies, after announcing by mail that it had just been registered with the Advisory Committee in Washington. This was the reverse of normal cooperative procedure between ACVA and the Advisory Committee, but Ja'miat 'al Islam was not part of the "three faiths" pluralism. Its leaders claimed that it had been formed in Turkey in 1868. Reaction within ACVA was unsympathetic, particularly among Jewish agencies. Within three years the Muslim agency had disappeared both from ACVA and from the registration lists of the Advisory Committee.[24]

Agencies representing the evangelical wing of Protestantism were slow to participate in government-funded activities. Among evangelicals the Seventh Day Adventists and the Salvation Army were exceptions, using their extensive overseas networks primarily for the distribution of surplus food under the 1954 Food for Peace legislation, P.L. 480. The National Association of Evangelicals, formed in 1940 as a theologically conservative counterweight to the Federal Council of Churches, never aspired to build the specialized bureaucracy that had grown up within the National Council of Churches; it preferred to leave most aspects of ministry to individual member churches. Evangelicals preferred the strength of doctrinal commitments to orthodox Protestantism over ecumenical unity among denominations, a bias that was ill-suited to the interfaith ACVA where leaders sought to "forget our differences as far as religious belief was concerned, [and] start from a basic belief in God Himself."[25] Evangelicals also openly talked of the need to relate service to faith, of the need for open evangelistic witness among the people they served abroad. In this extremely sensitive area, evangelicals never assented to the basic proposition that religious and secular ministries could or should be separated.

Another evangelical agency, World Vision, had been established in 1952 to assist children uprooted by the Korean War; for many years thereafter its founder, Dr. Robert Pierce (known to World Vision staff and supporters as "Dr. Bob") concentrated his efforts on this task. Unrelated to any particular denomination or interchurch body, World Vision was one of the first of a new breed of agency eventually known as "parachurch" institutions. Justifying their existence on the basis of the need for specialized ministries within the church, such independent agencies were strongly criticized by established church leaders as lacking accountability: they institutionalized the ministry of a person or small group, and owed no allegiance to a wider body of believers. Furthermore, World Vision was based in California, far from the voluntary foreign aid establishment; its style owed more to an almost entrepreneurial revivalism than to carefully cultivated diplomatic and congressional manners which other established agencies had learned from fifteen years based in New York and Washington.[26] Eventually World Vision came to see that there might be some benefits to working with the government; in 1962 World Vision Relief

Organization, Inc., was established alongside World Vision itself. Separated from its parent body World Vision by only a legal technicality, it was nonetheless a "secular" agency, and thus qualified to receive government assistance.

It would be erroneous to suggest, however, that only evangelical Protestants were encountering problems with the government over religious issues in foreign aid. By the end of the 1950s the bulk of government aid channeled through religious groups was not directed at refugees, but came through the surplus food program. Here the full range of Christian agencies faced difficult problems, notably over proselytizing with relief goods. In 1958, a dispute broke out among Catholic Relief Services, Lutheran World Relief, and Church World Service over charges that the agencies were using P.L. 480 goods to evangelize recipients in Taiwan where, despite larger numbers of Protestants than Catholics on the island, CRS was distributing 84 percent of U.S. surplus food. According to the *Christian Century,* "new Roman Catholic churches which were built in places where there was no Catholic population were equipped for storage and distribution of relief supplies, instead of the usual parochial schools. Priests used the U.S. surplus commodities that come to them so cheaply as come-ons for converts, and stay-ons for the come-ons."[27] It was hard to avoid the conclusion that use of government assistance conferred a certain passive benefit to the church and its institutions. Theological analyses by refugee specialists of the time make it clear that the World Council of Churches and the Catholic church were careful to delineate benefits to the refugee as well as benefits to the church in the work of the agencies.[28]

The two largest Protestant agencies, Church World Service and Lutheran World Relief, both faced critics within their own ranks who questioned the wisdom of government subsidies in overseas relief. How could agencies continue to claim that they were serving the wishes of a truly international humanitarianism when their major overseas efforts inevitably appeared to flow toward a select group of nations favored by the Department of State? And how did such overseas service relate to existing church mission activities in a given region?

Among Catholics, it was a different story entirely. Catholic theology and practice had long been accustomed to the European model, in which the Catholic church, through a concordat with the state, is recognized as the state church. Although no such formal agreement was ever a possibility under the U.S. system, Catholics still tended to work as closely with the government as was permitted. In the field of private foreign relief, this meant that by the 1950s, Catholic Relief Services not only dwarfed the Protestant and Jewish agencies, it had become the largest private relief agency in the world. Out of a field of twenty-four registered agencies, CRS alone received over 50 percent of the relief supplies from the State Department's International Cooperation Agency (the forerunner of AID) in 1958.[29] Thus for the Protestants the issue of government funding was not simply a philosophical inquiry into church/state theory. It raised a very practical question of survival in a field increasingly dominated by the partnership between the State Department and the Catholic church.

Though Jewish agencies were never as heavily involved with surplus food distribution as some of the other large religious agencies, they retained a strong interest in providing relief and migration services to Jewish refugees and immigrants. Hadassah had registered with the Advisory Committee for government assistance, and HIAS received resettlement subsidies for bringing Jews to the

United States; privately donated funds were thus released to sponsor immigration to Israel and other relief and development activities. Both agencies were more openly Zionist than the Joint Distribution Committee, which had nonetheless aided hundreds of thousands of Jews to immigrate to Israel from North Africa in the 1950s. Many of these Sephardic Jews eventually made their way to Israel with the assistance of Jewish agencies and ICEM.

1959: Year of the Refugee

In the United States, the United Nations' designation of 1959 as the International Year of the Refugee marked a high-water point celebrating the cooperation of private and public agencies in fifteen years of continuous service to refugees. Befriended by the leaders of CRS and other private agencies, Senators John Kennedy and Hubert Humphrey were outspoken supporters of channeling foreign aid through private voluntary organizations. The contributions of these groups would specifically be celebrated in the Year of the Refugee. It was in this spirit that a group of citizens representing public and private sectors met in the State Department in October of 1958 to plan a national response to the proposal that had arisen in Great Britain for an International Year of the Refugee. Chaired by Dean Francis Sayre of the Washington Cathedral, the assembled group resolved to take their case to the president. Dean Sayre, who had long been involved in refugee concerns and spent the summer of 1956 working with ICEM in Hungary, later recalled the White House meeting of representatives of the newly formed U.S. Committee for Refugees with Eisenhower and his cabinet:

> We were given twenty minutes before the assembled cabinet, and we began explaining the significance of the Year of the Refugee and how we hoped we might find some new support for refugee causes from the administration. The cabinet was immediately split. The Secretary of Defense objected to new refugee initiatives; Vice-President Nixon proposed $100 million in new government appropriations. The Secretary of the Treasury gave thumbs down on that. Ike said he thought we should try for the additional appropriations, but after the meeting he dropped the ball. The sabotaging of his intentions began immediately from the White House staff, the Treasury, God knows where.[30]

Sayre, working in the U.S. Committee for Refugees from a position designed to bring various refugee advocates into common public ground, found the task daunting. He was an effective public spokesman for refugee causes in his time with the committee, but he later offered a sober evaluation of the behind-the-scenes reality of refugee work:

> Behind the humanitarian concern of the churches, the other groups and the government in the pre-JFK days was a vicious power struggle. All the sectors were warring. If anything the Year of the Refugee was an effort to counterbalance governmental power with private power; the State Department officials of the day were snowing us. The unpleasant truth of the matter was that everyone had come to realize that refugees—bodies, really—meant power, different kinds of power for different people. The first thing I learned was this: don't romanticize it. Everyone knew about the power factor, but no one would ever admit it.[31]

The public events calling attention to refugee problems included a large lunch at New York's Plaza Hotel, at which Dean Sayre and Hubert Humphrey were the principal speakers. President Eisenhower issued a declaration officially recognizing the Year of the Refugee in May. In public, it was perhaps the last great hurrah for the "three faiths" grounding of refugee service, a celebration of everything good about private/public cooperation in a worthy cause. But the real news of the Year of the Refugee was more refugees.

Eisenhower's declaration in May occurred between two refugee flows that exemplified the new, non-European reality of world refugee problems. In March, rebellion against Maoist Chinese occupiers had caused thousands of Tibetan refugees to flee into India. On September 2, Congress passed emergency legislation freeing up a total of 4,500 nonquota immigration visas, most for Dutch victims of political turmoil in Indonesia, where the Netherlands' colonial control was about to come to an end. Through ACVA in New York, the voluntary agencies were again called into action, forming an advisory group to work with the State Department's Office of Refugee and Migration Affairs.[32]

The largest single flow of postwar refugees to the United States began to appear in Dade County, Florida, shortly after Castro took power in Cuba in early 1959. Never before had the United States been a country of first asylum. Initially, local Catholic charities, aided by an already sizable Cuban population in Miami, were able to carry the load, but by late 1960 authorities had concluded that Cubans would need to be resettled elsewhere in the United States. A conscious effort was made by the American Council of Voluntary Agencies and the State Department to assure that Protestant, Catholic, and Jewish agencies were in the lead in supplying assistance to the refugees and ultimately resettling them throughout the United States, even though Jewish agencies soon exhausted the flow of Jewish Cubans. Protestants were allowed to handle the overflow of resettlement contracts that Catholic Relief Service could not absorb, but only after agreeing that those resettled by Protestants would be allowed to attend the church and school of their choice once settled elsewhere in the country. For this resettlement service the agencies were paid $60 per refugee by the government.

The Kennedy Years to Vietnam

By the early 1960s, the future was both promising and confused for the world of religious voluntary agencies. The election of John Kennedy, a political supporter of the religious relief community, promised new interest in the role of voluntarism in foreign aid. Hubert Humphrey, long a great supporter of the role of voluntary aid in foreign assistance, was near the height of his power in the Senate. The Foreign Assistance Act of 1961, still the principal legislative mandate for U.S. assistance abroad today, incorporated for the first time a permanent mandate for government use of "private voluntary organizations." Both of these apparently hopeful signs proved again that political circumstances for the agencies and for their fragile cooperative efforts were not predictable.

The Kennedy presidency did give new emphasis to voluntarism abroad, perhaps best embodied in the founding of the Peace Corps. While not directly related to refugee assistance, the handling of the Peace Corps in Washington represents an important but little-known chapter of the evolving relationship between the federal government and religious agencies active abroad. As originally planned the Peace Corps would have simply farmed out contracts to the existing voluntary agencies, particularly to those with long-standing religious ties overseas. The early planners of the Peace Corps contracted a research firm run by a Quaker with ties to the AFSC and the Friends' lobby in Washington; his report on the feasibility of a Peace Corps that utilized existing voluntary organizations followed the enthusiasm of the Friends for the new venture.[33]

There were secondary considerations on the use of private agencies, the report noted. Foreign nations were often more receptive to private ventures than to those stamped solely with the mark of "official" U.S. foreign policy. Further, should a given Peace Corps project fail, "it will be less damaging to the reputation of the United States if [the project] is not identified as a purely official one." The policy board of the National Catholic Welfare Conference was so accustomed to the principle of church/state cooperation abroad that it approved cooperation without formal vote; a NCWC press release from the spring of 1961 even noted that religious congregations of priests, brothers, and sisters could be considered for participation in the new program.[34]

During congressional hearings on the Peace Corps appropriations bill, characteristic American pragmatism contended with an emerging spirit of strict separation of church and state more fully characterized two years later in the Supreme Court's *Abington* decision barring prayer in the public schools.[35] Senator Humphrey expressed the former in his comments during the Peace Corps hearings, when the issue of the use of religious agencies arose: "May I just say that I am a believer in the so-called doctrine of the separation of church and state but I am not a believer in inaction, and there are people who will rationalize this political principle to a point where you get nothing done." Sargent Shriver, director of the Peace Corps, expressed the ideal of separation of church and state in the context of expanded "nonreligious" cooperation between institutions: "We hope to enable" religiously based institutions "to expand existing nonreligious activities, to begin new nonreligious activities . . . including religious agencies which have been conducting nonreligious activities abroad for years."[36] Congress passed an initial $40 million appropriation for the Peace Corps, but left the church/state question unanswered.

The final outcome, influenced in large part by a debate in the press that reflected virtual ignorance of existing ties in refugee and relief between religious and governmental institutions abroad, was a bitter one for the church agencies that favored government contracts. By the fall of 1961, several church bodies, including the United Presbyterian Church, the Mennonite Central Committee and the Baptist Joint Committee on Public Affairs, had issued statements against direct church participation in the Peace Corps. Lutheran testimony at the time of congressional hearings had indicated that in a field where the religious community was divided over church/state cooperation, a "skewed pattern of church/state relationships may result."[37]

In the summer and fall, the secular and religious press took up the issue, calling attention to the possibility that contractual arrangements might violate the separation of church and state. The churches favoring cooperation were in a bind. The sudden public attention on their overseas work raised an issue that they could not win. Either they protested vigorously, risking extended discussion of their existing cooperative arrangements with government in refugee and relief matters, or they sat quietly by and watched the opposition in church groups and newspapers kill millions of dollars in new government contracts. The agencies chose the latter, and watched from the sidelines as the Peace Corps emerged as a separate, fully operational government agency. Bowing to public pressure, Shriver formalized the decision not to award contracts through existing agencies at a December meeting in Washington.

The question of expanding government cooperation with the religious voluntary agencies was a difficult one in 1961. Protestants, suspicious of Catholic ties with the government since World War II, were distressed by the congressional testimony of Bishop Swanstrom of CRS who, speaking for ACVA, asked that the principle of closer working relationships between the government and private agencies be included in the new Foreign Assistance Act. Some claimed that Swanstrom overstepped the bounds of propriety, presenting Congress with a Catholic position and stating that it represented the consensus of ACVA.[38] Again, however, this was not a controversy that the agencies wanted aired extensively in public.

Once the act became law, the question was not whether agencies would increase their cooperation with government, but how. From 1962 to 1965 the National Council of Churches conducted a rancorous, largely internal commission of inquiry into the question of Church World Service use of government resources. Opponents of increased government aid felt that Church World Service should not receive funds on a routine basis, but rather should agree to use them in response to specific emergency needs as they arose; otherwise institutional dependency on the government would be the inevitable outcome. Throughout the discussion, attention was drawn to the role of Bishop Swanstrom's testimony in bringing about the new intensified government cooperation, and of the challenge this raised to traditional Protestant worries about church/state ties.

Lutherans argued for somewhat lower levels of government subsidy than the National Council of Churches itself, but though Protestants criticized the Catholic view, all the major agencies were by then facing the same questions. The National Council of Churches held that 66 percent government resources and 33 percent private sources was acceptable; the Lutherans held to a 50-50 split. But the voices opposed to government funding within mainline Protestantism were already outgunned by the sheer presence of the Church World Service operation within the National Council of Churches. In 1952, the Church World Service budget, including refugee services and food programs, was just under $1.9 million, approximately 23 percent of the National Council of Churches' total budget for all departments of $8.2 million. By 1963, Church World Service had a budget of $41 million, of which some $26.4 million came from the government. This total represented 80 percent of all National Council of Churches funding for 1963, roughly reversing the funding ratio of eleven years earlier. Protestant opponents to government funding of overseas Protestant relief were trying to shut the barn door after the horse was already out.[39]

Involvement with refugee assistance continued somewhat separately from these direct church/state battles in the early 1960s. Cuban refugees continued to arrive until the Cuban missile crisis of 1962; during this period some 200,000 were admitted under the president's parole powers. Another 15,000 Chinese refugees in Hong Kong were paroled into the United States in 1962. The government could not address these problems without the help of private citizens, and private citizens could not address them without the authority of the government. Though the overseas locales had shifted, this aspect of the World War II relief system remained firmly in place.

New Church/State Dilemmas

In the midst of the public outcry over government assistance to religious institutions through the Peace Corps, the religious voluntary agencies saw that there was little to be gained by public discussion of church/state issues in voluntary foreign aid. The most that they could expect was further government willingness to approach the issues on administrative rather than legal or constitutional levels. After all, as George La Noue has noted, twenty years was too short a period to evaluate the results of an experiment that had itself grown from twin roots: the government's new position as mediator of a global balance of power, and the impulse of American religious bodies to help meet the needs of suffering human beings wherever they arose. Both parties felt the need to restrain references to the elements of self-interest involved in foreign policy; both treated their programs as mandated by a commonsense humanitarian approach.

The issues involved in cooperation between religious and federal authorities abroad could not be adequately summarized under the traditional rubric of "church and state," let alone their "separation." Facing the possibility or reality of established churches in several of the original thirteen colonies, the framers of the Constitution had sought a formula that would permanently prohibit a religious establishment in America. The religion clauses of the First Amendment had succeeded in barring such an establishment; nevertheless, the expansion of government activities into welfare services at home had raised a secondary but related question: did not government funding of religious institutions to meet such needs also constitute a different, de facto form of establishment? If so, what was the meaning of "separation" under this new version of expanded governmental responsibility for the welfare needs of society?

In health and welfare services, the distribution of federal subsidies in this century has not been a question of "church and state," but increasingly a question of "church and labor and community groups and universities and veterans organizations and others . . . and the state." Churches find themselves in competition for scarce funds with a variety of secular and community groups; to rule churches out as competitors simply on the basis of their religious commitments would probably constitute a violation of the free exercise of religion, placing organized religion in an untenably isolated position that, as some recent analysts have pointed out, penalizes individuals for exercising their right of forming religious associations.

In 1948, a second Supreme Court case involving religion in the public schools had caused an uproar.[40] A plan by which the school district of Champaign, Illinois, had released students during school hours for sectarian religious instruction— conducted on the premises of the school—was declared illegal. Predictably, some members of the court dissented. Justice Stanley Reed called attention to the close association between religious and public authorities in American life, and noted that even Jefferson allowed for the teaching of religion at the University of Virginia. Referring to Justice Hugo Black's citation of Jefferson's "wall of separation,"

Justice Reed noted dryly, "A rule of law should not be drawn from a figure of speech."[41]

Those who favored increased government cooperation with religious bodies overseas in refugee work and technical assistance had no trouble making the same point before Congress and the executive branch during the Peace Corps controversy. Yet by the early 1960s, they faced an atmosphere in Washington and across the country demonstrably different from the one that existed during and just after World War II. Months after religious groups were finally refused contracts with the Peace Corps, the Supreme Court issued the first of two decisions on prayer in the public schools. The first banned the use of a state-composed prayer in New York; the second banned compulsory prayer and Bible reading in public school classrooms.[42] These cold blasts of official secularism sent shock waves through religious believers across America. For many others, however, they represented the legitimate growth of pluralist tolerance. In the public reaction to the Peace Corps controversy, the secular and separationist principles embodied in the yet-to-appear prayer rulings appeared over and over again in the editorials of major newspapers.

While participants in religious missions abroad may have followed these domestic controversies, their leaders had little reason to believe that the church/state disputes bore relevance to their situation overseas. Debate had arisen over specific problems—such as the proselytizing incident in Taiwan and the Peace Corps—yet it remained clear that agency and governmental personnel were still firm believers in a humanitarian zone of cooperation, their common ground overseas since World War II. Since the war religious agencies had accepted more than a billion dollars of government assistance, acting as responsible stewards and helping thousands of Americans to meet the obligations of religiously motivated service. Practically, the government could not care for refugees or displaced persons overseas, nor could it effectively carry out programs of technical aid without the grass-roots assistance of the worldwide contacts of the churches. It needed the churches overseas, and the churches needed the support of the government. Domestic critics might cavil over fine points, but that would not, as Hubert Humphrey said, get the job done. National church and governmental leaders were willing to call the first twenty years of postwar church/state cooperation abroad a success, citing numbers of refugees aided, people fed, or village wells dug. The second twenty years would be harder to call.

7

The Consensus Breaks:
Vietnam and Its Aftermath (1965–1980)

Even though hundreds of thousands of Cuban refugees had come to the United States in the early 1960s, the federal statutes defining a refugee were still based on the disruptions and human displacements in Europe following the Second World War. The Cubans, and the Hungarians before them, were admitted under presidential use of the parole power, a power that left many in Congress uncomfortable. The Senate committee reporting out a new immigration act in 1965 attempted to limit the parole power to "emergency, individual, and isolated situations . . . and not the immigration of classes or groups outside the limit of the law."[1] When Lyndon Johnson went to the Statute of Liberty to sign the bill, he pointedly ignored this warning and announced that Cubans would find an open door in the United States. Between December of that year and 1972 an additional 368,000 Cuban refugees entered the United States.[2]

Despite twenty years of domestic and international pressures, the escalation of social and welfare services to Cuban refugees in the United States only strengthened the complementary role of the voluntary agencies in the federal government's efforts to address the global refugee problem. By the mid-1960s the federal and state governments were offering a range of subsidies to voluntary resettlement agencies that were unknown in the 1940s. Refugee policies had been and remained militantly anticommunist, but for the most part religious and other voluntary agencies were willing participants in overseas assistance and, more recently, government efforts to integrate resettled refugees into domestic welfare services.

The experience with the Cubans, and with Egyptians who fled Egypt under Nasser and the steady flow of Eastern Europeans, only reinforced earlier definitions of a refugee as someone who had left his or her native land and crossed an international border to seek refuge. Church agencies had long pressed for ways to help people who were internally displaced in their own homelands, but the United States and others had rejected such suggestions as unworkable.[3] Even the World Council of Churches had agreed that the new Office of the High Commissioner for Refugees could not, in 1951, be given any responsibility for the millions of expellees who had been returned to Germany by Soviet-supported regimes in Eastern Europe.

The Bitter Divisions of Vietnam

Only two months before President Johnson stood at the base of the Statue of Liberty to dramatize his revised immigration and refugee policies, the government had asked officials of the major voluntary agencies to go to Vietnam to examine the growing problem of internally displaced Vietnamese fleeing that country's growing civil war. The delegation, sponsored by the American Council of Voluntary Agencies in New York, reported their findings in measured tones:

> Over the summer and early fall of 1965, as the character of the war in Vietnam changed sharply, increased numbers of Vietnamese, including Montagnard (or mountain) people, left their homes in acute distress and appeared in urban and coastal areas seeking security under Vietnamese and U.S. Government control. . . . As the numbers rose to six or seven hundred thousand, with estimates that they might rise to one million by the end of the year, concern mounted as to whether . . . the American people, in the midst of their concern over a steadily escalating war effort, fully understood and supported the necessary increase in both government and voluntary agency programs to serve these people in distress.[4]

This "necessary increase" in service to internally displaced Vietnamese arguably marked the beginning of a new and troubled era of cooperation between religious institutions and the U.S. government overseas. The humanitarian coalition in the postwar world had worked as long as no one directly questioned the exercise of international U.S. power. When the legitimacy and humanity of that power fell under suspicion, as it did in the case of wartime refugees and humanitarian assistance in Vietnam, the consensus between church and state abroad fell apart.

With the collapse of French rule in Vietnam after World War II, international negotiations at Geneva in 1954 divided Vietnam into two states in an effort to contain popular support for communist forces under Ho Chi Minh. Along with southern Catholics, nearly a million new refugees from the north (many of whom were also Catholic) formed the basis of the political support of the Ngo Dinh Diem government in South Vietnam. Many were flown to the south on CIA-owned airlines.[5] By the early 1960s the northern refugees constituted 60 percent of the Catholic population of South Vietnam.[6]

As part of the postwar strategy of containment of communist expansion, the United States sought to provide humanitarian assistance to help stabilize the situation. With little fanfare, programs were established and by 1958 Catholic Relief Services, Church World Service, and the Mennonite Central Committee were all administering government-sponsored relief. The team of voluntary agency officials inspecting the situation in 1965 cited the successful relief operation of the 1950s as a useful precedent for the then current plans to assist refugees in the south. Since these Vietnamese were technically "internally displaced persons" rather than refugees, the programs serving them were administered by the Agency for International Development rather than the Refugee and Migration Bureau at the State Department.

ACVA representatives sought an expanded international presence in Vietnam to bring the refugee problem under control. They hoped to explore the possibility of bringing an "international refugee agency" to the country, and some church agencies entertained the idea of helping refugees in North as well as South Vietnam. When they arrived in Vietnam, however, they found that neither of these options was of particular interest to the authorities. After all, a war was under way; the refugees had left their homes because of increased military action and pressures from the Viet Cong. Because the refugees fled into areas held by the South Vietnamese, the ACVA team reported that "the present policy of both Vietnamese and U.S. Governments is to regard refugees as an 'asset.' "[7] Consequently AID and other government officials encouraged a rapid expansion of voluntary agency services, but under the direct control of U.S. and South Vietnamese authorities. There was little official interest in aiding the communist north. In response to public questioning on aid to North Vietnam, Bishop Swanstrom of CRS said, "It would be a holy and just thing to do. But it is simply impossible." Additionally, the fact that the refugees were internally displaced ruled out a role for the UNHCR. The agencies would of necessity adopt a partisan role in carrying out their humanitarian aid to refugees. From the early stages of the Vietnam War, then, there was a close connection between U.S. voluntary agencies and the U.S. war effort—a pattern familiar both in Korea and in World War II. The difference in Vietnam was of course the unpopularity of the Vietnam War in the United States.

Official Catholic policymakers stated in 1966 that the U.S. presence in Vietnam could be morally justified; that Christmas Francis Cardinal Spellman visited the troops in Saigon and was quoted as saying "My country may it always be right. Right or wrong, my country." The United States, according to Spellman, was "the Good Samaritan of all nations." Among Protestants, the Christian and Missionary Alliance (CAMA), a conservative denomination with Presbyterian roots, had long been active in Vietnam; its missionaries knew the country and strongly supported the United States in its fight against Hanoi. But within Catholic and mainline Protestant circles protest against the war was steadily gaining ground; by the fall of 1967, 46 percent of the respondents to a Gallup Poll felt that the United States had made a mistake in sending troops.[8]

In August 1967 the liberal *National Catholic Reporter* sent Michael Novak, a young academic with a growing reputation as an antiwar spokesman, to spend a month in Vietnam reporting on the war. There Novak shaped the most direct challenge to the work of the voluntary agency community to emerge during the war. According to Novak, Catholic Relief Services had diverted up to half of the food aid it had been given for aiding Vietnamese refugees to the the Popular Forces, the South Vietnamese militia. The story was picked up by the *New York Times,* but vehemently denied at CRS headquarters in New York. The public relations battle over the issue raged for most of the rest of the year; some publications, including the Catholic *Ave Maria,* urged that American Catholics suspend their donations to CRS and channel them instead to CARITAS, the international Catholic charity network of which CRS was the American affiliate. Agencies such as the American Friends Service Committee decided not to accept government assistance for their work in Vietnam. The CRS had no such commitment; as was the case in many other countries, the volume of CRS's war relief programs far outdistanced that of its competitors, and most of it was in the form of government food assistance. Despite official denials that food was being diverted to the South Vietnamese militia, CRS quietly discontinued the program in early 1968.[9]

The ACVA survey of 1965 had predicted that the internal refugee population of South Vietnam would grow to 1 million. The war reduced this projection to a wistful fantasy. By 1971, more than 6 million Vietnamese were displaced in the south, creating an enormous logistical and humanitarian difficulty in fighting the war. American authorities attributed the growth of the refugee population to the 1968 Tet Offensive, noting that the military attacks by the Viet Cong forced innocent people to flee their farms and villages. Critics of the U.S. war effort were equally quick to point out that many had left their homes in the wake of a new U.S. military approach to guerilla warfare known as "pacification." Under the pacification program, entire regions were evacuated of their civilian populations so that saturation bombing would kill any remaining persons—presumably Viet Cong—in a given locale. Refugees clogged the streets of Saigon as well as rural holding centers, many of which were administered by voluntary agencies. The major agencies, namely the twenty-two that formed the Council of Voluntary Agencies in Vietnam (CVAV), began expanding their programs when the U.S. military commitment grew in 1966; by 1971, despite the fact that the refugee population had reached 6 million, most of the agencies had begun to scale back their involvements.

Government assistance to voluntary agencies was extensive. Of the twenty-two agencies in the CVAV, ten received project support from the U.S. government; several of the other twelve received ocean freight reimbursements but refused project assistance. State Department figures for 1969 (offered with the caution that such figures are always likely to be incomplete) show that out of a total of $13.2 million spent on projects administered by voluntary agencies, approximately $6.6 million or 50 percent came directly through government contracts. An additional $17.4 million of material aid, including P.L. 480 surplus food, was dispensed by the agencies in the same year. Of this total, $7.9 million came from government sources, and was divided among six voluntary agencies. Voluntary agency personnel were also offered free air transportation and commissary and postal service privileges. The obvious conclusion was that the U.S. government regarded the voluntary agencies as an integral part of the war effort in Vietnam.

When American commitment to the war declined, so did the spending for civilian relief that reached the voluntary agencies. By 1971 there had been three consecutive years of declining spending by the government, despite the fact that social problems in Vietnam were escalating. One agency director offered the following account of his agency's contract relations with the United States in Vietnam:

> We had the unfortunate experience of believing the promise that it was an extendable, open ended type of contract that would be and could be, if we so desired, extended. This did not prove to be the case. . . . The drop in finances and coverage necessitated sending back to the States, before the job was completed to our satisfaction, people who were brought on just for the contract work. We felt that we were left hanging . . . the abrupt non-continuity was quite detrimental to our overall program.[10]

Despite such problems with government aid, only one of the agencies in CVAV felt that it was improper to accept any government assistance.[11]

Among Protestants, Lutheran World Relief, Church World Service, and the Mennonite Central Committee united their efforts in an agency known as Vietnam Christian Service. It was here, and in the AFSC, the Unitarian Universalist Service Committee, and International Voluntary Services (an agency formed with Brethren and Mennonite support in 1954) that much of the religiously based criticism of U.S. war policy was located in Vietnam. Vietnam Christian Service officials argued that the mere fact that their funds came from abroad rather than from Vietnam (quite aside from the fact that it was one of the six agencies distributing government surplus food) made their presence in the country "political." The limited remedy for this problem was "to minister insofar as possible to all men in need even though they may themselves be divided ideologically, politically and militarily."[12]

An incident involving International Voluntary Services (IVS) in 1967 shows the limits agencies faced in pursuing a critical approach to U.S. military policy in Vietnam. IVS had come to Vietnam in 1957 with support from AID and the government of Vietnam. In the summer of 1967 forty-nine staff members of IVS in Vietnam sent a letter to President Johnson in which they stated that they were "finding it increasingly difficult to pursue quietly [our] main objective—helping the people in Vietnam." The letter was published in the *New York Times* in September. Additional public protests from IVS staff continued over the next three years, including a 1970 letter to President Nixon and UN Secretary General U Thant alleging that the U.S. conduct of the war violated the Geneva Conventions. Rancor generated by these and other public statements eventually caught up with IVS. In 1971, when the agency tried to renew its contract with the relevant Vietnamese ministry, IVS officials were shuffled from one ministry to the next. With no renewal in sight, IVS decided later in the year that it would have to terminate its Vietnam commitment.

The country director issued a public letter in August stating that IVS was being forced to leave Vietnam for "political reasons." In an article published in December, the director further charged that South Vietnam's President Thieu had personally requested that U.S. Ambassador Ellsworth Bunker refuse to renew IVS's contract with AID. Even a trip to Vietnam by the executive director of IVS in Washington was not enough to salvage the situation, which by then had received extensive coverage in the press. The last director of IVS in Vietnam analyzed the situation as one which had seen a sea-change in the attitude of IVS volunteers in the course of the war. The IVS had begun with a commitment to low-key development aid, but according to one analyst,

> The "new IVS" took on an almost opposite character. The new objectives were to end the war and to change the Government of Vietnam. These roles of witness to the war and of being political activist[s] were contrary to quiet acceptance of the status quo and to the subordinate position. To those volunteers who adopted the "new IVS" in whole or in part, it provided a more relevant response to the new situation in the country. The difference between the "old IVS" and the "new IVS" was in regard to what was the most productive thing to do in a wartime situation. . . . In order to get the greatest exposure for its testimony, IVS naturally drifted into an informal alliance with the press corps. This increased exposure in the press, although it was thoughtful and reasoned, served to put IVS in the political spotlight on the dove side of the question. IVS was no longer a quiet, apolitical development organization.[13]

Though few of the voluntary agencies went as far as IVS in their public criticism of government conduct of the war, none of the agencies were unqualified supporters of the war; they were too intimately exposed to the human suffering that it brought to Vietnam. Several, however, including CRS and the more conservative Protestant agencies such as World Vision and World Relief, remained cautious in stating their criticisms and their objectives. CRS limited its efforts to short-term relief; its director stated that "long-range social welfare goals are the hope of any agency, but the reality of war makes it necessary to try to meet needs as they arise."[14] World Vision had a similar statement, combining commitments to relief and to evangelism: "This is the philosophy of World Vision: to meet need and, as God provides and blesses, to present Christ."[15] Both World Relief (National Association of Evangelicals) and World Vision drew much of their field personnel from the experienced missionary staff of the Christian and Missionary Alliance.

For the first time in the post–World War II period religious agencies found themselves in an ongoing adversarial relationship with the U.S. government. "The goal of the U.S. Government was to help the Government of Vietnam fight a war against what was referred to as Communist aggression, [and] the U.S. Government saw the agencies fitting helpfully into the picture," said Robert Miller, director of Vietnam Christian Service from 1968 to 1971. "Since U.S. soldiers and planes were involved in the killing and wounding and the creation of refugees the U.S. Government felt some responsibility to take care of these war victims and saw the agencies as helping to do that. . . . [But] the goals of the agencies were primarily humanitarian and were basically different from those of the government."[16] It was this public charge that the U.S. government had no true humanitarian interests, that marked the end of the consensus between governmental and religious leaders.

A number of factors caused this shift, which in effect challenged the entire postwar development of religiously based services abroad that functioned as a complement to U.S. policies. The vastly expanded press coverage of the war brought home the contradictions of the war to civilians in Vietnam and in the United States. Vietnam brought a new generation of voluntary workers into the agencies, young people for the most part unfamiliar with the postwar history of religious and governmental cooperation in refugee matters. Far from being condemned to repeat the mistakes of history, many felt themselves to be in the vanguard of a new, more humane movement that would give voice to the cries of the poor and the refugee. If governments were ignoring or even capitalizing on their plight, it appeared to be the task of the private sector to offer the needed alternatives. If this meant a more open alliance with the press in airing grievances, so be it. If the responsible governments could no longer act in a humane fashion, they argued, they would have to be isolated, prodded, and if necessary attacked until they changed. In such a political climate it is not surprising that agency representatives came to see their function as compensating for government policies rather than complementing them.

The most important new idea underlying this shift was that the United States *created* refugee flows. Accurately or not, refugee problems had previously been blamed on Hitler, Stalin, Khrushchev, or Castro. It was relatively easy for religious and other leaders to side with U.S. authorities in aiding victims of these regimes. After all it was the United States that had funded the bulk of postwar assistance, which had moved displaced persons and others to their new homes and had established the principle of voluntary repatriation and the structure of the UNHCR. The notion that voluntary agencies could initiate policies opposed to governmental policies in the midst of a war was ahistorical, but that was precisely the view that many young volunteers held in the face of the tragedies of Vietnam.

There were points at which the agencies, individually and through the CVAV, challenged the legitimacy of U.S. refugee policy with some success. In 1971 pacification operations were expanded in the hill regions inhabited by the Montagnards, tribal villagers who had lived isolated for centuries in Vietnam. Agency personnel saw these villagers terrorized by their forced removal. Initially the U.S. military authorities claimed that the operation was entirely under the control of the Vietnamese, but agency personnel on the scene saw U.S. advisors and military hardware being used. Vietnam Christian Service representatives contacted sympathetic authorities in Saigon with reports of the terror being inflicted on these internally displaced refugees:

> All their cattle, much of their rice, and other possessions had to be left behind. Also, the ARVN [Army of the Republic of Viet Nam] were purposely breaking ceremonial jars and taking potshots at the animals. Before they left, the ARVN set the hamlets on fire. Upon arriving at Buan Kli "B" [the relocation center] the ARVN threw the people's belongings out of the helicopters thereby breaking many items. They had been in Buan Kli "B" fourteen days already and all they had received was tents to sleep in.[17]

In March the CVAV agencies drafted a letter to the government of Vietnam in which they protested the conduct of the pacification program:

> We question if the political and military factors can justify their locations in view of the social and humanitarian considerations. . . . As social workers, we are opposed to the indiscriminate relocation of Montagnards. . . . In view of our opposition to such relocations, the member agencies of the Council are very reluctant to assist in this work if carried out as in the past.[18]

The following month officials of IVS and the Mennonite Central Committee were called on to provide testimony to the Senate Subcommittee on Refugees and Escapees concerning the Montagnard relocations. At the same time agency workers in the field gave vivid testimony to newspaper reporters and the publicity began to have its effect. By May Vietnamese officials announced policy changes that had the effect of halting the relocation program.

There were such successes along the way, but the agencies were a minuscule part of the American presence in Vietnam. Starting in 1969 a group of employees of different agencies began meeting in Saigon to discuss ways they could alter U.S. war policy. Letters were sent, vigils at Saigon churches organized, reports forwarded to home offices and to the press that played a definite role in encouraging antiwar activities in the United States. But when asked in 1971 whether their agencies had had a broad impact on U.S. policies toward Vietnam, only one of the leaders of nineteen agencies said yes. Seven thought that there might be a possibility that they had altered U.S. policies, but eleven flatly said no. Some felt that their presence had altered government policies in limited, specific cases.

Whether the religious leadership was supporting or opposing government policy, it could not be ignored. This was true in Vietnam to the very last moments of the official American presence in Saigon. When Ambassador Graham Martin was called on to supervise the final chaotic American withdrawal in 1975, he faced agonizing choices about who would be given places on the few helicopters that were ferrying people out of the embassy compound. The director of Catholic Relief Services refused to board a helicopter unless he was accompanied by his Vietnamese staff; he knew they would face certain death under the communists. Martin cabled the White House in desperation:

SAIGON FLASH TO WHITE HOUSE

AMONG AMERICANS HERE IS FATHER MCVEIGH, HEAD OF CATHOLIC RELIEF SERVICES, WHO WILL NOT LEAVE WITHOUT HIS VIETNAMESE STAFF, WHO HE KNOWS WILL BE PERSE-CUTED. . . . HOW WILL PRESIDENT EXPLAIN TO BISHOP SWANSTROM, US HEAD OF CRS, OR FR. MCVEIGH'S GREAT AND GOOD FRIEND CARDINAL COOKE, WHY I LEFT HIM? I REPEAT I NEED 30 SORTIES TONIGHT. PLEASE GET THEM FOR ME. WARM REGARDS, MARTIN. SE-CRET.[19]

The U.S. effort to aid internally displaced refugees was over; the task of resettling Southeast Asians still lay ahead. Many government officials did not antici-pate anything like the resettlement flow that eventually took place in the latter half of the decade. In 1973, for instance, an official of the State Department's Refugee and Migration Bureau told a committee of the House of Representatives that the United States did not anticipate war refugees "coming to the United States . . . it would be our opinion that they could be resettled in their own country."[20] By 1975 their "own country," South Vietnam, no longer existed.

For many with religious motives, the golden cord binding the moral purposes of the government and the church in international humanitarian assistance was severed in Vietnam. On this analysis church groups were gradually realizing the width of the gulf that separated their purposes in aiding refugees from those of the state. For others sharing the same negative analysis of the U.S. presence in the region, continued cooperation with government programs remained a necessary evil, to be approached only with the greatest caution. Such views were for the most part to be found within the mainline and peace churches of Protestantism and in peace activist circles in the Catholic church.

The political problems involved in working alongside government refugee pro-grams were not easily solved by resolutions that disallowed any future church participation in such efforts. The precedents for cooperation in the postwar era were strong; private agencies, even those with solid church constituencies, for the most part were not in a position to establish programs on a scale capable of provid-ing useful assistance without government assistance and cooperation. Few church workers, if they thought about it, were interested in creating a situation that institu-tionalized hostility between religious and governmental workers overseas. Church World Service was one of the agencies most scarred by its Vietnam-era problems with U.S. foreign policy; in 1974 its director was replaced in an internal power struggle won by those most concerned to assert the independence of CWS activities from the priorities of U.S. foreign policy.[21] Use of P.L. 480 food was then further reduced and CWS stepped up its antigovernment rhetoric, but it never attempted a total break from U.S. government assistance in its overseas programs.

In further eroding what remained of postwar church/state cooperation in for-eign policy, the Vietnam War highlighted the critical role of religion in formulating (or destroying) that consensus. Reaction to the war frequently split political opinion within various churches and denominations. The government sought the participa-tion of all interested religious and private groups willing to provide humanitarian assistance, yet those who participated in these efforts overseas went on to become the source of critical testimony on the war that reached the United States outside of official government channels.

Panic and Despair in Israel

In the Vietnam War era many American Jews were torn by political pressures that made them "hawks" on Israel and "doves" on U.S. participation in Vietnam. In the anxiety over the Six Day War of 1967 and the Yom Kippur War of 1973 a new sense of the distinctiveness of being a Jew in the United States arose alongside the inevitable bond that now existed between American Jews and Israel.

In the course of these two wars, Israel expanded its territorial holdings to include the West Bank of the Jordan River, the Sinai Peninsula, East Jerusalem, and the Golan Heights. Within the Jewish community, "the liberation of Jerusalem after 1,900 years of foreign rule" represented the ultimate vindication of the post-war efforts to reconstruct a Jewish polity in the modern world.[22] Outside the Jewish community reactions were mixed. Arguably no political actions before or since have so alienated those mainline Protestant and Catholic leaders in the United States who were party to efforts at reaching a peaceful settlement of Palestinian claims. Israeli annexation of Egyptian, Syrian, and Jordanian territories appeared to preclude the hope of many political moderates for a separate Palestinian state that could coexist alongside Israel. The rise of new forms of Palestinian terrorism in the late 1960s was used to justify the claims of Israeli authorities that the occupied territories offered the strategic protection from Arab attack (particularly in the Golan Heights) that Israel required.

As Israel surveyed its manpower losses in the fighting, it became clear that a new emphasis on the *aliyah,* the sacred Law of Return, would be a pragmatic political move. After the 1967 war the Israeli Ministry of Labor commissioned an American professor, Eli Ginzburg, to study the needs of Israeli labor in the light of the ongoing efforts to encourage the global Jewish *aliyah.* Daniel Elazar called the postwar emphasis on the *aliyah* "a number one public issue in Israel," and hence one that figured prominently on the agenda of Jewish relief and charity organizations. Reform rabbis called for new attention to voluntary *aliyah* in the United States, beginning with programs in congregational schools.[23]

At the American Council of Voluntary Agencies in New York, interagency tensions rarely reached the working agendas of the committees charged with coordinating the increasingly diverse activities of the voluntary agencies abroad. But tensions did exist; outside ACVA circles, church mission leaders were distressed by the effect of Israel's presence and the Palestinian refugees on the decades of work they had built up among Middle Eastern Arabs. Jewish analysts in 1969 found reaction among other Christian leaders and theologians toward the state of the Middle East "dismal." Friends, Mennonites, Lutherans, Catholics, and others who had worked with the Palestinian refugees since 1948 were often torn between what appeared as conflicting sets of legitimate aspirations in which Israelis and Palestinians were struggling for control of the same pieces of land.

Securing human rights for Soviet Jewry—particularly the right to emigrate to Israel—played an increasingly important role in the the efforts of American Jews in the 1960s to aid Jews abroad. In late 1966 a coalition of some twenty-five Jewish agencies secured the signatures of 90 senators in a campaign to increase cultural and religious freedom for Soviet Jews; the following year 315 members of the House of Representatives endorsed a similar plea. Throughout the rest of the decade Jewish leaders in the United States conducted a broad public relations and social action campaign directed at increasing awareness among Jews and others of the problems facing Jews in the Soviet Union.

In a meeting in Brussels in February 1971 an effort was made to resolve tension between Jews who sought to emphasize improvement of the human rights of Soviet Jews and those who wanted the emphasis placed on the right of emigration and *aliyah*. It was a variation on an old argument in the Jewish community, recalling the debate during World War II on whether emphasis should be on relief and rescue or on resettlement to Palestine. Many international Jewish leaders were willing to defer to the wishes of Israel; because the Israeli Jewish Agency maintained a strong bias toward emphasizing emigration, this approach dominated the Brussels gathering. In the Soviet Union the immediate response in March and for months thereafter was expanded emigration. In Washington, a delegation of Jewish leaders met with officials of the Office for Refugees and Migration to inform them of Jewish actions that were expected to result from the Brussels meeting, particularly matters concerning the transit routes between Vienna, Italy, and Israel. They told State Department officials that the Jewish community was not asking for any financial assistance for the operation "at this time." Jewish leaders, according to one State Department official, "were in the habit of deciding in New York and Jerusalem what they were going to do and then informing us after the fact."[24]

In the early part of 1973 the focus of the campaign for Soviet Jews shifted to a direct effort to move legislation through the Congress that would tie U.S. trade with the Soviet Union to the critical issue of emigration from the Soviet Union to Israel. Outside of the United States and Israel, the largest community of Jews (approximately 2.6 million, though estimates vary) in the world remains in the Soviet Union. The effort, spearheaded in Congress by Sen. Henry Jackson (D-Wash.) and Rep. Charles Vanik (D-Ohio), came in response to a 1972 move by Soviet authorities to impose an extortionate "diploma tax" on émigrés with some form of higher education. For those who had followed Jewish efforts at influencing worldwide treatment of Jews through congressional legislation, the Jackson-Vanik struggle had a familiar look. The successful 1911 national campaign for legislation to abrogate U.S. trade treaties with czarist Russia over the treatment of American Jews traveling in Russia could be seen as "virtually a dress rehearsal" for the Jackson-Vanik effort.[25]

The Jackson-Vanik Amendment was eventually attached to an East-West trade bill offering "most favored nation" status to the Soviet Union on the condition that it lifted its emigration restrictions. The State Department and National Security Advisor Henry Kissinger expressed some reservations about the legislation, preferring "quiet diplomacy," but Senator Jacob Javits (R-N.Y.) argued that the amendment would place U.S.–Soviet détente on "a sound moral basis." After intense debate in Congress, the White House, and the Jewish community the amendment passed both houses of Congress by a large majority. Emigration figures indicate that the years following the Jackson-Vanik effort saw a decline in the number of Jewish émigrés.[26] However, when emigration began to expand again, swelling to an annual high of 51,000 in 1979, Congress also expanded its financial assistance to help with the relocation of Soviet émigrés in Israel. In 1976 it appropriated more than $100 million for that purpose.

In Vienna, the first destination for most Soviet émigrés, representatives from Israel's Jewish Agency met every Jew coming from the Soviet Union. A report written in 1975, contained the following description of the process:

> "They are wary. They fear that we are KGB agents. But we approach them, smile and say 'Shalom.' *We are the first to tell them 'Shalom.'* " The word has a mystical quality.
>
> Immediately upon arrival, those refugees who are making *aliyah* are separated from those opting to go elsewhere. . . . Those refugees who do not intend making *aliyah*—they are called *noshrim*—are taken to hotels in downtown Vienna where they become the responsibility of HIAS. . . . Although the Russian government will issue an exit visa to a Jew only if he lists Israel as his destination (except in a very few special cases), the Jewish Agency joins with most of the Jewish world in regarding this as a legal fiction. . . . The Agency does talk to every *nosher*. After the individual has had a night's rest, he is interviewed by an Agency representative. The Israelis admit that these sessions, which are held at the HIAS office, often become emotional. . . . The Agency people are candid in describing themselves as "salesmen," emphasizing the good points of Israel while minimizing possible difficulties. They also challenge the refugee's view of life in the United States and his motives in choosing America.[28]

In 1975 Israeli journalists reported a growing tendency of Soviet Jews to reject the *aliyah* in favor of alternative homes.[29] By the following year more than half of those leaving the Soviet Union were no longer choosing to go to Israel, but were instead going to the United States, Canada, Australia, and elsewhere.

There were important political considerations in moving Jews to Israel from the Soviet Union. From 1966 through 1979 some 226,000 Jews left the Soviet Union with exit visas for Israel. During this period Soviet Jews provided the largest pool of new immigrants to Israel. For instance, of the nearly 20,000 Jews who moved to Israel in 1976, nearly 7,300 were from the Soviet Union; the next largest group (3,000) came from the United States and Canada.[30] By the end of the 1970s a painful fact emerged; for whatever reason, more Jews were emigrating from Israel than were arriving. With hundreds of thousands of Palestinian refugees living within the occupied territories, maintaining a Jewish majority in Israeli-held areas was again a troubling issue. How could Israel maintain its democracy without enfranchising the Arab populations? Alternatively, how could it enfranchise the Arabs and still remain a Jewish state? In the short run, the only option was increased emphasis on the *aliyah* as the central justification for a Jewish polity in Israel.

Toward that end the refugee policy of the U.S. government was a critical factor. Congress continued to appropriate funds to finance Israel's refugee programs. Such assistance had been offered periodically since 1951, but the justification had shifted dramatically. In 1951 financial assistance for the absorption process was justified on the basis of the devastation the wars surrounding the formation of Israel had wrought across the Palestinian countryside. By the late 1970s Israel was promoting its role as America's strategic democratic ally in the Middle East; in order to remain so, it required constant expansion of its Jewish population. In the early years of the State of Israel the Zionist movement was controlled by the secular Israeli labor movement and its political ally, the Labor party. By the time of the second Begin administration (1981–83), the theological roots of Zionism, and the theological significance of Zionism as a national Israeli ideology, had moved to the foreground. American financial and political support for Zionist immigrants was now in aid of an overtly theological movement.

In some ways, it was preferable to U.S. authorities that Soviet Jewish émigrés resettle in the United States. The United States had always welcomed Soviet refugees in the postwar period; the Escapee Program had demonstrated that this could be justified on the dual grounds of humanitarianism and cold war politics. Sending the refugees to Israel was in fact a much more expensive proposition. HIAS estimated that it cost $3,500 per refugee in the mid-1970s to relocate and absorb Soviet refugees in the United States; a functional resettlement system, supported by voluntary private contributions, handled much of the work. As for those going to Israel, there were constant complaints about lack of coordination between the Jewish Agency and the absorption department of the national government, which often appeared to work at cross purposes. Since the process in Israel was governmental rather than private, it was more expensive. Estimates for relocation and absorption in Israel ran approximately $35,000 per refugee, ten times the cost of bringing them to the United States. And much of this effort was funded by the U.S. government.

Christian agencies, on the other hand, often worked in parts of the world where Christian communities were minuscule or nonexistent. Increasingly, the interests of many Christian agencies diverged from those of the U.S. government. In Chile, for instance, the United States encouraged the fall of the Marxist government of Salvador Allende in 1973. The U.S. authorities had no interest in caring for the 12,000 political refugees—mostly supporters of Allende—who fled Chile after General Augusto Pinochet took power. President Richard Nixon could have paroled the Chileans as previous presidents had Cubans and Hungarians, but by 1975 only twenty-six Chileans had been given U.S. asylum. The UNHCR had been authorized to mount only minimal programs in Spain and elsewhere for the refugees. Church World Service, the American Friends Service Committee, and other refugee agencies did what they could, but recognized that their efforts flew in the face of official U.S. government policy. By the end of the decade their efforts had been partially successful; several hundred Chileans were admitted to the United States.[31] This conflict typified a growing post-Vietnam political opposition to governmental refugee policy within church refugee circles; it was mild in comparison with what lay ahead.

The Carter Years

Jimmy Carter's determination to place new emphasis on human rights cheered many religious leaders familiar with the realities of political oppression common in most of the world. Though the Carter administration left the legacy of the Refugee Act of 1980, as well as the massive program for resettling Southeast Asians fleeing communist governments in the region, its record on the continuing flow of Haitians and Cubans to the United States created new confusion among refugee advocates in the relief and resettlement agencies. While Carter was supporting legislation that attempted to eliminate the anticommunist bias of U.S. refugee policy, he was unable to make up his mind on how the tens of thousands of Cubans fleeing their homes in early 1980 should be handled. The INS systematically excluded Haitians fleeing the regime of "Baby Doc" Duvalier from consideration as refugees. By the time Carter left office in 1981, the American public was disillusioned not only by the record numbers of refugees wanting to come to this country, but also by the inability of the government to apply coherent and consistent standards of assistance.

During the previous decade, however, the focus of refugee problems around the world had shifted dramatically, and many of the mechanisms established to handle the problem were now notoriously inadequate. Refugee programs of the U.S. government were firmly established within the State Department. Although this arrangement insured that the refugee problem would have the "firm support of the Secretary of State," in the words of Carter's first secretary, Cyrus Vance, it also meant that refugee programs would continue to be tied to diplomatic and military priorities of U.S. foreign policy.[32] Thus, while refugee programs in Eastern Europe and Southeast Asia were relatively well funded, programs in Africa (for whose refugee problems political concern in Congress and elsewhere was low) and Latin America (where refugee problems before 1980 generally amounted to neighboring nations offering temporary shelter to political elites ousted in military coups) held limited interest for the U.S. authorities.

The influx of Southeast Asians that began in 1975 reinforced public perceptions in the United States of refugees as people who fled their homes in a mass exodus and required resettlement, preferably in the United States. The large movements, begun during the Gerald Ford administration and continued under Carter and Reagan, were not in fact carried out in strict accord with the UN 1951 Refugee Convention and 1967 Protocol on Refugees. Many of the Vietnamese leaving their homes faced economic hardship, but arguably were not facing political persecution. (Haitians, on the other hand, were examined individually by the INS and required to offer proof that they had spoken out in direct political confrontation with their government.) There were other, domestic political considerations at work in the United States on behalf of the Vietnamese; Americans wanted to show that they still had sympathy for the people of the region. Therefore U.S. officials were willing to go beyond the requirements of the law.

Church and State on the Thai-Cambodian Border

The 1970s was a decade of horrors for Cambodia. After the U.S. bombing of the country during the Vietnam War, Prince Sihanouk's hapless monarchy had given way to General Lon Nol, who from 1970 to 1975 ran a U.S.-supported government; Lon Nol was overthrown by the nationalist Khmer Rouge led by Pol Pot, whose genocidal communism was hostile to the Soviets, the Chinese, and the Vietnamese; finally came the Vietnamese-backed regime of Heng Samrin. The events of the 1970s were a chain of suffering that touched the continuing American guilt over Vietnam. Members of Congress pleaded for assistance to the refugees, held hearings, and prodded the State Department. Protestant and Catholic religious leaders, led by Fr. Theodore Hesbergh of the University of Notre Dame, presented a letter to President Carter in October 1979 asking for increased private giving to address the crisis, as well as intensive U.S. involvement, both at the political level and in humanitarian assistance to the innocent sufferers. "What has taken place in Cambodia is a mass assault on the basic human right to life," said Hesburgh. "We cannot say that we do not know this, and we cannot permit political, financial or technical difficulties to bring about another holocaust."[33]

Shortly after receiving the religious leaders, President Carter ushered them into the White House press room and announced an increase in appropriations to Cambodia from $7 million to $70 million. Like the Christian leaders who stood with him on the platform, the president evoked the murder of 6 million Jews during Hitler's reign. He did so in part because no event in modern consciousness so proclaimed the humanitarian imperative of response to human suffering. For the sake of human decency such wounds as Auschwitz and Cambodia must be healed. This logic, with humanitarian action viewed as the efforts at healing society's man-made wounds, is so universal as to approach the status of natural law. President Carter was on safe ground, and Americans around the nation responded generously.

Shawcross argues that the use of the Holocaust image, along with many journalistic efforts to identify Pol Pot with Hitler, produced an emotional response but very little solid understanding of the political cauldron that dozens of religious and secular agencies were about to enter. Both Pol Pot and Heng Samrin were after all Marxists, alternatively supported by the Chinese eager to punish the Vietnamese and the Soviets eager to contain Chinese influence in Southeast Asia. Comparisons with European fascism of the 1940s touched emotional chords but did little to explain the United States' political interests in this intra-Marxist dispute, which would inevitably come into play in the government's involvements with U.S. religious groups arriving to help the refugees.

A better parallel would have been the early days of the U.S. Escapee Program mounted in Eastern Europe by the Eisenhower administration in the 1950s, which assumed the existence of significant shared political objectives between agencies of church and state. In both instances, powerful factions within the government were interested in marshaling domestic and international public opinion against a Soviet effort to install a surrogate government in a small country. Eisenhower and Carter both relied strongly on the Voice of America, which had broadcast into Hungary and later into Cambodia that people seeking food and safe haven could find them just across the border. And in both cases, representatives of American religious groups provided the bulk of voluntary agency support in the actual border camps.

Within days after the White House gathering Carter announced that his wife would visit the Cambodian-Thai border area, and the national Cambodia Crisis Committee was formed to coordinate private contributions for relief of the refugees arriving in Thailand, with Rosalyn Carter as honorary national chairwoman. This national spotlight helped the committee raise over $60 million from private and corporate sources for relief along the border. In late November agencies working in Thailand were informed that as a result of Mrs. Carter's visit, "a fund may be made available from [the office of] religious affairs in the White House for projects proposed by Christian agencies."[34] In making her visit, the First Lady stood in the tradition of Eleanor Roosevelt, using her office to personify the humanitarian values inseparable from the democratic ideal in the minds of many Americans.

Handling the political situation on the ground in Thailand was more complex. U.S. and Chinese officials shared a common interest in limiting Soviet/Vietnamese interest in the region. China shouldered primary responsibility for the military activity in the Khmer camps while the U.S. offered humanitarian aid and expressed hopes for a neutral government in Phnom Penh that, in the interest of regional stability, would not be hostile to Vietnam. The Thai military tolerated these operations within their territory, but their general hostility kept relief agency workers in close touch with friendly officials active in the operation.

Thailand had little interest in including Christian and other voluntary agencies in the planning of relief operations. American agencies were in frequent touch with the Kampuchean Emergency Group, the extension of the U.S. embassy based in the border town of Aranyaprathet, but they had few other levers in the planning of field operations, and were often the last to hear of tactical decisions on moving refugees, levels of assistance, and other plans that eventually were put into operation. Some agencies made efforts to establish high-level contacts with the Thais—CRS, for instance, encouraged the queen in her efforts to organize the wives of high-ranking Thais in American-style voluntary service to the refugees. But most agencies were dependent upon good relations with the U.S. embassy staff or individual leaders with whom they maintained contact. They were there not only as representatives of churches, but also as employees of the UN or the U.S. government. If the UN could not protect its own humanitarian goals from the political pressures of the border, the voluntary agencies were in an even weaker position.

Agencies seeking to help Cambodians essentially had two options: to work out of Phnom Penh and aid Cambodians living under Heng Samrin, or to work on the border and aid Samrin's opponents. The UNHCR would eventually open repatriation negotiations with Phnom Penh, but no voluntary agency could work on the border and still find an open door in Phnom Penh. Restrictions on aiding enemy countries were relaxed for the few who sought to work inside Cambodia. Church World Service chose to work in Phnom Penh, and in a masterpiece of post-Vietnam strategy, mostly used Cuban Protestants in its offices there to allay Vietnamese suspicions about U.S. objectives. CWS was joined in Phnom Penh by the Mennonite Central Committee. World Vision eventually chose to there instead of the border region when a former employee from its pre-1975 stint in Phnom Penh emerged as an official of the Heng Samrin regime. He invited World Vision to return and to rehabilitate its Phnom Penh children's hospital, which had been ransacked by the Khmer Rouge.

This left the border operations to Catholic Relief Services and a variety of conservative, largely evangelical Protestant agencies. Many were recruited by present and former U.S. government officials eager to insure a warm welcome to all who sought to avoid entanglement with the Vietnamese. First on the border was CRS, which arrived in June 1979 (months before the international outcry later in the fall) bringing food supplied by the U.S. government. Government officials realized that they would need an agency the size and expertise of CRS to move food to the border and to establish a variety of support programs.

Into the Reagan Era

Once the refugees had been resettled in the United States, the roughly one dozen resettlement agencies and their local affiliates handled most of the work. Among the agencies with World War II roots were the Migration and Refugee Services of the U.S. Catholic Conference, Lutheran Immigration and Refugee Service, Church World Service, and the YMCA. World Relief, though active overseas since the 1940s, only began resettlement services in the United States in 1979. The ability of the resettlement agencies to handle the flood of refugees was remarkable, but in many localities the volume of the casework overwhelmed the capacities of congregations, agencies, and support groups. Many of the refugees came from such remote cultures—the Hmong of Laos are perhaps the best example—that extensive efforts were required to assimilate them into American life. Frustration and administrative tangles became standard elements of an otherwise successful operation.[35]

The 1970s also saw a new expansion of international evangelical relief and development efforts. A 1974 gathering of several thousand evangelical leaders from around the world in Lausanne, Switzerland brought a new emphasis to social ministries in Protestant circles that had previously focused international efforts on the evangelistic spread of Christian faith. World Vision and World Relief, both evangelical agencies, were joined by new relief agencies (such as World Concern of Seattle; Food for the Hungry of Scottsdale, Arizona; the Christian Reformed World Relief Commission of Grand Rapids; and Compassion of Denver), each of which began refugee care overseas. Missionary bodies like the Wycliffe Bible Translators, Sudan Interior Mission, and the Christian and Missionary Alliance organized separately incorporated secular arms, hoping to utilize government assistance or expand their definitions of mission beyond traditional evangelical concepts (or both). Some eventually found their way into refugee activity abroad; numerous other agencies eventually joined them in government-assisted activities without taking the traditional step of forming a "nonreligious" secular affiliate designed to address church/state questions.

The 1980s began with passage of the Refugee Act of 1980, legislation that many refugee advocates had sought for years in efforts to regularize U.S. refugee policy. The new law established a permanent refugee coordinator with access to the White House, virtually eliminated the unpredictable parole power of the attorney general, and established annual consultations to set reasonable approximations of refugee admissions for the coming year. No sooner had the president signed the bill into law than the voluntary agencies and the government became embroiled in open conflict over how to respond to the waves of Haitians and Cubans arriving in Florida. These early developments underlined what had repeatedly been demonstrated during the previous thirty-five years: it was unrealistic to expect refugee politics to conform to any preexisting law, no matter how sensitively devised to protect the interests of all parties involved.

Across the board, the stage was set for the development of new church/state tensions in refugee work abroad in the 1980s. Protestant, Catholic, and Jewish communities brought new twists into their relations with the government. If traditional procedures no longer covered the variety of religiously based agencies seeking involvement with the government's refugee programs, several of the traditional agencies themselves devised more independence from governmental priorities. Church World Service and the American Friends Service Committee, both awakened to new perspectives by their Vietnam experiences, reduced their levels of cooperative activity with government-sponsored projects overseas. Catholic Relief Services, the largest relief agency in the world, faced mounting pressures from within to examine its extensive ties with Washington. Jewish communities, often split over the best response to Israel's growing difficulties, faced new questions over movements designed to aid Jewish refugees and immigrants. With political polarization commonplace in most of the religious communities serving refugees abroad, the "three faiths" coalition of the postwar years seemed a distant memory by 1980.

It was true that many agencies retained the ability to form functioning coalitions to meet refugee needs abroad. This was true during the Nigerian-Biafran conflict in the late 1960s; it was true in assistance chaneled to Afghan refugees in Pakistan, and in relief efforts in Somalia and Ethiopia in the early 1980s. In many of these instances, agencies that questioned government priorities in other fields were willing to participate in government-supported refugee programs for the sake of aiding people in need. But many senior agency officials whose careers had begun in the 1940s acknowledged that the situation had changed substantially. The work of Christian and Jewish agencies overlapped with less frequency; differing views over the proper disposition of the Palestinian refugees created underlying tensions. Mainline Protestant and Catholic efforts were styled differently from the often brash efforts of evangelical Protestants. And the expanding work of secular agencies such as Save the Children, the International Rescue Committee, Oxfam, and others diminished the pride of place religious agencies had long held in the field.

The continuing expansion of the world's refugee population offered the grim assurance that there was more than enough work to go around. When Jimmy Carter left office in 1981, Ronald Reagan inherited a refugee program that retained much of its anticommunist leanings. It had, however, necessarily outgrown its European base and expanded to follow the appearance of new refugee populations. In 1980 these populations were largely in Southeast Asia, Latin America, and Africa. To bring our overview up to date, then, we now turn to three countries in those regions—Thailand, Honduras, and Sudan—to examine some specifics of church/ state relations abroad today.

8

Honduras: Trouble on the Border

Central America has come to epitomize the foreign policy traumas of the 1980s for the United States; the same is true for U.S. refugee policy. Whether we look at the arming of refugee camps, the U.S. government's politically grounded lack of interest in particular refugee populations, or the domestic sanctuary movement, all of the inequities of official policy may be seen in this one region. Not surprisingly, much of the conflict has been between religious agencies and the government, and more often than not the conflict has been explicitly cast in church/state terms.

This chapter focuses on the rift that developed between U.S. officials and voluntary agency personnel working with Salvadorans who fled the civil war at home and were interned in camps run by the UN High Commissioner for Refugees in Honduras. Church agencies and others working in western Honduras sought, much as they had in Vietnam, to function as advocates of the refugees in the face of U.S. policy that insisted that they did not qualify as bona fide refugees. Agencies responded to the Honduran refugee crisis with assertions of parallels between the errors of Vietnam and the errors being made in Central America. In the process the limitations that private agencies faced in attempting to create genuinely independent alternatives to governmentally determined refugee policies were brought into focus. Those limitations applied to the work of the UNHCR as well as to the private voluntary agencies. Disagreement over the proper handling of Salvadorans spilled over to the conduct of UN refugee programs, which were frequently responsive to U.S. financial and political pressure. A total breakdown of cooperation between UN, U.S., Honduran, and private agencies seemed just around the corner, and when tensions were at their highest, religiously grounded resistance on the part of the voluntary agencies and the refugees played a central role.

Honduras became the strategic center for U.S. political and military engagement of the entire Central American region. However the wider strategic issues developed, there was no avoiding the refugees, and they came to Honduras from all the surrounding countries. The Nicaraguan Miskito Indian refugees were allowed to roam freely from their camps in the broad savannahs and marshlands of the east, but Salvadoran and Guatemalan refugees in the west were fenced in camps tightly controlled by Honduran military and secret police. The different styles of administration mirrored the attitudes of the U.S. government to the populations in question. The flight of the Miskito Indians confirmed U.S. claims that the Sandinistas were persecuting Nicaraguans. The Salvadorans, however, came largely from guerilla-held regions of El Salvador; Guatemalans fled military repression and forced resettlement. To aid the Salvadorans was to aid the guerilla cause rather than the U.S.-supported government of El Salvador.

It was this Salvadoran refugee flow that engaged most of the U.S. Catholic and Protestant relief agencies in Honduras. While the treatment of the Miskito Indian refugees merits its own story, the struggles that arose in the Salvadoran camps amply illustrate the variety of political and military factors that today must be taken into account in analyzing church/state issues abroad. The U.S. ambassador to Honduras in this period characterized the refugee situation on the Honduran-Salvadoran border as "a rugby match, everybody with their arms around each other and kicking each other in the groin. . . . [It is almost] impossible to see what's happening from outside the scrimmage."[1] It was not, as most participants would agree, a setting designed to strengthen cooperative understandings between U.S. church groups and government officials.

El Salvador is the most densely populated country in Central America. Its major source of employment is agriculture, but the vast majority of agricultural land has been, and continues to be, in the control of a wealthy minority. Salvadorans have long migrated to sparsely populated Honduras in search of land on which to subsist. The socioeconomic tensions in El Salvador increased during the 1960s as wealthy landowners expanded their control of the nation's wealth, devoting the majority of the arable land to export crops such as coffee and controlling the fledgling industrial base, initiated in large part with aid from the U.S. government under President Kennedy's Alliance for Progress.

According to a UN study, the percentage of landless peasants in El Salvador rose from 12 percent in 1960 to 40 percent in 1975.[2] During this period, the economic migration of Salvadorans to Honduras continued to increase due to ever-worsening conditions for the Salvadoran peasantry. By the mid-1960s, over 300,000 Salvadorans had unofficially migrated to Honduras.[3] The social tensions caused by such a large population of Salvadorans led the Honduran government to expel most Salvadorans in 1969. The result was a border conflict known (because it erupted in the course of a soccer match between the two countries) as the "Soccer War." Though the war itself lasted less than a week, it left emotional and political strains between the two countries. With Salvadoran troops poised to move into the Honduran capital of Tegucigalpa, only a truce hastily arranged by the Organization of American States prevented an expanded conflict.

The civil war in El Salvador began in earnest after the coup of October 15, 1979. A group of young, reform-minded military officers gained power and sought to implement land reform, hold elections, and control military violence. These officers soon lost power to more conservative senior officers, who wanted to guarantee that the power of the military would not be threatened. As the military and the various factions of the national police stepped up attempts to suppress guerilla activities in the countryside by targeting known or suspected guerillas and their sympathizers, civilians began to flee. Often moving in groups of several hundred, entire villages picked up their few precious belongings and left their homes, hoping that safety lay on the other side of the Lempa River in Honduras.

Like the rest of Central America, Honduras had little experience with international methods of addressing refugee problems. Even as late as 1979, the term "refugee" had a restricted meaning in Latin America. It meant either a European who had fled social collapse during and after World War II, or "asylees," usually ousted juntas or elites from other Latin countries. Their treatment was regulated under regional conventions. Organized response to large numbers of semipermanent international refugees was still largely unknown in Central America in 1979. Honduras was not a party to the drafting of the UN's 1951 Refugee Convention or 1967 Protocol on Refugees, and only acknowledged more limited hemispheric agreements. It therefore stood outside the European-centered procedures that had evolved for providing assistance, protection, and durable solutions in refugee crises. With the arrival of thousands of Salvadorans in 1980, Honduras was faced with an emergency. At that point it simply ignored the fact that it was not party to international refugee agreements and invited the UNHCR to begin a program of international assistance.

There was in Honduras an additional factor in the refugee crisis. The U.S. embassy in Tegucigalpa was, in the privately held view of nearly all participants, the chief mover of refugee policies in Honduras in the early 1980s. Both the ambassador and the deputy chief of mission of the embassy in 1982 had previously faced special responsibilities for refugees in Cambodia and other parts of Southeast Asia during the Vietnam War. In Southeast Asia, "aiding refugees" generally meant helping the victims of communist aggression in the region. This viewpoint motivated the aid given to the Miskito Indians in the east, but was not applicable in the Salvadoran camps.

There, most of the refugees were from guerilla-held regions of El Salvador adjacent to the Honduran border. The U.S. embassy was not willing to admit that the Salvadoran refugees were refugees under the terms of the UNHCR convention. Since the State Department was at the time certifying that human rights conditions were improving in El Salvador in order to fulfill a congressional condition for the continuation of military aid, the U.S. embassy in Tegucigalpa classified the Salvadorans in Honduras as "economic migrants." This drastically limited their status under U.S. immigration law and refugee policy; they were not under this definition eligible to enter the United States as refugees.

Though the struggle over the fate of Salvadoran refugees in Honduras received considerable coverage in the press, the underlying church/state conflicts between the U.S. refugee agencies and the Reagan administration were barely mentioned. This is understandable; few of the participants were willing to highlight the difficulties that would detract from the central question of the fate of the refugees. Yet when religious and governmental agencies began to pursue widely differing goals in dealing with the refugees, the church/state dimensions of the rift came to the fore. In the words of a staff member of the Foreign Affairs Committee of the House of Representatives, by the early 1980s the fate of refugees in western Honduras had become "the most politicized refugee situation in the world."[4]

Within the first four years after the crisis began in 1979 the church/state conflict had emerged at every point. Church workers and refugees were murdered, religious agencies receiving U.S. assistance had repudiated administration policies, and church factions were bitterly divided between supporters and opponents of U.S. policy. The UNHCR (its work in Honduras largely funded by the United States) was suspected by the voluntary agencies of being too closely linked to the U.S. embassy. Virtually the entire community of voluntary agencies—for the most part representing U.S. and Honduran religious bodies—experienced some paranoia about the presence of the Central Intelligence Agency. Such varied issues as the selection of an agency to coordinate a refugee camp, the protection of refugees from military attack, and the freedom of refugees to move from place to place brought the weight of religious conscience and religiously grounded action against U.S. foreign policy in Honduras, El Salvador, Nicaragua, and Guatemala.

Conflict Breaks Out on the Border

Of the many such issues, the dispute over whether the refugees from El Salvador should be moved farther into Honduras away from El Salvador was the most rancorous. What looked like a bureaucratic disagreement among relief workers and governments was in fact a profound conflict between church agencies and U.S. foreign policy in the region. By 1985, lessons that had already emerged in the late 1940s were brought home anew to church workers of the post-Vietnam generation. Although private agencies could challenge the legitimacy of specific government decisions on refugee policy, escalation of those challenges into open political confrontation raised broader issues that threatened to submerge humanitarian consensus under long-standing animosities between U.S. political and religious leaders.

The UNHCR, noting that the refugee camps were generally within 10 kilometers of the Salvadoran-Honduran border, began pressing at the end of 1981 for the camps to be moved further inland. In this, the UN agency was simply playing by its own rules and by regional agreements of the Organization for American Unity. The UNHCR policy governing the establishment of refugee camps advises that they be located at least 50 kilometers inland in the country of asylum. The Salvadoran border region was full of Honduran paramilitary bands, Honduran Army soldiers, and supporters of various factions in the Salvadoran civil war; protection of the refugees, a primary function of the UNHCR, proved difficult. Furthermore, the UNHCR held out the hope that once the refugees moved further inland, the Honduran government might provide the refugees with land that they could farm temporarily to achieve a measure of self-sufficiency. To UNHCR officials, such a plan was preferable to the difficult logistics and expense involved in moving large quantities of food along the poor Honduran roads to the border region. This plan also appealed to U.S. embassy officials, for quite a different set of reasons: moving the Salvadorans would remove an easily accessible center for feeding and housing guerilla sympathizers.

Catholic Relief Services had been among the first agencies to bring assistance to the refugees in western Honduras beginning in May 1980. When CRS realized that the few hundred they were aiding were just the beginning of the coming refugee influx, they requested authorization from the AID office in Tegucigalpa to divert 35,000 pounds of U.S. government food to the refugees (CRS was under contract with the U.S. government to distribute the food to Hondurans). The AID office granted the request. When a subsequent request arrived from CRS to divert additional AID food to the Salvadoran refugees, the AID officials responded with an offer: in exchange for the additional food, they wanted CRS to compile a list of the refugees by age, sex, and home inside El Salvador. The UNHCR routinely collects such information, but officials of the Catholic agency felt that to do so for a particular government with political interests in the situation violated their role as a neutral humanitarian agency. It appeared to them that they were being asked to collect political demographics with no guarantees of how the embassy might eventually use the information; they decided to decline the offer. "AID projects tend to collect a lot of political information on the side," said one CRS worker.[5] The information requested seemed extraneous to the task of meeting the growing needs of the refugees.

The church agencies reasoned that as new arrivals crossed the border, their safety would be best insured by the readily accessible camps and their requisite crews of intergovernmental and voluntary personnel. Though each of the agencies working in the area had stated policies of neutrality and disinterested humanitarianism, the majority of their regional staffs were hostile to official U.S. policy in Central America. To them, even though a move inland had technical justification in UNHCR policy, a true reading of the best interests of the refugees would keep them near the border. There, the UNHCR itself could exercise more fully its "protection mandate," assisting refugees such as the relatives of those who had already been massacred along the border. What benefit, asked agency workers, would the refugees gain from the move? Inland, they would only encounter hostile Honduran peasants, with ramifications understood by many agency personnel familiar with the history of the Soccer War and the persistent economic migrations from El Salvador.

The problem lay in what can best be described as the political character of the refugee population. The Honduran province of Santa Rosa bordered the Salvadoran province of Morazan, the chief stronghold of the leftist guerillas fighting the various governments in San Salvador and hence the origin of most refugees. Aiding the refugees, therefore, was interpreted by some—including U.S. embassy officials—as providing assistance to the guerilla movement. Church workers often professed lack of interest in whether persons who reached the camps were actually supporters of the guerillas, but the circumstantial evidence, if measured by the hostility of military forces on both sides of the border, was strong.

For example, on March 18, 1981, some 5,000 refugees succeeded in their fourth attempt to cross the Lempa River to safety. Some had been on the road as long as six months. Their previous efforts to cross the river had been halted by the Honduran Army, which had fired from positions on the Honduran side. While still in El Salvador, many had been pursued from their homes by the Salvadoran Army and paramilitary death squads. The Salvadoran Army was still tracking them as they reached the border itself, firing from mortars and from helicopters that strafed the hills and forests below. In the course of their attempts to cross the river, more than 50 died before they outwitted the Honduran military on the other side on their fourth attempt. This particular group came largely from the Cabanas province, another guerilla stronghold.[6] Such movements of refugees alarmed both Honduran and U.S. officials in Tegucigalpa.

The religious motivations of the refugees and the relief workers of various agencies was quite obvious. Common in many refugee homes was a picture of the murdered Salvadoran Archbishop Oscar Romero, patron of and martyr to the struggle they all now sought to survive. Agencies and churches frequently conducted open-air masses and prayer meetings. One observer wrote of his experience attending a mass at which thousands of refugees celebrated the first anniversary of their crossing of the Lempa River: "The Biblical event that most spoke to their experience was that of Moses leading his people out of Egypt with the Red Sea parted to let them cross. . . . At the Mass the names of the fifty killed in those three days were called out by families, amid sobs, the only open expressions of grief that I heard in my time with them."[7] The biblical Exodus is central to the writings of many Latin American liberation theologians, and the theme of casting off oppression resounded in the religious life of the camps. Countless refugees and Honduran Catholics gathered as "Delegates of the Word," base communities committed to common life and prayer focused on the Bible. This *praxis,* or theology in action, was the new form of Christian engagement with the world called for by the liberation theologians. CRS and CARITAS (CRS's international Catholic affiliate) frequently worked with the local movement of Christian base communities, popular Catholic fellowships based upon Bible study, informal worship, and commitment to group solidarity. The military regarded such developments with suspicion; when one such base community of sixteen Salvadoran "Delegates of the Word" was arrested in Tegucigalpa in April 1981, they were quickly deported to El Salvador. Agency officials understandably shared the concerns of the refugees for secure asylum. In the early 1980s several relief workers were killed while aiding refugees along the border, along with a number of refugees.[8] The political implications of the theological commitments of the refugees and the agencies did not go unnoticed by governmental authorities charged with responsibility for the refugees.

Even a matter as straightforward as coordinating relief efforts carried overt political overtones. In 1980 all the agencies serving the refugees in Honduras (including Catholic, Baptist, and Mennonite groups) met to work out coordination with the governmental authorities. One agency, CEDEN, was an indigenous Honduran relief agency supported by some thirty mostly evangelical Protestant denominations and missions active in Honduras. The coordinating role would have to be assumed by a single agency or committee of agencies that together had enough experience through their own prior involvement with the refugees. The choice of the UNHCR in Honduras was the team of CRS and CARITAS. Both agencies had ties to the national church hierarchy as well as grass-roots contacts with the *campesinos* of western Honduras; they understood the tensions that existed between Honduran peasants and Salvadoran migrants within the country.

The choice of CRS/CARITAS was vetoed in Geneva through pressure on the UNHCR from the U.S. mission, which took its cue from Washington and the embassy in Tegucigalpa. CEDEN was given the coordinating role. While there were independent reasons for the selection of CEDEN—it had established a strong record of relief in times of national disaster—there was open speculation on the "real" basis for the decision. Many believed that it was the result of U.S. pressure to name an agency less likely to ally itself with the guerilla sympathies of the refugees. The CEDEN members included the indigenous or affiliated churches of many of the U.S. fundamentalist and evangelical missions active in Honduras.[9] Such groups were newly in favor with various officials within the Reagan administration; surely the U.S. government was taking such considerations into account in pressing its choice.[10]

At the time CEDEN did not openly espouse liberationist interpretations of the situation. The perspective of liberation theology—grounded in resistance to civil authority and a preferential option for choices supporting the poor, in this case the Salvadoran refugees—was implacably opposed to the refugee policies of the U.S. or Honduran governments. Liberation meant freedom for self-determination and participation in the political process on the part of the refugees. Acceptance of this liberation analysis of the refugee problem placed staff members of such agencies as the American Friends Service Committee, the Mennonite Central Committee, Church World Service, CARITAS, and CRS in conflict with virtually any government policy which did not in their view have the best interests of the refugees at heart. Government officials hoped that CEDEN's ties to conservative evangelicals might offer a more congenial, complementary perspective to government decisions.

Whatever their theological roots led agency workers to believe was the correct interpretation, they all faced the same complex reality on the border. Published reports stated that hundreds of Salvadoran refugees had disappeared in the first six months of 1981, most killed by military and paramilitary forces from both Honduras and El Salvador. There were as yet no UNHCR protection officers; any protection functions were unofficially carried out by the agencies working in the border camps at La Virtud, Guarita, and Colomoncagua, which housed the majority of Salvadoran refugees.[11]

Forced Relocation

In November 1981, the UNHCR reached a decision, made in conjunction with the Honduran government and the U.S. embassy: some of the refugees, those living in La Virtud, would begin moving to an inland site, Mesa Grande. Representatives of UNHCR and the Honduran National Refugee Commission announced that decision to the refugees at La Virtud, telling them that they would either participate in the move, beginning on November 15, or return to El Salvador. The transfer was begun on schedule, over the protests of the refugees and many of the church agencies, but it took months as the refugees, frightened about the loss of their homes and of moving farther from El Salvador, moved as slowly as possible. In the eyes of most agency workers, the UNHCR was abandoning the central humanitarian focus on the needs of the refugees and siding with the interests of the United States and Honduras.

In one of the most sustained private advocacy efforts in modern international refugee work, voluntary agencies began an effort to keep the rest of the refugees from being moved farther inland. From their perspective, a move inland would only expose refugees to further harassment from hostile Hondurans. The Honduran government itself had waited until January 1981 to recognize Salvadoran refugees formally, and even then the civilian and the military wings of the government worked from different perspectives. The civilian government had never promised permanent resettlement inside Honduras; in mid-1982 Minister of Foreign Affairs Edgardo Paz Barnica stated flatly that relocation of the refugees in third countries was the ultimate goal for Honduras. What, then, asked agency officials, was the value of engineering another admittedly temporary move for the refugee population?

One goal of the voluntary agency effort in fighting the transfer was to support a stronger protection role for the UNHCR in Honduras. In the beginning the UNHCR supported the idea of camps located close to the border, a position that it maintained as late as March 1981.[12] The refugees' need for protection was evident, and the UNHCR initially reasoned that keeping international workers close to the border would provide the best methods of protecting the Salvadorans. However, the Honduran military remained a serious obstacle. Its position was stated clearly in 1982: "For the past two years, Salvadoran guerillas intervened in our country, flagrantly violating the laws and freedoms of Honduras. . . . That is why the armed forces have undertaken not to tolerate the presence of these unscrupulous assassins in our country."[13] This was diametrically opposite to the diplomatic "economic migrant" position of the U.S. embassy, but the effect was similar. Life was not going to be easy for Salvadorans who fled to Honduras; once there, they found not a safe haven, but rather a new set of antagonists, chiefly the Honduran military and the U.S. embassy.

By this time the Democratic opposition in the U.S. Congress had begun to notice the difficulties along the Salvadoran border in Honduras, and seized them as ammunition in their opposition to the regional policies of the Reagan administration. Twice in the second half of 1981, a Democratic staffer from the House of Representatives visited La Virtud, arriving for his second visit in November. As he understood it, the rationale for placement of camps along the border was to make "future [refugee] crossings safer and easier and . . . deter indiscriminate abuses by local military."[14] After discussion with private agency personnel, he came to the view that the U.S. government was eager to deny the use of Honduran soil to Salvadoran guerilla sympathizers, not to insure Honduran neutrality toward the civil war in El Salvador, but in order to pave the way for Honduran involvement in a regional effort to defeat the Salvadoran guerillas. A U.S. Army captain who had visited the camps during the same period seemed to buttress this theory when he told several observers that the refugees "are the guerillas," and that therefore "they have no human rights."[15]

The U.S. embassy strongly disputed that such statements represented U.S. policy. There was little doubt, however, that both the Honduran and Salvadoran military were exceedingly hostile to the refugees. From the report of the congressional staffer's visit:

> Entering La Virtud, we saw refugees in a line with guns pointed at them by Honduran military. The refugees were signing a census for food distribution.
> . . . At 11:52 a.m. two files of military personnel passed the open door of the building we occupied. These approximately 20–25 soldiers went directly to the Honduran barracks. . . . The Hondurans we were interviewing said they were "Salvadoran," adding that the Salvadoran military had come into town on previous occasions. Just after this incident I left for lunch with the French doctors. At approximately 12:30 p.m., we were interrupted by a volunteer who ran into the doctors' residence shouting "Come quick. ORDEN [the Salvadoran military police] is in the camp and taking people away." We immediately jumped into a jeep and drove down the winding dirt road that runs from La Virtud to the camp. At the point where the road from La Virtud meets the road out of the camp we

encountered approximately 12 men armed with standard Salvadoran issue M-16s. They were escorting approximately 20 refugees. Fifteen refugees, males ranging from 15 to 45 years of age and an eight-month pregnant woman had their hands behind their backs and their thumbs tied together. . . .

On encountering the persons coming from the camp, our group began to shout that the refugees had to be released, that we knew where they were taking them, that we were the international press and representatives of the United States, and that they were not going to get away with this. . . . Most of our group got out of the jeep, moved toward the men, began to shout again to release the refugees and began to obviously take pictures. At this point another person and I got back in the jeep and drove through the armed group back up the road to the Honduran army barracks. . . . I pleaded, demanded, and argued for assistance which was refused. I was even refused an observer. We raced back to the camp.

The armed group, with the captured refugees, had started up the riverbed which leads some four and one half kilometers to El Salvador. Our group of visitors and relief officials, with some refugees, began to follow shouting the whole world will know. Finally, at about 2 and ½ kilometers, one refugee worked his thumbs loose and turned toward us. The others began to resist and finally they too turned and made for us. The armed men hesitated and then continued toward El Salvador. We escorted the freed hostages back to the camp. . . . There was great joy among the refugees and many dropped to their knees to pray.[16]

This observer was convinced that such an incident could not have taken place without a climate of consent from U.S. embassy officials, who had variously stated that the border with El Salvador needed to be "cleared, sanitized and/or closed."[17] By early 1982, the church relief societies had become strongly polarized along lines determined by support or rejection of U.S. and Honduran refugee policies. Supporters of the government's refugee policies—evangelical agencies such as the California-based World Vision or conservative churches represented within CEDEN— were judged by Catholic and mainline Protestant groups to be naive accomplices in governmental plans, trading their compliance with military authorities for governmental approbation.

It was clear that the U.S. government officials monitoring the refugee situation in western Honduras believed that political and humanitarian concerns were to be sharply distinguished. This position accorded with traditional humanitarian standards that held that relief should be nonpolitical and nondiscriminatory. But this view could only be justified if one ignored the governmentally sanctioned distinctions between the incarcerated Salvadoran "economic migrants" and the relatively free Nicaraguan Miskito refugees in eastern Honduras. The church/state conflict arose from the perceptions of church officials that the political climate demonstrated by these distinctions was obscuring the needs of the victims, which should have been at the heart of the humanitarian ethic. It was a church/state matter only because it was church groups who confronted the government on behalf of the refugees, and because religious commitments lay behind the confrontation. Nothing like it had occurred overseas since the refugee struggles of Vietnam.

Those opposed to the government's plans to move the refugees faced further upheaval. In a complex series of political maneuvers, the increasingly liberal director of CEDEN was removed in January 1982, and the agency was stripped of its coordinating role. Many attributed this series of events to covert political intervention on the part of the U.S. and Honduran governments, and to the fact that

CEDEN's director had now emerged as an advocate of the Salvadoran refugees and was therefore unwilling to accept guidance from the UNHCR or the U.S. embassy. After six weeks of futile efforts to name a new coordinating agency, the UNHCR took the unusual step in mid-March of itself becoming the coordinating agency for the Salvadoran refugee operation. In thus becoming "operational," the UNHCR went beyond its routine supervisory functions established in other refugee settings around the world. Yet here there was no choice; the parties involved in the relief operation—notably the church agencies and the governments—were increasingly unable to talk with each other.[18]

The appointment of UNHCR as the coordinating agency was announced shortly before a senior delegation of State Department refugee officials arrived in Honduras to monitor refugee operations among both the Salvadorans and the Nicaraguans in Honduras. In conversation with UNHCR officials during the visit, the senior State Department delegate expressed satisfaction with UNHCR's new coordinating role.[19] However, Washington analysts also sensed that the UN was quietly sympathetic to the Salvadorans, and officials in the office of the U.S. Coordinator for Refugees—a post created by the Refugee Act of 1980—decided that it was time to "kick the ass of the UNHCR" for the slow movement of refugees from La Virtud and Guarita to Mesa Grande, which the U.S. government had supported from the beginning. When the State Department team flew into La Virtud for an inspection, observers from the American Friends Service Committee and other voluntary agencies ("a dirty band of hippies," sniffed one of the State Department officials) discussed the situation with them. "The U.S. gives millions of dollars in military aid to Honduras . . . why can't you ask them to secure the safety of these refugees?" asked an AFSC worker. The senior U.S. official responded, "We have no say over that." As an afterthought, he turned to another worker in the camp and said, "If you would stick to the Lord's work instead. . . ."[20] For such refugee officials, there was to be no mixing of religious and political concerns; one simply drew the line.

The UNHCR Struggles for Neutrality

In the relocation effort two border camps were retained, but only on a temporary basis; the new camp of Mesa Grande further inland continued to fill with unhappily relocated refugees. The same day in March 1982 that the U.S. government officials visited the soon-to-be-closed La Virtud, the refugees stated their position on the move in a letter to the UNHCR:

> Since the month of November we have endured every kind of attack against our dignity by the Salvadoran and Honduran armies. . . . Since then we have experienced every kind of repression to the point where we cannot even go two blocks from this place because the refugees are being captured, disappeared and assassinated.
>
> This is another indication that there is no neutrality in Honduran territory, but rather a direct collaboration on the part of the Honduran and Salvadoran armies. For this reason our safety is not assured either here or in Mesa Grande where they would like us to be relocated. For all these reasons we ask you to help us seek a refuge in a different, neutral country.[21]

In deciding whether to move the refugees, the UNHCR was caught between the refugees and the voluntary agencies on one side, and a donor government and the national authorities on the other. As the situation developed in the early months of 1982, the UNHCR publicly expressed its displeasure with several church groups for sending outside observers to the region.

Such observers routinely pointed out the insufficiency of the UNHCR's limited protection efforts along the border. Observers associated with the National Council of Churches, the National Council of Churches of Canada, the American Friends Service Committee, and the World Council of Churches all visited the camps, some staying two weeks or less. When the observers returned home, their often aggressive attacks on U.S. policy in the region inevitably meant more headaches for the UNHCR staff trying to mediate between hostile camps in both the governmental and the voluntary sectors. Although many UNHCR officials privately supported the advocacy efforts of the church agencies and others, most felt there was nothing to be gained by a direct attack against U.S. government policies or against its Honduran embassy, with which the UNHCR had to deal on a daily basis. While the UNHCR publicly repudiated observers from religious agencies (who were essentially free agents beyond its control), it also sought alliance with the voluntary world against the governmental pressures on its work.

The agencies, however, grew increasingly restless about what in their view was the UNHCR's inability to offer protection or otherwise work in the best interests of the refugees. The Honduran National Refugee Commission, the Honduran government's official body, had signed a document stating that they were eager to deal with the refugees within the spirit of the 1951 UN Refugee Convention, but since the military dominated the commission, there was little debate about the commission's interpretations of the "spirit of the Convention."[22] The Hondurans would conduct their affairs as agents of a sovereign nation, and the UNHCR and others could only accept and adapt.

For the Honduran military international law was applicable only as a tool for advancing its pragmatic goals, which rarely centered on the welfare of the Salvadoran and Guatemalan refugees.[23] Honduran officials eventually told U.S. congressional investigators that the government would agree "conditionally" to sign the UN accords dealing with refugees. Their conditions meant that refugees in Honduras would have no freedom of movement and no right to seek employment or naturalization. Such limitations, given the UNHCR's willingness to agree with U.S. and Honduran approaches to the Salvadoran refugees, struck many voluntary agencies as part of a larger picture of governmental willingness to sacrifice the interests of the refugees for broader military and political objectives. Most of the agencies believed they had no alternative other than an advocacy approach that pitted moral and religious commitment against political expediency.

While the variety of participants makes it difficult to describe the Salvadoran refugee problem strictly as a church/state dispute, church agencies that felt particularly responsible for the refugees spoke out against governmental policies. A group of Canadian church leaders, the Inter-Church Committee for Refugees, issued a blistering attack in September 1982 on the UNHCR's work with the Salvadorans in Honduras.[24] Like the UNHCR itself on many occasions, the Canadian church leaders were prudent enough not to mention one powerful player, the U.S. government and its local representatives. Instead they focused on the danger posed to refugees by Honduran military garrisons stationed near the border camp of Colo-moncagua and the lack of protection at a small camp for some 500 Guatemalans, El Tesoro. They also demanded a minimum of twelve full-time protection officers in the border regions. The Inter-Church Committee and others believed that interna-tional attention, combined with support from friends in the U.S. Congress, would create enough of an outcry that pressure could be brought to bear on those responsi-ble for the deplorable conditions. Many church agencies helped mobilize public opinion against official policies by presenting their own reports of events, reports that often ran counter to official governmental versions.

Despite the efforts of the church agencies, the situation only continued to deteriorate. The UNHCR sent a delegation headed by the deputy high commis-sioner to Honduras to evaluate the charges of the Inter-Church Committee in late 1982. The delegation soon learned of the reality in Honduras: the UNHCR was precariously balancing its commitment to oversee refugee relief and protection efforts against its need to respect, if not advance, the political and security objec-tives of its major donor government. The UNHCR, if it sided with the agencies and the refugees against the U.S. embassy and the Honduran military, would more than likely be sent packing in the midst of an unpleasant crackdown. Alternatively, it had an obligation to remain and see it through, to preserve a semblance of objectiv-ity in a situation in which every possible solution was deemed evil by some party. In addition to the future of the refugees, the future reputation of the UNHCR was on the line. It would have to stay and find a delicate balance. That balance would not be calculated to please the religious agencies or the refugees themselves.

Following this high-level UNHCR visit, one problem that had irritated the UNHCR for months was summarily eliminated. The church agencies were told by the UNHCR that no new "international observers" would be allowed to visit the western camps, and that protection issues were to be the sole responsibility of the UNHCR, not the private agencies. These were direct blows to mainline Protestant involvement in the situation, which had spearheaded much of the advocacy on protection issues but, by early 1983, had been forced to limit most of its involve-ment to such "observer" status. The UNHCR wanted to avoid any further criticism. By early 1983, the Mennonite Central Committee and the CARITAS/Catholic Relief Services team were the only two religious agencies remaining in western Honduras with broad full-time responsibilities.

Observers noted that early 1983 was marked by UNHCR pressure on "certain agencies" to dismiss members of their staffs and to hire certain others. Claims were made that the UNHCR had cooperated with the Honduran military in the investiga-tion of an agency worker at Mesa Grande. And still, the UNHCR continued to insist that on the basis of its own regulations, there was a clear humanitarian mandate for moving the refugees farther inland.[25]

Church Agencies Fight Relocation

By April, the UNHCR had advanced new, more specific proposals for the relocation of the refugees. One such suggestion, that CARITAS purchase land for this purpose in the Honduran province of Olancho, reached the ears of the Archbishop of San Salvador, Arturo Rivera y Damas. During a visit to the refugee camp of

Colomoncagua, the archbishop denounced the plan, noting that Olancho was a center of hostility toward Salvadorans, and an area in which Honduran landlords had waged terrible vigilante warfare against both Salvadoran and Honduran *campesinos* for nearly a decade.

The prelate announced that CARITAS would never place itself in the role of landlord in that setting. Joining with the local Honduran bishops, Rivera y Damas told the refugees that the church leaders wanted "to be the echo of your voices." Aside from the voluntary agencies, few others seemed interested in the archbishop's warning about the Olancho relocation plan. Only in June did the UNHCR acknowledge that the Olancho sites had been a poor choice, citing the fact that during the 1969 Soccer War, 200,000 to 300,000 Salvadorans who had migrated to Olancho and neighboring Yoro province were forcibly expelled back to Salvador. "Resentments toward Salvadoran refugees might still be strong," said a rather understated internal memorandum.[26]

In September 1983, a year after the report of the Inter-Church Committee for Refugees appeared, a second report on the same set of issues was released after an independent visit to the camps by the directors of the British Refugee Council (BRC) and Oxfam (Canada).[27] Like the earlier Canadian church report, this one was timed to coincide with the annual October meeting of the UNHCR's executive committee in Geneva, where donor governments would review the agency's accomplishments and goals. This report concisely set forth the positions of the Honduran government, the UNHCR, the refugees, and the voluntary agencies.[28]

In preparing their report, the two agency directors took the time to speak directly with refugees representing different groups in different camps. Concerning the proposed relocations, they noted that the Honduran government had already labeled the refugees as "subversives," and questioned how this would sit with the Honduran peasants in the areas to which they were to be moved. The refugees had invested time and effort in making their lives bearable at their current locations. They refused a UNHCR offer to send representatives to visit the new proposed sites, and later signed a petition stating that "for these reasons we say once and for all 'No!' to relocation, and if they want to relocate us by force, it would be better to let us return to die in our places of origin in El Salvador."[29]

The refugees continued to be backed in their efforts to resist relocation by many of the church personnel in the camps. The agencies, the report notes, were responsible for functional tasks such as health, housing, and food distribution. Equally important were the roles they played in less defined areas such as "communications" and "personal counselling and support." Because the agency personnel lived in the same environment and faced similar problems, "the agency workers see themselves as basically 'with the people,' supporting them, listening to them and responding to them. This is, in their view, the relationship they want and must have as supportive individuals. That is, they must respect the refugees' decisions, they must voice the desires of the refugees, and they must be channels of communication to the UNHCR and to their own agencies on behalf of the refugees." The agency staff stressed to BRC observers that the refugees were being relocated for local and regional military reasons, and criticized the methods the UNHCR had used to present its position to the refugees. The agency staff also defended the lives that the refugees had built in their present locations. Many claimed that they would "stand with the refugees in opposition to relocation and would not abandon them."[30]

Shortly after this report was debated in Geneva the UNHCR abruptly dropped its humanitarian justifications for the proposed move inland. During a meeting with agency leaders on October 31 in Colomoncagua, the UNHCR officials for the first time stated that the relocation "was being pushed by outside influences and being promoted for military reasons." An observer summarized the state of affairs as follows:

> Until October 31, the UNHCR only hinted that the underlying motive for relocation is military. Their public admissal of that pressure by outside force allows for a legitimate examination of a series of events and positions taken by various parties, in view of the relocation for military reasons.
>
> For several months, there have been rumours of a US-engineered invasion into El Salvador from Honduran territory to attack the guerillas in a pincer movement. The troops would enter from over the Honduran border into the northern guerilla-led provinces of El Salvador while the El Salvadoran Government troops would move up from the capital and the south.
>
> The . . . treaty signed at the end of 1983 by the Governments of Honduras, Guatemala and El Salvador, allows each of those countries to call on one or more of the others for military support in case of an internal problem.
>
> Troops from those countries are presently training at Puerto Castillo and Trujillo, two American-administered training camps in the Atlantic coast of Honduras. The training of the present group should be over by the end of February or the beginning of March [1984].

Discussion of the situation in the field turned, as it often had in the past, to the role of the American embassy in Tegucigalpa:

> Colomoncagua borders on the guerilla held province of Morazon. It is often hinted at as a possible invasion site [because of] the already constructed infrastructure of dwellings, storehouses, latrines, roads and a new water system. . . .
>
> The staff at the American Embassy has been quite open about their interest and influence in the relocation. [The relevant staff members], who have a refreshing frankness about the subject, are very clear in announcing that the border zone must be cleared quickly and efficiently and that that is the reason for the relocation. They do not spend any time dressing it up in humanitarian reasons. They want the refugees out as fast as possible. . . . [An official] indicates that the U.S. Embassy is involved in planning the logistics.[31]

Church workers had been pointing to the possibility of increased military activity in and around the camps for nearly two years. Now their suspicions were confirmed by the UNHCR. The invasion did not materialize, but the suggestion that it could have been launched from vacated facilities for several thousand refugees was not implausible.

On New Year's Day, 1984, a representative of the UNHCR met with the refugees in Colomoncagua to inform them that plans had been made for relocation on land that would be temporarily loaned by the Honduran government in Yoro province. A representative for the refugees informed the UNHCR that it would have to take responsibility for anything that might happen during the relocation. At that point, all the refugee leaders silently rose and left the room. Four days later, the Mennonite Central Committee sent a letter to the U.S. embassy, restating the opposition of the refugees to the move. At the very least, the Mennonites asked that the embassy allow the relocation to "move at as slow a pace as necessary to ensure refugee cooperation." "We stand on the side of suffering people," said the Mennonites. "We ask that you use the influence of the U.S. Government to prevent rather than instigate additional violence towards people who have already suffered so much."[32]

Somehow the advocacy role of the church groups had crossed a line, appearing to some to challenge the foreign policy prerogatives of the federal government. The Reagan administration officials were irate. The normally temperate Secretary of State George Shultz publicly denounced the activities of U.S. church groups in Central America before Congress in the spring of 1983; the U.S. ambassador in Tegucigalpa had some months earlier similarly claimed that one of the senior church officials working with the refugees was "not a relief worker, but a political activist." Ambassador to the United Nations Jeane Kirkpatrick had similar unsympathetic views on the four U.S. Catholic women who had been killed in El Salvador at the end of 1981, claiming that their political ends had overshadowed their religious work.[33] Religious workers were, in the eyes of U.S. officials, having a hard time distinguishing "the Lord's work" from illegitimate political involvement. As a result, U.S. church/state cooperation abroad had reached a new low in the Central American refugee crises by the early 1980s. To those who pondered the matter, the dream of cooperation on a global scale between the great moral and religious authorities of the republic was fading.

At home in the United States the Central American refugee crisis was igniting new tensions. For every one Salvadoran held in Honduran camps, ten or twenty simply headed north to the United States. If they entered the country illegally they were subject to deportation by the Immigration and Naturalization Service. Church workers in the Southwest helping refugees sought to stand between the Salvadorans and the INS. In 1982 the sanctuary movement began publicly confronting U.S. officials with a strategy designed to incorporate public advocacy for Central Americans with direct efforts to challenge U.S. foreign policy in the region. As never before, refugee issues were demonstrating their ability to cross international boundaries; domestic political disputes followed Americans abroad and followed them back home again, much as refugees themselves crisscrossed national boundaries.

The sanctuary movement added a new twist. Though U.S. church/state tensions were real on the Salvadoran/Honduran border, so far no one was proposing that they should be addressed in U.S. courts under the religious freedom protections of the First Amendment. Yet the sanctuary movement, as we will see, attempted to do just that. In response to the prosecution of movement leaders by the INS, sanctuary workers sought to bring the role of the churches in the moral and political clashes of Central America under the protection of the First Amendment. The movement itself was rooted in the adversarial traditions of private voluntarism that had evolved since the Vietnam War, but it made a fatal error in believing that religious visions of international justice would carry the day in an American courtroom. In the eyes of the Reagan administration in Washington and the U.S. embassy in Tegucigalpa, the outright abandonment of complementarity to U.S. Central American policy in the voluntary sector was going too far.

9

Thailand: Coping with Yellow Rain

Anticommunism has for better or worse formed the backdrop of U.S. foreign policy in the postwar period. Though interrupted somewhat by the détente of the early 1970s, strong anticommunism underwent a revival in the early Reagan years, which had a direct bearing on American refugee policies. Even though the Refugee Act of 1980 eliminated many statutory features of institutionalized anticommunism, officials again faced new pressures to favor refugees from communist-dominated areas.

Though most church agencies had vigorously supported this emphasis in the late 1940s and for much of the 1950s, anticommunism began to lose favor as a foundation for humanitarian cooperation between church and state abroad. After the Vietnam War, many of the agencies sought either to provide direct assistance to Vietnam (the most famous effort being a shipload of wheat donated by Church World Service in 1977–78) or to aid both sides in the ongoing conflicts in the region, mainly in Cambodia and Laos. Many felt that some restitution should be made for U.S. intervention in the region, and that humanitarian assistance to refugees and others displaced or disrupted by the war was only one small way of accomplishing this.

Though refugee camps in Thailand were administered by UN organizations, it was clear that the emphasis placed on Southeast Asian refugees could not have occurred without the direct interest and involvement of the United States. Per capita expenditures on Southeast Asian refugees vastly exceeded those for Africans in similar straits. Morton Abramowitz, the U.S. ambassador to Thailand under President Carter, was widely known for the direct interest he and his staff took in Thai refugee matters. Thailand offered asylum on the condition that the Western nations—again, primarily the United States—establish generous resettlement policies. The Thais did not want a single alien permanently resettled in their territory, yet by the early 1980s several hundred thousand remained in more than two dozen camps that stretched from the northern hill country to the tip of the southern peninsula bordering Malaysia.

Of course, some voluntary agencies were either unaffected by collective guilt from the war, or unabashedly willing to continue an identification with the programs and policies of the United States in the region. Catholic Relief Sevices, for instance, followed the same policy in Southeast Asia as it did elsewhere, assiduously seeking out areas of overlapping concern between the U.S. government and the Catholic church. The effort to care for Cambodian, Laotian, and Vietnamese refugees in Thailand was heavily dependent on CRS and on evangelical Protestant agencies, several of which were just beginning to become involved in refugee assistance. As was true in Central America, the evangelical agencies that came into their own in the 1970s and early 1980s were among the most reliable allies U.S. officials had in conducting international refugee assistance. Many did not have the qualms that other agencies did in associating themselves with programs openly identified as anticommunist. Among long-standing agencies this willingness to work with the U.S. government was frequently perceived as a naiveté on the part of newcomers eager to make a place for themselves in the international relief establishment. This chapter looks at the way one such agency, World Vision of Monrovia, California, became increasingly sophisticated in its response to political components of U.S. refugee policy in Thailand.

In the early 1980s, members of the Hmong tribe of Laos continued to flee the Vietnamese communist regime that had taken over the country in 1975. Thousands found themselves in a camp in northern Thailand where medical services were run by World Vision and its Thai affiliate, the World Vision Foundation. More and more Hmong refugees were claiming that they had been the victims of poison gas attacks on their villages, conducted for unknown reasons by unidentified perpetrators. These claims, which soon engaged the attention of government officials of all ideological stripes, drew World Vision into a political dispute that would have tried any agency, religious or secular, whose primary interests were humanitarian rather than political. Caught between conflicting U.S. approaches to the cold war of the 1980s, World Vision had to forge its own version of the proper response to U.S. actions that further politicized the plight of refugees.

World Vision's capacities had grown rapidly worldwide after the war. Its enormous success in raising funds privately made World Vision virtually independent of the pressures that came with the need for government assistance, and yet it retained its ability to work alongside continuing U.S. government relief efforts in Southeast Asia. "Government is not the enemy," a World Vision executive emphasized in 1983.[1] That year, some ten years after the withdrawal of U.S. troops from the region, refugees were still fleeing the war zones. Some 200,000 rebellious Cambodians and former members of the South Vietnamese government and armed forces were massed in a no-man's-land of camps on the Thai-Cambodian border. World Vision chose to reopen a hospital it had established in Phnom Penh. In the Gulf of Siam, and in the waters off the coasts of Hong Kong, Singapore, Malaysia, and the Philippines, ships continued to encounter the Vietnamese "boat people," many of whom were ethnic Chinese, the shopkeepers and small businesspeople of South Vietnam. By 1983 the exodus by sea had been under way for more than four years. Those who escaped had had enough gold to illegally book passage and enough terror to prefer life on an overcrowded, vulnerable boat than in their own homes. World Vision had been among the private agencies to call attention to the suffering of the boat people, and had outfitted a vessel designed specifically to intercept and rescue them at sea.

In March 1982 there appeared in the *Bangkok Post* an article by a journalist who had visited Ban Vinai, a camp for some 35,000 Hmong refugees just south of the Mekong River in northeast Thailand.[2] She had gone to Ban Vinai specifically to study the allegations that Hmong refugees had been chemically attacked in Laos with "yellow rain," a deadly mycotoxin that caused vomiting and bleeding on contact, and frequently resulted in death. The camp was at that time administered by World Vision and CAMA Services, Inc., an affiliate of the Nyack, New York-based Christian and Missionary Alliance which handled general administration. Both had come to provide humanitarian assistance.

The article minced no words; it alleged that World Vision medical workers intentionally held back information about the nature and extent of yellow rain use against the Hmong, and did so for political reasons. From her article would flare an international controversy over chemical warfare in Southeast Asia, one that typified the new generation of political pressures faced by U.S. religious groups working abroad. Surrounded by intelligence gathering, endless battles in the press, and ambivalence in the American embassy in Bangkok, World Vision had to find a way to respond to the yellow rain controversy. The religious agency was caught in political currents beyond its control, while the Reagan administration's attention was on the strategic aspects of the yellow rain issue.

The Hmong

In northern Thailand, the border with Laos is formed by the Mekong River. Cutting through and along the hills of Thailand, the Mekong seems made for an idyllic evening enjoyed from the wooden balconies of houses lining its steep banks. On the river below, fishermen, silhouetted against the sunset reflected in the water, haul in their nets from longboats and children laugh in the gathering darkness along the water's edge. What electric light there is is soft, warming the wood of the balconies but overwhelmed by the flaming reds and purples of the sunsets. As it flows past quiet Thai towns, the river here is peaceful, yet the ghosts of war still linger on its shores.

The reverberations of the war were still affecting the Lao hill tribes living across the Mekong from the northeast Thai province of Nong Khai. After the Thai fishermen and the children had retired for the evening, Hmong tribesmen and their families quietly stole across the river to asylum in Thailand. The numbers of Hmong refugees were less than those in the late 1970s, and by 1982 some Hmong refugees were even returning to Laos, after a joint project by UNHCR, the American Friends Service Committee, and the Mennonite Central Committee had worked out a moderately successful repatriation program. The UNHCR could not guarantee their safety once back in Laos, however; the Lao government imposed limits on outside monitoring. And more Hmong refugees arrived in Thailand every day.

The only thing that the Hmong felt could guarantee their safety in Laos was weaponry, a resource none of the humanitarian or religious agencies could offer. The Hmong had always been known as fierce fighters. In the West, colorful geometric quilts made by Hmong women were sold in upscale department stores and marketed through self-help programs sponsored by World Vision and CAMA Services. The women also made more gruesome quilts, showing battlefields full of heavily armed men in combat, the surrounding hills littered with corpses and grieving families. This was the world the Hmong had fled; many feared it was what awaited them if they returned to their homes in Laos.

There were special reasons for the flight of the Hmong to Thailand. The tribe had served as CIA operatives and mercenaries in the region at least since the early 1960s. During the height of the war in 1971, a report from the congressional General Accounting Office charged that assistance slated to go to war refugees in Laos had been diverted to covert military operations run by the CIA among the Hmong. In Congress, Senator Edward Kennedy charged that "until recent times, the U.S. AID refugee program was simply a euphemism to cover American assistance to persons who agreed to take up arms against the [communist] Pathet Lao." Those people were the Hmong, and they were not likely to be popular under the Vietnamese government installed in Laos in 1978.

This was the historical context when World Vision became the chief medical supervisor at the Hmong refugee camp at Ban Vinai, a few miles south of the Mekong in Nong Khai province. About 100,000 Hmong still remained in the camps of northeast Thailand in late 1981. While the Hmong detested camp life, it was also clear that those resettled in the United States were having difficulties adjusting. Some succumbed to a "sudden death syndrome" for which investigators could find no cause. Abandoned lots in some U.S. cities began sprouting rice and other crops as the Hmong refugees strove to create some semblance of their old lives in Laos.

Although numerous relief agencies were involved in resettling the Hmong, World Vision assisted the movement of most of the Hmong who eventually reached the United States. Among those selected for resettlement was General Vang Pao, the military commander of the Hmong during their alliance with the Americans. In March 1981 Vang Pao wrote a letter to Vice President George Bush. For six years the Vietnamese and the Russians had overrun his country, and it was his own people who were suffering most. How could the United States neglect its staunchest allies in the region? Vang Pao believed that the Vietnamese would not only expand their ideology, they would fulfill their notion of regional manifest destiny by Vietnamizing Laos, filling the land with ethnic Vietnamese. Vang Pao got right to the point with Bush:

> Due to the question of the [American soldiers still missing in action] they [the U.S. government] make certain not to acknowledge and publicize the mass genocide of tens of thousands of Hmong . . . the refugees are virtually imprisoned, [victims of] circumstance, pawns of the United States-Vietnamese War. While the Administration speaks about human rights, men, women and children die from chemical agents in Laos. . . . Also, many hope that modifications in foreign policy of the new Administration will eventually permit the Laotian people to return to Southeast Asia and particularly to Laos after the Vietnamese Communists have been driven out.[4]

Ten days after writing the vice-president, Vang Pao issued a public statement that reiterated his charges that the United States was purposely ignoring the chemical warfare against the Hmong and called for a congressional investigation into the Hmong allegations about yellow rain. Vang Pao believed there was a studied effort to obscure the contributions of the Hmong during the Vietnam War:

> We Hmong were the United States' surrogate and secret army in Laos for 15 years . . . [we] gathered critical intelligence on troop supply and tank move-

ments . . . fought the Communist Lao and North Vietnamese . . . sabotaged
North Vietnamese-Soviet tanks . . . helped rescue American pilots . . . and suffered over 30,000 dead men, almost 10% of our Hmong population.[5]

Why, he asked, was not greater attention paid to the question of yellow rain,
directed as it was against American allies?

The U.S. government was itself undecided over the best approach to the
yellow rain question. Hmong tribes began reporting the use of chemical agents
against them in 1977; reports were also filtering in to government sources that
Cambodian refugees were being similarly attacked inside Cambodia. Yet there was
a serious problem with verification. No Western representative had been an eyewit-
ness to an attack of chemical warfare inside Laos or Cambodia; the medical symptoms of affected refugees could also be attributed to bronchial infections and other
causes. Furthermore, there was always the question of the best strategic response,
which hinged on one's view of the best approach to Vietnam's colonial aspirations
in the region. If an ongoing struggle with Vietnam lay ahead for the United States
and its regional allies, pressing the yellow rain question could serve as powerful
anti-Soviet, anti-Hanoi testimony. On the other hand, if one thought that some
reduction of the Soviet presence was possible, or even that Hanoi might be weaned
away from the Soviet Union, it was in the best U.S. interests to let the issue of
yellow rain slide. Officials in Washington and at the embassy in Bangkok were of
two minds on this question.

The Yellow Rain Controversy Deepens

In early 1982, shortly after the first article appeared in the *Bankok Post,* the World
Vision staff in Thailand were in close contact with the U.S. embassy in Bangkok on
the "gassing issue"; because of growing inquiries from the press and others, it
seemed best to cooperate with the U.S. officials. World Vision made their medical
files on Hmong victims available to officials of the embassy, semiofficial government representatives, and the press. On the political question, they were passive.
"We are obliged to leave the political implications to other agencies or people who
have the expertise to investigate these matters and the potential power to do
something about the problem," wrote a World Vision official in Bangkok. But even
as World Vision was cooperating with the embassy's investigation of yellow rain, it
was encountering difficulties. Samples of contaminated tissues or scrapings of dust
purported to be yellow rain had been sent to the embassy, but the embassy did not
(as promised) report back on its findings. World Vision asked for an evaluation of
the evidence to aid them in answering reporters' questions, but the embassy did not
respond.[6]

The headline of the *Bangkok Post*'s March article on the use of yellow rain
among the Hmong read "The Poisoning of the Hmong," accompanied by a gruesome picture of a deformed baby. The photo was over five years old, and not at all
representative of the children at Ban Vinai. The journalist, who believed that the
Soviets were using chemical warfare, saw World Vision's policy of avoiding the
political issues in favor of the medical ones as inhumane. To her, it was simply an
attempt to avoid facing or confirming the claims about yellow rain, and to do so was

to stand on the side of the oppressors, the Vietnamese and the Soviets. World Vision officials saw this as playing fast and loose with the facts. World Vision records consisted largely of descriptive reports of events in Laos, which could not be confirmed or denied. If, as she claimed, adequate evidence had existed since 1980 about yellow rain, it would have been published in medical journals by then. In a letter of response to the *Post,* World Vision noted that her claims that "accurate" evidence existed on the use of poison gas in Laos were false. According to their letter, "No set of signs and symptoms of 'survivors' are *exclusively* suggestive of abnormalities associated with exposure to poison chemicals."[7] After receiving mixed signals from the U.S. embassy, World Vision sought a middle course that would protect its medical mission in Ban Vinai.

By the end of March, the controversy had reached the House of Representatives. Even though World Vision could get no adequate update of the evidence from the U.S. embassy in Bangkok, subcommittees of the House Foreign Affairs Committtee called in witnesses in March 1982 to give testimony based on independent investigations conducted among the Hmong and Khmer refugees. Chemical analyses had shown that substances found on leaves and in water "were not of natural origin, but were placed there by the intervention of man."[8] Since 1977 refugees had been reporting a variety of gassing or chemical incidents, involving "red gas," "yellow drizzle," "white smoke," "white liquid," and "a very pungent blue-green mist." It was speculated that a variety of chemical agents had been used experimentally.

One witness representing Freedom House, a human rights organization in New York, backed up General Vang Pao's arguments by citing his own conversations with the Hmong: "I frequently asked them what they thought were the motives for the use of chemical weapons. The most common reason was that the Vietnamese were seeking revenge for the Hmong's cooperation with the United States during the Vietnam war."[9] He called for a diagnostic medical team in Ban Vinai to study the evidence more effectively. Since a key chemical element for identifying yellow rain is metabolized within four hours after it enters the body, there was still no specimen confirming that any individual had been gassed. There were only external samples and unverifiable reports of gassing attacks in Laos, many of which were contradictory and subject to change over time.

The congressional hearing was on March 30; on April 4, 213 Hmong suddenly surged across the Mekong in search of asylum in Thailand. Of these, 38 claimed to have been victims of yellow rain. In a separate incident the previous day, 5 witnesses who also crossed the Mekong claimed their village had been gassed, killing 16 people within twenty minutes. World Vision doctors forwarded the information to the U.S. embassy. In their view, by such action they were maintaining their medical objectivity and participating in the search for reliable information about the problem. On April 24, there was another hearing in the House Foreign Affairs Subcommittee on Pacific and Asian Affairs. This time, a former World Vision employee testified. He had been a medical officer at Ban Vinai since 1979 and medical director of the camp from February 1980 to April 1981. He presented himself as a field expert on the yellow rain issue.

He noted that it was only since April 1980 that evidence existed in sufficient quantity; refugees were then talking about "colored dust from the skies that kill[s]."[10] During his stay at Ban Vinai the doctor had met the journalist responsible for the *Bangkok Post* article, who was making her first visit to the camp. Together in late June, they visited the U.S. embassy to ask for further investigation of the gassing claims. A representative from the Centers for Disease Control of Atlanta was brought in for an opinion; he told the embassy that although there did seem to be an uncommonly high number of complaints about gas poisoning, he would not personally be competent to carry out an investigation. The World Vision doctor told Congress that he had become convinced of the use of yellow rain in February 1980. In December he had started a file on suspected cases of gassing, and for the next three months sent three suspected victims from the refugee camp to two U.S. government officials, a political officer and a military attaché from the U.S. embassy. Working from a hospital in nearby Udorn, they were to supervise a detailed analysis of the cases.

Cooperation with the embassy was a political decision, but the only one the doctor felt he could make. He had not been contacted by the International Committee of the Red Cross, the venerable Swiss agency that is often among the first agencies to investigate humanitarian concerns amid political tangles. And his contact with the UNHCR field officer stationed in the camp was limited. Technically the UN officer was his supervisor, but on the question of yellow rain the UN officer "was openly skeptical. On this issue we strongly disagreed." The only other authorities who seemed likely to take an interest were in the U.S. embassy. Yet despite apparent embassy interest in the issue, and despite World Vision's own interest in clarifying just what was happening to the Hmong, the embassy officials in Udorn were not releasing any reports on the cases they had studied. Reporting to the Congress on the whole series of events, the doctor alluded to "evidence" still in place when he left Ban Vinai, consisting of "a significant number of people (several hundred) who had survived what they claimed to be poison gas exposure."[11] World Vision officials later noted that the personal file on gassing the doctor had kept during his stay at Ban Vinai consisted of the record of exactly one patient.[12]

By May of 1982 public interest in the yellow rain issue necessitated a clarification of World Vision's nonpolitical goals of Christian service. The process of sending yellow rain reports to the embassy was altered. First, the embassy was politely asked to cease the almost daily telephone calls to Ban Vinai to ask for the latest totals of yellow rain victims. World Vision announced that henceforth the British, Australian, New Zealand, and Canadian embassies would also receive information on yellow rain. Furthermore, instead of telephoning the camp staff, the American embassy would be informed of new yellow rain materials by World Vision's Bangkok staff, "at the same time the UNHCR Representative is informed." The United States and the United Nations had almost come to represent opposing political perspectives, and the World Vision opted for a studied neutrality which involved providing the same information to all interested parties.[13]

Before the month was out, World Vision executives in California took things a step further. They advised their field staff in Thailand to stop giving reports on yellow rain to the American embassy. Instead, they were to channel reports, particularly tissue and blood samples, through the UNHCR for testing. A letter was drafted to the U.S. embassy by World Vision's Bangkok staff, stating that "to maintain our credibility as a non-political agency . . . World Vision will cease to send blood samples or other material to your office for clinical analysis."[14] World

Vision planned to inform the U.S. government that neutrality in humanitarian assistance required that it discontinue its reporting to the embassy.

The letter was never sent. World Vision decided that ending reporting to the U.S. government would not solve their difficulties in Thailand. If the U.S. officials would not act on the samples it had forwarded, World Vision also believed that the UNHCR did not take reports on the gassing seriously; a complaint was forwarded to the Geneva headquarters of the UN agency. It seemed as though no one would spend enough time on the samples to report back on their analysis. Either that, or the officials involved had other reasons for slowing the availability of reliable information on yellow rain. In any case, World Vision field staff began a more formal process of sending their reports to several agencies and embassies, including the United States. Despite such private efforts to keep some order and objectivity in approaching the yellow rain issue, there was no agreed-upon conclusion on how toxicologic analysis should proceed. World Vision was attempting to cover all possible bases in the hope that some acceptable procedure for dealing with the evidence would emerge. Its officials felt that the attitude of the UNHCR personnel who refused to take the question seriously was the most dangerous stance—they reminded UNHCR officials that the issue, how to "assess the claims by refugees of serious contraventions of the Declaration of Human Rights," was well within their legal mandate.[15]

In early June, the U.S. Coordinator for Refugee Affairs Eugene Douglas paid a visit to Ban Vinai, where he spent most of his time discussing yellow rain. World Vision's camp director explained to his visitor from Washington that his agency espoused no political position in the dispute. Their interest, as medical directors of the camp, was in medical issues. They sought to bring the yellow rain controversy to a wider audience only in the interest of better medical treatment. "While we are interested of course in human rights, we are not in Ban Vinai to address that question, nor are we equipped to solve it," he told the U.S. official, who responded that he understood and supported that position.[16]

This was not enough. World Vision needed to state its own position in a way that demonstrated its political independence from the U.S. government. There were by then as many people affirming to Congress the existence of chemical warfare against the Hmong as there were denying it. World Vision's close ties to the embassy in Bangkok were well known, making it appear that the agency was the surrogate of U.S. interests. Yet the embassy was unable to generate objective, scientifically acceptable studies of the evidence it had received. Such contradictions were not readily visible to those outside the dispute, who frequently equated World Vision's work with U.S. government interests. This charge, which could be heard in press and voluntary agency circles, began to affect World Vision's ability to carry out its responsibilities at Ban Vinai.

By late June 1982 a memorandum on an "issues management approach" to the yellow rain question was circulating in World Vision offices. "Issues management" was a bureaucratic way of suggesting that public relations on this issue would be disastrous if the situation got out of hand. World Vision officials believed that if they increased their pursuit of the truth about yellow rain, challenges would emerge in at least four areas. First, who would believe World Vision's statements about the evidence for yellow rain? This reflected their frustration in dealing with the U.S.

embassy in Bangkok. Believers and doubters would no doubt be polarized according to preexisting political attitudes to the Vietnamese and Soviet presence in the
region. Second, it was plausible that the whole thing was Hmong propaganda. If
this was true, World Vision would have spent time and money pursuing a political
phantom, which is difficult to justify to donors. Third, and perhaps most dangerous,
was the charge that World Vision was in "complicity with American foreign policy
in Southeast Asia." If it was true that the agency was being used by the U.S.
government in the yellow rain dispute, they would appear at best naive and at worst
disingenuous. Finally, the effects on World Vision's local affiliate, the World Vision
Foundation of Thailand, needed to be considered. Religious relief agencies from
outside the country had a hard enough time without public scandals tying them to
superpower intrigues.

Was World Vision's position on the issues believable to journalists and to the
public? "It would be very easy to make us look like a bunch of bleeding hearts
reacting emotionally to a people with whom we had developed close links . . . it is a
view certain to emerge as some journalist's story if we make strong statements
supporting the Hmong side of the issue," the memo stated.[17] Partisanship—whether
right or wrong—was not to be displayed to the public. These were not matters that
relief agencies normally explained to their donors; the issue merely confused people
whose primary interest was in helping others in need. Concern over the "bleeding
heart" image suggests that World Vision perferred to be portrayed as independent
agents of mercy who stood above partisan politics.

Was the yellow rain issue a Hmong propaganda exercise? Certainly anyone in
the United States familiar with Hmong actions under General Vang Pao knew that
the Hmong could be using the yellow rain issue for overtly partisan ends. The
memo suggests a careful path through conflicting political claims:

> The Hmong are not so foolish that they fail to see this issue as an opportunity to
> bring international pressure on the Laotian government. . . . It was said more
> than once to me that the Hmong see themselves as "the new Israel," chosen by the
> US to inherit the promised land of Laos, then deserted by their source of power
> and hope, disinherited, and now being spread abroad. They are one of the most
> active refugee groups in Thailand in agitating for their interests. Additionally they
> are a close-knit tribal society with well-developed intrasociety communications
> and authority patterns. They are able to pass intelligence across the Mekong and
> across the Pacific. . . . Hill-tribe people they may be: stupid they are not.
>
> The problem for World Vision is that the credibility of any statement on
> yellow rain is undermined by the knowledge that to some extent such statements
> are orchestrated and encouraged by a group involved in a political struggle. Of
> course, in isolation, this fact alone has not stopped us from standing up on human
> rights issues in other places, notably El Salvador. The difference in Ban Vinai is
> that we are not able to show reporters the bodies of innocent people murdered in
> their beds at night, but only the symptoms and statements of sick people. Death is
> easy for a journalist to interpret; disease is much more difficult.[18]

Thus World Vision was well aware that the refugees they served were often far from
the images of innocent suffering so useful to agencies in raising funds at home. The
Hmong were certainly capable of spinning webs of self-interest that might entail
dangerous political consequences for others, including World Vision.

The charge of direct complicity between World Vision and U.S. government policies was inevitable. After all, in past experiences in Vietnam "conservative" agencies had aligned with the United States and "liberal" agencies had sought greater independence. Journalists interested in "proving complicity" between a conservative Christian agency and the government in the yellow rain issue needed only to point to World Vision's initial steps of sending medical samples to the Bangkok embassy, and to the agency's frequent and open contact with embassy's political and intelligence officers. This was a no-win situation for World Vision. A presentation of the true state of confusion over the issue was liable to make their management efforts look incompetent; to let the situation smoulder meant coping with continual accusations from the press that they were being used by the U.S. government. Neither characterization was strictly true, but it was unlikely that this would be acknowledged by the press.

Journalists might also search for "complicity" between the local World Vision office—run by a Thai national—and the Thai government. Thailand after all wanted the refugees out, either repatriated or resettled in a third country. Attention to the refugees' political activities would only complicate this process. Yet complicity inevitably had the negative implications of clandestine, underhanded agency contact with self-interested governments toward evil ends. These were journalistic stereotypes that World Vision wanted to avoid. For the World Vision Foundation of Thailand as well as for World Vision headquarters in the United States, the question of self-interest was closely tied to the organization's freedom to stay in Thailand.

A closer look at World Vision's Thai-based staff revealed a young organization often unsure of its standing, a Christian institution in a largely Buddhist society. An "issues management" perspective in this setting meant acceptance of the fact that the Thai government had ordered the yellow rain issue played down. World Vision's Thai director interpreted this to mean that the agency should not treat yellow rain in Ban Vinai as a "human rights" (that is, "controversial") issue. To go beyond the medical facts of the cases in public discussion "will result in a lack of future cooperation from the [Thai] government. Such uncooperativeness will make our ministry much more difficult, although it may not close us down." Complicity was not so much at issue for World Vision as was its continued freedom to work in Thailand. Such freedom for private agencies always depended on favorable relationships with local authorities. In the best interests of all concerned, and taking the long view, World Vision felt no one ought to criticize the statement that "our primary interest in the issue is medical." Thus the memo suggested a simple policy statement that distilled the political and humanitarian demands of the situation in a form that might also assure a long-term future for World Vision in Thailand. In talking with the media, some issues ought to be avoided while some would benefit from further discussion. The yellow rain debate was a case for "containment," but all such decisions would profit from international agency control in the early stages of a given crisis.[19]

A new effort was made to upgrade the medical analysis of patients and samples within the U.S. government. In September, the State Department's Bureau for Refugee Programs offered partial funding for an "information project" on chemical warfare; the project director telephoned World Vision headquarters in California and asked if World Vision might supplement the State Department's grant with a modest contribution of $10,000 or more. World Vision officials noted that the director of the project was himself a former foreign service officer. Although they agreed to cooperate with the State Department, World Vision officials decided not to provide any funding. In view of some of the personnel who would be involved, there was little doubt in their minds as to the direction of the research.

Though it was fair to say that the UNHCR could do nothing about the use of yellow rain inside Laos, various agencies on the scene hoped that the UN body would play the role of objective mediator, sponsoring appropriate medical and chemical tests. After all, one of the chief functions of the UNHCR was legal and physical protection of refugees; surely this fell within their mandate. Responding to a World Vision request, the UNHCR chief in Bangkok spoke of "humanitarian" concerns over the use of "chemical toxins," but never once mentioned the word "protection." He virtually dismissed the entire dispute: "none of the symptoms among those allegedly exposed could be directly related to any chemical toxin. . . . Consequently, it is my conclusion that the refugees claiming exposure to chemical toxins in Laos have been and are receiving the best possible treatment from the World Vision doctors in Ban Vinai." He further suggested that World Vision forward its requests to the special Experts Group the UN had mandated under the General Assembly to investigate yellow rain.[20]

The UNHCR had several reasons to avoid fanning the flames of the yellow rain dispute. First, it had a strong desire not to upset its major donor nations. If the UNHCR read the existing evidence as proof of chemical warfare it could upset the delicate negotiations for repatriation of refugees in Laos or Cambodia. Laotian officials had agreed to limited repatriation programs in their country; even this small success would be brought to a halt if the UNHCR confirmed reports that yellow rain was being used in Laos. By 1982 the refugee problem in Southeast Asia was beginning to take on the marks of a long-term, no-win dilemma; resettlement ceilings in the United States and other countries that had accepted Southeast Asians were dropping. In this context the UNHCR needed to preserve its few demonstrable successes in repatriation as well as its ability to deal with all parties in particular disputes.

The U.S. government seemed hopelessly divided. While the State Department in Washington was preparing a public white paper on the existing evidence of chemical warfare, no results from tests on blood and tissue samples were available, even though samples had been either forwarded to the embassy by World Vision or obtained under its supervision.[21] The embassy workers assigned to the issue were not doctors or scientists, but political and military personnel. They were aided by a retired Air Force doctor in the employ of the International Rescue Committee. Beginning in 1982, his salary was paid directly by the State Department. He spent virtually all of his time on the yellow rain issue: he visited camps, interviewed patients, queried them on the nature of Vietnamese chemical production and on the nature of chemical attacks. He offered his expertise to the other religious and voluntary agencies, providing a lecture on chemical warfare to World Vision staff in Ban Vinai. In his view, most of the agencies were skeptical that yellow rain was being used. He was convinced that on the whole the gassing reports were genuine.

As the chief field investigator for the State Department's information project on yellow rain, he was sensitive to the political ramifications of the issue. He told congressional investigators, "A number of U.S. Government personnel in [the Department of Defense], Intelligence, State Dept. and Congressional staffs . . .

seem to have been less than happy that the investigation was even undertaken . . . for some it has been an embarrassment to be proven wrong and for others, it complicates their assigned tasks, especially in disarmament talks." As for other countries interested in yellow rain, whom he called the "'shy' governments," they appeared eager to stay out of what looked like a superpower dispute and displayed "a frightened paralysis of action not unlike that seen in Europe and much of the democratic world prior to the onset of World War II."[22]

In discussing the work of the voluntary agencies before Congress in February 1983 he singled out World Vision, claiming that the fact that World Vision worked not only in Thailand but also in Cambodia and Laos distorted its position on yellow rain. Rather than acquiesce to substantial evidence that chemicals were being used in Laos, he argued, World Vision sought primarily to protect its own interests in that country, which meant staying out of the dispute. Incredibly (in the case of World Vision), he interpreted the voluntary agency presence in all three countries as evidence of a radically politicized "one-world" philosophy, evidenced by their "felt need to continue 'on both sides' regardless of any degree of inhumanity or modus operandi that might be displayed in any host country. In general, among the 'religious Volags,' the Catholics and more fundamentalist Protestants would be supportive of the 'Yellow Rain' research efforts." His list of agencies in this group included Seventh Day Adventists, Mormons, and the Unification Church, as well as a Thai Catholic group.[23]

In the course of the previous year five medical workers from Ban Vinai camp, four of them employees of World Vision, had provided testimony to Congress. Each one had stated essentially the same story: they believed that chemicals were being used against the Hmong in Laos, but they could not prove it conclusively; "if victims are seen shortly after their exposure to [a] chemical lethal weapon, medical evidence alone may prove conclusively the poison gas syndrome," stated one witness from the Ban Vinai camp. Such evidence did not exist. Even though each of these medical workers eventually stated a belief in the yellow rain hypothesis, World Vision still maintained a cautious, neutral stance. There remained a desire on the part of some governmental officials to push through "conclusive" findings, even though few reputable scientists would agree that they existed. Even the voluminous files of the investigator from the International Rescue Committee/State Department included embarrassing recantations of yellow rain stories from refugees who later admitted that they had pressed their claims for political motives. Under such circumstances, there appeared no reasonable alternative for a private agency other than to sit tight, do its job, and steer around the political currents. This required sophistication and a realistic view of the quality of mercy that could rise above those currents.

To call this stance apolitical, the term often used derisively to stereotype evangelical and conservative relief efforts, is to miss the point entirely. It is true that many such agencies have grown up in an atmosphere rooted in conservative Protestant faith missions in which Christian work was by its very nature considered to be above politics. But contemporary political conditions around the world—often fueled (as in this case) by long-standing cold war tensions—have forced World Vision and similar agencies to come to terms with their relationship to the wider social and political settings in which they operate. The yellow rain dispute at Ban Vanai shows an agency grappling with events that no longer fit an apolitical model of religious presence in the world, in which church agencies must work through their relations with their own government, host governments, local affiliates, and the press in order to serve those in need, the refugees. The motivations of religiously grounded refugee work and of U.S. foreign policy may indeed overlap, but at many points the work itself is inevitably an ineffective mixture of competing institutions and motives. World Vision wisely sought a course that downplayed conflict with external authorities for the sake of preserving their ability to serve those in need.

10

Sudan: Rescuing Ethiopia's Black Jews

No other refugees and homeless people have received such consistent attention from U.S. policymakers in the postwar period as the Jews. Although the issue has taken on human rights dimensions, its roots are political and religious. Israel today requires an expanding Jewish population, which has meant renewed emphasis on the religious Law of Return or *aliyah*. The political significance of an expanded Jewish population in Israel is obvious, but its religious meaning was newly emphasized in the late 1970s by a variety of national and religious authorities involved in the migration process. While most refugee flows emerged specifically in the face of religious or political persecution at home, the migration to Israel was itself charged with religious meaning: Jews would find their true homeland by making the *aliyah*, a message Israeli leaders broadcast to Jews dispersed around the world.

Church/state dimensions of the involvement of the U.S. government with Jewish or Israeli agencies are complicated by the desire of all parties to avoid rekindling anti-Semitism and by the unstable political situation in the Middle East. In presenting their case for U.S. assistance, Jewish officials frequently emphasize the secular nature of their relief and humanitarian work and play down religious components. Jewish leaders, much like their Christian and secular counterparts, have routinely sought to harmonize their interests in aiding refugees with those of the U.S. government, and this was the case with the Ethiopian Jews. Though Jewish political and humanitarian leaders were willing to submit the issue to political negotiation, religious Jewish activists treated the *aliyah* of the Ethiopian Jews as a nonnegotiable religious obligation. The Israeli political and religious leadership was also strongly divided.

In contemporary refugee work there is no parallel to U.S./Israeli cooperation in the modern *aliyah*. Since the founding of Israel the United States has played a critical role in financing this migration. As Israel emerged as America's strongest ally in the Middle East, there were strong secular and strategic reasons for the United States to assist in a process considered central to Israel's survival. In the case of the airlift of Ethiopian Jews to Israel, however, there is little evidence that the United States wanted close identification with the process. As the situation developed the government had few options but to allow minority interests within the Jewish community to determine its policy.

A Religious Mandate

In an extraordinary set of clandestine operations conducted from 1978 to 1984 involving the U.S. government, U.S. Jewish agencies, Israel, and Sudan, the extensive refugee operations in eastern Sudan were used as the cover for moving Ethiopian Jews (in Ethiopia called *Falashas,* or outcasts) to Israel. The American Jewish community was no stranger to the illegal movement of Jews across international borders; Operation Moses, as the Israeli part of the Falasha airlift was known, found its spiritual ancestry in the illegal movement of Jews to Palestine prior to the founding of Israel. The movement of the Falasha was in this sense nothing new; even before World War I American Jews had supported international efforts to save the lives, even entire communities, of endangered Jews. When possible these movements had been legal; when not, not. The Falasha effort was among the most controversial and dangerous, hence the secrecy surrounding its details. In the end, when the operation collapsed under international publicity in 1985, it was only the intervention of State Department officials, Vice-President Bush, and the Central Intelligence Agency that saved the lives of the Falasha still stranded in eastern Sudan.

According to Isaiah 11.11–12,

> It shall come to pass in that day, that the Lord shall set his hand again the second time to recover the remnant of his people, which shall be left, from Assyria, and from Egypt, and from Pathros, and from Cush, and from Elam, and from Shinar, and from Hamath, and from the islands of the sea. And he shall set up an ensign for the nations, and shall assemble the outcasts of Israel, and gather together the dispersed of Judah from the four corners of the earth.

The Cushites were the remnant outpost of Jews living in Ethiopia, at the far reach of the world Isaiah might have known. It did not go unnoticed among modern Jews that Isaiah included Cushites in the *aliyah.* The Cushites were identified in the tenth chapter of Genesis as the sons of Ham, a son of Noah. The most ancient legend held that they were the offspring of Solomon and the Queen of Sheba. In New Testament times Philip had encountered an Ethiopian, presumably of Jewish background, in the Gaza Desert on his way to worship at the temple in Jerusalem. The Ethiopian was treasurer in the court of Queen Candace—a name, incidentally, also applied to the Queen of Sheba in Ethiopian legends.

The Falasha became a cause célèbre in nineteenth century European Jewish circles when visitors to Abyssinia encountered their communities and brought back tales of their primitive Jewish life. In the United States, committees were organized to assist the Falasha in Africa before 1940, but little consideration was given to their removal to Palestine.[1] Even after Israel was founded in 1948, efforts to aid the Falasha were limited to relief and rehabilitation in Ethiopia, conducted under the auspices of ORT, the Joint Distribution Committee, and smaller groups with specialized concerns. Only in the 1970s was it possible for Israel and other Jewish communities to consider the question of the Falasha coming to Israel.

Several factors combined to press the urgency of removing them from Ethiopia. In 1973 the chief rabbi of Israel's Sephardic (or Oriental) Jews declared that the Falasha were to be recognized as Jews, and hence eligible for inclusion in the *aliyah* under Israel's "sublime symbol of self-help," the 1950 Law of Return. In 1975 he was joined in this opinion by the chief rabbi of the Ashkenazi (or European) Jews.[2] As a result of the Yom Kippur War, Israel and Ethiopia broke diplomatic relations, eliminating an official channel for assistance to the Falasha. By 1976, the future of the Falasha, as of other sizable Jewish communities outside Israel, was inevitably tied to Israel's desire to expand its shrinking Jewish population. To Jewish activists concerned specifically about the Falasha, these factors all pointed to a rescue operation.

From the beginning controversy dogged their efforts. The American Jewish community was split over the proper approach to the Ethiopian Jews. Black, mostly illiterate, and living in a premodern agricultural setting, the Falasha practiced a pre-Talmudic Judaism that would be foreign even within the Orthodox Jewish communities of Israel. Furthermore, staging an actual rescue operation in Sudan was complex. There, as in most of black Africa, blacks eager to maintain good relations with the Arab population of North Africa became vocally anti-Israel after the 1973 war. Some black leaders were willing to blame the general problem of African refugees on "Zionism" and covert Israeli political operations.[3] In the Sudan, under General Gafar Nimeiry, Arab-language newspapers in Khartoum occasionally ran excerpts from the bogus *Protocols of the Elders of Zion,* an anti-Semitic document that originated in Russia and was promoted in the United States by Henry Ford in the early part of the century. Government officials in the United States were skeptical about Jewish claims that the Falasha were receiving especially harsh treatment. State Department evaluations of the human rights situation in Ethiopia in the early 1980s argued that although human rights were distinctly limited under the Marxist regime of Lt. Colonel Haile-Mariam Mengistu, evidence that the Falasha were singled out for persecution was lacking.[4]

Mainline Jewish agencies, while not openly agreeing with State Department assessments, sought a moderate approach, suggesting that although emigration to Israel was the most desirable solution in the long run, short-term political complications argued for the establishment of assistance programs in Ethiopia. In 1974 the Joint Distribution Committee began a small program that provided $25,000 per year.[5] Such evaluations and limited assistance were challenged by Falasha activists in the United States, who alleged that the Ethiopian Jews had been targeted as traitors, removed from their land, and placed in ghettolike situations. In July of 1981 the regional governor of Gondar, the province where most of the Falasha lived, ordered the long-term programs of the international Jewish Organization for Rehabilitation and Training terminated. This meant that ORT operations involving wells, roads, farming aids, and sanitation, as well as support for twenty-five synagogues, were brought to a halt.[6]

American Falasha activists turned to Israeli officials for assistance in their efforts to establish an Ethiopian *aliyah.* There had been hesitation in official Israeli circles, but the election of Menachem Begin as prime minister in 1977 augured well for more attention to the situation. The earliest efforts of the Israelis were tied to diplomatic negotiations to buy the freedom of the Falasha to emigrate. In August of 1977, sixty Jews were brought to Israel as part of a deal with the Ethiopian government; another sixty-one followed later in the year. But an admission by Moshe

Dayan in February 1978 that the Israelis had been selling arms to the Ethiopians raised the clear possibility that the movement of the Falasha had been tied to the arms deals. This revelation spelled the end of negotiated agreements between the Israelis and the Ethiopians.[7]

Following Dayan's announcement in early 1978, American Jews presented new plans for a Falasha *aliyah* to the Begin government. As with previous movements of Jewish refugees, two essential matters were to be addressed: rescue from abroad and absorption inside Israel. The rescue operation involved a variety of private Jewish groups. And there was no doubt that it was risky: it meant bringing Jewish civilians as well as agents of Mossad, the Israeli intelligence branch, to Sudan. The Falasha were told that they would be taken to Israel if they were willing to travel across the border to Sudan and wait temporarily in camps already filled with hundreds of thousands of Ethiopian and Eritrean refugees. The wider flow of refugees provided a cover for the movement of Jews in a country overtly hostile to their presence. Once the rescue portion of the operation was over and the Falasha reached Israel, responsibility for their absorption would shift to the Jewish Agency, the governmental arm of the Zionist movement.

The Operation Begins

There was nothing simple about the operation, which eventually began in Sudan in 1978. People with Israeli passports were not officially permitted inside Sudan, and official hostility toward Jews was well known. Had word leaked out to the Muslim Brotherhood in eastern Sudan that Israelis and Americans were transporting black Jews as part of the refugee operation, there might well have been serious civil disturbances. Sudanese state security officials, whose cooperation was required so the operation could proceed quietly, were paid large sums of cash, from both private and government sources, reputedly running into the millions of dollars.

There were remarkably few American voluntary agencies in eastern Sudan, due in part to the Sudanese government. Whereas dozens of agencies had flocked to help in a comparable refugee problem in neighboring Somalia, only a handful of outside agencies worked in the region of Gedaref, where the Falasha were staying in refugee camps. The International Rescue Committee was in Sudan on a contract with the State Department; the indigenous Sudanese agencies Sudanaid (Catholic) and the relief arm of the Sudan Council of Churches (largely Protestant, but including Catholic participation) functioned in the camps with support from American and European counterparts. By 1983 CARE was working on water and reforestation projects, and a small independent U.S. Catholic organization, Lalamba, had left Ethiopia and followed the refugees across the border, reestablishing its efforts in Sudan with a State Department grant. Agencies were staffed by a few American expatriates, virtually all of whom were under thirty and unaware of the Ethiopean Jews' presence in the masses of refugees.

The larger refugee operation was superintended by the Sudanese Commissioner for Refugees and the UNHCR, which staffed a suboffice in Gedaref. If many voluntary agencies were unaware of the early stages of the Falasha situation, the UNHCR could not make such a claim. In the beginning, according to UN sources, a standard route was established: Falasha were moved in buses to Khartoum, where they were met by Israeli Mossad agents working from a house in the city. When circumstances allowed, they were placed on chartered flights from the Khartoum airport for Israel. Despite lax security in Sudan, there was no way that a movement involving the transport of hundreds of Ethiopians inland remained other than an open secret. Those Falasha sent in the early busloads were reportedly disguised as Italian tourists, complete with makeup, holiday clothes, and toys for the children; from that point on, UN officials familiar with the operation referred to the Falashas as "the Italian cases." Though the UNHCR could not officially support such an operation that singled out a group of refugees for special attention, they were powerless to stop it.

By 1980 Falasha activists in the American Association for Ethiopian Jews (AAEJ) in the United States saw a correlation between the numbers of Falasha reaching Israel and the amount of pressure the AAEJ brought to bear at any given time on the matter; in other words, they doubted Israel's commitment to establishing a strong Ethiopian *aliyah*. This situation was as unacceptable to the AAEJ and its supporters as the increasingly vocal efforts of the AAEJ were to the leaders of the American Jewish establishment. Therefore a Committee on Ethiopian Jewry was formed within the National Jewish Community Relations Advisory Council. Before this move, no inclusive organizational structure promoting the cause of the Falasha had existed; the AAEJ had served that function for twenty-five years, but its methods were increasingly unacceptable to more moderate Jewish leaders.[8]

Little has been said about the role of the U.S. government in the Falasha operation. In the early years, officials would have liked nothing more than to see the whole operation go away; it was a headache in their relations with the Sudanese, the Israelis, and the Ethiopians. But in 1980 significant legislation, the Refugee Act of 1980, made possible the next step of the operation in Sudan. Before 1981, the United States had not conducted a single refugee resettlement program in Africa. There were several reasons for this, despite the growing masses of refugees throughout the continent. First, it was the stated desire of Africans that refugee problems be handled at home. The Organization of African Unity had drafted a refugee convention in 1969 stating that refugee problems were "a source of friction among many Member States" and that "all the problems of our continent must be solved . . . in the African context."[9] Many African states were wary of resettlement programs which, necessarily selective in who they chose, siphoned off the educated Africans to the West. The African nations wanted to avoid such a "brain drain." Second, African refugee problems generated little political urgency for U.S. strategists; Vietnamese and Afghan refugees and Soviet Jews received far more attention and support. It was easier to provide limited support for local settlement and assistance, and hope that the problems could be resolved by Africans in the long run.

In 1981, however, some members of Congress argued that the lack of U.S. resettlement programs in Africa represented a racist approach to the continent's refugee problem. Under the new Refugee Act, it seemed appropriate to demonstrate an effort to reach an evenhanded solution to the world refugee problem. In a notable example of domestic U.S. politics taking priority over the wishes of other nations, the State Department later that year undertook its first and only African resettlement program. It was based in Gedaref, Sudan.

Two camps near Gedaref, Tawawa and Um Rakuba, held most of the Falasha that reached Sudan. From those camps, Falasha were moved secretly to Israel, by several escape routes. Some followed routes established by Israeli intelligence officials through Khartoum. Some were taken to Sudan's coastline on the Red Sea, where they were met by boats and taken to Israel. Some were smuggled south via Kenya; others were flown to South Africa on servant visas. Others were moved directly through the resettlement program of the U.S. government, so that by the end of 1983 some 5,700 Falasha had reached Israel.

Unable to halt the operation, U.S. officials had apparently adopted the "if you can't beat 'em, join 'em" approach, yet even this was done in an atmosphere of secrecy quite apart from the aboveboard resettlement effort openly sanctioned by the Congress. Voluntary agency officials in Gedaref were for the most part unaware of the complexities of the operation going on around them, even unaware that several of them had hired Falasha sympathizers from among the refugee population. As part of the resettlement effort the U.S. government financed education classes to teach English and elementary cultural background to refugees selected for resettlement. And as Africans had feared, it was common for selected refugees to have a high level of skills; many had held professional positions in Ethiopia, others spoke English or had been staff workers with the voluntary agencies in the region. By late 1982, however, agency teachers suddenly encountered entire classes of refugees who not only spoke no English, but had no professional skills or other background suitable for resettlement in the United States. They were in fact peasants and farmers: unknown to the agency workers, they were Falasha. At the same time, Sudanese officials and others responsible for supervising the movement of Ethiopians scheduled for resettlement in the United States noticed that they often received two different sets of "official" listings of refugees, or that special efforts were made to secure places for refugees from Um Rakuba or Tawawa. Some departing under the U.S. resettlement program were indeed going to the United States; others, once they were out of Sudan, were transferred to planes to Israel.

One of the factors behind this stepped-up movement of Falasha to Israel was the increasing political activism of the Falasha supporters in the United States. Officials of the AAEJ frequently visited absorption camps in Israel and were unhappy with what they found. Indeed, they launched attacks against Yehuda Dominitz, director of the Jewish Agency in Israel, for the alleged restrictions of Falasha once they reached Israel. The AAEJ believed that Dominitz was only willing to work with the Falasha problem as far as the establishment Jewish leaders in the United States were willing to push him. Dominitz could exercise control over the flow of Falasha by stating that absorption camps were full, or by claiming that excessive publicity by AAEJ leaders was creating a political problem. Indeed, in line with the collusion AAEJ saw between the Jewish Agency and U.S. Jewish leadership, the United Jewish Appeal, the clearinghouse for all international funding raised in the U.S. Jewish community, circulated a confidential memorandum that (following most views in the State Department) suggested that the AAEJ's work was amateurish and endangering the lives of those involved in rescue efforts. In protest against efforts by Jewish leaders in the United States and Israel to clamp down on their efforts, the AAEJ withdrew from the Committee on Ethiopian Jewry, which had been established in 1980 as an effort to moderate its efforts. To AAEJ leaders, Jewish and governmental leadership had fallen into the same pattern as those who responded to Hitler by claiming that nothing more could, under the circumstances, be done.

The AAEJ and its fellow activists held a single trump card in this standoff: as long as Falasha kept appearing in eastern Sudan, the pressure could be kept up on authorities to do something. And despite the political wrangling going on in Israel and in the United States, the Falasha kept coming. Thousands—the majority of those still left in Ethiopia—had reached eastern Sudan by early 1984. In ill health, frightened, and unsure of the arrangements that awaited them, they had been persuaded that the dangerous trip across Ethiopia and the uncertain wait in Sudan were worth the chance to reach Israel. In 1983 several secret airlifts, one plane at a time, took place in the desert scrubland near Um Rakuba. As word of the secret operation spread, the possibility of quietly shipping the Falasha overland to Khartoum as part of the regular transport of refugees being resettled in the United States evaporated. Remarkably, however, local Muslim militants apparently had not yet heard of the black Jews in their midst. Some time remained, but the measures needed were becoming more drastic, and the political clout of interested governments—particularly the United States—was increasingly needed to overcome hostility within the Sudanese government. In March 1984, nomads spotted the landing of a plane—a Hercules C-130 American transport—and news of this unannounced landing in the desert spread quickly. So quickly was official involvement spreading, in fact, that after years of silence concerning what had previously been a matter of concern only within the Jewish community, the *New York Times* abruptly ran an editorial stating that "the plight of the Falasha ought to be on Ethiopia's agenda."[10]

A Swedish nurse working in the camps visited the U.S. embassy in June 1984, asking if something could be done to get the Falasha out of the camps. He approached Jerry Weaver, the refugee coordinator at the U.S. embassy in Khartoum. This was not the first time Weaver had heard of the Falasha. He was quite familiar with the problem: the constant stream of Jewish refugee activists, many displaying a "Lone Ranger" style that announced that their presence was what the Falasha were truly waiting for, had been a part of Weaver's life for years. Like other embassy officials, he hoped that Jewish refugee workers—indeed, all voluntary agency personnel in the country—would understand that refugee problems were primarily in the hands of governments. The previous year, one individual named "Jack Charity" had simply gathered a small group of Falasha and headed south, hoping that UNHCR workers would help him cross the border into Kenya. Another couple had descended on Gedaref, full of news of what the outside world was doing for the Falasha. As a result the refugees were left terrified and unsure of whom it was they were supposed to be dealing with. Weaver correctly perceived that such indivduals had no sense of the complexity and danger they were courting in a country as volatile as Sudan. They were doing little to address the overall problem, which in 1984 amounted to moving some 12,000 Jews out of the country. This was not a problem for the Lone Ranger, or even for a dozen of them.

New Pressures Mount

Despite continued resistance in the Jewish Agency to a stepped-up movement of Falasha, some humanitarian solution to the problem was needed. The Falasha in Sudan were so frightened that most refused to leave their huts in camps; packed tightly together, disease spread; they refused to eat, and death rates mounted steadily. Weaver made sure that the State Department funds were available to send food specifically to Falasha camps. Jewish activists in the United States, including an official in the office of the U.S. Coordinator for Refugee Affairs, pressed for action, but according to Weaver, he and his colleagues in the State Department "wanted something straightforward that would not create an embarrassing situation for the Government of Sudan."[11] The UNHCR was also in a difficult situation. Its previous representative in Gedaref had heard of the Falasha and took an interest in the situation. His personal assistant, an Ethiopian, was caught by Sudanese security officers providing assistance to the Falasha and jailed. Since the UNHCR was forbidden to show preference for one refugee group over another, the incident was cause for serious embarrassment. The UNHCR Gedaref agent was quickly posted elsewhere and replaced by an American who had worked with Church World Service and CARE and was willing to help secure a U.S. solution to the Falasha problem.

Jews and others impatient with the mixed messages coming from Israel revived pressure tactics. On the op-ed page of the *New York Times* of September 15, Falasha activist Simcha Jacobovici spelled out the political dimensions of the situation to a world that hardly knew the Falasha existed, let alone the complications over their fate in Israel, Sudan, or the American Jewish community. "At least 1,300 black Ethiopian Jews, mostly children, have died in refugee camps outside Ethiopia," he wrote, carefully avoiding any mention of Sudan. He directed criticism against then Prime Minister Yitzak Shamir, Yehuda Dominitz, and other Israeli "bureaucrats" who were impeding a solution. From May to June, "not only were none rescued by Israel but also all major Jewish organizations, including the World Jewish Congress and Joint Distribution Committee, chose not to provide any financial, medical or food aid. . . . What is needed, without further delay . . . is a massive rescue airlift from the camps and from Ethiopia. This will occur only if it is demanded in Israel and abroad."

The call was heard. By early fall 1984 Weaver had decided that no solution would be found without the active support of sympathetic and powerful members of the Sudanese government. He sought an audience with the vice-president, General Omar Tayeb. According to Weaver, Tayeb agreed to provide assistance as long as the CIA was involved. Weaver relayed this condition but said it was turned down flat by Washington. Weaver was to be in charge; he was the refugee coordinator in the U.S. embassy, and he was the man who best understood the situation. In October Weaver went to Geneva, ostensibly for the annual meeting of the executive committee of the UNHCR. There he held extensive meetings with State Department officials and representatives of the Jewish Agency and the Israeli government. Sudanese officials in Geneva charged with facilitating the coming airlift were also kept informed. Operation Moses was falling into place. Weaver was to handle all finances of the operation, and in this regard, he later insisted on two incredible claims: that no bribes changed hands and that no U.S. government money was spent on the effort.

Operation Moses

On November 20, 1984, Weaver and his co-workers in the Israeli Mossad had arranged for four buses to gather outside the camp at Tawawa, where some 250

Falasha were whisked off to the Khartoum airport, about seven hours away. They were met by a Belgian chartered plane and the first Operation Moses plane soon took off for Israel. This pattern continued for nearly seven weeks as thousands of Falasha were finally allowed to reach their destination. In a press account of December 10, Reagan administration officals denied that the United States had any involvement in the ongoing airlift, which by then, some three weeks into Operation Moses, had illegally moved some 3,000 Falasha to Israel. Diplomatic, governmental, and Jewish sources told reporters at the time that the airlift was taking place "as a result of the famine in Ethiopia." The U.S. involvement was claimed to be limited to $15 million allocated for the absorption of the refugees inside Israel. The same week, an article in the *Washington Jewish Week* quoted Leon Dulzhin, chairman of the Jewish Agency, as saying that Israel was experiencing "a sudden jump in immigration, far beyond the figures we projected for this and the coming year."[12] His remark was made at a fund-raising dinner in New York; Dulzhin was unaware that it would appear in the press. After this, the press was silent on the matter for the remainder of the year. No one had directly implicated Sudan and the operation continued; it was scheduled to run through January 17.[13]

It came to an abrupt halt January 3 after Yehuda Dominitz was interviewed in a magazine published by the Gush Emmunim party, well known for their efforts to settle the territories occupied by Israel after the 1967 war. When the outside press picked up this official confirmation of Israeli involvement in the effort, Israeli censors temporarily gave up trying to control any governmental acknowledgments of the airlift (a news blackout on the airlift in Israel followed shortly). At a news conference an official of the Israeli Foreign Ministry said, "When the time will come, it will be our honor to disclose the people and the governments who helped." In Sudan, meanwhile, the predictable happened: an embarrassed Sudanese government halted the flights. In Ethiopia, the government denounced the airlift as "illegal trafficking" in Ethiopian citizens and a "gross interference" in the internal affairs of Ethiopia. It claimed that the Sudanese had been offered money to draw them into a conspiracy with unnamed "foreign powers."[14]

There was little doubt that internal political debates over the Falasha in Israel had brought about the premature publicity on the operation. "It is my plea," said President Chaim Herzog of Israel on January 7, "that we do not make this splendid rescue of Ethiopian Jewry into an ugly chapter of accusation and slanders leveled by political groups against each other."[15] It was more a matter of keeping the existing deep political divisions out of the press than preventing unprecedented slanders in the future. The Jewish Agency and others in Israel stood accused of racism, and even worse: of abandoning the Zionist promise that all Jews without exception had a home in Israel. Until the U.S. government formally entered the picture, the uncoordinated private rescue operations had created provocative and dangerous conditions for participants and for the refugees in Sudan, not to mention trouble caused for the Reagan administration in its relations with the Nimeiry government. American diplomats were often furious in private over the rescue missions mounted by Jewish activists. (As late as the fall of 1984, a State Department official directly involved in the Falasha affair maintained that the Falasha were not being singled out for persecution within Ethiopia.)

Two further questions remained. The premature halt of Operation Moses left hundreds of Falasha still stranded in Sudan; estimates ranged from 900 to 4,000.[16]

What was to happen to them now that publicity had destroyed the secret airlift? Second, what was happening to the Falasha once they reached Israel? It was the second question that next drew the attention of the press, when the United States protested to Israel later in the month about reports that Falasha were being settled in the Israeli-occupied West Bank. This policy had been in place well before Operation Moses, though Israeli officials were now quick to claim that the fact that one processing center in the West Bank was handling Falasha did not mean they would be permanently settled in that area. The U.S. government was on record as opposing Israeli settlement policies in the West Bank, and the use of U.S. economic aid to Israel for absorption costs of new immigrants was forbidden in the occupied territories. News that the Falasha were being sent to the front lines of the West Bank was more than the United States would tolerate.[17]

Israel still needed American help in addressing the matter of the Falasha still stranded in Sudan. Contrary to Jerry Weaver's claim that the U.S. financial role in Operation Moses was limited to the congressionally mandated absorption costs in Israel, the *New York Times* claimed on January 18, 1985, that the costs of the charter flights by the Belgian Trans European Airways "were paid for by Israel with money received from America." Israel was simply in no financial position to handle the exhorbitant costs of the operation, and it would need to return to the United States for aid in rescuing the Falasha remaining in Sudan.

In March 1985 Vice-President Bush visited Sudan with a sizable entourage. There he conducted meetings with President Nimeiry, who agreed to allow the United States to airlift the remaining Falasha out of the country, provided that no Israeli planes were involved in the operation and that the refugees were given visas to countries other than Israel. Once the Sudanese leader had given his approval, the CIA was called in to manage the operation. Though CIA officials frequently take interest in refugee flows, it is unusual for the CIA to administer a program directly, as was the case in the final rescue operation. Some 800 Falasha were flown out on Hercules C-130 transports between March 21 and 23. The operation was paid for by CIA funds and from U.S. refugee allocations.[18]

As far as the U.S. government was concerned, the affair was closed. Jerry Weaver, his life reportedly threatened by Arabs outraged by the Falasha movement, was hurriedly sent home from the Sudan on March 25. On April 6 a coup toppled Nimeiry's government; the new military rulers of Sudan announced later that month that senior Sudanese officials who had participated in Operation Moses would be placed on trial. The trial was televised in the evening in Khartoum for weeks in the fall. In November several voluntary agencies suspected of participating in the Falasha operation were expelled from Sudan. Far from controlling the situation, the Reagan administration had been placed in the unenviable position of pulling Israel out of a tight spot; It had been placed there by the outspoken and persistent efforts of an activist minority in the Jewish community. The AAEJ pursued its politics of intervention and created a tragic set of events it could no longer shield or manage. The AAEJ and its supporters believed religiously in the *aliyah,* particularly its relevance to the Falasha. That belief led them to international political intrigues that in the end demonstrated that the *aliyah* could take precedence over the political and diplomatic interests of any government that stood in its way, including the Israeli government. The London-based *Economist* sided with the Falasha and their managers, stating that they properly "got the benefit of permissible discrimination."[19] Yet the attitudes of American and Israeli activists toward official constraints were not unlike those of church sanctuary workers helping Central Americans who had come to the United States to escape civil strife at home.

In order to achieve the final rescue of the Falasha, however, the Jewish community in Israel and the United States stood together (those who still had objections made their weight felt by exposing the operation prematurely). Caught in the pressures of deciding what would become of several thousand Jews stranded in a hostile Muslim environment, reluctant establishment leaders among American Jews faced a choice of abandoning their fellow Jews—an intolerable choice—or bringing their weight to bear on behalf of U.S. government intervention. That intervention, coming as it did during a renewed Sudanese civil war, contributed directly to political instabilities that resulted in the collapse of Nimeiry's government.

Honduras, Thailand, and Sudan each provide vivid examples of the real and potential difficulties facing church/state cooperation abroad in the 1980s. Whether we look at open advocacy designed to counter government policies, governmental equivocation over sensitive political matters that bear on the health and safety of refugees, or religiously inspired crusades on behalf of particular populations, common solutions between religious and governmental authorities appeared, if at all, only under political duress. The same was true during World War II, but at that time the U.S. government was not seen as an unreliable partner or as the enemy of humanitarian concerns. In the 1940s, religious agencies not only dominated refugee work, they provided the government with stable, reliable leadership and political backing at home. Neither of these conditions prevails in the 1980s. All parties seem increasingly intent on pursuing their own definitions of the best interests of particular refugees. The inevitable result in the midst of this turmoil is a new level of confrontation between church and state. Under these circumstances, theological dimensions of humanitarian rationales, as well as legal and admininstrative frameworks of cooperation, fall under new scrutiny.

11

Theological Commitments within Humanitarian Structures

The preceding chapters have all dealt with the modern evolution of religiously grounded ties to state policies for aiding refugees. The growth of religious pluralism in the United States and elsewhere required that specifically theological rationales and motives give way in the public forum to the language of humanitarianism, a language that both governmental and religious bodies could share to explain and occasionally justify the complex and often conflicting motivations behind their various involvements. Renewed stress on theological motives within religious communities in recent years has meant that the common currency of humanitarianism has come under new strains.

From common sense and from international humanitarian law we have identifed three components in the humanitarian ethic. Such work must retain a primary focus on the needs and welfare of innocent victims, whether they be victims of natural catastrophes or man-made political disasters. Second, the aid must aspire to a status of neutrality, variously defined as "nonpolitical," "apolitical," or above partisanship. Finally, there must be no discrimination in the distribution of aid. While the broad category of humanitarianism is itself neutral enough to calm many lurking misgivings, understanding humanitarian practice that involves religiously grounded agencies today requires new attention to the significance of theological motivations. As a subcategory within humanitarian bodies, religiously grounded organizations have increasingly veered from the straightforward standards of humanitarianism just set forth. Protestants, Catholics, and Jews all have based their communal involvements in refugee matters in theological rationales that have contributed both to their interest in particular refugee populations and to their ties with governments. Those theological considerations have shaped the distinctive character of their differing contributions and interests, and are critical for an understanding of current realities and future potential for church/state conflict in the conduct of U.S. refugee policy.

The question of authority in setting goals for field operations is a case in point. A Protestant missionary in Honduras posed the question theologically. It was clear to him that aiding refugees could be seen as a direct response to Jesus' statement that should his disciples offer a cup of water, even "to the least of these," they would be serving Jesus directly. It was a mandate from the scriptures. "What I want to know," asked the missionary, "is when we help these refugees and give a cup of water, in whose name is the cup given? Christ or Caesar?" An exclusive tilt in one direction or the other on the part of religious or governmental workers will certainly cause problems.[1]

The role of theological constructs and religiously grounded philosophy in refugee work has not gone unnoticed by U.S. officials. In 1983 the State Department and a new religious advisory group formed by the U.S. refugee coordinator called a major conference in Washington to discuss the role of religious and moral traditions in U.S. refugee assistance.[2] The overriding theme of the conference was the value of extending the traditional complementarity between private and public authorities in refugee work. This was a controversial theme by 1983; one of the clear agenda items for government speakers at the conference was denunciation of the fledgling efforts of the church-based sanctuary movement, which was directly challenging U.S. deportation and asylum policies. Another theme that emerged was the insufficiency of traditional theological frameworks for determining national policy.

Among the theological precedents cited was Jesus' parable of the Good Samaritan. In Luke 10.30–37 two Jews, a priest and a Levite, both pass by a man, also presumably a Jew, who had been beaten by robbers and left by the side of the road to die. A Samaritan, from a culture then reviled by many Jews as impure, stopped and aided the man, dressing his wounds and taking him to a nearby inn. The Samaritan was clearly the only person who qualified as a true neighbor of the victim.

According to one speaker at the conference, there is "deep desire" on the part of many American citizens and officials to "play the role of the Good Samaritan" in confronting today's refugee problems.[3] However, intervening factors make the personal attention of the Samaritan to the wounded man a less than satisfactory analogy to the problems confronting U.S. policymakers. Said one conference participant, expressing his view of the limited capacities of individuals and societies in addressing refugee issues:

> If an individual comes to your door one night and says, "I am down on my luck. It is cold outside. I haven't any food. If you could just give me a meal and a place to stay the night I will be on my way tomorrow and that will give me a chance to make it," most of us would want to take the person in. If a family appears on your doorstep and makes the same request you would call the county welfare office for assistance to the family. And if a village shows up on your doorstep and makes that request you call the police. Numbers make a difference, and the numbers in the world have changed.

The same speaker raised this issue in response to another Christian story, that of Martin of Tours who gave his cloak to a beggar. "What if St. Martin had encountered 20 beggars? Would he have cut the coat into 20 little pieces, inadequate for each? Should he have chosen one?"[4] Such questions acknowledge that the choices involved in refugee issues in our day are inevitably tragic, and that the existence of a theological precedent does not automatically tell us what the appropriate response should be, particularly when public policymakers must harmonize contradictory demands and strictly limited resources.

Government leaders at the conference emphasized that while they needed and relied on the assistance of religious agancies in refugee work, the government should remain the arbiter of who would and would not be assisted. From the earliest efforts of Roosevelt and his staff to address the refugee problem "on a broad religious basis," government officials have realized the importance, crudely put, of having God on their side. The "three faiths" coalition of the wartime era effectively submerged real differences among Protestants, Catholics, and Jews under the broad language of humanitarianism. All in fact brought their own theological priorities and visions to aspects of the common task.

Believers of each faith face pressing theological concerns in their work overseas. Each, though springing from related theological traditions, offers different answers to the question posed by the missionary in Honduras: in whose name, to what ultimate ends? Those answers, often bypassed in the attention given to refugee assistance today, are both intimate and public, and nearly always passionate. They stem from the relationship of individuals to broader patterns they see in Christian and Jewish theology. Yet experience in the modern world has demonstrated that religious bodies are not launched on a simple trajectory leading from specific, closed dogmas to open, universalist tolerance of all views. An obvious example is the involvement of Zionists with refugee assistance. Early Israeli Zionists were often militantly secular, justifying the movement of Jews to Israel on political and national grounds. By the late 1980s, the strongest proponents of Zionism had shifted to a fundamentalist theological interpretation of their purpose in collecting Jews in the Land of Israel.[5]

Theology in its broadest sense is human reflection on God's workings in the world. Within Christianity and Judaism one's relationship with God exists within a received set of historical accounts, parables, and commands that explain the way God works in the world and through people. Tied as they are to the deepest roots of Western civilization, such stories continue to inform Christians and Jews as they consider their vocation in the modern world. Theology does not always determine the actions of religious institutions, however, and singling out the roots of religious motivation should not be seen as an effort to impose theological determinism on religious relief agencies.

Once a religious body had decided to make a commitment to refugees, it finds that it is acting in a sphere far beyond the moral imperative of caring for the homeless. It must also learn to navigate political disputes generated in the Congress, the military, and the various agencies of the executive branch, to mention only the domestic American scene. Theology will not always determine how these battles are fought, but it is fair to say that religious bodies would never have entered the fray in the absence of substantial theological rationales. As some modern relief workers struggle to articulate the significance of theology in their work, others are eager to claim that their work is "not religious," often meaning that they are not interested in actively evangelizing refugees. But to generalize from such comments that theological commitments are not relevant to international refugee relief is to belie the inner motivations of the majority of those who provide the actual assistance—and of many who supervise the programs within the U.S. government and elsewhere. It is also to abandon the internal roots of religious action that have been granted wide protections under U.S. law.

Theological Moorings

The Hebrew narration of history begins with God's creation of a good world, the world of Eden, and quickly advances to the predicament of human homelessness. Adam and Eve, the first parents of humanity, sin. They become refugees from the divine presence through their desire to be equals of the Creator. Through this act of rebellion they lose their home in the Garden of Eden and break communication with God. The first words Yahweh addresses to Adam after Adam and Eve have eaten the fruit of the Tree of the Knowledge of Good and Evil are in the form of a question: "Where are you?" They are banished in shame, east of Eden. This simple account carries truths that have resurfaced in every generation down to the present. Henceforth, Judeo-Christian religion has been concerned with the theme of return: to the homeland, to the people, but primarily to heal this primal separation from God. The depth of this homelessness of the human soul was memorably summarized by Augustine of Hippo as he surveyed the decay and collapse of the Roman Empire in the fourth century: "O God, you made us for yourself, and our hearts find no rest until they rest in you." Today both Jewish and Christian leaders have argued that their involvement with refugees around the world represents a theologically mandated response to this human plight of homelessness.

In the Hebrew scriptures those who remained faithful to the God of Israel were constantly taught the importance of extending help to their fellow creatures. Such help mirrored Yahweh's covenant of faithfulness to the lost of Israel. The very act of service—first to the House of Israel, then to others—would be a foretaste of the restoration of humanity's place in creation. The deepest reality of the covenant was the attitude of trust and loyalty between the parties. The word often translated into English as "mercy" is the Hebrew *chesed,* which means loyalty or steadfast love. Some scholars have suggested that the best reading of *chesed* is "covenant-love." The concept has been of recurrent importance in the structuring of Jewish and Christian ties with earthly authorities.

Zeal for the covenant has frequently contributed to exclusionary activities, which today are often identified with the darkest side of religion and politics. The Jews were not always the victims of events that created wanderers and refugees; occasionally they were the perpetrators. Abraham sent the sons he had fathered by concubines "unto the east country" so that they could not challenge the power of his son Isaac. Among Christians, the Puritans of the seventeenth-century Massachusetts Bay Colony created a theocracy that essentially excluded even fellow Protestants such as Quakers and Baptists. Fear of the evils created by overly close ties between spiritual and political authorities lies behind American traditions designed to foster the independence of church and state.

The Exodus of the Jews out of Egypt remains today a theological keystone in Jewish life. Exemplifying God's action in history on behalf of an oppressed people, it also speaks to the centrality of the *aliyah,* the Law of Return, in the modern Jewish community. Perhaps no other series of events in the Bible, with the possible exception of the death and resurrection of Christ, has been so frequently drawn into political analogies of the American experience. The English Puritans of the seventeenth century read the meaning of their journey to America in its light. They saw America as the land of the New Adam where redeemed humanity would institute the righteous will of the Lord.

Today, Latin American liberation theologians and conservative Jews in Israel alike have read their own history into the experience of Israel's journey out of the bondage of Egypt. In one reading the Egyptian Exodus portrays the state as a force frustrating the purpose of God on earth, a human creation to be subverted and disobeyed in the name of a higher law. From another perspective the Exodus was the first historical manifestation of what would centuries later be inscribed as an elemental human right in Western democracies: religious liberty. It was in the crucible of the wandering in the wilderness between Egypt and the Promised Land that God gave Israel the law at Mt. Sinai. Out of this experience of isolation came the two great commandments, love of God and love of neighbor. The entire tradition of service to the stranger and refugee itself is rooted in the understanding of Yahweh as the ultimate refuge or stronghold of God's people.

Christians have always understood the birth, death, and resurrection of Jesus of Nazareth as the seal of God's new covenant with his people. He is for them the promised messiah, coming to establish a new era of the Kingdom of God on earth. By the time of the birth of Jesus, Jews were no longer masters of their own nation, but subjects of the Roman Empire. Jesus himself was at one time a refugee, when his family fled to Egypt to avoid the Roman authorities. It was in this historical setting that Jesus brought to the Jews the startling news that the Kingdom of God was breaking into human experience through his arrival and through the subsequent working of the Holy Spirit.

The essence of the kingdom would be the restoration of the love and justice of God the Father, Yahweh. Those who had left their homes in Eden, those who were the victims of miscarried justice, could return (as under the Old Testament provisions for sanctuary). This message, carrying the themes of expulsion and return, was foreshadowed by the events in the life of Jesus. Another thread from the Hebrew scriptures that recurs in the New Testament is the lesson of Christian responsibility toward the stranger and the commitment to provide hospitality and care for those in need. The author of the Letter to the Hebrews admonishes Christians always to keep the doors of their homes open to strangers, since by taking them in, they may be unknowingly entertaining angels (Hebrews 13.2).

In a recent publication directed at potential donors, the evangelical agency World Relief (of the National Association of Evangelicals, the conservative Protestant counterpart of the National Council of Churches) used another parable of Jesus to explain the rationale of its entire mission. The parable of the Sheep and the Goats tells of God's judgment which, like a shepherd separating his sheep from goats, will illuminate the truth or falsehood of human choices. As described in Matthew 25.31–40, God will appear in his glory as Universal King, sending the goats to one side and placing the sheep at his right hand, saying

Come, you who are blessed by my Father; take your inheritance, the kingdom prepared for you since the creation of the world. For I was hungry and you gave me something to eat, I was thirsty and you gave me something to drink, I was a stranger and you invited me in, I needed clothes and you clothed me, I was sick and you looked after me, I was in prison and you came to visit me. Then the righteous will answer him, "Lord, when did we see you hungry and feed you, or thirsty and give you something to drink? When did we see you a stranger and invite you in, or needing clothes and clothe you? When did we see you sick or in prison and go to visit you?" The King will reply, "I tell you the truth, whatever you did for the least of these brothers of mine, you did for me."

World Relief's publication "State of World Need in the '80s" takes the varied categories of service mentioned in this "Matthew 25 Christianity" as touchstones for its international efforts. How can one know whether one falls among the sheep or the goats? It depends on what we do, how we act on the options God puts before us. And for World Relief, people only act when they believe. This connection between belief and action is drawn explicitly: "What we believe, we do. Everything else is just so much religious rhetoric."[6] World Relief is not alone in its use of this passage for justifying its overseas activities. From their origins in the 1940s Catholic Relief Services, Lutheran World Relief, mainline Protestant Church World Service, and others have used the words of Matthew 25 to legitimize their ministries abroad to refugees and other needy people.

With few exceptions refugee work is today carried on in a political environment largely determined by interested states. In this climate there is little likelihood that religious perspectives (such as the primacy of assistance to those in need, or the refugee as a sign of our need to return to God) will dominate international political efforts to address the problem. Thus the compromise formula on which all such cooperation is based: for those areas of good works in which (for many and varied reasons, to be sure) both church and state have interests, the resources and political authority of the state may be combined with the resources and humanitarian authority of religious bodies. Whether we are looking at World War II-era displaced persons or Central American refugees in the 1980s, common grounding in biblical commitments to refugees and the stranger has not meant a uniform approach to U.S. government policies. Any full understanding of the role of religious agencies in refugee work must be framed in a wider context of differing theologies of church and state. From this vantage point, Protestants, Catholics, and Jews have taken the words of the Bible and arrived at very different approaches.

Judaism: Covenant Faithfulness

More than the average American Christian, Jews have confronted over and over again the reality of human homelessness that dates from the expulsion of Adam and Eve from Eden. At the 1983 conference on the religious and moral foundations of U.S. refugee policy, Nobel Peace laureate Elie Wiesel, survivor of Hitler's concentration camps, quoted a Hasidic commentary on God's question to Adam after the fall, "Where are you?" The rabbi asked, "Is it conceivable, is it possible, that God did not know where Adam was?" His response, according to Wiesel, was that God knew; it was Adam who suddenly had no sense of where he was. The Jewish predicament for much of recorded history was augured in these primal accounts: they would leave their homes as wanderers, into an era of diaspora and homelessness.[7]

One expression of *chesed,* or the covenant-love of God for Israel, is *zedakah,* kindness and charity expressed as justice. Moses Maimonides, who lived most of his life as a refugee, wrote in the twelfth century in *Laws of Gifts to the Poor* that "there is no greater obligation than the redemption of captives, for the captive is like the hungry and thirsty and the naked, and stands in danger for his life."[8] Jewish communities traditionally have taught the centrality of this commitment, particularly toward fellow Jews; it is impossible to comprehend the passion invested in the rescue of Ethiopian Jews without it. In his history of the Joint Distribution Committee, Oscar Handlin explained the strong pull that *zedakah* exercised on the Jewish conscience: "Centuries of experience had created a sense of mutuality; the group took care of its own, both out of the consciousness that no one else was likely to help and out of the reluctance to see its reputation suffer among other peoples."[9] This tradition was maintained and strengthened by American Jews in both senses referred to by Handlin.

In the 1930s and 1940s American Jews sought help in the cause of Jewish refugees wherever needed. The sense among the Jewish communities that no one else was likely to come to their aid was more than confirmed by the repeated delays from the non-Jewish world in responding to Hitler's early persecutions. Zionists intent on achieving their ends practiced *bitzu'ism,* a term that has been roughly translated as "implementationism," the need to get the job done with relative indifference to ideology or political roadblocks.[10] Within the Jewish world Hitler's actions served to unite various competing factions. The author Stefan Zweig wrote in 1942: "Later, at some future date, we shall again gladly and passionately discuss whether Jews should be Zionists, revisionists, territorialists or assimilationists; we shall discuss the hair-splitting point of whether we are a nation, a religion, a people or a race. All of these time-consuming, theoretical discussions can wait. Now there is but one thing for us to do—to give help."[11]

The largely secular, labor-dominated Zionist movement has always had a profoundly theological core, the *aliyah*. Since World War II, no theological concept has so influenced the ties between American Jewish groups and the U.S. government as the fulfillment of the *aliyah*. With the formation of the State of Israel in 1948, these passionate discussions of Judaism were transformed into the political debates of a nation at war with its neighbors—and frequently with itself. For 2,000 years the Jews had been living in diaspora; once their homeland was restored, the *aliyah* took new prominence in Jewish commitments to refugee and immigrant movements. Zionists interpreted the Jewish moral imperatives of the saving of souls and the ransom of prisoners in specific terms, namely, that Jews must be gathered to the safety of a Jewish state.[12] Theology followed politics: Israel's viability now depended on the ability of Zionist leaders, the wider Jewish community, and its international supporters to move Jews to Israel. The theological grounding of the *aliyah* exercised a powerful hold on the world's surviving Jewish communities. Countless numbers of rabbis and individual Jews in the late 1940s returned to the words of Isaiah 27.12–13:

> . . . and ye shall be gathered one by one, O ye children of Israel. And it shall come to pass in that day that a great trumpet shall be blown; and they shall come that were ready to perish in the land of Assyria, and they that were outcasts in the land of Egypt; and they shall worship The Lord in the holy mountain at Jerusalem.

James G. McDonald, America's first ambassador to Israel, cited this passage in his memoir of his time in Israel in the late 1940s to explain the enthusiasm the Jewish people experienced over the restoration of Israel.[13] He found the deepest meanings of the new state of Israel within the theological and political aspirations of the Jews to return to their homeland. However, he and most of the leaders of the new state knew that all the power of good intentions and righteous theology would not solve Israel's political problems. Time was limited; the *aliyah* would have to be speeded along as quickly as possible amid internal debates and external threats.

As in the case with other religious communities, the Jewish theological and cultural climate has generated a particular set of approaches to the state. Daniel Elazar and Stuart Cohen argue that Jewish political life in all of its diversity is still remarkably dominated by the biblical concept of covenant. They write that

> Jewish political institutions and behavior reflect this covenantal base in the way they give expression to political relationships as the embodiment of a partnership based upon a morally grounded compact and, like all partnerships, oriented toward decision- and policy-making through negotiation and bargaining. Here the concept of *hesed* (covenant obligation) plays a crucial role in providing the basis for the operational dynamics of the covenant relationship . . . blocking a natural human inclination in contractual situations to interpret contractual obligations as narrowly as possible.[14]

In foreign affairs this has frequently meant the inclusion or human rights, particularly those of needy Jewish communities, in U.S. foreign policy objectives. The power and prestige of the U.S. government has, along with the private efforts of American Jews, been an essential component for the accomplishment of the *aliyah*. This was true when U.S.-Russian trade agreements were terminated in 1911 over the question of Jewish rights, and during the formation of the War Refugee Board of 1944, the early immigration efforts of the 1950s, the Jackson-Vanik Amendment of 1974 tying Jewish emigration to U.S.-Soviet détente, and the movement designed to bring Ethiopian Jews to Israel in the late 1970s and early 1980s.

The establishment of Israel revived theological commitments among the Jews. The executive of a major Jewish fund-raising agency active in refugee resettlement in the United States said in 1984 that he believed that among Jewish laity, religious commitments to Judaism were replacing the more modern emphasis on Judaism as a set of cultural, ethnic, and political ties. These commitments have always existed; the movements of Jews from Yemen, Morocco, Ethiopia, and elsewhere would not have carried such weight without the *aliyah,* the Law of Return, behind them. With the election of a second Begin administration in 1981, however, the emergence of a new fundamentalist rationale for Zionist efforts to bring Jews to Israel became evident in Israeli politics.[15]

As in Christian circles, Jewish agencies involved in refugee aid are required to keep explicitly religious activities separated from those funded by the U.S. government. Although Orthodox Jewish relief bodies have been registered with the State Department since World War II, the increased Orthodox role in refugee affairs in recent years has on occasion jolted the long-standing ties between the State Department and the Joint Distribution Committee, HIAS, B'nai B'rith, and other agencies that traditionally have represented their interest in refugees as ethnic and cultural.

Emphasis on the *aliyah* has come in the context of the Jewish political style, which has been shaped by the traditions and theologies of covenant. Elazar and Cohen see the Jewish community returning again and again to the three pillars of the covenant with Yahweh: the Torah, the priesthood, and the structuring of civic relationships. One strain of American Jewish voluntarism, exemplified by such agencies as the Joint Distribution Committee, represents an effort to combine covenant fidelity with ties to civic realities outside Jewish circles. The JDC built its authority in the Jewish community in part on its ability to represent Jewish and universal aspirations on the wider stage of the non-Jewish world. Such efforts within U.S. Jewish communities bridged ancient isolation from the broader civic and political order at a time when there was as yet no independent Jewish political entity.

Covenant faithfulness has meant a continued strong emphasis on the autonomy of Jewish communites from the outside world. Institutionally (at least as far back as the fund-raising efforts of the government's National War Fund in 1943) this has meant the independence of Jewish fund-raising activites from national fund-raising efforts and the continued freedom to concentrate on needy Jewish communities abroad. Given the close ties between Jewish agencies and U.S. government-sponsored refugee relief and resettlement programs—recalling Jewish involvement from the time of the pioneering War Refugee Board of 1944—Jewish agencies have been able to maintain autonomy in their programs through the traditional emphasis on offering help "first to the House of Israel." Lest this offend some readings of the pluralistic spirit of modern democracy, one can only say that the postwar era is also the post-Holocaust era. It is difficult to think of a single argument that could ethically challenge the desire of Jewish communities to focus on their own internal needs.

A focus on these ancient covenant virtues of *zedakah* and *chesed* are often interpreted in the non-Jewish world as excessive self-absorption on the part of the Jews. Though apologists for the "three faiths" public humanitarianism have emphasized its unity to the U.S. public for years, part of the need for this philosophy may stem from the very diversity of the different faiths and communities in the United States. A too visible focus on Jewish refugees, for instance, was seen by government officials as a liability during World War II and was therefore minimized.

Such a political climate takes a cumulative toll on a minority community and generates a variety of responses. American Jewish intellectuals have identified points in the last 40 years in which they and their fellow American Jews have undergone emotional waves of homelessness and abandonment. Undoubtedly part of this emotion springs from the fact that many American Jews feel a dual loyalty to the United States and to Israel. Public political criticism of Israel is taken by some as a personal attack on the American Jewish community, Israel's chief supporters. One response to such attacks is to increase support for Israel and for the wider interests of Jewish communities, and one way to do that is to build bipartisan ties with the U.S. government. Like their Christian counterparts, Jews have actively sought to work with the State Department, the Congress, and other offices responsible for U.S. foreign policy on matters of mutual concern.

Aside from military agreements with Israel, there is arguably no field of such long-term mutual concern to the United States and Israel as the continued flow of Jewish immigrants to Israel. The United States has since 1945 consistently assisted Jewish voluntary agencies moving Jews to Palestine and Israel. This commitment has not gone unchallenged. George Warren, the State Department's senior officer on refugees and migration after the war, was strongly pro-Jewish and sought to aid Jews migrating to Israel and the United States. In a State Department still known for the strength of its Arabists, this attitude was balanced in part by separating control of Palestinian refugees from Warren's wider refugee operation.[16] Since the mid-1970s when emigration *out* of Israel became the norm, there has been new pressure to compensate by increasing the number of Jews migrating to Israel. In the case of Ethiopian Jews, independent American Jewish leaders pushed ahead when they felt Israel and the United States were moving too slowly. Such perceived political needs are some distance from pure theological concerns, but the contemporary migrations of Jews would not have taken place without the covenant bonds of Hebrew theology and cultural Jewish identity it has nurtured.

Protestantism: Between Mercy and Justice

Evangelism, church-planting, hospitals, and schools formed the backbone of Protestant mission programs before World War II. This agenda was (and, to some degree, still is) impervious to short-term political change of the sort that generates refugee populations. There was a certain timelessness to this style which disdained such short-term political problems as refugees as a distraction from the true work of the Kingdom of God. While this attitude would soon recede (it had to; too many mission stations were swamped with refugee crises during and after the war) it would not disappear.

Critics of this style often fail to note that this Protestant attitude of separateness is often based on experience and on theological conviction. The call for separation from the world for the sake of God was after all at the heart of God's covenants with Israel. Puritanism with its conviction of human sinfulness necessarily emphasized the covenant law at the heart of God's grace. Niebuhr claimed that ideally Protestantism "is the form of Christianity which sees the peril of human self-confidence most clearly."[17] Although separation from worldly powers could not totally remove Christians from life in a fallen world, Protestant believers look primarily to the goodness of God rather than the goodness of humanity. Martin Luther had divided the world into two kingdoms, the Kingdom of God and the Kingdom of Caesar. Under Caesar, he taught, *all* aspects of life, including social justice, depended upon "chains, the sword and the law."[18]

In this realm of Caesar, the *agape* or deep spiritual love of Christ was inevitably subordinate. In order to protect expression of that love in Christian communities, a firm line had to be drawn between religious and political activities. Various forms of Protestant piety can be traced to the search for this shifting line between the things of God and the things of Caesar. As Protestant leaders recovered the biblical mandates for caring for refugees, their work inevitably drew closer to the foreign policymaking process both in Washington and abroad. The leadership of mainline Protestantism since the mid-1960s has been dominated by the view that the church could and should oppose what has been called "a public philosophy of force" in foreign policy matters. Serious opposition to governmental use of force demanded an increasingly firm line of separation between Protestant efforts and those of the government overseas. Niebuhrian realists, mired in ambiguity, gave way to a new generation of Protestant activists. Between Vietnam and a growing nuclear threat, many Protestant leaders were pushed to a logic that demanded outright opposition to military spending, armed incursions, and even less controversial state functions. Mainline Protestant reactions to U.S. foreign policy since 1970 have been openly hostile, frequently (and accurately) calling attention to limitations placed on the work of voluntary associations (such as churches) abroad. The theological roots of this internationalist idealism may be traced to a conference Protestant leaders called in England in 1937 to address the new problems that totalitarianism in Europe was creating for the church in its relationship with the modern state. At the Oxford Conference on Church, State and Community, non-Catholic church leaders from around the world met to search for a new understanding of the relationship between Christ and Caesar. It was a depressing moment in world history, and Christian leaders felt the need of new light as they sought to bring the Gospel before the nations. Christian leaders were nervous about the political uses being made of the churches.

Far from dealing in abstractions, the conference participants knew all too well the precarious and dangerous state of affairs religious believers faced in the twentieth century. In most Western countries the 1,600-year tradition of a state church was either moribund or had been replaced with new arrangements. The long-term effect was a continued subordination of religious interests to those of the state. "A little-known subordination of church to state," wrote the advance planners of the conference, "is found in the fact that the church is seldom favored for its own sake, but only in so far as it is regarded as useful for the welfare of the state or as part of the historical inheritance of the nation. Thus modern states are severing themselves from Christian influence."[19]

The modern situation confronted the church with the possibility that God's plan must somehow be newly articulated in order to counter the distortions of Hiterlism, the materialism of Marxism, the nationalism of Mussolini, and the behavioristic and humanistic theories developing in Western democracies. "Is there," asked the conference leaders, "a Christian understanding of man distinguishable from all of these?" If there was, it was to be found in the relationship between the church and the community (meaning the society or nation as a whole) in which the church found itself. Western democracies assumed a distinction between state and society; this implied that society, particularly through the church, might limit state action by demonstrating that the state is not autonomous, but the subject of God's judgment. The church, in other words, must retain the independence of Solomon, bringing justice to a corrupt and sinful world.[20]

In sum, Christians were to work toward "permeating the public life with the spirit of Christ."[21] In a pragmatic vein, Christians were also to promote "the means of adjustment to altering conditions"; the conference called on believers "in more fortunate countries [to] press the demands for justice on behalf of the less fortunate."[22] Most important, however, the focus was not on the secular adaptations necessary for religious life in the contemporary world, but on the freedom of the church to pursue its own unique identity:

The first duty of the church, and its greatest service to the world, is that it be in very deed the church—confessing the true faith, committed to the fulfillment of the will of Christ, its only Lord, and united in him in a fellowship of love and service. . . . The call to ourselves and to the world is to Christ.[23]

From this passage can be distilled the rallying cry of Oxford, "Let the Church be the Church." In affirming this theological truth, conference delegates insisted that the church could and should maintain its own standards of truth, justice, and freedom independent of those imposed by government. Here was a fragile butterfly struggling to emerge from its Constantinian cocoon.

The call to Christians to press the claims of justice went hand in hand with the recognition that their weapons were not those of the nations. Oxford delegates agreed that the state maintained the responsibility for the enforcement of law and order, but that the state itself could not properly be called the source of justice; that source was God himself. According to this theological reading, the state was the servant of justice, not its lord. The conference's summary statement specifically argued that justice must be expressed through a demand that sovereign states willingly limit their own sovereignty by abandoning their claims to be the final judges of their own causes. Through such statements the delegates indicated their hope for new forms of international federalism—such as the League of Nations and the emerging body of international and humanitarian law—which acknowledged the transcendent source of the deepest human values.[24]

Compared with the advances of Oxford and the contradictions that lay ahead in the Vietnam War and its aftermath, mainline Protestant theology on refugee matters was bland in the 1950s. Its new excitement arose with its willingness to experiment with the universalism of global service. Its ventures into refugee problems in India, Hong Kong, and the Middle East were part of wider Protestant efforts to announce a universal presence of the Kingdom of God. Equally valuable was the emergence of "technical assistance" in Third World countries, an early term for what is now referred to as development. Both options of foreign service offered a new means of conceptualizing the relationship between the Christian and the non-believer. In the earlier missionary model, conversion of the individual was the primary goal, followed by the convert's involvement in Christian institutions such as schools, hospitals and, centrally, the church. A theology of service placed more emphasis on Christian witness, expressed not so much by preaching conversion as by an increased willingness on the part of Christians to see Christ already present in those they served.

The themes of Oxford were reiterated at the 1966 Geneva Conference on Church and Society, where an international gathering opened the way to more radical interpretations of the role of the church in modern society. One participant, reflecting new concerns over revolution in Latin America, wrote that "Father Camillo Torres, the Colombian guerilla priest, was the hero and martyr of the conference." Yet the Geneva conference was strongly criticized for failing to develop a theology that supported its new openness to the secular and to God's active participation in the events of history. Theology with socially conservative implications "was not effectively present" at Geneva, according to John C. Bennett. The efforts of participants to reach a common theological grounding of their social analysis "came to little . . . there was no common body of doctrine that was held by such a diverse group from which theological convictions could be deduced that would illumine the discussions of social issues."[25]

Words of the prophets that once suggested a common ground for government and religious officials working side by side in humanitarian service had by the time of the Vietnam War often become the rallying cry of those who took a strong stand against the U.S. government's actions in the war. This spirit grew as more and more relief agencies moved into the field of development overseas. In the late 1960s the Peruvian Catholic theologian Gustavo Gutierrez crystallized the beginnings of a movement known as liberation theology, essentially an effort to read the Scriptures "from below," with the mind and heart of the poor themselves, thereby giving renewed meaning to the Bible's call to "let justice roll down like a mighty river."

Seeing Christ present in the poor and the political refugees of Central America often did little for the ability of agency workers to see him present in the actions of U.S. government officials charged with administering U.S. regional policy in Central America. Not surprisingly the liberation impulse in Protestant (and much Catholic) thought has grown suspect in the eyes of many government officials. Despite changes in legislation directing that foreign aid serve the "poorest of the poor," liberation theology appeared to challenge government priorities at every point; it certainly undermined established notions of complementarity between private and public authorities. In an unprecedented action in the spring of 1983, Senator Jeremiah Denton of Alabama called Senate hearings to examine alleged ties between liberation theology and Soviet-influenced Marxism in the region, placing religious groups on notice that outspoken opposition to U.S. policies abroad could lead the government to make its own determinations of what was acceptable and unacceptable theology. The hearings were called because much Catholic and mainline Protestant voluntary action had moved from a complementary to a compensatory stance vis à vis U.S. foreign policy. In broad terms this stance disapproved of what Protestant leaders saw as the state's deviation from biblical standards of justice. Reflecting on this course of ecumenical Protestant thought in a 1967 book, ethicist Paul Ramsey suggested that what Protestants needed was "to return to Oxford and begin again."[26] At the very least this pattern of hostility toward the state had by the 1980s contributed to an unstable climate in the delivery of refugee assistance.

Conservative Protestantism: Evangelism over Politics?

Conservative Protestants in refugee work have never fully accepted the approach to mission that focused on the presence of Christ already present in the other. Christ's message remained something that must be taken from one person to the next. His message must be endlessly received, repeated, and renewed; it must frame relationships, business affairs, and the inner life. Jesus' commandment (in Matthew 28.18–20, often called by evangelicals "The Great Commandment") to spread the Gospel "to all nations, even to the ends of the earth" continued to determine the ethos of their involvement with refugees.

Perhaps the best means of understanding the relationship between evangelical theology and refugee work is from the perspective of those working in a given setting. Perhaps no current situation illustrates this so clearly as the efforts of evangelicals to coordinate their ministries to refugee camps in Thailand. From the early stages of the refugee influx in 1975 evangelical missions and agencies from the United States played a dominant role among private voluntary agencies. Twelve of fifteen voluntary agencies in Thailand in 1976 were of Christian origin; more than half of the twelve represented evangelical Protestants. The Committee for the Coordination of Services to Displaced Persons in Thailand (CCSDPT) was formed and led by this early group of agencies. In the early days monthly meetings of CCSDPT—held for the purpose of sharing information among private and public officials involved in refugee problems—were routinely opened with prayer.

There were always opponents to evangelism in the camps. It was claimed, with reason on occasion, that evangelicals were too aggressive; that evangelism took advantage of the disruption in the lives of the refugees, or showed disrespect for local custom and tradition. In some ways, however, the evangelism question only raised the broader one of the fate of the entire religious enterprise in refugee work. In the last analysis, the need for good manners and working relationships dictated that a claim of religious authority could not stand as the central sanction for a pluralistic effort such as CCSDPT. The same was undeniably true in the broader context of refugee aid. Religion was welcome in the effort, provided it did not try to fulfill its ancient role as the bearer of transcendent meaning and truth. Compared to this task, secular work in refugee camps was a limited and narrowly defined job. It is not unusual today to find employees in mainline Protestant, Catholic, and Jewish relief bodies who will insist that their refugee work "has nothing to do with religion."

Negative attitudes in governmental circles toward evangelism did not sit well with the Protestant agencies who had administered refugee programs in Thailand from the early days of the crisis. Even as the leaders of Christian agencies were joining with others to create CCSDPT in 1976, many Christian leaders were growing concerned about the future of Christian witness within the refugee camps. Though these conservative Christians willingly shared in the common tasks of the camps, from emptying garbage to administering camp hospitals, they retained a commitment to integrating social and spiritual ministries to refugees. In 1976 they formed an informal network specifically to address the religious situation they confronted in their refugee work. Meeting every three months, leaders of the major evangelical bodies sat down to discuss their common concerns for the refugees of Thailand. Their discussions did not center on the agenda of the UNHCR or on that of the Thai or U.S. governments. It was, without apology, an attempt by a self-proclaimed loyal remnant to frame their efforts in the camps in the light of the coming Kingdom of God. In the first seventeen months of the crisis, Christian missions and relief agencies provided $2 million of a total of $2.6 million spent on the refugee problem by voluntary agencies.[27] Thus it was with a real sense of achievement that they gathered in January 1977 to discuss their future plans.

Several groups formed the core of the Christian Ministries Seminar, as the meetings came to be known. CAMA Services, Inc., the relief arm of the Christian and Missionary Alliance (CAMA), was strong in the region because of longstanding CAMA missionary ties in Southeast Asia. World Relief, the relief arm of the National Association of Evangelicals, worked closely with the CAMA in Thailand. Overseas Missionary Fellowship had, until its expulsion from China, borne one of the most respected names in the world of faith missions, China Inland Mission. Though still hoping to return to China, OMF had since branched out to other countries in Southeast Asia and the Pacific. Thailand Baptist Mission, the

Southern Baptist missionary presence in the country, was also an early supporter of the gatherings. "While the pros and cons of the refugees' decision to flee made an interesting debate topic for some," wrote a leader of World Relief, "the actual presence of tens of thousands of destitute peoples presented an unmistakable call for action. Many heard the call."[28]

Many other Christian agencies joined in this effort to coordinate evangelical witness in the camps. Theirs was not a spirit of secrecy, but one of open confidence in their responsibility for Christian witness. When they encountered opposition, it was portrayed as wrong-headedness; the rightness of the path they had chosen was demonstrated in the joyous fruits of their labor. Said one:

> It must be honestly admitted that not all Christian organizations, missions and churches in Thailand looked with unanimous favour on the advisability and necessity of Christian ministry to Indochina refugees. . . . Nevertheless, many clearsighted individuals would not be dissuaded, and soon a number of missionaries, after years of hard work with limited response, were pleasantly surprised at the warm reception accorded them and their Message by refugees. Some began to devote much of their time to their new ministry.[29]

In the coming months and years much of the agenda of the Ministries Seminars would focus on the statistics for baptisms and church attendance in the refugee camps throughout Thailand. Numerous pamphlets for the curious and the converted ("The Glories of Grace," "Fleeing Error, Seeking Truth") were gradually made available to church leaders in the Lao, Khmer, and Vietnamese languages.

Church/state questions in all of this went largely unposed, even though the agencies routinely accepted U.S. government funds either directly or through UN bodies. Some religious agencies received direct grants from the government for their refugee work, grants which freed private funds for evangelistic and other directly Christian activities. During the first six months of the crisis in 1975, church agencies had dominated the relief efforts. When the UNHCR appeared in October, the operation became quasi-governmental, with church agencies relegated to "supplemental" tasks (improved medical and educational services). Logistical control and planning shifted to governmental and military circles. As in other refugee situations involving U.S. religious relief, church/state concerns lay below the surface.

From the government's side, simple pragmatism of the "don't fix it if it ain't broke" school dominated. Relief was reaching the refugee population, much of it administered by volunteers who did not appear on the government's payroll. Furthermore, the presence of Americans in the relief effort offered some additional leverage to the U.S. government as it became aware of the political implications of the refugee problem. By demonstrating spontaneous interest in refugee relief the private agencies unavoidably helped to place the Vietnamese government in a negative light.

The U.S. officials were happy to encourage American volunteers along the Thai borders with Laos, Cambodia, and Burma. Ignoring evangelism—even if it struck some participants as too strong a link between the government and the church—was a small price to pay to have workers friendly to U.S. policies in the camps. It would not be the U.S. government that would raise questions over evangelism. It was the evangelical agencies themselves that were eager to patrol their own ranks to weed out pressure tactics and abuses of trust in conjunction with evangelism. Prudent leaders among the evangelicals realized that continued free-dom to evangelize depended upon maintaining restraint and order. Easily carica-tured abuses (giving money in exchange for a pledge to convert, tying the provision of services to religious demands) were shunned publicly in order that more mature contacts could continue privately.

In 1982 serious difficulties arose when Seventh Day Adventist workers persis-tently offered refugees small sums of pocket money along with encouragement to seek salvation in the Seventh Day Adventist Church. Since the Adventists often made common cause with evangelical groups on other issues, evangelical leaders within the Ministries Seminars approached the workers in question to challenge their tactics. Only months earlier the Ministries Seminars had addressed the prob-lem of inappropriate evangelistic techniques. "Aid should not be used as a weapon to encourage a particular political allegiance, nor a particular religious allegiance," the agencies were told by one of their leaders. Nor should it be used "primarily as an excuse to evangelize."[30] Undeniably there were pitfalls built into nearly every effort to find a "clean" form of evangelism. If donated clothes from the United States were given to the leadership of a refugee church, refugees joined the church to get free clothing. In other situations refugees made professions of faith, knowing that Christian refugees, by virtue of their contact with workers in the voluntary agencies, were frequently among those resettled in the United States.

Yet the evangelism question persisted in UN circles; in 1982 a UN camp official sent a complaint to the UNHCR Bangkok office concerning unacceptable evangelis-tic activity. Participants acknowledged that difficulties included the Seventh Day Adventist technique of distributing pocket money to refugees in exchange for con-version. (Adventists, while not denying that money and other items were distrib-uted to refugees challenged this description of their work.) The dispute erupted into an ill-fated attempt by the UNHCR to prohibit evangelism in the camps, and evanglical leaders in the Ministries Seminars decided that it was time to confront the Adventists.

Protestant leadership today spends an inordinate amount of time denouncing other Protestant efforts at engaging the modern world. Many who have participated in these intra-Protestant disputes have learned the importance of pluralism and compromise in public debate. When pluralism is invoked to defend such essentially internecine feuds as doctrinal distinctions within evangelical theology, the intellec-tual ice can get a bit thin. Yet according to documentation from members of the Ministries Seminars, this was where they found the Adventists skating when they tried to raise the question of community standards in evangelism. The Adventist logic held that to "hide our differences and not teach our distinctives is demeaning to the intelligence of the refugees." This sounded more like the entrepreneurial flattery of a customer by a salesman than a solution to a pragmatic problem, namely, the coexistence of religious activities with nontheistic and and occasionally hostile perspectives in a refugee camp. By their actions and choices Adventist field personnel argued that one is free to promote one's beliefs by whatever means deemed necessary. This position did not facilitate discussion with UNHCR officials. It erroneously assumed total freedom in a situation that carried with it numerous built-in constraints. It was hardly surprising, then, that putting it into practice collided with other visions of authority in the camps.[31]

Much of the criticism of evangelistic activities came from staff attached to the

UNHCR. While the UN officers realized that they had no ultimate authority over the religious activities of voluntary agencies, they nonetheless had their preferences. Some were open to evangelism, but this was probably a minority view. Most UN professionals regard the overt presence of religion as an unprofessional intrusion on their work. Yet even those who voiced these objections were tolerant of Buddhist centers or Sunday mass; it was the stereotype of the aggressive American evangelical that pained these international civil servants.

By 1980 friction between the evangelical agencies and the United Nations sent leaders in the Ministries Seminars searching through UN documents for an accurate reading of what the United Nations really *did* believe about religion and religious freedom in the modern world. Several of the evangelical leaders decided it was time to remind the UN of its own ground rules. In the question of camp evangelism in Thailand, the agencies attempted to build their case on conformity to UN standards. They did so by reasserting the refugee's "right to human dignity, hope, freedom of conscience, and free access to ideas." Because the evangelicals supported this concern for the whole person, they affirmed their support "for freedom of conscience and religion for all refugees." These beliefs were then supported by the UN Universal Declaration of Human Rights of December 10, 1948. Article 19 of the declaration spoke specifically to their concerns:

> Everyone has the right to freedom of opinion and expression; this right includes freedom to hold opinions without interference and to seek, receive and impart information and ideas through any media and regardless of frontiers.[32]

To the church leaders, this meant that no religious position should be prescribed for refugees "by anyone exercising authority in the camps, even in the name of preserving national or cultural identity." According to the document they prepared, no pressure, whether direct or implied, "should be used to influence religious beliefs through the offer of special food, clothing, other material inducement, or opportunity to migrate to third countries. This militates against the sincere expression of belief which is the essence of true religion."[33] In a few words these Christians had summarized the ideals of their evangelical calling to share the word throughout the world. Verbal presentation of the Gospel would remain a key element in their vision of ministering to the whole person.

Critics of such evangelical engagement contend that a "narrow" theological focus on conversion blocked consideration of the political use that the U.S. government and others have made of evangelical agencies. It was clearly different from the approach taken by many of their mainline Protestant brethren. To the extent that it did not focus exclusively on evangelical converts, it was arguably within broad humanitarian standards. For many of these evangelicals theological reflection on relations with the state was unknown. Their theology and the enthusiasm it inspired was immediate and experiential. For a very different set of theological and pragmatic reasons, Catholics have traditionally arrived at a functionally similar stance toward the state.

Catholicism: "Marvelous and Manifold"

> Just as the symmetry of the human body is the result of the disposition of the members of the body, so in a State it is ordained by nature that these two classes

[church and state] should exist in harmony and agreement, and should, as it were, fit into one another, so as to maintain the equilibrium of the body politic. . . . Mutual agreement results in pleasantness and good order; perpetual conflict necessarily produces confusion and outrage. Now, in preventing such strife as this, and in making it impossible, the efficacy of Christianity is marvelous and manifold.[34]

Pope Leo XIII, 1891

Through the centuries as the Catholic church has sought (in Pope Leo's words) "harmony and agreement" with governments, it has never viewed itself as merely one constituent among many. As the eldest guardian of Christian faith, the Catholic church has divided the world into the City of God, governed on earth by the Catholic church, and the City of Man.

Refugees played a role in the formation of this doctrine, classically set forth by Augustine of Hippo in *The City of God*. In 410, Rome, the ordering force of the world Augustine had known, collapsed; Alaric the Goth sacked the Imperial City. Almost immediately wealthy Roman refugees began appearing in Hippo and other cities of North Africa. Their presence recalled for Augustine the status of Christian believers in this world. They were *peregrini,* resident aliens in a world turned from God, called perpetually to a certain "difference," yet recognizing the importance of their business here "within this common mortal life." Weaving together themes of mortal responsibilities in the midst of heavenly pilgrimage, *The City of God* is far from an escapist tract. It seeks to set forth the role of the Church, the new "consecrated commonwealth" of Israel, in a world of transition and tragedy.[35]

From Augustine to Leo XIII and since, the Catholic church has been an acknowledged master at relating to governments, first denouncing, then accommodating. Before World War II, Catholic sentiment in the United States was strongly isolationist. The war did not qualify as a "holy war" in part because the U.S. government, like all governments, was "founded on pride, rapine, perfidy, murder."[36] Yet once the war came, the church hierarchy adapted the more cooperative view enunciated by Pope Leo. During the war the Catholic church sought to prevent strife by rebuilding the proper "equilibrium" between the City of God and the City of Man. From World War II onward, a complementary approach to humanitarian cooperation with the U.S. government abroad has effectively carried the day in the Catholic hierarchy.

We can go so far as to say that in the United States, the Catholic view of cooperation with the state has shaped the postwar ethos of church/state cooperation in international humanitarianism. The Catholic church could accomplish any number of things that government or other religious bodies could not. Entire orders appeared in the nineteenth century devoted to aiding immigrants to the United States. The church provided education and lessons in democratic citizenship to millions of immigrants and their children. We have seen that government officials risked arousing anti-Catholic sentiments in 1943 in order to incorporate Catholic efforts into wartime humanitarian service. The church also offered diplomatic listening posts in every important capital and access to public opinion in dozens of nations; its announced purpose in these settings was to achieve harmony and mutual agreement among various parties. Such capacities, on a scale unmatched by Protestant or Jewish efforts, have made it possible for the Catholic church to suggest responses to international humanitarian problems that have been difficult for governments to refuse.

The Catholic church has been able to sustain good working relationships with the U.S. government in part through its traditional emphasis on acts of mercy (or, in terminology that has fallen into some disfavor, charity) toward the poor and the needy. In his 1979 homily at Yankee Stadium, Pope John Paul II used Jesus' parable of the Rich Man and Lazarus at the Gate to describe the relationship between the rich and the poor nations in today's world. In Luke 16.19–31, Lazarus, who has been a beggar outside the gate of the house of a rich man, dies and goes to dwell in the bosom of Abraham. Subsequently, the rich man dies and finds himself in a world of torments. Looking up, he sees Abraham far away in the distance embracing the beggar Lazarus. How could it be that Lazarus is blessed with heavenly rest and he is not? Such stories taught that in the divine economy, justice would truly be married with charity, confounding human standards and appearances. It is a story much beloved among Christians from today's poor developing nations, and it carries a striking message of hope for agencies such as Catholic Relief Services as well. Such stories, the pope told his audience, were not simply the fragile memories of a time long past; they are the very substance of Christian faith in the world today. A story such as Lazarus and the Rich Man, said the pope, "must always be present in our memory; it must form our conscience."[37] Within the Catholic church such parables have informed individual consciences and vast institutions alike.

While social service institutions fulfilled mandates of religious service, they also brought appreciation from government officials charged with meeting public tasks. In the late nineteenth century, Catholic hospitals were already receiving federal assistance for their work with the urban poor. The creation of the National Catholic War Council in 1917 and War Relief Services in 1943 provided vehicles for the refugee effort; both (we need only recall the long struggle over Catholic participation in early government-funded Indian mission programs) represented a new legitimation of Catholic participation in efforts to define and act on a national humanitarianism. The experience of Catholic institutions with the massive immigrant influx in the early part of the twentieth century, both in the United States and in Europe, also contributed to the relative ease with which services to refugees were expanded after the war.

The role of the Catholic establishment in this international effort, whether on behalf of refugees or others in need, has been framed primarily in terms of the political philosophy of subsidiarity to the state, rather than in the more Protestant framework of independence from the state. Religious freedom has for Catholics most often been a product of dialogue, of an effort to reach common principles (often spoken of as natural law) between church and state. A wall of separation between church and state has appeared to them to be an unnatural construction, both politically and theologically. Catholic theologian and cultural analyst Walter J. Ong has written that "New Testament prescriptions concerning the relationships between church and state . . . [have] nothing like the prescription purported to be enshrined in the long Indian name for the Connecticut lake which means 'You-fish-on-your-side-I-fish-on-my-side-nobody-fish-in-the-middle.' There is nothing said of 'territory' or 'areas' of sovereignty." Ong points out that in the New Testament religion and the state are both personalized—Christ and Caesar—and that their relationship will itself be the product of personal dialogue and relationships between both sides.[38] Such views are also congenial to the formation of broadly shared concepts such as humanitarianism.

The political philosophy of subsidiarity, promulgated by Pope Pius XI in the 1931 encyclical *Quadragesimo Anno,* provided a rationale for Catholic institutions to enter into a dialogue with modern governments that would lead to solid institutional relationships in expanding welfare states. Issued to commemorate the fortieth anniversary of Leo XIII's *Rerum Novarum, Quadragesimo Anno* sought to articulate a Catholic philosophy that would produce a moderate course between communism and unrestrained capitalism. Subsidiarity defined the proper relationship between church and state in that process. The essence of subsidiarity was that a larger institution (the state) should delegate to smaller or subsidiary institutions (the church and others) tasks which those lesser institutions were best suited to perform. Pius XI said this:

> It is an injustice, a grave evil and a disturbance of right order for a larger and higher organization to arrogate to itself functions which can be performed efficiently by smaller and lower bodies. This is a fundamental principle of social philosophy, unshaken and unchangeable, and it retains its full truth today. . . .
> Let those in power, therefore, be convinced that the more faithfully this principle be followed, and a graded hierarchical order exist between the various subsidiary organizations, the more excellent will be both the authority and the efficiency of the social organization as a whole and the happier and more prosperous the condition of the State.[39]

When the governments of Europe and the United States moved aggressively in the 1930s into welfare tasks traditionally fulfilled by the church, subsidiarity dictated a continuing strong role for religious institutions, if necessary by the use of government aid.

When the national Catholic hierarchy organized relief services during the world wars, it was making a significant departure from established Catholic mission practice. Foreign missions, as defined by a variety of papal statements, existed in order to establish the church.[40] This embraced the concept of saving souls, or making converts, but was not limited to this task. More fundamental was the existence of the church, its Word, its sacraments, its institutions, and its hierarchy. Once this internal, functioning core was in place, the conversion of men and women could proceed with confidence.

War Relief Services, because of its integration of religious and secular efforts, agreed to perform tasks that did not necessarily emphasize the primary nature of the church. This more limited mission focused on the provision of services to refugees and the needy and the support of similarly functioning Catholic institutions abroad. This is not to say that CRS or its predecessors abandoned distinctively religious tasks or that traditional orders or converts did not benefit by their participation in humanitarian refugee aid. The effort to combine religious and secular mission has understandably brought confusion to the ranks. In an extreme example, the director of CRS activities in Thailand in the early 1980s stated that "CRS is not a religious institution." CRS may have made formal agreements to eschew evangelism as defined by Elmer Gantry stereotypes, but its leaders through the years certainly would not have scorned the idea that the CRS was to emulate the role of the Good Samaritan. This is basic Catholic political philosophy, reflecting two key elements: a concern for maintenance of "right order" (fulfilled by a relationship of subsidiarity with the state) and a constant return to the life of the individual as the point of intersection of the interests of church and state. The image of the Good Samaritan, actively meeting individual needs, captures some elemental religious aspects of the church's interest in cooperation with the state. The fact that this provision of assistance under a Catholic banner has left many recipients open to Christian witness is still very much a part of the motivation for many within CRS.

In 1975 Pope Paul VI issued the encyclical *Evangelii Nuntiandi,* which set forth a full Catholic definition of evangelization. Along with emphasizing the content of the Christian faith, the pope stated that "it is primarily by her conduct and by her life that the Church will evangelize the world, in other words, by her living witness of fidelity to the Lord Jesus—the witness of poverty and detachment, of freedom in the face of the powers of the world, in short by the witness of sanctity." This sanctity must emerge in "the unceasing interplay of the Gospel and of man's concrete life, both personal and social." The message of evangelization is about "the rights and duties of every human being, about family life without which personal growth and development is hardly possible, about life in society, about international life, peace, justice and development."[41] This vision includes the works of mercy and justice carried out by American Catholics engaged in the problems facing refugees today.

For some years CRS has had to ask whether religiously grounded humanitarianism committed to cooperative ventures with the state can actively incorporate liberation theology perspectives. In the early 1960s thousands of Catholic priests and religious from the United States, working both through CRS and through local missions, were called forth for ministries in Latin America. They had the opportunity to view firsthand the miserable conditions of the poor and the accepted alliance between the Catholic church and the political and economic elites of the region. Many could see that the tradition of subsidiarity, so productive in the industrialized democracies, contributed in Latin America to the formation of a ruling triumvirate of the church, the military, and the aristocracy. Many were drawn to the emerging liberation theology, which, in line with various New Testament imperatives—the story of Lazarus and the Rich Man for one—explicitly sought to place God on the side of the poor rather than alongside entrenched elites. First formally acknowledged at a conference of Latin American bishops at Medillin, Colombia in 1969, liberation theology has since driven a wedge into Catholic church/state relations in both North and South America. Often using Marxist categories of analysis, it has on occasion blocked the efforts of church leaders at finding common ground with governmental authorities, replacing consensus with what has amounted to open confrontation.

The liberation style, with its emphasis on breaking the chains of oppression, of bringing "liberty to the captives," has clearly played a role in the work of Catholic Relief Services in Central America. By 1981 the accepted pattern of CRS following the U.S. government into areas of political turmoil was the subject of fierce debate among CRS staff in the region. The cooperative stance commonly described as subsidiarity or as the complementarity of church and state was still the norm pursued by CRS executives in New York and Washington, but it was increasingly unpopular with CRS affiliates, field staff, and local Catholic workers in the region. This was certainly true in the dispute over refugees on the Salvadoran-Honduran border. In Brazil, an executive of CARITAS, the international Catholic affiliate of CRS, wrote to CRS headquarters that the close ties between CRS and the U.S.

government would make it impossible for CARITAS to work with CRS in Brazil. Similar cries were being heard from local Catholic leaders in eastern Africa and elsewhere. In 1982, five of the six Central America country directors were removed because their political commitments were causing severe tensions with Washington and within the organization. This move eventually led to an investigation by the CRS board of the organization's ties to U.S. government policies and programs.

Refugee work had not, before the emergence of liberation theology, been the occasion for an open rift between church and government leaders. Catholic officials attending the Second Vatican Council in Rome (1962–65) had already reaffirmed the commitment of the church to refugees from social, political, and religious unrest.[42] It had been clear from established working relationships that the only approach that made sense was one in which the church functioned in a subsidiary role in what remained essentially a governmental-run operation. Yet the Second Vatican Council was also the source of a new Declaration on Religious Liberty, authored in large part by the American Jesuit John Courtney Murray. This document was strongly marked by American democratic values, notably the concept that government should be limited so as not to encroach "on the rightful freedom of the person and of associations." "Religious freedom . . . has to do with immunity from coercion in civil society," the declaration continued, and no religious body is "to be restrained from acting in accordance with its own beliefs, whether privately or publicly, whether alone or in association with others, *within due limits* [emphasis added]."[43]

Before the late 1960s Catholic refugee workers had had few occasions to test what was meant by "due limits." Theological analysis began to insist that any form of charity that did not have an equal or overbearing concern for justice at its core was suspect, a disguised means of maintaining the status quo. In 1984, writing on behalf of Pope John Paul II, Cardinal Casaroli attempted to clarify Catholic thought on this matter. There was no hesitation in reaffirming traditional Catholic commitment to aiding refugees. According to Casaroli,

> refugees appear to be the most stricken [of all suffering people]; for their very survival they depend completely on other people, strangers and unknown, even for the most elementary necessities of life: housing, clothing, acceptance.
>
> Christ the exile, obstructed, excluded, discriminated against, lacking even a stone on which to lay his head, begging, seems to live on today in the millions of · refugees.

As the personal representative of Christ on earth, the pope could not but be close to refugees and their plight. The cardinal quickly added his own "within due limits" clause; he made it clear that the church did not ultimately seek a role that could be described as revolutionary. Its assistance to refugees, while fulfilling Christian mandates of justice and charity, "obviously does not mean to contest or in any way deny the right of every civilized and ordered community to protect its own territory, to take proper measures to safeguard its legitimate national interests."[44]

At its core Casaroli's message reasserted subsidiarity as the desired ideal. The same has been true in more recent Vatican statements on liberation theology. On April 5, 1986, the pope again explicitly set forth subsidiarity as the proper context within which liberationist perspectives could receive official sanction.[45] In the last analysis such a perspective assures that the church will not contest the state on ultimate matters of sovereignty relating to refugees. This, it may be argued, is not so much a capitulation of the church to the state as a prudential judgment based on the desire to meet human needs while preserving and advancing existing standards of liberty. Liberation theology has taken a different approach to the church's relationship to the state; in common with certain threads of Protestantism it has focused precisely on this contest of ultimate sovereignty. This has sometimes meant standing in judgment of the state, but it has also meant an intensified search for the presence of a transcendent spiritual kingdom existing in this world beyond the boundaries of the nation-state.

The postwar era has seen both contraction and expansion of theologically grounded challenges to state policy in refugee matters. Within this period, religious agencies have gone through similar transitions in assessing their role in wider humanitarian concerns. In a sense the "three faiths" approach to religious participation in public policy dating from World War I was a means of expressing the way Protestants, Catholics, and Jews shared "one faith": faith in the public and global goals of the United States and their role in those goals. The language of humanitarianism remains a means of expressing this faith in secular terms that can be readily accepted by a secular government. A philosophy and functioning moral core of humanitarianism is still central to any cooperative project between the private sector and the government in foreign policy.

The expansion of secular private relief has brought the practice of secular humanitarianism to the fore. This has not eliminated the presence of theological motivations in refugee work. The post-Vietnam era has seen a resurgence of openly theological distinctions within religious agencies, posing a new sort of challenge to a "three faiths" approach to humanitarianism. Whether the specific matter is advocacy for refugees in the face of perceived governmental indifference or hostility, or the role of direct religious evangelism in the context of a wider secular and pluralistic context, issues of religious freedom have been revived in the conduct of U.S.-based humanitarianism. The question that must now be answered is whether domestic approaches to religious freedom have a bearing on the relations between U.S. citizens working abroad and officials of the U.S. government charged with carrying out foreign policy.

12

The Courts and Religious
Free Exercise Abroad

Questions of religious freedom pervade international refugee assistance. The First Amendment's free exercise clause does not guarantee unlimited religious freedom for U.S. citizens; rather, in concert with the establishment clause, it announces the existence of a sphere of religiously motivated actions that remains independent of government authority. The primary vehicle of this freedom is the prohibition against government establishment of a particular religion or of religion in general. American participation in international humanitarian relief owes a serious debt both to the independent, voluntaristic sphere of action defended from government encroachment in the Bill of Rights and to the Constitution's refusal to sanction a "special relationship" between a particular religious body and the state. The dimensions and shape of this voluntary sphere in U.S. foreign policy have been debated by refugee proponents and others throughout the postwar period.

Religious freedom has not been among the limited set of Bill of Rights guarantees upheld when questions arise about the actions of U.S. government officials toward U.S. citizens abroad. Only one directly applicable case has come before the courts; in it the court upheld the government's right to limit the flow of religious relief funds sent to North Vietnam during the war.[1] In the history of refugee work overseas, religious freedom abroad has not been accorded the central role that it has in our domestic cultural and legal traditions. Perhaps the potential conflict of ultimate sovereignties is too great. The government is not eager to provoke confrontation on the topic of religious freedom; when religious freedom is yoked with foreign affairs, the reluctance of the courts to intervene is understandable.

How might the courts go about approaching the question of religious freedom abroad? Consider first the hypothetical case of a religious agency that was interested in assisting refugees from Chile after the 1973 fall of the Marxist government of Salvadore Allende, and found various avenues of assistance blocked. At that time, thousands of supporters of Allende fled Chile to Spain, Argentina, and other Latin nations. This refugee movement received only very limited assistance from the U.S. government and the UNHCR. The United States had disapproved of the Allende government, and had no intention of assisting Allende partisans in their search for asylum abroad. Therefore, the United States did not fund UNHCR help for these refugees; it would not issue export licenses or provide any direct funding to the religious agency interested in giving assistance. But because the U.S. government is, after all, in the business of supporting refugees around the world and commonly uses religious agencies to provide relief and assistance, was the right of the members of the refugee relief agency to practice their religion by aiding Chilean refugees violated by a political decision of the government?

A quick and simple answer is no. If such a charge were admitted to a court, the court might argue that since there are many other opportunities to help refugees, the government's decision to restrict its assistance to certain refugees does not constitute a substantial infringement of the religious freedom of members of the relief agency. Even though some agencies were concerned about the lack of U.S. interest in Chilean refugees in the 1970s—or Haitian, Salvadoran, or Guatemalan refugees in the 1980s—the agencies themselves have hesitated to bring free exercise claims to the courts. Aside from the basic confusion about the applicability of U.S. law to the relations of U.S. citizens and their government outside the territorial United States, the independence of such agencies has been compromised to some extent by the fact that they receive financial assistance and political protection from the government in their work abroad. Taking such claims to court would constitute "biting the hand that feeds you" and would not be looked upon lightly in Washington. Even those agencies that for the sake of their own independence have been the most cautious about accepting funds have been extremely reluctant even to introduce the language of free exercise of religion into their relationships with the federal government overseas.[2]

This is not to say that the questions will never be posed. Federal prosecutors handling the government's case in 1985 against the sanctuary movement convinced the U.S. District Court in Phoenix, Arizona, to limit testimony to the facts of the case (in their view, whether or not participants in the sanctuary movement had broken immigration laws) and to exclude testimony based on the religious motivations of participants or on their analysis of the "immoral" nature of U.S. policy in Central America.[3] Thus, religiously based activism does not (at least in the eyes of the government's lawyers) today enjoy notable protection under the free exercise clause.

We therefore begin our analysis of the role of the free exercise clause in church/state matters abroad with a brief look at the history of the way it has been interpreted and applied domestically by the Supreme Court. The process has varied since the earliest cases involving Mormon polygamy. The current method is a balancing test, weighing state interests against the claimed infringement of religious freedom. When possible courts have used less sensitive grounds than religious free exercise for settling disputes. If the prosecution of workers in the sanctuary movement is any indication, the government may simply seek to disallow arguments based on religious motivation and focus narrowly on statutory violations. Such a strategy could backfire, revealing the inability of the government to tolerate religiously grounded dissent from its policies.

Traditional Legal Approaches to Religious Freedom

New religious movements and sects through the years have taken advantage of the First Amendment protections and their appeals to the Supreme Court have framed a good deal of our interpretations of the free exercise clause. This was true of the Mormons in the late nineteenth century, the Jehovah's Witnesses in the 1940s, and adherents of a variety of sects in the 1970s and 1980s. The question of the free exercise of religion did not reach the Supreme Court until 1878. As we have seen from the early debates about church participation in schools run by the government in the Indian Nations, the 1870s were a period of concern among Catholics and Protestants over the legality and fairness of church ties to the government. The 1878 case *Reynolds* v. *United States* set the freedom of Mormons to adopt polygamy in Utah against the right of the government to define limits of religious practice. The *Reynolds* court cited Thomas Jefferson's "wall of separation" letter to the Danbury Baptists as an "authoritative declaration" of the scope of both religion clauses. Because of this wall, "Congress was deprived of all legislative power over mere opinion, but was left free to reach [its authority over religiously grounded] actions which were in violation of social duties or subversive of good order."[4]

The Court, in other words, was stating its prerogative to limit religious actions that seriously challenged the existing social order. It did so by using an analysis that left individuals free to believe anything they desired ("mere opinion") but left the state in active control over religiously inspired action. Taken at face value, this analysis could effectively destroy religious freedom, confining it merely to personally held beliefs, perhaps only to those beliefs that have no demonstrable social consequences. In retrospect, the belief/action dichotomy in the Mormon cases can be faulted on further grounds.[5] Since the decision explicitly affirmed conventional morality over the rights of a minority, it left the Court free to limit the free exercise of minority groups (or even that of the majority, should their actions be subversive of "good order"). Furthermore, since *Reynolds* was not concerned with the role of religion in promoting social change—its holding specifically supports then-current understandings of the desirability of monogamy—it holds within it the basis for expanding governmental limitations on the active practice of religion should it become too troublesome.

Statements deploring injustice to refugees, to the domestic poor, and in the developing world are much in evidence in religious bodies today. Religious workers ought to recall that precedents for governmental limits on their freedom date back at least to Cherokee cases of the early 1830s, when the executive branch simply disregarded Supreme Court rulings that supported the efforts of missionaries attempting to block military efforts to relocate the Indians. As he ordered troops to move the Indians President Jackson's response to the Court's Cherokee decisions was simple: "[Chief Justice] John Marshall has made his decision; now let him enforce it." The precariousness of religiously grounded adversarial activity under U.S. law becomes even more obvious when we realize that the belief/action test of religious free exercise has never been repudiated; it has merely been joined by several other methods of testing the legality of various statutes.

For nearly fifty years after the last Mormon case the Supreme Court did not directly address questions of religious liberty. When it did, in 1940, it was the Jehovah's Witnesses who turned to the courts for protection of their religious liberty. The landmark case *Cantwell* v. *Connecticut* reaffirmed the belief/action distinction ("The [freedom to believe] is absolute, but, in the nature of things, [freedom to act on religious belief] cannot be") but added a second standard for limiting free exercise, the existence of a "clear and present danger" to society from the acts in question. Such dangers were defined as "immediate threats to public safety, peace or order," categories broad enough that they could be invoked in any number of instances involving perceived threats to the conduct of the nation's foreign policy.[6]

As the entire world was being enveloped by the conflicts of the Second World War, the Supreme Court continued to hear a number of cases arising from the conduct of Jehovah's Witnesses. In two different kinds of cases—concerning the freedom of Witnesses and their children to refuse to salute the flag and the legality of local taxes levied on the distribution of religious materials—the Court registered verdicts that would subsequently be reversed. In the first flag salute case in 1940, the Court ruled that the children of Jehovah's Witnesses were not exempt from the local board of education's requirement for saluting the flag during school hours.[7] Justice Frankfurter, in what might be read as a judicial response to the unsettled political situation in Europe, cast the salute to the flag in the context of promoting national security. "National unity is the basis of national security," he wrote, and safeguarding that unity took precedence, in the Court's judgment, to unbounded freedom to follow one's conscience in matters of religion. Justice Frankfurter wrote that the school board's requirement for saluting the flag was "not aimed at the promotion or restriction of religious beliefs," but was "a manifestation of specific powers of government . . . essential to secure and maintain that orderly, tranquil and free society without which religious toleration itself is unattainable."[8] Jehovah's Witnesses were advised that like all Americans, they might from time to time be required to make "adjustments" in their practice to conform to their duties as citizens.

Within three years, the Supreme Court heard a virtually identical case and reversed its ruling, holding that "compulsory measures toward 'national unity' " were dangerous by their very nature. That verdict will continue to reverberate in contemporary conflicts between church and state abroad:

> As governmental pressure toward unity becomes greater, so strife becomes more bitter as to whose unity it shall be. Probably no deeper division of our people could proceed from any provocation than from finding it necessary to choose what doctrine and whose program public education officials shall compel youth to unite in embracing. . . . Those who begin coercive elimination of dissent soon find themselves exterminating dissenters. Compulsory unification of opinion achieves only the unanimity of the graveyard. . . . If there is any fixed star in our constitutional constellation, it is that no official, high or petty, can prescribe what shall be orthodox in politics, nationalism, religion, or other matters of opinion or force citizens to confess by word or act their faith therein. If there are any circumstances which permit an exception, they do not now occur to us.[9]

This defense of religion operating freely and without entanglement with the government is among the strongest in case law. Yet federal policy toward religious groups active in government policies abroad in the postwar period reflects the spirit of the former decision as well as the latter.

Furthermore, as the Court has done elsewhere, it used the second flag salute case to place religious freedom at the top of a domestic hierarchy of rights protected under the Bill of Rights.[10] Religious freedom has not to date appeared in the list of civil rights that courts have protected in the overseas contacts between U.S. citizens and their government. We might hope that religious freedom, when directly tested abroad, would be given comparably strong consideration as a protected right of American citizens. In practice, it appears that the distinction between belief and action has been the functional standard. When the U.S. refugee official told religious relief workers to "stick to the Lord's work" in the Salvadoran refugee camps in Honduras, he was implying the existence of a privatized zone of religious freedom in which only actions with no public consequences would be given freedom from governmental oversight or control.

We have noted the accepted wisdom that "due limits" on religious freedom expand during wartime. Yet the Supreme Court at the height of World War II not only extended religious freedom on the sensitive issue of saluting the flag, it also changed its mind about whether cities could restrict religious evangelism by imposing taxes or license fees. The second of the two evangelism cases produced the strongest language to date in defense of religious freedom. Outdoor itinerant evangelism, declared the Court, "occupies the same high estate under the First Amendment as do worship in the churches and preaching from the pulpits. It has the same claim to protection as the more orthodox and conventional exercises of religion." The justices also argued that governmental freedom to tax evangelistic activities would close the door on those evangelists who "do not have a full purse. Spreading religious beliefs in this ancient and honorable manner would thus be denied the needy." The Court emphasized that the minority status of evangelists was protected by the First Amendment:

> Plainly a community may not suppress, or the state tax, the dissemination of views because they are unpopular, annoying or distasteful. If that device were ever sanctioned, there would have been forged a ready instrument for the suppression of the faith which any minority cherishes but which does not happen to be in favor. That would be a complete repudiation of the philosophy of the Bill of Rights.[11]

Inherent in this reasoning is the logic of both religion clauses of the First Amendment. Minority freedoms are protected by limiting the right of government to impose judgments based on its estimate of the correctness of a given religion. Whether such standards might be directly applied in the defense, say, of evangelicals working in Thai refugee camps, remains an open question. Any standards that judged such evangelism more harshly than religious practices of other groups certainly could not withstand the logic of these early free exercise decisions.[12]

After the period of active consideration of free exercise claims during World War II, the Court turned to establishment issues and rarely directed its attention to free exercise questions until the 1960s. However, by the end of the war, interpretation of the constitutional doctrine of free exercise of religion had been transformed from a simplistic distinction between belief and action (in which the government was left holding all the power to determine when certain actions were appropriate) to a modified version of this doctrine, in which additional criteria (such as the presence of a "clear and present danger") were applied in setting the course for government limitations on actions inspired by religious belief. The Supreme Court justices of the 1940s leaned toward protecting the right of individuals to *act* on their religious beliefs. This paralleled developments in which religion moved out of the purely internal, personal realm and into public life, particularly in the field of legislatively and administratively sanctioned welfare services. These developments could be seen in the various involvements of religious agencies in the war effort, from the founding of the USO (originally a classic "three faiths" group formed to further the war effort) to the expansion of the military chaplaincy and religious involvement in overseas relief, refugee, and rehabilitation activities. Such developments were encouraged as normal expressions of support for a war widely deemed necessary for the survival of democratic government. Common sense, patriotism, and compassion dictated that religious groups support government efforts to win the war at home and abroad.

Religious Freedom in Three Keys

When Americans work overseas, their religious freedom is primarily controlled by the laws and practices of the foreign states in which they reside.[13] Our interest in examining religious freedom abroad is limited to transactions between American citizens overseas and the U.S. government. In the course of our inquiry at least three types of relationships between religious bodies and the government can be identified which test existing levels of religious freedom. The next step is to ask how the courts might test free exercise claims under each set of circumstances.

The first type of church/state pattern may be called independent relationships, in which religious bodies pursue their mission separately from government, looking occasionally to government services and support. Most missionary societies fall into this category. In the current mix of church/state relations abroad, contacts between the government and missionary societies probably come closest to fulfilling the Madisonian ideal of church and state independently operating in their respective spheres. For the most part, these societies and mission boards have not been directly active in refugee assistance and care. When they have been, it usually was through the temporary loan of field personnel to relief agencies. Missionaries themselves used to independent pursuit of their religious mission are often frustrated when they suddenly encounter U.S. government regulations and limitations.

While some may question the term "independent" in the face of missionary cooperation with government intelligence gathering, such cooperation is generally voluntary and incidental to normal mission activities. President Gerald Ford and CIA chief William Colby in 1976 refused to agree that the CIA would stop using missionaries as informants, arguing that this would inhibit the freedom of those Americans who out of patriotic commitment wanted to aid their government. In truth, voluntary assistance to the CIA by missionaries is one of the least important challenges to religious freedom abroad under the First Amendment, though its relevance to the local perception of missionary intentions is a matter best addressed by religious agencies themselves. Missionaries may want to consider how these contacts limit the independence of their mission work, but voluntary cooperation between missionaries and the Central Intelligence Agency is no more constitutionally offensive than religiously motivated testimony before Congress on matters of public concern.

A second type of involvement, cooperative relationships, generally (though not always) involves some degree of federal support for religious activities overseas. Contracts and grants with the U.S. government as well as contracts between religious agencies and UN bodies caring for refugees fall into this category. When federal assistance is involved, statutory limits will be imposed on religious freedom. For instance, the strong defense of freedom to pursue evangelistic activities found in Supreme Court decisions is irrelevant in contexts where the government is paying for the services of a religious agency. Once a strict interpretation of protections against establishment have been set aside (as in current federal funding of religious agencies in welfare and refugee assistance), so must protections of free exercise be loosened. Government is by law compelled to protect religious freedom, but it is under no compulsion to fund free exercise of religion by individuals or agencies.[14] The focus of contracts between religious agencies and the government is neither establishment nor free exercise, but on the terms of completing a carefully bounded service or set of tasks in the public interest.

The third type of involvement between church and state abroad affecting religious freedom consists of the efforts of religious bodies to act in opposition to the government, or to set standards for religiously motivated actions that overreach or transcend the actions of government. Such "overreaching" of government standards was common in Jewish efforts to aid refugees during and immediately after World War II. It is occurring today in the open protests and activities of some religious groups working with Central American refugees. In such cases conflict between church and state over foreign affairs should not be automatically avoided. Private agencies have on occasion taken the first courageous steps down a road that eventually helped define subsequent government policy. For instance, religious attempts to transcend and redirect government policy were very much in evidence when agencies working in Southeast Asia began to help boat people leave Vietnam in the 1970s. Religious agencies may also exert unwelcome pressures on government. In the Sudan, U.S. government personnel commonly complained about the domestic pressures exerted by Jewish groups eager to see greater U.S. support for the movement of Falasha out of Ethiopia. Such alternative or opposition policies may emerge in agencies that operate independently of government or in those that operate with federal grants or contracts.

The unsettling precedents of the Cherokee cases of the 1830s and today's intense judicial debate over the jurisdiction of the court system outside the territorial limits of the United States expose the weakness of the courts in resolving conflicts between civil liberties and governmental authority in foreign affairs.[15] Were the courts to intervene in contemporary religious challenges to the authority of the state overseas, they would have the legal tools at hand to limit religious freedom sharply. This could be done through a variation of the belief/action distinction or under such rubrics as "clear and present danger," "national security," or "compelling state interests." Whether a court would have similar powers to extend the religious freedom of Americans overseas is another question.

In recent years the Supreme Court has developed a balancing test for reaching decisions on free exercise claims. Although earlier standards have not been discarded, the movement toward "benevolent neutrality" as a proper description of the state's position toward religion has necessitated further advances in the logic of free exercise decisions.[16] The resulting balancing test requires that the courts pursue two separate steps in analyzing free exercise claims. The first step is to weed out cases not properly dealt with under the religion clauses. For a particular case to merit consideration, three questions must receive an affirmative answer: Is the belief motivating the action religious? Is the belief sincerely held? Will the government regulation in question "substantially infringe" the exercise of religion by the claimant?[17] If the answer to any one of the three is no, the government regulation stands. If the answer to each question is yes, the court then attempts to balance the free exercise claim against the government's purpose in its regulation.

Since tests such as this one are distilled from lengthy court decisions rather than systematically expounded as a set of requirements might be in the Federal Code of Regulations, their application varies with the particular circumstances of a case. Whether or not the court applies the full balancing test depends upon the depth of the challenge to the government's interest. If the challenge is a serious one to paramount interests of the state, the test will be applied with full force.[18] When the interest challenged is less important, courts have been less rigorous.[19] We may safely assume that any free exercise challenge that infringes on issues of national security or upon the government's right to conduct foreign policy will come under the full weight of existing law.

Three Potential Court Responses

How would the courts deal with a free exercise claim today in any of the three types of church/state relationships just discussed? Missionary boards and societies that have no institutional or contractual ties to the U.S. government obviously hold the strongest legal ground in bringing free exercise claims against particular governmental regulations, provided that their activities do not substantially entangle them with government in other ways. Since these societies are incorporated to fulfill a specifically religious mission, the motivation of their members must be assumed to be religious; there is little likelihood that they would travel abroad if such motivation were not sincere. However, the government has attempted to distinguish religious action from political action, holding the latter subject to prosecution.[20]

As with the other types of religious agencies active abroad, the question of substantial infringement of religious free exercise of mission societies may turn on the interpretation of regulations governing the responsibilities of government officials toward U.S. citizens residing abroad. It is not uncommon for U.S. officials to warn missionaries to consider leaving a region in which political upheavals appear likely; embassy personnel on occasion advise missionaries to refrain from evangelistic activities because of potential political repercussions. If it could be proved that certain missionary societies were denied visas to a given country as a result of collusion between U.S. and foreign officials, or that passports were denied to members of some societies and not to members of others (as happened during the early 1950s), there would be cause for concern about substantial infringement of religious freedom.[21] An illustrative case arose during the Carter administration concerning the right of a religious radio station to broadcast in a politically sensitive area of southern Lebanon.[22]

For agencies that accept governmental support, direct or indirect, the question of religious freedom has particular boundaries. This has been true since the earliest compromises in strict interpretations of the separation mandated by the establishment clause brought the need for the government to circumscribe free exercise. Recall the 1912 controversy over whether Catholic religious who taught in government-funded schools on Indian reservations would be allowed to wear religious garb and insignia while in the classroom. At that time opponents of religious garb in classrooms argued that the practice could easily identify the power and prestige of the state with a particular religious body. This administrative decision has not functioned as a firm precedent. Many relief workers abroad during and after World War II wore governmental uniforms identified with the insignia of their own private agency; Catholic nuns and priests wearing religious garb have at various times routinely handed out Food for Peace supplies to refugees and others in need. The question has been raised by other religious groups concerned over governmental identification overseas with the Catholic church, but no case concerning this matter has ever reached the courts. Presumably, it is seen as a matter of whether or not the Catholic church through its relief agencies fulfills the terms of its contractual obligations with the government rather than a matter of religious freedom.

In 1981 the State Department's Bureau of Refugee Programs published contractual guidelines stating that "none of the funds made available to the Grantee under this agreement may be used for the purpose of proselytism."[23] Is this an illegitimate infringement of the free exercise rights of an agency contracting with the government? If so, the agency is under no compulsion to sign the contract. However, once they do, it could be argued that they are forswearing explicit religious witness in any operations connected with the government contract. The point here is simple: once the pattern of absolute separation of church and state has been altered by cooperation in social welfare, restrictions on the scope and nature of religious mission are inevitable, and government is entirely within its rights in restricting the use of funds or supplies for activities that advance religion. To put it in the context of the Supreme Court's free exercise test, the contractual limitation against proselytizing does not amount to a "substantial infringement" of the free exercise of a grantee. Since the agency is presumably free to carry on its work elsewhere without the government's funding, a court would probably rule that the limit imposed on their exercise of religion is incidental.

Financial cooperation between religious bodies and the government inevitably results in a loss of religious freedom; such is the dialectic between the religion clauses as they have been interpreted in the twentieth century. Religious institutions are allowed to expand through such funding arrangements but their specifically and distinctively religious functions are then restricted by law. Religious bodies have been required to establish separately incorporated "secular" arms, but as we have seen, this has often been a paper adjustment and never really empties the agencies of their religious motivations, goals, and practices. We will return to the adequacy of these arrangements in the next chapter. Yet implicit in the postwar church/state relationship abroad is the willingness of religious institutions to pursue public goals as defined by governments. This is the contractual dilemma faced by all religious groups that assist refugees.

Three factors weigh against an entirely negative assessment of this limitation of religious freedom. First, the possibility exists that religious bodies can accept federal assistance while still maintaining religious activities. Several agencies have made serious efforts to differentiate their governmental and private funding, and have proceeded to conduct religious worship, teaching, and evangelism on private time and with private resources. Second, the role of the United Nations as a middleman for U.S. funds, while not totally eliminating U.S. control, has served as a buffer. Religious groups such as the Baptists, who normally insist on a strict separation between church and state, are much less resistant to accepting federal funds when they are laundered through the UN system. This situation has helped create a community of support and shared interests between the UN agencies and private voluntary agencies. Finally, all private voluntary agencies active abroad, religious and secular, argue that accepting federal dollars puts them in a position to actively influence U.S. policies. This is certainly true in the case of U.S. refugee assistance; without the active pressure and involvement of religion, the current system of refugee care and resettlement would never have come into existence. The problems arise, as in so many other dilemmas that face us today, only when short-term gains in assisting human beings are measured against the long-term effects on the relationships that exist between institutions.

The final instance considered here, in which religiously motivated individuals or institutions (working independently or cooperatively with government) test their freedom to overreach, transcend, or oppose government policies, may well become the most heated topic involving church and state abroad in coming years. Such confrontational situations could compel the government to exercise restrictive authority (beyond that authorized in contract or grant agreements) over religiously based activity. In some instances, the restrictions may originate in personal animosity between government and private officials, such as that between State Department officials and Jewish leaders during World War II. If the uses and misuses of governmental authority over American religious groups abroad are addressed through the court system, the standards that the courts have developed over the years—the belief/action distinction, the existence of a "clear and present danger" or "compelling state interests," and the current free exercise balancing test—together with the considerations inherent in the conduct of foreign affairs and the pursuit of national security combine to form a powerful arsenal for limiting any behavior that is at odds with an administration's definition of the national interest.

The only existing precedent in case law supports the antipathy of the government toward religiously inspired initiatives that run counter to its policies abroad. In 1973, the courts upheld the U.S. Treasury's blocking of a $25 contribution an American Quaker had attempted to send in 1967 to a Canadian Friends organization that provided medical supplies to both North and South Vietnam. The Treasury invoked the 1917 Trading with the Enemy Act; the plaintiff claimed that the government was thereby interfering with his religious freedom. But the appeals court ruled that blocking the check did not amount to a substantial infringement of religious free exercise, and the Treasury's ban on a private citizen's assistance to a state hostile to the United States was upheld as a "proper governmental purpose."[24]

Critical attitudes toward government refugee policies appeared in religious circles with the arrival of modern refugee problems in the 1930s. Continuing through World War II, the Mutual Security Act, and the early 1950s, religious agencies helping refugees have protested a variety of governmental decisions limiting humanitarian projects. Successful strategies have been carried out in a variety of ways: congressional testimony, court cases, mass protests, print advertisements. In particularly controversial matters agencies may simply encourage employees to pursue opposition privately. The personnel of several religious agencies in refugee care have been active in the sanctuary movement, providing expertise gained in their work both here and abroad. However, no agency engaged in contractual or grant agreements with the federal government is eager to be publicly associated with a movement so openly critical of administration policies. In such instances, prudence dictates that the prompting of religious conscience be channeled into the actions of individuals.

Religious Free Exercise and Government Pragmatism

The efforts of the courts to establish contemporary standards of religious free exercise have been uneven; more charitably, in the words of Chief Justice Warren Burger, courts have attempted to establish "play in the joints" so that both sides, church and state, might claim victories along the way.[25] Clearly, Judeo-Christian traditions alone provide ample grounds both for cooperating with government and for resisting state actions in refugee work. It is futile for governments, particularly the U.S. government, to believe that the simple imposition of pragmatic, political ends will snuff out commitments to refugees that have existed for millennia. We may hope that a spirit of compromise will continue to allow aid to refugees that meets the concerns of both religion and government.

Certain options, however, remain in the hands of government officials for controlling religiously grounded efforts that stray too far from an administration's priorities. Their use would represent a serious new challenge to religious freedom overseas. One in particular should be mentioned here, the revocation of the privileges of tax exemption and the government's refusal to permit certain religious agencies to participate in government-sponsored programs abroad. The government is capable of using the Internal Revenue Service (IRS) as a means of making its wishes known to private agencies that violate Internal Revenue Code regulations, stray too far from official policies, or pursue unorthodox political approaches. The IRS is also capable of placing its own interpretations upon its congressionally defined mandate. This interlocking field of administrative and legislative authority is a minefield that is drawing increasing attention from those concerned with religious freedom in America. Domestically, there is a growing history of cases challenging the not-for-profit tax exempt status of religious organizations.[26]

Traditionally, tax exemption has been considered a key element in efforts to keep church and state separate. Contemporary opponents of this view have argued that exemption represents the unconstitutional establishment of religion, giving favored status to religion. Supporters of tax exempt status for religious bodies have held that taxing churches would only lead to greater entanglement between government and religion that exists under current arrangements. They often cite Chief Justice John Marshall's trenchant observation that "the power to tax is the power to destroy" as the elemental proof that exemption is necessary not only to avoid establishment problems, but also to insure the continued free existence of religious institutions.[27]

The idea that government might use the power of taxation to limit or destroy particular religious groups' attempts to serve society may at first appear too cynical to entertain. Recent domestic case law, however, suggests that this scenario is not fanciful. The courts and the executive branch have set the stage for making a strong case against religious bodies acting in ways that vary substantially from administration policies. In a separate opinion in the 1983 case involving the tax exempt status of Bob Jones University, Justice Lewis F. Powell strongly objected to the Court's reasoning on just this point. "The Court asserts that an exempt organization must . . . not act in a manner 'affirmatively at odds with [the] declared position of the whole government.'" This, he explained, suggests that "the primary function of a tax-exempt organization is to act on behalf of the Government in carrying out governmentally approved policies . . . such a view . . . ignores the important role played by tax exemptions in encouraging diverse, indeed often sharply conflicting, activities and viewpoints." In this opinion Justice Powell found a ready audience among religious leaders disturbed over precisely the same points. Those who paid close attention to the decision realized that they were being told that their pursuit of covenant faithfulness or the Kingdom of God was acceptable only so far as it was not deemed to be "affirmatively at odds" with government policy.[28]

In this case the Court based its judgment on the university's conformity to agreed-upon public policy, paying relatively little attention to the more confrontational issue of religious freedom. On this point, the Court cited its earlier ruling that the state "may justify a limitation on religious liberty by showing that it is essential to accomplish an overriding governmental interest."[29] The same strategy would probably be applicable overseas: as we have already noted courts generally prefer to pass judgment on secondary matters rather than on primary First Amendment rights. Such avoidance of direct confrontations between church and state is only normal; there are enough differences between them that there is no need to look for more. But a strategy of avoiding the issue indefinitely may have unintended results: it may intensify the differences, or it may bury religious freedom under the weight of secondary restrictions.

Open public debates over the latitude government accorded for private voluntarism expose the slow and often painful efforts of modern democracies to reconcile internal differences.[30] It is conceivable that the government could in the future, either legislatively or through the courts, hold that tax exemption is available only to those agencies which administer programs that complement government policy. Under the terms of a 1950 presidential order still renewed annually, the United States is technically in a state of emergency regarding relations with the Soviet Union.[31] Under such circumstances the formulation of private, alternative, or compensatory approaches to foreign policy finds little support among government policymakers. As Justice William Brennan argued in the Pentagon Papers case, infringements of First Amendment rights once reserved for a time of war might now be extended to other situations.[32] The president might issue an executive order barring religious or other private relief outside the United States that did not support his foreign policy, or simply replace the efforts of private voluntarism with a single government-run humanitarian body. Furthermore, a redefinition of tax exemption as a government subsidy would make it easier for an administration to explicitly favor those agencies it believes will operate programs that advance its own objectives.

If the government chose to question the tax exempt status of a religious agency working abroad, a vast quantity of information is already at its disposal. Virtually all groups—missionary society or relief agency, financed entirely with private funds or assisted by government—fall under government scrutiny at some point. The statistics on private tax exempt agencies are stored by the IRS in an information system greatly expanded in recent years through the use of computers. The Internal Revenue Manual, the book of procedures used by employees of the IRS, explains the thirty-one descriptive categories applicable to tax exempt organizations. Though churches and their auxiliaries are not required to provide such information, many do so out of a desire to maintain (for the sake of their donors) a clear certification from the IRS as a nonprofit organization. The categories used to describe exempt organizations include

> A status code which indicates actual or potential deficiencies in the organization's tax exemption, a code indicating the amount of the organization's assets, a code for the organization's gross receipts as shown on its most recent return, and the year the most recent audit was conducted. One of the status codes indicates an intention by the Internal Revenue Service to conduct a pre-examination of a church which has never received a determination regarding its exempt status from the Service.[33]

One such code, the activity code, includes nine categories of religious activities, which differentiates "mission" and "missionary work" (is one more explicitly religious? Just what is the difference in the view of the IRS?). Under the category of "advocacy" there are thirty-five codes for topics such as anticommunism, pacifism and peace, separation of church and state, and racial issues. These data may be revised, according to the Internal Revenue Manual, "without the approval or consent of exempt organizations." "Thus," according to attorney Sharon Worthing Vaino, "there exists a fantastic system which is capable of keeping track of the tax-exempt organizations in the country with a particular ideological persuasion."[34]

In a dispute over whether a religious organization was too religious to receive federal assistance abroad, a government official stated that he was "inclined to the view that we should be guided more by the ultimate nature and usefulness and target of their overseas activities than the identities of those through whom the work is done."[35] This pragmatic attitude toward religious agencies on the part of government officials is common and perhaps justified: they are charged with executing policy, not examining the consciences of individual citizens or groups. Such attitudes through the years have allowed cooperation between the government and any number of agencies that incorporate religious activities in their overseas relief. With its emphasis on pragmatic results and relative indifference to motivation, this view has promoted the involvement of religious bodies in government-sponsored assistance. Yet it is a piece of political pragmatism nonetheless, not a serious effort at public moral dialogue over admittedly difficult terrain.

If motivation is of little or no significance, how could any actions claim religious warrant, thus falling under the protection of the free exercise clause? Supreme Court rulings have pressed for a limited definition of religion under the establishment clause, but the free exercise clause demands a broad definition of religion rooted in the freedom of the individual to act on religious motivations and beliefs. This judicial approach parallels the expanded definitions of religious mission used to explain the involvement of religious agencies in relief and development activities abroad. It is nonetheless at variance with the administrative and formal arrangements between the government and religious agencies, which currently demand, implicitly or explicitly, segregation of religious activities into a limited area. There is no way absolutely to segregate the religious and secular actions of a given individual or agency. To do so would require a governmental definition of religion, a course that the courts have perennially denied to state and federal officials. The

Court has held that government aid for religious institutions, even if it is earmarked for secular purposes, may not be allowed "when it flows to an institution in which religion is so pervasive that a substantial portion of its functions are subsumed in the religious mission."[36]

Yet when the religious motivations of individuals are held to be of little or no significance, their actions quickly take on a purely secular political appearance requiring an evaluation based only on their "usefulness" to government. To view religious agencies as tools for pragmatic ends can be exceedingly dangerous in complex political settings. In the Scopes evolution trial in 1927 Clarence Darrow affirmed the fundamental difference between the ends of religion and those of the state. "The realm of religion," he said, "is where knowledge leaves off, and where faith begins, and it never has needed the arm of the State for support, and wherever it has received it, it has harmed both the public and the religion that it would pretend to serve."[37] Darrow's concern was not fundamentally different from that of Madison: the role religious bodies might play as political factions. Under this aspect religion becomes merely another competing political force to be dealt with by government. To the extent, however, that religious agencies have sought shared humanitarian standards with each other and the government, they may have the grounds for transcending this impasse. We will return to this possibility in a later chapter.

At one level religion is a competing force in modern society; its claims must contend with those of the economy, the media, the environment, and countless other areas of human activity. Historians, religious scholars, and legal specialists have argued that the significance of the church/state question has declined with the emergence of other equally powerful private interests. Yet the church/state dichotomy remains central to the habits and laws of American democracy, in part because the development of theology is the search for truth about the human condition, and the democratic search for religious liberty is the most important and consistent effort in history to establish the goals of a free society. In an era when federal programs frequently attempt to limit the role of religious institutions to their practical utility in short-term policies, ignoring centuries of theological tradition and the parallel evolution of religious and humanitarian freedoms in democratic society is suicidal. Yet so also is the notion that a particular version of religious truth will ultimately conquer governmental efforts to order civil society. It is in the interest of all—particularly refugees, the living symptoms of political and religious "malfunction"—that cooperative efforts be made to order human freedom within a framework of law shared by both church and state.

13

Paying the Piper: The Role of Government Assistance

The idea that private agencies can maintain unfettered independence and also accept material and financial assistance from the U.S. government has been proven false in the experience of any number of religious agencies that work overseas. One by one each has had to face the reality that whoever pays the piper calls the tune. In one small example, a missionary agency, eager to receive assistance in the early 1980s for its efforts to transcribe heretofore unwritten African languages, used its separately incorporated "secular" arm as a funding channel for an Agency for International Development contract. The local AID official visited the project in Africa after six months for a routine inspection. On arrival, he asked his missionary hosts to store his beer in their refrigerator. It was not an item the missionaries normally stocked, and they expressed reluctance. "Don't you know the Golden Rule?" asked the AID inspector. "Doesn't it say 'He who has the gold makes the rules?'" The beer went into the refrigerator.

Today government assistance to church agencies covers refugee aid, famine and disaster relief, and development assistance. In using government funds as they have, have religious agencies active abroad violated the spirit of the establishment clause? Alternatively, has the government, by limiting its application of the establishment clause in such instances, made unlawful use of religious charity, turning it to political ends by distributing assistance inside a sphere that should ideally be considered religious or humanitarian? The history we have examined in this book points to a continual expansion of the use of government funds for overseas activities by religiously based agencies. This has not been a measured growth, but has developed by fits and starts governed by various political and historical factors.

Certain factors such as the ties of religious agencies to local populations or their knowledge of the region have caused the government to strengthen its foreign assistance ties with particular agencies. In the case of refugee movements this has on occasion been the sole determining criterion for establishing a funding relationship with the government. In 1982, for instance, the State Department gave a grant to Lalamba, a U.S. group that calls itself the world's smallest voluntary agency, to operate health services to Ethiopian refugees in eastern Sudan. Under normal circumstances (if they can be said to exist in refugee issues) Lalamba's unabashedly and pervasively Catholic character might have been a problem in a government contract. But given the health needs of the refugees and the political interest of the United States, Lalamba's religious purposes were treated as secondary.

During the 1940s the government justified aid to religious agencies on the grounds that they were the logical people to come to the aid of their coreligionists in Europe. It is now clear that such ties are no guarantee of governmental support when there are intervening political considerations. Simply because Christians are aiding Christian refugees along the border between El Salvador and Honduras, there are no bilateral grants forthcoming from the U.S. government to such agencies. At the insistence of Pakistan's Islamic government American religious agencies were initially excluded from direct governmental patronage on the scene of what was at the time the world's largest concentration of refugees.

The government's assessment of the feasibility of using religious or other private agencies overseas often depends on its reading of public opinion on foreign policy, religious issues, or domestic politics. Perhaps the most celebrated public furor over church/state funding ties in foreign aid came not over refugees, but at the time of the establishment of the Peace Corps. Despite the entire postwar history of church/state cooperation overseas, the initial planning of the Kennedy administration to use church bodies in the Peace Corps caught the attention of the press. Responding to initial press criticism, a staff memorandum on the church/state question argued that "aid to religion, if relatively minor and non-discriminatory, was generally accepted as a proper and appropriate government activity."[1]

Three days before scheduled congressional hearings on the subject in June 1961, the *New York Times* ran a major front-page article raising questions about church/state ties and the Peace Corps. Three days later the Washington *Post* editorialized:

> Generally speaking churches which sponsor welfare projects in other lands are basically interested in proselytizing regardless of how much emphasis is laid upon economic, social and educational aid. Will this underlying motive be changed when the Government begins to provide the funds?

The opinion of the press was nearly unanimous: the wall of separation between church and state was crumbling. The Chattanooga *Times* charged that using federal tax dollars for "church missionary operations" was merely an extension of President Kennedy's intention of providing federal dollars for church schools at home. The public outcry was in the end enough to overpower official government plans and the idea of using church agencies was scrapped (not because of "constitutional issues"; the decision was described as an "operating judgment" of the government).[2]

How Do Government Funds Limit Mission Activities?

In using government funds in overseas refugee work, religious agencies are not attacking the separation of church and state. Fundamentally, they are asserting the rightness of their participation in an international humanitarian effort, and agreeing that any such effort must be a joint undertaking of private and public authorities. There are institutional benefits and limitations that go along with this participation. For religious agencies, the limitations include restrictions on the explicitly religious character of activities associated with government-assisted relief and political limits rooted in federal priorities.

Two examples may suffice to illuminate these limits. As we have noted, contemporary funding procedures include contracts between the State Department and individual voluntary agencies. In 1981 the State Department's Bureau of Refugee Programs signed one such contract giving the Seventh Day Adventist World Service Organization (SAWSO) $750,000 for work among refugees along the Thai-Cambodian border. There was a clear secular—though political—objective shared by the State Department and SAWSO: strengthening access and services to forces loyal to Son Sann, one of three factions of the anti-Vietnamese coalition of Cambodian refugees living in the border camps (the other two were headed by Prince Sihanouk and Pol Pot). The SAWSO field workers took a strong partisan interest in Son Sann, hoping among other things that a future Cambodian government free of Vietnamese influence would be receptive to an Adventist missionary presence.

In the camps, the Adventists were also known for an aggressive brand of evangelism, scorned even by evangelical Protestants. The State Department felt such evangelism was best left out of government-funded refugee programs. Therefore, the contract the Adventists signed contained wording that incorporated the "no proselytism" language advanced in contractual guidelines in Washington that same year (see Chapter 11). In this step the government was addressing the religious rather than the secular purpose of SAWSO's presence in the camps.

An unspoken understanding exists between religious agencies and governmental officials in refugee work that evangelism activities should be discreet, but rarely had the issue been addressed directly in contracts. Can this contractual prohibition be read to apply to all proselytism? Does it mean that proselytism cannot even be a part of activities privately financed by SAWSO using personnel funded under the government grant? Whatever the answer to these questions, the "no proselytism" clause echoes a theme nearly as old as the republic itself, announced first in the Indian missions of the 1790s by Secretary of War Knox. If religious institutions are to work on projects involving a mixture of private and public funds, they must trim their sails: they must accommodate secular goals. The attitude of the government has been remarkably consistent on this point, yet individual administrations have always had difficulty enforcing this, particularly in our day. Many contemporary politicians in America and elsewhere have come to realize that attempts to suppress religious fervor can easily backfire.

It would be unfair to draw the conclusion that State Department or other government offices uniformly seek to suppress American religious activity abroad in favor of governmental goals. Equally common are government officials who conscientiously warn religious groups about the pressures they will face, either from the U.S. government or in the local setting abroad, when they accept funding. In a concurring opinion in the 1963 prayer cases, Justice Brennan wrote that

> it is not only the nonbeliever who fears the injection of sectarian doctrines and controversies into the civil polity, but in as high degree it is the devout believer who fears the secularization of a creed which becomes too deeply involved with and dependent upon the government. It has been rightly said of the history of the Establishment Clause that "our tradition of civil liberty rests not only on the

secularism of a Thomas Jefferson, but also on the fervent sectarianism . . . of a Roger Williams."[3]

Foreign service officers at home and abroad frequently exercise what is, in their judgment, prudent diplomacy in urging that Americans temporarily restrict sectarian religious activities in sensitive political settings. Such officers believe they are doing their job in pursuing the best interests of American foreign policy. But does such a prohibition on proselytism as that in the SAWSO contract exhibit an unacceptable degree of "interference with religion"? Many observers of and participants in American religion would say it does, though this fact notably failed to keep either party from signing the contract. If it has become a routine part of government practice, dozens of other such contracts with this provision have been signed by religious agencies in recent years.

It is frequently local issues of political standing or balance of power that determine the actions of the U.S. government abroad toward U.S. citizens, not domestic legal interpretations of the religion clauses of the Constitution. Church/state law played a very definite role in a refugee project of the Episcopal Presiding Bishop's Fund for World Relief in southern Sudan, a project financed almost entirely by the State Department. Again, as has often been the case, perceptions of U.S. law served as the backdrop for an administrative settlement of the conflict that arose rather than as the framework for a legal action. Church/state law functioned here something like a yardstick for measuring the terms of the settlement that was eventually reached.

The political capital of southern Sudan, Juba is predominantly black, predominantly Christian. As recently as 1972, Juba had been a stronghold of the Anyanya guerillas, a Christian-led movement that had marshaled the south in a seventeen-year civil war to resist Islamic rule and ultimately to achieve partition from the north. Animist tribes are still a sizable minority, but Christianity is the predominant cultural glue for black southern Sudanese. It has not notably stirred southern politicians toward statesmanship, however; one provincial governmental arrangement after another has collapsed since the end of the civil war, frequently brought down by charges of buying influence and personal corruption. With material conditions pitifully stagnant after more than ten years of peace with Khartoum, any southern politician who defended the actions of General Nimeiry's government was likely to emerge wealthy but politically powerless.

In late August 1983, the final blow came as Nimeiry announced that the three-tiered Sudanese judicial system, containing elements of British colonial jurisprudence, common law, and Islamic *shari'a* would be scrapped, and *shari'a* would become the law of the land, including the south. Some observers read this as an understandable concession to the Gulf states of Saudi Arabia and Kuwait, both of which had been prominent supporters of General Nimeiry, but Christians in the south saw it as the last betrayal. The civil war began again in earnest.

A routine entry among "project countries" in the 1982 annual report of the Presiding Bishop's Fund for World Relief of the Episcopal Church indicated the church had spent $30,000 for "spiritual and material ministries" in southern Sudan. Officials of the fund had established working relationships with the Episcopal church of Sudan through its hierarchy in Juba, and resolved to pursue a much larger project together providing assistance to some of the roughly 150,000 Ugandan refugees then in the region. The project—increasing the fund's financial commitment to the region more than a hundredfold—grew from a $3.5 million contract with the Department of State's Bureau for Refugee Programs. Such grants have been a standard form of government cooperation with religious agencies abroad since the establishment of the U.S. Escapee Program in 1952. The fund itself began in 1938 as a separate relief agency within the Episcopal Church.

The Presiding Bishop's Fund was, then, in signing on with the U.S. government, treading ground that had been trodden by dozens of religious voluntary agencies over the decades. In such arrangements church groups routinely worked with their overseas affiliates. A supportive network of national church members undeniably lent credibility to projects negotiated on the other side of the globe; the existence of such networks meant that assistance would reach the refugees more quickly than if Westerners alone handled arrangements.

Continued influxes of Ugandan refugees were beginning to outstrip the efforts of the UNHCR suboffice in Juba. Raids by paramilitary forces loosely aligned with Ugandan President Milton Obote extended civil disruptions dating from the departure of Idi Amin in 1978, terrorizing tribes in the northwest of Uganda and sending many wounded and sick into involuntary flight to Sudan. For Rev. Samir Habiby, executive director of the Presiding Bishop's Fund, a project in the region represented a logical extension of existing cooperation between the Fund and numerous Anglican leaders of East Africa. Furthermore, the senior Anglican leader of Sudan, the archbishop of Juba, welcomed involvement of the American Episcopalians in his home see; a refugee project would demonstrate the active concern the church took in improving material conditions. The involvement made sense for other reasons as well; many of the Ugandan refugees were themselves Anglicans and many Sudanese Anglicans had sought asylum in Uganda in the 1960s and 1970s.

There were some drawbacks. Funding for refugee projects in southern Sudan was normally dispensed through the UNHCR; the UNHCR not only had no more funds, but did not work directly with the Presiding Bishop's Fund. The Fund had been active in a variety of development and relief activities abroad and had been a longtime participant in Church World Service, but they had no experience organizing and administering refugee camps. Despite some hesitation on the part of career refugee officials in the State Department, the opportunity in Juba looked tailormade to their superiors and to Episcopal officials: the local infrastructure of the Sudanese Anglicans, the regional offices of the Sudan Council of Churches, the American Episcopalians, the Anglicans among the refugees, and the U.S. government shared a commitment to addressing regional refugee problems.

In this optimistic spirit the Southern Sudan Refugee Assistance Project (SSRAP) got under way in early 1983. First duties for the new director included establishing contacts with the UNHCR. The UNHCR looks askance at such bilateral arrangements for refugee care; under administrative agreements with the government of Sudan, the UNHCR itself was in charge of all camps in the country. But to make a fuss would be to lose sight of the primary objective, improved care for the refugees in the region. The SSRAP director had little difficulty assuring UN officials that he wanted to work closely with them.

His other close contacts were formed with officials of the Anglican church and the Sudan Council of Churches. With the assistance of the archbishop, he sited the project headquarters just behind the stone Anglican cathedral, on land belonging to the church; as a sign of partnership, one of his first construction projects was a simple garden, a fenced area of brick paths and flowers, with a gazebo and hand-made wooden chairs that the bishop might use for receptions once SSRAP completed its three-year project.

One administrator of the Sudan Council of Churches was outspoken in his distrust of such arrangements. While foreigners routinely register with Khartoum in order to work in the country, he noted that the Sudanese churches themselves were in a much more precarious position, holding only a de facto legal status with the Khartoum government. Even more difficult for him was the effect of foreign government funding on church-based agencies. "Two things are clear: the government of Sudan will profit from these arrangements, not the church, and second, any evangelistic activity, in the case of the U.S. government, contravenes the terms of the contract," he said.

> This is far from the African idea of Christian mission. Many people believe that the church hierarchy is becoming secularized through its contact with churches and funding from the West. This contributes to discontent with the hierarchy; revival movements now break out, as groups ordain their own pastors. Take the refugee project, SSRAP. Many people will not accept the fact that the hierarchy has approved cooperation with a project not associated with the inner, evangelistic life of the church.[4]

In Juba, however, such issues were only a small part of what SSRAP's director faced in his first experience as a contractual agent of the U.S. government. The provisions of the contract had hardly registered with him; in his view he was there representing the Presiding Bishop's Fund, eager to establish cooperative links with the Episcopal church of the Sudan and to elevate Sudanese to administrative posts in the project. To him, the U.S. government had funded a $3.5 million experiment in cross-cultural service to refugees and to local Sudanese and left its administration to the Episcopal church. Within the course of a few months SSRAP had active programs in four refugee settlements, and even claimed to have significantly cut mortality rates by employing native medicine men as part of their health care program. Plans were in place for bringing in a specialist in solar technology who would teach the refugees how to manufacture solar water pumps.

Before 1983, the United States had not had a full-time refugee coordinator on the staff of its Khartoum embassy. The Reagan administration expanded its involvement with the country's refugee problem with several new voluntary agency projects in 1982—and this meant that an appointment was overdue. Named to the post was an AID official who had already spent six years in Sudan. Crossing the line from development aid to refugees made sense in his case; several of the new projects, such as irrigation systems and reforestation in eastern Sudan, were funded by AID. Nevertheless, though both refugee and aid agencies were associated with the State Department, their procedures and contracts were not identical. When the new government-appointed refugee coordinator visited SSRAP in May, he began calling attention to some of the differences.

On arriving at the project headquarters, he raised questions: Why were the project vehicles marked with Episcopal church of Sudan/SSRAP logos? Wasn't this a project of the U.S. government, not the Sudanese Episcopalians? How did SSRAP respond to charges that its hiring policies favoring Episcopal and other Christian workers violated nondiscriminatory hiring clauses in the contract? And why did SSRAP build the project headquarters and storage facilities on church land? All these questions implied that the separation of church and state had been directly violated. The U.S. refugee coordinator bluntly informed SSRAP that it had seriously misinterpreted its mandate under the contract. Logos would have to be removed, hiring practices changed. He advised SSRAP that pending a ruling on the question from the State Department, it would be wise to suspend all SSRAP operations, particularly any scheduled construction.

The SSRAP director had considered some of the issues in advance and in preliminary meetings with State Department officials had had a clause inserted in his contract vaguely incorporating an additional document stating that SSRAP expected to maintain a close working relationship with the Episcopal church of Sudan. He now discovered that the addendum had no legal standing. Ostensibly on church/state grounds, his project was being halted by the U.S. government. Some refugee professionals in the State Department had entertained reservations about the arrangement from the beginning, knowing full well the religious/political tensions that existed between the northerners and southerners in Sudan.

In Khartoum, where all foreign exchange and credits were carefully watched, the arrangement had a distinctly political dimension. There, the intention of the Presiding Bishop's Fund to work with the Episcopal church of Sudan and other Christian agencies such as the Sudan Council of Churches appeared to officials to be giving support to Christian leaders who were active in the nascent revolt against Muslim leadership. Khartoum officials had been informed in advance that ownership of the project's resources would revert to the Episcopal church of Sudan once the project ended. Nevertheless, the refugee project planned for the Juba region was, to the Nimeiry government, a bilateral agreement between the United States and the Democratic Republic of the Sudan. As such, Sudanese officials believed it belonged to Khartoum, not to the local infrastructure of Christians. Technically this was not true, but the principle remained the same to Sudanese officials. "We are not obligated to give special treatment to the church in Juba," said one official. "Anything built with this grant belongs to Khartoum."

In brief, amid some of the most severe interreligious tensions anywhere in Africa, the U.S. government had agreed to fund a Christian agency as its contractual agent to work in southern Sudan. When it became clear that the Khartoum government was unhappy over such a large sum finding its way into agencies tied to Christian churches in the south, the U.S. government was required to clarify the arrangements. To that end, domestic church/state issues were invoked on the grounds that use of government funds for church facilities (such as the bishop's garden) was illegal, and the project was administratively halted for several months while officials in Washington and Khartoum debated the outcome. Whether or not U.S. church/state standards were really the important question (Episcopal officials pointed out that buildings built overseas as part of U.S. government agreements with church agencies frequently reverted to local church officials once a project ended), church/state friction in Washington definitely came into play. Senior church and government officials in the United States were furious; the dispute in Juba "reached the highest levels of the State Department," according to a State Department official active in sorting out the eventual fallout. In the end, the project continued once consensus was reestablished between church and government authorities.

In Juba, it was just one more link in a chain of events that was driving black Christian leaders to join the resistance in military training camps in Ethiopia and in remote sections of southern Sudan. "The combination of U.S. Government funds with the anti-church stance of the Khartoum Government is a dramatization of the larger issues we face," said one church leader. "The church hierarchy is becoming secularized through such contacts with the west, and losing the support of the people. This only increases our local problems." A senior military official from the Anyanya movement agreed. "This agreement was negotiated with Khartoum, with no involvement of local officials. Here, because Khartoum seeks to Islamicize the south as well as exploit its vast oil and mineral resources, we face hard choices. When the United States sides against the Christians, and our people are being killed by the Muslims, if someone, even from Ethiopia or Libya, offers you a gun you will take it."

In the course of this controversy several things became clear. First, the U.S. government participated in the project primarily for its value as a political carrot with the Sudanese government. Domestic and foreign church connections were integral. Second, the standards of separation of church and state were applied as a means of accomplishing governmental ends, not as a means of protecting the church or maintaining standards of religious liberty. The State Department's sudden concern for the disposition of property in a contract with a religious agency could have had as much to do with internal disputes over the awarding of the contract within the State Department in Washington as it did with religious liberty or local politics in Sudan. Third, whether it was done for proper or improper motives, the halting of the project on church/state grounds shows again, from a slightly different angle, that the State Department's claim that the Constitution stops at the water's edge is not entirely accurate. Church/state law may be used for any number of purposes; when a particular situation overseas involves a sizable award of government funds, establishment problems are inevitably mixed with substantial political considerations.

The Triumph of Subsidiarity

To trace the growth of assistance to religious agencies we must understand the agencies' distinctive internal attitudes toward participation in government-funded programs. Decisions on the use of federal assistance often are rooted in specific Judeo-Christian and American attitudes toward the state. Church relief bodies have inherited traditional religious attitudes about the use of government assistance, and as we have seen these attitudes differ among Protestants, Catholics, and Jews, as well as the secular public. For the government, securing the appearance (and substance) of evenhandedness toward various religious groups has been a continual effort. Within the voluntary community, variations on the Catholic philosophy of subsidiarity have carried the day. Despite the persistence of more separatist views, some form of cooperation with the government, including the use of federal dollars, has been the postwar norm.

No political philosophy has more thoroughly rationalized church-based use of government aid than subsidiarity. This view has its critics both inside and outside the Catholic church, but it has forced the church's competitors in the provision of relief abroad either to seek government aid or to drift to the edges in the joint public/private relief effort of the last four decades. "If the money came from the Devil himself, it could still be used to help those in need," a New York official of Catholic Relief Services said recently.[5] Such openness to a variety of financial sources has been foundational in building CRS into the largest voluntary association in the world. Similarly, the Migration and Refugee Services of the U.S. Catholic Conference in Washington has achieved its preeminence in immigration and refugee resettlement services through effective use of governmental allowances based on the number of refugees and immigrants served.

These extensive efforts were not created ex nihilo by government funding, which was in many ways a response to the existing size and organizational scope of the Catholic church. In a paper prepared for a 1974 State Department seminar on the role of the Catholic church in U.S. foreign policy, a career foreign service officer noted that while the UN had 19,000 development experts around the world, and the U.S. government employed 12,000 U.S. citizens and Third World nationals in development programs, the Catholic church had 250,000 nuns and priests working as missionaries in underdeveloped areas. These statistics constitute the sort of temptation that "conjures up all kinds of visions" for government planners looking for ways to extend their programs. When the study's author added the realization that involvement of church personnel could only lend credence to John Kennedy's dictum that "we carried out a foreign aid program because it was *right,*" the future of church agencies as channels of government assistance appeared bright.[6]

Though many Protestant leaders would today profess disinterest in the question of the relative power of the Catholic church and Protestant churches in the United States, the entire period of state welfare services beginning in the 1930s has been accompanied by a current of anti-Catholicism, much of it directed against the growth of Catholic power through practices stemming from the philosophy of subsidiarity. In the 1940s and early 1950s Paul Blanshard and Protestants and Other Americans United for the Separation of Church and State (today shortened to "Americans United") launched numerous attacks against growing Catholic power in Washington. Almost none of this public domestic debate was directed toward government funding of religiously based relief abroad, but Protestants and others active in the field were well aware of the different perspectives on funding within the religious community. It was not that Protestants themselves refused power and assistance in Washington; they simply were unhappy, after years of unofficial Protestant hegemony in education, foreign policy, and other key areas, at the prospect of competing with Catholics on equal terms.

The Supreme Court decisions of 1947 and 1948 that appeared to prohibit any domestic government assistance to religion profoundly shocked the mainline Protestant leadership, who correctly saw Protestant as well as Catholic necks on the block. Opposition to the new separationism of the Court was added to the problems facing Protestants in their relations with the rest of American society. On the one hand, they predicted correctly that strict separationism would contribute to an increasingly privatized role for religion, assuring in the words of Theodore Roszak that it would become "privately engaging, if socially irrelevant."[7] On the other hand, while separationism appeared to address their concerns about growing Catholic power, it allowed for no Protestant "exception," formal or informal. The only major religious community pleased with the rulings were the Jews, who felt that a strong separationism protected them from oppression by the Christian majority.

By the 1950s Protestant leaders had justified the use of government resources with their own adaptations of subsidiarity, which focused on the limits church agencies should place on their use of federal aid. To some extent it was mere pragmatism; relief officials did not see the necessity of using hard-won private donations to pay for ocean freight expenses when such subsidies were readily available from the government. As noted in Chapter 5, Lutheran World Relief, the most conservative of the large Christian agencies on the funding issue, argued that an agency could accept no more than 50 percent of its resources from the government and still retain its independence. Church World Service placed the figure at 66 percent. Catholic Relief Services topped the other two by suggesting 75 percent as a reasonable figure.

Protestant leaders needed to maintain growth rates competitive with other agencies in the field (clearly impossible without government assistance) as well as answer critics within their own ranks who insisted on a traditional Protestant concern about ties with the state. After a long series of meetings, studies, and debates within the National Council of Churches, mainline Protestants eventually accepted a compromise position that allowed for government assistance to Church World Service in meeting emergency needs but declined aid on a "sustaining" basis. Considering that the agencies were themselves "sustained" by a continual series of international emergencies, whether refugee flows or other human disasters, the distinction was somewhat academic, but it served to meet criticisms from within the churches.

The Vietnam War intensified left-wing resistance to any form of direct identification with the foreign policy of the United States in both Catholic and Protestant circles, of which funding was the most direct. Resistance to the war policy was not limited to pacifist Protestant denominations, but included the National Council of Churches, Lutherans, and Catholics as well. Yet when the migration of boat people and other refugees from Vietnam began in 1975, most Americans, including many who had opposed the war, felt a strong desire to provide aid and asylum. Government funds were released under special legislative and executive action and inevitably found their way to the voluntary agencies. Today, Protestant agencies active with refugees abroad hold every conceivable opinion on the matter of government funding; the missionary and relief and development wings of Protestantism routinely debate the appropriateness of such aid. In both camps there are strict separationists, enthusiastic acceptors, and short-term emergency cooperators. In analyzing the effects of such positions, caution should be used in equating use of federal funds with subservience to government ends. Some of the agencies most likely to support U.S. policies abroad pursue the most stringent policies toward limiting the use of government funds.

This has been true of the recently formed Operation Blessing, the relief arm of the Christian Broadcasting Network, which is active in aiding refugee populations that supply manpower for the anti-Sandinista contras in Central America. The dean of the Christian Broadcasting Network University's School of Public Policy, Herbert Titus, in 1985 articulated a position that scorns religious cooperation with public welfare. "If any civil ruler attempts to use his taxing power to force people to care for the destitute, it invokes the coercive power of the state and destroys God's commandment to meet the needs of the poor out of love," wrote Dean Titus. "Love, to be love, requires that one give voluntarily without threat of legal liability, and that one receive unconditionally, without limit by legally-enforceable standards. State-enforced welfare or wealth distribution programs violate the law of God."[8] There could be little place for the use of government aid by groups committed to this vision. The alternative, practiced with some visible success by the Christian Broadcasting Network, is the collection of a biblical tithe. Yet even Operation Blessing with its emphasis on God's attention to refugee and relief needs in Central America has found it helpful to use U.S. military transportation for shipping its relief goods abroad, and its policies in bringing aid to Miskito Indian refugees have paralleled administration efforts to provide support for the contras.

Similarly, socially liberal denominations and church groups may find financial ties with the government expedient. In recent years the Episcopal church has, through the church's Presiding Bishop's Fund for World Relief, drawn close to the refugee interests of the Reagan administration. The pacifist Mennonite Central Committee accepts government funding as long as it believes such funds will not hinder the independence of their religious mandate. The World Council of Churches, among the most liberal of church bodies and known for its critical attitude toward U.S. approaches to the developing world, has maintained funding ties with the U.S. government since the mid-1940s for the purpose of assisting European refugees.

The evolution of evangelical Protestant thinking on the question of government funding has also been prodded by political factors, namely, the realization in the 1960s and 1970s that evangelical efforts were being outstripped by other agencies with fewer scruples concerning the use of federal dollars in their overseas projects. The National Association of Evangelicals' World Relief Commission maintained a small but effective program using Food for Peace and ocean freight reimbursements in the 1950s, but evangelicals were by and large not at that time ready for large-scale government programs that challenged the notion of separation of church and state. Postwar evangelical theology took a strong separationist stance, in the conviction that this policy—and its attendant disdain for the use of government resources—hewed to the core of civic virtue in church/state practice.

Evangelicals clung to this strong separatist vision in the context of overseas assistance much longer than their mainline Protestant brethren. World Vision began experimenting in earnest with government assistance in the early 1960s, but evangelicals did not become a significant factor in government-funded relief until the mid-1970s, the period coinciding with the post-Vietnam refugee flow. In 1975 the Seattle-based World Concern began a seven-year effort to register with AID (this may be contrasted with the experience of other religiously based agencies that the government deems desirable, which can be officially registered within a matter of days or weeks).[9] In the eyes of AID officials World Concern could not adequately demonstrate its ability to separate its secular from its religious mission. The registration struggles in the 1970s of World Concern and of the Summer Institute of Linguistics, the separately incorporated development wing of the Wycliffe Bible Translators, pointed to a new concern within the government over the use of federal funds by religious agencies.

Jewish agencies have pressed for strong governmental support for programs that assist Jewish refugees. To obtain a clear picture of the use of government funds by Jewish agencies serving refugees, one must consider two facts: the success of their private fund raising and the enormously increased burdens on the Jewish community since the establishment of Israel. These factors have affected the entire range of domestic and international Jewish philanthropy, but the refugee question has frequently been the most visible and contentious.

Throughout the twentieth century Jewish agencies have been successful in raising funds privately within Jewish communities. They built their own reputations in the early years of the century before structures of governmental assistance were in place. Tremendous fund-raising efforts characterized Jewish foreign assistance during World War I. Ten million dollars were raised for European and Middle Eastern Jewry in ten days in 1917; Cyrus Adler estimated that during the war he personally raised another $10 million in Philadelphia. Another $3.6 million in private U.S. funds went to Russian Jews during the famine of 1922–23; all of it came from a community that numbered only 500,000 at the time. In 1925–26 a $15 million campaign by the Joint Distribution Committee raised over $18 million.[10] Throughout the Depression years of the 1930s millions were raised privately every year for refugee relief and for the Jews in Palestine.

Before the establishment of Israel, support for Jewish needs was strong among national Protestant and Catholic leaders, but the government was often reluctant to identify itself with Jewish causes by providing aid to Jews. We may recall here the initial reluctance of Franklin Roosevelt to appear to support a "mere Jewish relief set-up," as well as the protracted opposition to refugee assistance and rescue efforts within the State Department during World War II. This put pressure on Jews to raise their own money for overseas relief. Limited Jewish participation in the National War Fund left the bulk of private Jewish fund raising independent of coordinated national efforts. War Fund officials were concerned that identification of Catholic or Jewish groups as recipients would inhibit giving by other Americans to the fund. While Jewish groups did participate in such wartime consortia as the United Service Organization for the armed forces, they concentrated their fund-raising efforts on Jewish causes.

When the Roosevelt administration finally established the War Refugee Board in 1944, it was largely in response to pressure from Jews and their allies in refugee advocacy. It was understood that apart from administrative responsibilities centered in Washington, the bulk of the activities would be carried out and financed by Jewish agencies. Although Jewish agencies attempted to convince War Refugee Board leaders that extensive government assistance would be required for the rescue operation, John Pehle, the director of the board, insisted that government funds be limited to those available through discretionary funds in the executive branch. "The last thing I think you want to do," he told his staff, "is go to Congress."[11] Actually, little more than $1 million in congressional war relief appropriations (out of a wartime total of $85 million) was quietly passed along to the War Refugee Board, along with $547,000 in presidential discretionary assistance. Jewish agencies themselves provided the bulk of the financing for the board's activities, some $16 million.

While Jewish fund raisers have continued to deliver a far higher level of per capita giving than their Protestant or Catholic counterparts, government funding of Jewish refugee movements has remained a feature of U.S. foreign policy.[12] With the development of a political rationale that Israeli vigilance and democracy based on a Jewish majority had become the cornerstone of geopolitical stability in the

Middle East, the maintenance of a flow of Jewish settlers to Israel has in the last decade taken on new political significance. That flow has regularly been supported by dollars from the U.S. government, much of it channeled through the Intergovernmental Committee for Migration.

This brings us to the second critical factor in Jewish attitudes about government funding of refugee matters: the establishment of Israel and the sudden opportunity of Jewish communities to fulfill the politico-religious mandate of the *aliyah*. The magnitude of the costs to resettle Jews from around the world in Israel has brought American Jewish leaders again and again to the Congress for funds in the postwar period. The use of federal appropriations to send Jews to Israel is unique. Other than indirect multilateral assistance through the UNHCR and ICM, the United States normally limits its financial commitments to third country refugee resettlement to those refugees coming to the United States itself.

It would be false to suggest that American Jews transferred their problems to the lap of the government. It is true that Israel and the international Jewish community grew increasingly dependent on the political prestige exerted by their U.S. supporters; this political factor has no doubt in the long run been more important than funding ties between the U.S. government and U.S. Jewish organizations aiding refugees. Furthermore, the generosity of American Jews to their fellow Jews abroad increased after the war. Oscar Handlin in his history of the Joint Distribution Committee caught the postwar mood of the Jewish community on the matter of international Jewish need: "The whole concept of overseas relief, as it had been known since 1914, required revision. Aid was no longer a form of charity but rather an obligation to rehabilitate in which costs did not count." Between 1946 and 1952, American Jews contributed $342 million to help resettle and rehabilitate Jewish war refugees and settlers in the new State of Israel.[13]

The movement of Jews to Israel has, like many other transfers of refugee populations, become deeply entwined with national security concerns. In the early years after the establishment of Israel the Jewish population grew rapidly, rising from 1.45 million in 1952 to 2.15 million in 1963.[14] Typically, U.S. government funds (channeled through ICM) were used to help finance the actual movement of Jews between their countries of origin and Israel. Resettlement and absorption expenses of Jews reaching Israel traditionally have been subsidized by congressionally mandated assistance to Israel.

The attention of American and Israeli Jews focused increasingly on the largest remaining concentration of Jews living under oppressive conditions: Soviet Jewry. In addition to their personal concerns for the safety of Soviet Jews, Israelis recognized that (aside from American Jews) the emigration of the Soviet community of between 2 million and 3 million Jews was the only remaining possibility for vastly increasing the Jewish population of Israel. Such a movement required the active support of the U.S. government. By 1970 paid advertisements such as the following became common in the *New York Times* and other publications:

WE, BY OUR SILENCE, DOOM THE SOVIET JEW. WE, BY OUR APATHY, SHED THIS BLOOD. We reject the respectability. We will do what must be done. We wish to shake the world and spotlight the Soviet Jewish problem so that the United States government will be forced to demand justice for people if the Soviets want Western friendship.[15]

William Orbach, author of a 1979 book *The American Movement to Aid Soviet Jews,* has stated that the issue of Soviet Jewish emigration joins diverse issues of morality and power: morality because it is right, and power because Israel needs the immigrants to diminish "the danger of its being overwhelmed by its numerically superior neighbors." The détente of the early 1970s provided the backdrop to intense Jewish pressures on Congress that eventually produced the Jackson-Vanik Amendment, tying U.S. trade to Soviet policy on increased emigration opportunities, an obvious reference to the Jewish community. The emigration of Soviet Jews declined in the mid-1970s, but jumped forward in 1979 when over 51,000 Soviet Jews were allowed to emigrate. In that year over 50 percent of the resettlement funds distributed by the State Department's Bureau of Refugee Programs to private agencies went to groups aiding Soviet Jews.[16]

Thus, despite pockets of resistance, within the various U.S. religious communities a general sense has emerged that the use of federal dollars and subventions is acceptable, even necessary in assisting refugees. Historically, the struggles of the Jewish leadership from the 1930s onward for increased attention to the plight of Jewish refugees—and their demonstrated competence in creating channels of providing assistance—led the way to the practice of aiding refugees by channeling government assistance through religiously affiliated groups. Politically, this has coincided with a basic support in Catholic circles for cooperation with government welfare programs. Leaders in the recent explosion of evangelical Protestant agencies, whether they receive government assistance or not, might be surprised to see the similarity between their stance and the traditional Catholic and Jewish perspectives. In the current political climate, the odd men out are that assortment of strict separationists, leftist critics, and theological liberationists who from their varying perspectives find government funding of religiously grounded activities abhorrent to the best interests of American democracy.

The Unavailable Figures

It must be said at the outset that only fragmentary information is available about the cumulative nature and extent of government assistance to religious agencies aiding refugees. Detailed State Department records from the early postwar years are frequently inaccessible; many agencies have either not adequately cataloged their archives or keep them closed to researchers. Some agencies are notoriously uninterested in making their current contract arrangements with the government public, perhaps with good reason. Furthermore, official summaries of government expenditures issued in Washington often do not contain records of grants or contracts issued to voluntary agencies through local embassies around the world; such funds do not necessarily appear in the budgets of the central office at home. It is also common for local AID and embassy missions to fund the activities of indigenous voluntary organizations. In some parts of the world, such as Africa and Latin America, the majority of such indigenous agencies have religious origins and motivations. These agencies are not required to meet the domestic registration requirements of AID, which involve a commitment to separation of religious and secular aspects of the agency's work.

Even within the Washington-based budget structures of the federal government, refugee allocations have widely varying sources and destinations, despite efforts to centralize programs through the State Department's Bureau of Refugee Programs. Development activity for refugees in Africa and elsewhere has been channeled through the Agency for International Development; in Central America Peace Corps volunteers—themselves overseas to provide development aid rather than relief—have been assigned to work alongside agencies providing short-term assistance. The Office of Foreign Disaster Assistance is responsible for funds that reach voluntary agencies working with Palestinian refugees, and the American Schools and Hospitals Abroad fund pays for yeshivas and other facilities for Jewish refugees in Israel. Resettlement agencies now aid refugees to find new homes in the United States through the Department of Health and Human Services. In addition, discretionary funds are available to the president for meeting refugee emergencies; their disbursement is not always recorded in the government's cumulative records of voluntary agency funding.

A similar set of accounting problems exists in tracing U.S. dollars spent through the UNHCR and other intergovernmental bodies. The auditing facilities of the UNHCR are far less developed than those of the U.S. government, and the UNHCR is always open to the possibility of donor abuse. In 1983, for instance, a major U.S. religious agency serving refugees in Thailand had no funds left even to pay its own administrative expenses. Calling on its extensive contacts in Washington, it arranged to have an additional $500,000 of federal funds earmarked for its Thailand program—and laundered through the UNHCR. Such practices are the exception rather than the rule, and officials involved perhaps should be given the benefit of the doubt. Complex international relief operations generate complex problems. But they illustrate the dangers of relying on official figures, private or governmental, for determining the extent of federal funding to the refugee efforts of different religious communities.

A 1983 General Accounting Office audit of the use of U.S. refugee funds in Africa stated that 95 percent of U.S. aid through the UNHCR was "untraceable."[17] "Why should American funds be traceable?" replied a UNHCR funding official when presented with this statistic.[18] One way of avoiding donor abuse is to avoid the practice of earmarking the funds of a particular government to voluntary agencies from the same country. While some voluntary agency leaders today bemoan the servitude of the UNHCR to U.S. foreign policy goals, they are often much happier using U.S. government money that has come to them through the UNHCR "laundry." Even Baptist leaders with their built-in instincts toward the separation of church and state have said that it is not the same thing for them to accept funds from the UNHCR as from the U.S. government.

In its 1946 survey of the displaced persons problem in Europe, the American Council of Voluntary Agencies stated that "the primary responsibility for the care and welfare of the displaced persons rests with government and military authority and the work of voluntary agencies is supplementary to this primary responsibility."[19] Relief supplies were available through UNRRA and the IRO, but the administration of voluntary agencies was financed by private contributions. Government assistance was directed toward foreign policy objectives in relief activities and toward enhancing the effectiveness of private funds, not toward sustaining private voluntarism itself. After the government's initial step in funding direct ocean freight costs in 1947, there remained a cautious attitude toward funding private agencies.

Under the Displaced Persons Act, for instance, Congress actually rejected an amendment that would have provided the agencies with direct grants for settling displaced persons permanently once they reached the United States. Congress instead authorized a loan fund which covered travel expenses, but required that the agencies repay the government. There were no welfare payments to the refugees or to their sponsors. As part of the admission process agencies were required to provide assurances of housing and employment for all displaced persons.

The Displaced Persons Act contained no authorizations for covering the resettlement costs of the refugees brought to the United States by the voluntary agencies. The act assumed that private giving through the agencies would adequately cover expenses. Thus, though the act may fairly be counted as the beginning of long-term working ties between church agencies and the government in refugee resettlement, it was not the beginning of the funding relationship in refugee matters. The act, by tacitly relying on the private resources of agencies, assured their integral role in the refugee care process. It was not until later, when refugee flows continued after the war and private giving was unable to keep pace with the flow, that some of the agencies turned to government contracts.

The next major expansion of federal assistance to voluntary agencies came with the legislation that provided U.S. surplus food for distribution abroad (the Agricultural Act of 1949), and the implementation of technical assistance under President Truman's Point Four proposals. Agencies began separating their refugee activities from broader commitments to provide relief (often in the form of agricultural surpluses) and other assistance. As the Congress sought support and practical help from the public in implementing U.S. foreign policy commitments, the voluntary agencies regularly supported legislation that increased subsidies to their assistance programs in the late 1940s and early 1950s. If at times the distinctions between military and security assistance were as thin as the line drawn between religious and secular activities, the attempt to make such separations nonetheless continued to undergird the rationale for church/state cooperation abroad.

With the focus still on rebuilding Europe, in 1951 Congress appropriated $10 million for the establishment of an intergovernmental agency for migration. The founding of the UNHCR in Geneva the same year (though without U.S. funding) addressed legal protection and material aid for refugees. Care for the thousands of refugees and escapees still streaming out of Eastern Europe—the area where voluntary agencies had played the largest role abroad—was covered under appropriations of $4.3 million authorized by President Truman to be spent on the new Escapee Program. While these appropriations were sent to a variety of sources, the Escapee Program has continued to provide financial assistance through the years to agencies working with refugees from Soviet communism, notably Hungarian refugees in 1956, Soviet Jews in the 1970s, and Polish refugees in the 1980s.

The Escapee Program marked the first time the government offered voluntary agencies contracts for specific refugee tasks it wanted accomplished abroad. No cumulative figures for the first five years of the program have been published. However, in a letter to a researcher in 1964 an official of the State Department did offer cumulative contract totals for the years 1959–64, when escapee activity in Europe had declined somewhat. Among participating agencies Catholic Relief Services held $5.4 million in contracts; the World Council of Churches held $3.6 million; and the Tolstoy Foundation held $1.2 million. HIAS and the Joint Distribution Committee both held under $500,000, and the Lutheran World Federation under $100,000.

The Far East Refugee Program was a separate division of the Escapee Program. The same letter provides contract totals in the Far East (much of it centered on Chinese refugees in Hong Kong) for agencies for the ten-year period 1954–64. Contract totals for religious voluntary agencies are as follows:

Catholic Relief Services	$2,490,000
Church World Service	$1,141,000
Lutheran World Federation	$1,131,000
World Council of Churches	$542,000

Several other religious voluntary agencies received small grants; no Jewish agencies were active under this program. Government assistance to religious agencies in this period peaked in 1960–61, when they received approximately 80 percent of all Far East contracts.

Since the State Department's Bureau for Refugee Programs and its predecessors have never been formally bound by the State Department's standard registration requirements for voluntary agencies, it should be noted that the Far East Refugee Program also made use of missionary societies during this period. The largest recipient of government assistance was the Catholic Foreign Mission Society of America (Maryknoll), with $920,000 in government contracts. Its closest Protestant competitor, the Oriental Missionary Society, received $35,000.[20]

It was in this setting, with government subsidies approaching or exceeding half of their income, that the major Christian agencies were forced to assess what were "proper" levels of government aid consistent with their status as private voluntary agencies. As had been true since the war, however, events had more to do with the development of church/state funding ties than with ideal versions of proper church/state relations. The Cuban refugee crisis of 1960–61 began a new era in government involvement in funding the work of all the refugee resettlement agencies. With some 40,000 Cubans in the Miami area in need of assistance and resettlement, the federal government authorized the release of contingency funds available under the Mutual Security Act of 1954 to voluntary agencies able to provide resettlement services. In a report to President Eisenhower in January 1961, a presidential assistant assigned to the task recommended that the resettlement agencies "should be given firm assurance of continued support through provision of adequate Federal funds for expenses incident to resettlement, the principal cost of which is transportation." The report suggested that the agencies cover expenses "necessary to meet the temporary needs of refugees prior to resettlement."[21]

The agencies did not concur in this final judgment, asserting in a quickly released counterstudy that "the Federal Government of a country of first asylum should be responsible for the initial care and maintenance of the refugees." After his inauguration President Kennedy signaled a new funding commitment in refugee welfare, sending his Secretary of Health, Education and Welfare Abraham Ribicoff to Miami in early February. Kennedy himself announced a nine-point Cuban Refugee Program on February 3, which included an initial $4 million allocation for refugee welfare from Department of Health, Education and Welfare contingency funds. Thus began a tradition of extending welfare services to asylum seekers within the United States, often administered with the direct assistance of the voluntary agencies. The resettlement agencies became intermediaries between the Department of Health, Education and Welfare (later Health and Human Services) and the refugees, administering large amounts of federal welfare and resettlement assistance on their behalf.[22]

Before the Vietnam War, then, the efforts of religious bodies to aid refugees both at home and abroad were firmly rooted in a system of cooperation with U.S. authorities that was increasingly dependent on governmental assistance, both material and financial. The triumph of subsidiarity was virtually complete. This growing dependency reinforced the complementarity of religious and governmental efforts, making it virtually impossible for private agencies to participate in refugee assistance without reference to the administration's priorities. Certain programs could be minimized or dropped, but the importance of government assistance in providing services could not be obviated. Church World Service, for instance, sharply curtailed distribution of Food for Peace supplies after numerous analysts in the early 1970s argued that food handouts created dependency rather than development; Church World Service began appearing less often as a contractor for refugee assistance abroad. Yet the agency remained active in refugee resettlement, accepting the same subsidies as other agencies and participating in the government-assisted "joint voluntary agency" approach to selecting refugees overseas for resettlement.

Recent Government Funding of Religious Agencies

The majority of funds channeled through the State Department's Bureau for Refugee Programs in the 1980s goes to international organizations: the International Committee of the Red Cross, the UNHCR, the UN Border Relief Operation in Thailand and Cambodia, and the United Nations Relief and Works Agency, which serves Palestinian refugees. According to figures released by the State Department, in 1982 $252.7 million (68 percent) of a total of $371 million in contract agreements went to the organizations listed (much of this was then subcontracted to voluntary agencies). Of the remaining $118.3 million, $69.3 million (19 percent) goes directly to religiously affiliated agencies.

According to an internal audit analysis, $49.3 million of the refugee assistance from the State Department to voluntary agencies was spent for resettlement and placement costs for the 97,900 refugees resettled in the United States in FY 1982.[23] Since formal contractual relations between voluntary agencies and the government in the resettlement field did not begin until 1975, this formal subsidy arrangement, much of it spent on expenses incurred once the refugees reach the United States, can be counted as an outgrowth of the influx of Southeast Asian refugees at the end of the Vietnam War.[24] Again, the agencies that have been active since World War II have been the recipients of the largest federal subsidies. (It should be noted, however, that one of the largest grants from the Bureau of Refugee Programs in 1982, $12.5 million, went to the United Israel Appeal for the resettlement of Soviet Jews. The previous year the United Israel Appeal received $25 million from the bureau for resettling Soviet Jews "or other similar refugees" in Israel.) The agencies' demonstration of competence, as well as the continued stability of the constituencies they represent, has resulted in a solid role for them as the State Department's scope of its of refugee resettlement funding expanded.

Most of these agencies were also recipients of Food for Peace and holders of contract agreements with AID and other agencies involved in foreign assistance. As should be clear from this brief review of funding ties, contract figures from the Bureau of Refugee Programs will not give a complete picture. Catholic Relief Services, for instance, appears in the 1982 agreement listings only once, under a $100,000 contract for a health center in a single refugee camp. Yet in Thailand and Honduras, to mention only two countries where CRS provides refugee relief, this amount represents only a small fraction of the CRS food and care efforts. Such programs invariably use subsidized Food for Peace alongside other supplementary services financed privately or through the UNHCR or other international body.

A comparison of the levels of government food, freight, and grant and contract aid to several religiously based agencies gives some sense of the widely varying attitudes of the agencies toward federal funding and assistance. Using figures supplied by AID for the post-Vietnam years 1975, 1979, and 1980, Table 1 indicates the percentage of each agency's total income that was derived directly from U.S. government sources.

Before offering interpretation of these figures some initial qualifications must be stated. In some instances the simple analysis of percentages is misleading. In the case of Catholic Relief Services, for instance, government subventions as a percentage of total income declined in this six-year period. This happened because of a significant expansion of CRS itself. From 1975 to 1980 the actual dollar value of government assistance to CRS increased from $169.9 million to $240 million, a shift that cannot be accounted for entirely on the basis of inflation, and which does not appear in the statistics of Table 1. Furthermore, the agencies listed operate on very different scales. CRS (1980 total income: $349.2 million) and the Joint Distribution Committee (1980 total income: $62.8 million) are the largest on the list; Rav Tov, the Orthodox Jewish agency formed to assist Jewish refugees and immigrants, operated the same year on a budget of $1.7 million.

Nevertheless, Table 1 gives some indication of the roles of internal agency attitudes and external events on determining the levels of government assistance.

TABLE 1.   Percentage of total agency income from governmental sources (Food for Peace, ocean freight reimbursement, government grants and contracts) (based on data supplied by Agency for International Development)

	1975	1979	1980
American Friends Service Committee	2.5%	3.3%	3.5%
Joint Distribution Committee	6.8	12.8	35.9
Catholic Relief Services	75.4	78.3	68.7
Church World Service	14.4	27.5	43.6
Lutheran World Relief	25.0	20.4	24.0
Mennonite Central Committee	5.4	1.7	1.6
Rav Tov	*	*	64.4
Seventh Day Adventist World Service	55.4	59.8	70.7
World Relief	4.3	0.3	38.2

* Not registered.

The "peace church" agencies, the AFSC and the Mennonite Central Committee, have maintained consistently low levels of government assistance, accepting ocean freight reimbursement and occasional small grants and contracts, but no Food for Peace. Lutheran World Relief also maintained a consistent level of around 25 percent of government assistance, a cautious post-Vietnam attitude, judging from its analysis of the early 1960s which proposed 50 percent as a cap for government aid. Several agencies, notably World Relief, the Seventh Day Adventist World Service, and Rav Tov, each used greatly increased levels of assistance during this period, often a reflection of the view that if the government was in the business of aiding private agencies, they wanted their fair share. In the two latter agencies, pressures from this expansion contributed to internal difficulties in the early 1980s.

The years 1979–80 were, quite independent of funding plans made by the agencies themselves, full of developments requiring humanitarian attention. The boat people crisis, the Cambodian border operation, and the increased emigration of Soviet Jews were followed quickly by the arrival of more than 100,000 Cuban refugees in March–April 1980. In many ways it is a tribute to these and other agencies that in the face of these emergencies they were able to expand the extent of their services abroad so rapidly, whether financed by federal or private sources. From the perspective of those in need, it matters little what the source of the funding is, as long as help arrives in time. Yet this pragmatic perspective, sufficient as it may be to justify the use of government funds by religious groups, hardly answers the difficult legal questions raised by such funding ties between church and state.

14

Government Funds: "An Awful Engine of Destruction"?

When Americans speak of the separation of church and state, they are usually vaguely referring to the "no-establishment" tradition enshrined in the First Amendment's religion clauses. Agreement as to what the establishment clause actually means has never been universal and the debate continues today. Whatever interpretation the courts give to the establishment clause in the future, its application to contemporary involvement of U.S. religiously based agencies and the government in refugee work overseas will center on the question of federal funding. It is clear that current practice owes more to a view that favors accommodation of church and state than to Thomas Jefferson's concept of a "wall of separation."

Though religious freedom and the separation of church and state have often been treated as foundations of American democracy, some observers have expressed skepticism along the way, particularly when church and state have gone abroad. English churchman Max Warren, a longtime observer of American missionary activities around the world, noted in the 1950s that "not even an American can separate church and state."[1] Contemporary experience in refugee work abroad confirms Warren's judgment. We must now consider whether the legal nonestablishment tradition has anything to say to this situation. Justice Douglas's 1963 statement that the most effective way to establish an institution is to fund it reveals the depth of contemporary preoccupation with limiting government funding of religious bodies. Though funding of a variety of religious relief agencies is a far cry from the state church system, neither can such funding be consonant with an "impregnable" wall of separation. It represents what has been called the mixed model of church/state ties.[2] This approach goes well beyond the thoughts and intentions of the Founding Fathers. Remembering their actions in underwriting missions to the Indian Nations, however, we can say that the mixed model has been normative in certain areas since the founding of the republic.

Prevailing attitudes toward the separation of church and state often grow directly from Supreme Court decisions that attempt to locate the "wall of separation." Cases that directly involve overseas activities of religious bodies are still rare, and little attention has been paid to the history of laws regulating relationships between religious bodies and the government abroad. No matter where one stands

213

in this debate, the interpretation of domestic law in related church/state topics substantially determines the tone and enforcement of congressional legislation and related administrative regulations of church/state funding ties. Thus, our investigation of relevant establishment clause issues must also address the history of the interpretation within the court system of the complex issue of the "establishment of religion," particularly regarding the use of government assistance raised by taxation.

The Establishment Clause and External Relations

Religious institutions serving refugees today participate in a complex battle over the proper relation between government and religion in shared concerns about public welfare.[3] Even though there was nothing resembling the current welfare state in colonial America, the issue of establishment of religion in refugee work abroad is a continuation of a discussion that has been with us since the early days of the republic. The question of refugees, with its direct political implications, has never allowed the application of neutral principles of state welfare assistance. In practice it has more resembled Chief Justice Burger's "play in the joints" than theories of strict separation.[4]

One method courts have used in interpreting the establishment clause has been to put forward arguments based on the "intent of the framers." This consists in an effort to recreate exactly what the authors of the Constitution had in mind when they wrote the First Amendment, and to apply this intent to present situations. The problem with this method stems from the difficulty of ascertaining what the framers as a group actually meant by the religion clauses, as the records indicate that different participants in the Constitutional Convention had different understandings. Furthermore, politicians and others perennially oversimplify the record. As noted earlier, the shorthand image of a wall of separation did not even appear until an 1802 letter from President Thomas Jefferson to a group of Connecticut Baptists. Though Jefferson's thinking on the subject of church and state was an important factor in colonial efforts to reach a national consensus, he himself was in diplomatic service in France when the Bill of Rights was actually written. Nevertheless, his "wall of separation" has entered American folklore as the "correct" understanding of the historical purpose of the establishment clause. This is in part due to the use of the expression by the Supreme Court in its earliest case dealing with the religion clauses, *Reynolds* v. *U.S.* (1878).

The possibility of religiously grounded civil conflict lurked just beneath the surface of early colonial religious establishments. James Madison observed that the existence of state churches created a climate in which different churches seemed "as ready to set up an establishment which is to take them in as they were to pull down that which shut them out."[5] While recognizing that church and state shared many common interests, Madison and other leaders were nervous about such political self-interest on the part of churches, and wondered if America might not in her laws somehow set an example by minimizing the religio-political intrigues many associated with the churches in Europe. "It remained for North America," he wrote, "to bring [this] great & interesting subject to a fair, and finally to a decisive test."[6]

In the early days of the republic, the establishment clause was not held as an official bar to the commingling of religion and foreign policy. While Jefferson preached enlightened American opinion to civilized Europe, the message was communicated at the same time to America's neighbors at home, the Indians. As we have seen, Congress turned to missionaries as the logical bearers of the *Novus Ordo Seclorum,* the new order of the ages. Rather than a slavish alliance between church and state, or a strict separation, the government encouraged church bodies to demonstrate religious freedom as one of the beneficial results of the new order. As part of its encouragement the federal government provided financial assistance to church missionaries. This humanitarian and missionary impulse in foreign affairs, which has been called everything from sentimental imperialism to the highest hope for humanity, stood in some contrast to reigning attitudes toward domestic church/ state ties.

From the days of the Continental Congress the government sought the cooperation of church missionaries in making contact with Indian tribes. This was, in turn, an extension of a church/state partnership that had existed at the time of the settling of New England. The Massachusetts Bay Colony, for instance, provided land, buildings, and churches for towns of "Praying Indians" in the seventeenth century. While both church and governmental officials acknowledged the beneficial results of this partnership in missions to the Indians, it was never an easy road. From the very beginning the government sought to limit the nature and the extent of any mission which it funded in whole or in part. We may recall Secretary of War Henry Knox's dictum that "no attempt shall be made to teach the peculiar doctrines of revealed religion except to those Indians to whom any of its mysteries have already been revealed," in other words, no evangelism.[7] Missionaries of the day were not likely to accept such a stricture and little attempt was made to enforce it. Presbyterian missionary Samuel Kirkland received from the government $1,500 a year from 1793 to 1812 to pay for the expenses of his Indian school in upstate New York.[8] The Civilization Fund of 1819 provided government aid to church groups willing to send missionaries and educators to the Indians.

More serious from the long-term perspective of the churches was the government's Indian Removal Act of 1830. The sudden removal of Indians from their homelands irreparably damaged the work of the missionaries, who in the eyes of the Indians they served were then tied to government interests. When church leaders pursued actions that differed from government strategy they were prosecuted.

Despite conflicts, this early period saw the beginnings of a long partnership between the government and the foreign and home mission boards of the churches. Church agencies were the primary source of field personnel for the government's Indian programs for over a century, providing social services and operating primary and secondary schools. During this period numerous interchurch and church/state squabbles occurred as Catholics sensitive to the federal government's marked preference for Protestants raised questions of both free exercise and establishment. Protestants concerned about growing Catholic influence fought back, but the Catholic argument carried the day: an unofficial establishment of Protestantism in government-funded work infringed on the religious freedom of Catholics to compete for the funds. In short, Madison's fear that government involvement with religious institutions would inevitably lead them to the status of factions proved only too true.[9] The resulting relationships between the government and religious bodies exhibited favoritism, discrimination, and graft. An unhealthy disruption of society along religious lines began to take place.

The *Bradfield* and *Quick Bear* Cases

How should the government best care for persons who for economic, political, or historical reasons become wards of the state? Before the furor over government funding to religious missions to the Indians died down, two cases previously mentioned reached the Supreme Court, *Bradfield* v. *Roberts* (1899) and *Quick Bear* v. *Leupp* (1908). They demonstrated that the U.S. government was eager to have church agencies as partners in social welfare both domestically and under treaty arrangements with the Indian Nations.[10] The two cases confirmed a pattern that was already in place and would later be extended both at home and abroad, namely, that pragmatic needs and overlapping concerns in welfare matters dictated that a continuing mixture of governmental and religious efforts could and should be accommodated.[11]

In a series of appropriation acts from 1895 to 1899 the Congress, mindful of the religious controversies, ended subsidies to sectarian Indian schools. However, in signing treaties with different Indian tribes, the government had, over the years, granted the tribes so-called treaty funds that would be held in trust by the Treasury for the eventual use and benefit of the Indians.[12] Once direct government support for the Indian schools was eliminated by Congress, the resourceful Bureau of Catholic Indian Missions pleaded with President Theodore Roosevelt to release these funds for the support of Catholic mission schools. The Catholics were informed that if they could produce consent documents from the Indians being served, the funds would be made available. Once news of Catholic success spread, Protestant leaders resolved to take the matter to the courts.

Quick Bear, a Sioux Indian recruited by the Protestants, joined several other Indians in pressing a complaint against Indian Commissioner Francis Leupp, alleging that Leupp's treaty fund contracts with the Bureau of Catholic Indian Missions were illegal and violated the will of Congress to terminate funding of sectarian schools. The Catholics countered Protestant support of the Indians by providing a Catholic lawyer as "special counsel" to the government; the government eventually turned its case over to the special counsel, who argued it before the Supreme Court.[13] The Court's final decision was that since the trust and treaty funds actually belonged to the Indians, the government was merely holding private funds rather than dispensing tax dollars. It therefore supported the government in its arrangements with the Bureau of Catholic Indian Missions.

The rationale of separating treaty and trust funds from tax appropriations evident in *Quick Bear* has been consistently applied to government involvement in religious welfare abroad. Surplus property and commodities owned by the government and transferred to religious agencies have received similar exemption from consideration as infringements on the no-establishment rule of the First Amendment.[14] The *Bradfield* case established the precedent for church/state contractual relationships in social welfare. Provided that a Catholic hospital was open to all, its religious affiliation was "of not the slightest consequence" to the government; since both the hospital and the government had an interest in meeting the same needs of the same population, and since the government assistance provided a benefit primarily to the sick rather than to the church, contracting of services by the government offered no constitutional offense.[15]

In the Indian schools matter, the decision focused on the need to distinguish government welfare assistance to religious institutions from tax dollars; there was little doubt that the schools on the Indian missions were religious in character. In the *Bradfield* case, it focused more on the "arguably non-religious" character of the service rendered by the hospital. Overseas refugee work has involved the transfer of virtually every sort of government aid to religious refugee agencies, and the effort to demonstrate that the agencies are nonreligious, or that separation of religious and secular ministries exists, has been less than adequate. Furthermore, modern relief activities take place in unsettled political conditions far removed from those of a hospital or an Indian reservation, and are open to greater exploitation from a variety of perspectives. Even the Indian Nations disputes demonstrated that government involvement with religious agencies in politically sensitive areas was capable of dividing the population along religious lines.

Are Refugee Relief Agencies "Religious"?

Before addressing the matter of establishment issues dividing the public along religious lines, which has itself become part of the contemporary debate on religious establishment, the *Bradfield* ruling that separately incorporated agencies spun off from churches are not "religious institutions" requires attention. If the Court's analysis here is sufficient, there is no need to debate further the propriety of contemporary church/state ties in refugee work. In the same ways that government officials treated the issues as "mere matters of expediency and economy" and weighed them as such against claims for and against the role of organized religion in government-sponsored Indian programs, so would any court today use the *Bradfield* decision to weigh the government's desire to provide services to refugees against the seemingly more "abstract" principles of religious freedom and the separation of church and state (see Chapter 2).

In their contacts with government today, agencies stress their humanitarian, nonsectarian qualities; to their own constituencies, however, most repeatedly emphasize the religious aspects of their mission. Concern about the expanding role of Protestant evangelicals makes the question of government funding in refugee work appear more urgent; many question whether the work of evangelicals meets the criterion of being sufficiently secular. Yet the question is more complex than the presence or absence of direct evangelism in an agency's program. While direct evangelism may certainly qualify as a religious act, any definition that limits religion to specifically religious or sacramental actions would be far too narrow a definition to suit most religious believers, especially those working abroad with refugees.[16] Acts of mercy involved in refugee work are religious acts for many relief workers, building upon the commands of Jesus in Matthew 25. In practice, the technicality of incorporating relief agencies separately from parent church bodies is of limited value in cordoning off religious practice from the secular purposes of government.

Tension between expansive and limited definitions of religion has created a complex problem for the courts in the modern era. Laurence Tribe has noted that the need to accommodate increasingly diverse religious traditions under the First Amendment has broadened the legal definition of the free exercise of religion to include humanistic and nontheistic beliefs. "It is equally clear," according to Tribe, "that in the age of the affirmative and increasingly pervasive state, a less expansive notion of religion was required for establishment clause purposes lest all 'humane' programs of government be deemed constitutionally suspect."[17] Tribe proposes that free exercise cases be decided on the basis that the activity in question is "arguably religious," and that establishment cases should address the "arguably non-religious" character of the activity. In a 1953 free exercise case the Supreme Court held that "it is no business of courts to say that what is a religious practice or activity for one group is not religious under the protection of the First Amendment."[18] Free exercise definitions of religion must emerge from the social functions of religious belief, not from majority definitions of religion. If either majority definitions of religion or expansive free exercise definitions were applied to establishment issues, he argues that the establishment clause could become "an awful engine of destruction."[19]

Over the years, the grouping together of religiously based and secular agencies for the administration of the U.S. grants and contracts in refugee, relief, and development work may have obscured the emergence of a new type of relief and development agency, the "parachurch" agency. The heritage of such agencies (including such groups as Food for the Hungry of Scottsdale, Arizona; World Vision of Monrovia, California; Compassion International of Denver; and many others) owes more to the history of the missionary movement than to agreements to provide services of recognizably secular purpose. Parachurch agencies have fulfilled specialized ministries in evangelism, mission, advocacy, welfare, and other fields on a scale not possible for local congregations or regional church bodies. In this sense they more closely resemble the organizational structure of many charitable Jewish agencies than they do the efforts of denominations or ecumenical groups to build internally administered relief agencies. Usually established by independent groups of believers committed to certain goals in mission work, many approach their goals with an eager, occasionally entrepreneurial spirit.

While the religious motivation of the agencies is frequently stressed to the public, their status as religious institutions in the eyes of the government under current provisions has been unclear. Whereas church-related welfare bodies seek separate incorporation as secular agencies, parachurch agencies often justify their existence on the basis of their specialized ability to meet particular religious obligations. Many of the new parachurch bodies, particularly those serving evangelical constituencies, are reluctant to identify themselves primarily with the provision of secular welfare, preferring to integrate welfare services into previously existing religious priorities such as church planting, evangelism, and religious education. When necessary they, like churches, establish separately incorporated relief arms to accommodate government funds. Thus any effort to classify the religious character of institutions serving refugees abroad today faces a monumental tangle of institutions and institutional definitions of "religion."

For establishment clause purposes, and in line with the logic of the *Bradfield* decision, the government classifies religiously based agencies that work with refugees as secular. This practice, dating from the World War II era, finds primary expression today in the Internal Revenue Code and related secondary gateways to funding eligibility such as the registration process of the Agency for International Development. For the purposes of private fund raising many agencies accept the IRS designation as a church; for their funding relations with government they form separately incorporated arms (for example, World Vision International also includes the "secular" World Vision Relief Organization as a channel of government assistance). For government purposes the agencies are classified as secular, while most persons serving in them would insist on interpreting their work as the fulfillment of a religious obligation. Such contradictions are commonplace in the effort to accommodate overseas church/state cooperation to constitutional standards. The central question in determining the legality and the permissible extent of federal involvement with religion is whether a particular form of involvement compromises the intent of the free exercise or the establishment clause.[20]

Whether refugee work abroad compromises the establishment clause must depend on how the intent of the clause is understood. We have examined something of the intent of the framers, as well as subsequent problems of defining religion. Norman Cousins has described the resulting dilemma as follows: If we take a broad reading (backed by Supreme Court decisions) that "almost any action by the Federal Government in support of religion is in violation of the First Amendment," direct church/state cooperation in refugee work is prohibited. Alternatively, and more in line with Tribe's desire to examine establishment issues on their "arguably non-religious" character, Cousins argues that "the Constitution speaks for itself, and that if the Founding Fathers, who declared against an established state church, were opposed to any or all Federal concern for religious activities in America, they would have said so."[21] They were not, and did not.

Recent Court Attitudes on Establishment Questions

When government officials named the evangelical agency World Relief as its choice to administer the camp for Nicaraguan Miskito refugees in Honduras, was it "establishing" World Relief—or simply making a political judgment? Has the government, by giving Catholic Relief Services a vastly larger role than other religious groups in surplus food distribution and refugee care and resettlement, "established" the Catholic church? Did disproportionate government assistance to Jewish agencies aiding Jews who left the Soviet Union in the late 1970s "establish" the agencies that resettle Jews in the United States and Israel? When government agencies denied funding to a group of evangelical agencies working abroad, were the evangelicals in the position of an oppressed "minority" unable to break the stranglehold on government funds channeled to an unofficially established coalition of more "respectable" religious and secular bodies? None of these questions is answered by the logic of the *Bradfield* decision. They have all arisen within the modern (post-1930s) system of welfare entitlements, and they all involve the volatile politics of foreign affairs rather than the more settled domestic situation at home.

The modern welfare state has generated a host of similar entanglements between religious and governmental institutions. From 1947 through the 1970s essentially four approaches to the establishment of religion emerged from the courts. Each was an attempt to formulate the proper relationship between institutions of religion and institutions of government. None adequately addresses the current situation of funding ties between church and state in overseas operations.

The first approach, the "no-aid" theory, strongly emphasizes the concept of a wall of separation between church and state. While this view has not been discarded, subsequent decisions have moved in different directions, particularly concerning cooperation in state-sponsored welfare services. Here a second approach, the "evenhandedness" theory, attempted to allow cooperation between church and state as long as no particular religion was favored. A strict concept of a wall of separation has here been replaced with efforts to determine a "floor" and a "ceiling" of acceptable church/state interaction. The third approach of the Court has been the idea of the "benevolent neutrality" of government toward religion. This represented a government stance that neither advanced nor inhibited religion, and left room for "play in the joints" between the two religion clauses. Finally, the most recent of the Court's approaches is summarized in what is known as the *Lemon* test, after the 1971 case *Lemon* v. *Kurtzman*. Incorporating elements of previous standards, the test is a three-part examination of the establishment questions in any given case. Since in overseas refugee work it would be hard to argue that a wall between church and state is firmly in place, it will be of some value to review how the Court has reached its current understandings of the establishment clause. While the image of a floor and ceiling has taken on substance in the course of a series of court decisions on domestic church/state matters, the political instabilities of international relations may call for yet a different vision when church and state go abroad.

The No-Aid Theory

Dating from the *Everson* decision of 1947 ("No tax in any amount, large or small, can be levied to support any religious activities or institutions, whatever they may be called, or whatever form they may adopt to teach or practice religion"), this strong version of the wall of separation has been watered down by the Congress and the Court in a variety of circumstances.[22] Indeed, anyone familiar with Court and legislative actions sanctioning domestic church/state cooperation in welfare work could see that either the definition of religious institutions had to be narrowed, or the no-aid view substantially qualified, for such cooperation to come about. The no-aid view appeared partially in response to the wave of publicly aired suspicion that appeared in the late 1940s as the Catholic church in the United States moved aggressively into government-assisted welfare and education, both at home and abroad. Establishment matters are never simply the application of an abstract constitutional theory; they inevitably spring from (and occasionally rechannel) the existing levels of political participation and power among religious groups.

It should also be noted that despite the no-aid rhetoric of *Everson,* the Court nonetheless held that the matter at issue, the use of publicly financed transportation for parochial schoolchildren, was constitutional. This decision has been compared to the so-called child-benefit theory which held certain forms of government aid lawful because the benefits accrued to the state and the child, not to the religious school.[23] When a governmental interest is being served (as is the case with the care of refugees abroad), ways around the no-aid theory have been found. Thus, as Thomas Jefferson himself authorized government support of Catholic Indian missions only one year after authoring the phrase "a wall of separation," the Court's no-aid ruling deferred almost immediately to the perceived need to maintain government-supported services and social order. In the area of foreign aid, this is the case in provisions of the Foreign Assistance Act of 1961, in which overseas religious institutions receiving federal backing are included in the broad category of "private and voluntary organizations."[24]

Perhaps the strongest statement of the no-aid theory is found in the dissent of Justice Wiley Rutledge in the *Everson* case. He argued that the state had no business funding even the bus fares of students attending Catholic schools. To him, the Court's willingness, in allowing bus fare subsidies in *Everson,* to say that "all we have here is 'public welfare legislation' " destroyed the strict separationist intent of the Constitution's religion clauses. Rutledge feared that the Court's argument "seeks, in Madison's words, to 'employ Religion as an engine of Civil policy.' "[25] On Rutledge's view, the framers of the Constitution taught that the condition of religious liberty was that religion should remain free from both state interference and state sustenance, and this condition extended to the "public welfare" activities of the churches. This view essentially combines Madison's view that religion and government occupy separate spheres and Jefferson's wall of separation which allowed no overlap. While some may find this "complete division" to be a politico-historical phantom, many legal, religious, and political professionals still defend it as the heartbeat of American democracy.[26] Protestant ethicist John C. Bennett, for instance, recently defended the *Everson* "no-aid" concept as protecting the nonreligious minority from the possibility of a multiple religious establishment.[27]

Nevertheless, no-aid theories have had little effect in the practical world of refugee work abroad. When State Department and private relief officials stress that private agencies working independently of government do not have the resources to address global refugee problems, they are telling the truth. But strict separationism, if politically irrelevant at present to international church/state welfare cooperation, continues to function as a powerful spotlight directed at the pitfalls just down the road. Toward this end it is worth quoting Justice Rutledge's warning on the effect of dispensing public money in the midst of a multiplicity of competing religious interests:

> When [religion] comes to rest upon that secular foundation [e.g., public funding] it vanishes with the resting. Public money devoted to payment of religious costs, educational or other, brings the quest for more. It brings too the struggle of sect against sect for the larger share or for any. . . . The end of such strife cannot be other than to destroy the cherished liberty. The dominating group will achieve the dominant benefit; or all will embroil the state in their dissentions.[28]

During the early struggles for religious freedom, Madison believed that such intrigue must be prevented by a governmental blindness to religion that could only be achieved by as little contact between the two as possible.

Refugee care on its current scale would simply not exist without cooperative arrangements between the government and religious relief agencies. In order to make an argument against such cooperation that carried political as well as legal weight, strict separatists would have to be able to demonstrate that some other acceptable method for handling refugee problems was at hand. Given the number of interested parties in any such dispute, a simple demonstration that the current arrangement violates domestic church/state law would hardly pull enough weight against the long-term, seemingly intractable problems for the world's refugees and for Americans responding to their plight.

The Evenhandedness Theory

Under a second approach taken by the Supreme Court, the government may aid religion in certain limited ways, as long as no single religion is given preference over another. In 1952, five years after the strict separationism of *Everson,* Justice Douglas wrote the Court's opinion in *Zorach* v. *Clausen,* in which he argued that a total separation of church and state literally applied would create alien camps within the society, "hostile, suspicious and even unfriendly." "We are a religious people whose institutions presuppose a Supreme Being," wrote Douglas. His opinion draws on the "three faiths" vision of religion in American life current at the time, explicitly mentioning Catholics, Protestants, and Jews. (It is perhaps worth noting that as late as 1931 the Supreme Court stated that Americans are "a Christian people.") Justice Douglas voiced concern over the perception that government was hostile to religion, or that government favored secular over religious approaches. He stressed governmental evenhandedness in stating that "the government must be neutral when it comes to competition between sects."[29]

Within a few years, the concept of government evenhandedness toward all religions was discarded by the Supreme Court on the grounds that "neither a State nor the Federal Government can constitutionally . . . pass laws or impose requirements which aid all religions as against non-believers."[30] Here the Court considered the infringement of the rights of secular Americans by a multiple religious establishment, a second aspect of evenhandedness. At issue was a Maryland requirement that public officials in that state take an oath that included reference to belief in God. This was held to be an inappropriate state encouragement of religion, indeed of theistic religion. The Court noted that Buddhists and Taoists did not hold conventional Western concepts of God, and that the oath was as inappropriate as if Congress passed a law that held "that no federal employee shall attend Mass or take any active part in missionary work."[31] Since this decision (*Torcaso* v. *Watkins*), the Supreme Court has not returned to the evenhandedness approach.

Variations on this theme are common in political choices made by government in refugee-related matters. The federal government worked with the theme in the early days of cooperation with religious groups in overseas refugee work. Typical was Franklin Roosevelt's 1938 advisory group, the President's Advisory Committee on Political Refugees, which included five Protestants, three Catholics, and two Jews, a formula roughly approximating public perception of the status these groups held in American life. At the time of resettlement of refugees under the Displaced Persons Act of 1948, federal resources were allocated to private, largely religiously based resettlement agencies. The agencies were generally presumed to work with their coreligionists in Europe; Lutherans were resettled by Lutheran Immigration and Refugee Services, other Protestants by Church World Service, and so forth. Among refugees resettled under the Displaced Persons Act, statistics on religious preference were kept. Forty-seven percent were Catholic, 35 percent were Protestant, and 16 percent were Jewish.[32] Thus, levels of government assistance followed the number of representatives of a given faith in the refugee population itself.

Though it did not conform to a demographic profile of the American population, this allocation of the task of resettlement made practical sense in the European setting. When a joint Protestant, Catholic, and Jewish approach was applied to the influx of Cuban refugees in the early 1960s (at the time of the *Torcaso* decision), the overwhelmingly Catholic character of the population made the "three faiths" approach seem overly formal and (even though there were some Protestant and Jewish refugees) on occasion inappropriate. The Asian and African refugee problems of recent years have made the coreligionist approach to evenhandedness still more difficult.

Proportional approaches to governmental evenhandedness in its dealings with religious or secular bodies have now been discarded. Since all such efforts have been administrative rather than congressionally mandated actions, there was little need for the government to place a rigid scale of proportional representation at the center of its choices of operational partners in refugee work. In a 1983 case dealing with tax deductions for parents sending their children to private schools, the Supreme Court explicitly rejected any view of evenhandedness toward religion based upon the proportion of the population affected by a given decision.[33] Opponents of government assistance to parochial schools have argued that it would unlawfully favor the Catholic church's extensive system of parochial schools. In the 1983 case *Mueller* v. *Allen* Justice William Rehnquist wrote for the Court that it would be virtually impossible to determine a fair system for evaluating "the extent to which various classes of private citizens claimed benefits under the law." Any such effort, such as an annual governmental survey to determine what classes of person benefited from the deduction, "would scarcely provide the certainty that this field stands in need of, nor can we perceive principled standards by which such statistical evidence might be evaluated."[34]

If proportional schemes are unworkable in the relatively stable domestic setting, it is inconceivable that they would carry legal weight in the chaotic world of refugee work. Evenhandedness may be a worthy ideal, but in the heat of World War II, the operative concern of the government was to draw as many loyal private bodies as possible—religious or secular—into support of its programs. In practice, the size and scope of refugee resettlement contracts between religious agencies and the federal government are regulated by long-established working relationships, many of which date from this period.[35] Those agencies that participated in early resettlement efforts supported by the U.S. government have retained their dominance in the field and today bear in relation to each other a similar scale of operations as existed during the four years of the Displaced Persons Act, from 1948 to 1952.

In sum, the evenhandedness theory of government involvement with religion, including evenhandedness to religious and secular groups alike, has had little practical role in the development of church/state relations in international relief work. Whatever the government's policy, individual religious bodies hold different views of the value of working with government. Even if the government allotted its assistance based on the number of people represented by a specific group, there would be those who would turn down such assistance on principle. Since most groups that qualify for government assistance and seek it do receive something, it can be argued that the government has been politically willing to spread its assistance to the broadest possible spectrum of Americans. Beyond this, the specifics of church/state cooperation abroad are a combination of history, political necessity, humanitarianism, and specific institutional capabilities.

The Benevolent Neutrality Theory

The phrase "benevolent neutrality" appears in a 1970 Supreme Court decision, *Walz* v. *Tax Commission:*

> The general principle deducible from the First Amendment and all that has been said by the Court is this: That we will not tolerate either governmentally established religion or governmental interference with religion. Short of those expressly proscribed governmental acts, there is room for play in the joints productive of a benevolent neutrality which will permit religious exercise to exist without sponsorship and without interference.[36]

This statement by the Court is a far cry from the strict separationism of *Everson.* Indeed, many commentators have considered the Court's shift from no-aid to benevolent neutrality as part of a process of maturation in judicial understanding of the religion clauses. To the extent that the Court's neutrality toward religion is benevolent, it follows (in a secularized version) the philosophy of Roger Williams, urging that the state keep its distance from, as well as positively encourage, religion.

The Supreme Court has cited a decision of Judge Alphonso Taft in the 1860s as precedent for its philosophy of governmental neutrality to religion. For Judge Taft, neutrality meant "absolute equality before the law, of all religious opinions and sects," and that the government "is neutral, and while protecting all, it prefers none, and it *disparages* none."[37] Judge Taft thought this approach offered the greatest opportunity for the fulfillment of the ideal of religious liberty. Benevolent neutrality attempts to reconcile the two religion clauses. The religion clauses are not, stated Chief Justice Burger, "the most precisely drawn portions of the Constitution"; they should be viewed as stating an objective rather than fixing a statute. The *Walz* case quotes Justice Douglas in *Zorach,* in which he states that the Court favors an attitude that "shows no partiality to any one group and lets each flourish according to the zeal of its adherents."[38]

Accordingly, the Court held in *Walz* that tax exemption for churches did not violate the establishment clause. In this case Justice Douglas appeared to modify his previous stance, based on his concern over the growing reliance of religious institutions on government. Dissenting in *Walz,* he opposed tax exemption for churches since in his view it amounted to a government subsidy; he added that "the extent to which [churches and religious institutions] are feeding at the public trough [today] in a variety of forms is alarming." Tax exemption does not advance or inhibit religion, argued Justice Burger in *Walz;* it is "neither sponsorship nor hostility."[39] From such considerations springs the substance of benevolent neutrality toward religion.

In assessing the importance of the "benevolent neutrality" approach for church/state establishment issues overseas, we need to know how Chief Justice Burger's statement that religious freedom can best exist "without sponsorship" and "without interference" from the government can or should be applied. Churches and other religiously motivated groups engaged in refugee assistance abroad have, through their related relief and development bodies, repeatedly sought the sponsorship of the

U.S. government, directly and indirectly, both financially and diplomatically. This has remained an acceptable form of church/state cooperation since World War II, in part because the agencies could not conceivably play the role that they have in international assistance without the power and prestige of the U.S. government (as well as that of the United Nations) behind them. Given the level of federal resources now engaged in overseas relief and development, it would be more accurate to speak of governmental *sponsorship* of religiously based activities than of church/state *partnership*. It is not a relationship of equals; it is a vast public entity accepting the aid of much smaller private agencies. In exchange for assistance, the private agencies essentially agree to establish programs that complement those of government.

What of governmental "interference" in the refugee relief activities of religious agencies? If government funds an activity, in whole or in part, it is natural that some level of monitoring will take place. The monitoring is done to assure that governmental objectives are indeed accomplished. Some agencies feel that monitoring of their use of funds has resulted in the "interference" Justice Burger would prohibit in his definition of "benevolent neutrality." Disputes have arisen over governmental blockage of those goals that the religious agency, in its identity as a private voluntary association, seeks to accomplish in addition to governmental goals it has accepted by accepting funds.

Here relief and development agencies, whether church or parachurch, face squarely and dilemma of their status as "secular" agencies. While they may be "secular" on paper, the agencies are populated by people of religious faith. Their sectarian goals in serving abroad frequently include the building of international relationships with fellow believers, construction of churches in refugee camps, development training designed to benefit indigenous religious communities, religious teaching directed to fellow believers, or evangelism directed to those who come from other backgrounds or from no religious tradition at all. Christians see such activities as a vital expression of the universal character of the Gospel.

Chief Justice Burger's ideal of the benevolent neutrality of government "which will permit religious free exercise to exist without sponsorship and without interference" is not easily transferred abroad. It may be a useful description of domestic governmental practice toward religion, but it is hard to speak of the government's "neutrality" in international affairs or in its related dealings with U.S. religious groups active abroad. The "secular" character mandated under the original *Bradfield* case for welfare agencies with contractual relations with the federal government is arguably more difficult to sustain under the pressures common in remote refugee camps than it is in domestic care facilities or welfare service centers.

The Lemon *Test*

The last approach to the establishment clause we will examine is the so-called *Lemon* test fixed in the 1971 decision *Lemon* v. *Kurtzman*. Because this test has served as the primary means of determining establishment cases since then, it is (along with *Bradfield*) the case to which a court would probably turn in an establishment question involving American religious groups overseas. Each of the three questions or "prongs" of the test needs to be answered affirmatively in order for a court to rule that a particular law or provision does not violate the establishment clause. Each of the inquiries has a history in previous Supreme Court rulings, and each can be traced to the mixture of early attitudes on the establishment of religion represented by Madison, Jefferson, and Williams. The questions are (1) does the law in question serve a secular purpose? (2) is the effect of the law primarily secular, rather than advancing or inhibiting religion? (3) does it avoid administrative and political entanglement between church and state?

Secular purpose

The secular purpose question poses the least difficulty for church/state cooperation abroad. Simply stated, a given law must have a secular purpose which is not intended to either advance or inhibit religion.[40] Since government cannot order or regulate a given situation by claiming its view is correct and that of a given religion is wrong, it does so on the claim that its regulation serves a secular purpose.[41]

Care of refugees abroad, as well as their resettlement in the United States, is certainly justifiable as a secular purpose, and it would be difficult, if not impossible, to demonstrate that such tasks were also intended to advance or inhibit religion. In the late 1940s, it might have been argued that the Displaced Persons Act advanced the Protestant, Catholic, and Jewish religions by expanding their numbers within the United States, but there was no such test at the time. Furthermore, the use of such an argument to the detriment of suffering war victims seems cruel. In the current context of refugee work, the refugee populations come from such varied religious and secular backgrounds that it is difficult to say that particular religious traditions are being advanced or inhibited. The legislative mandate for the involvement of private relief agencies in refugee work today springs from the Refugee Act of 1980. That law, in accord with international refugee conventions, states clear secular purposes in refugee assistance. Similarly, in the Foreign Assistance Act of 1961, the backbone of U.S. foreign policy law, the general purpose of the act is to advance "the foreign policy, security, and general welfare of the United States by assisting peoples of the world in their efforts toward economic development and internal and external security." It is under such manifestly secular statutes that religious agencies work with private, governmental, and intergovernmental assistance. The secular purpose test springs from Madison's view that church and state must act independently enough that they take no direct cognizance of the other's rightful sphere of interest.[42] Since the test concentrates on the intent of the legislation rather than on its implementation, it is probable that a court would agree that church/state ties implicit in foreign aid and refugee relief legislation passes this first test.

Primary secular effects

The second of the three "prongs" of the *Lemon* test attempts to go beyond the intent of a given piece of legislation and address the effects of its implementation. The primary effect of legislation must be secular. If the primary effect is to advance or inhibit religion, the law fails this second test.[43] Like the first test, the roots of this test have been traced to Madison's view that the respective spheres of religion and government should be kept as independent from each other as possible. In *Lemon,* a "primary effect" is one that is direct or immediate rather than remote and incidental.[44] Government funding of evangelism or of buildings used for worship would constitute a direct effect, while tax exemption or church use of government surplus food or property, since they do not directly involve the transfer of taxpayer funds, are indirect.[45] Thus a $2,000 expenditure of government funds for a religious sanctuary in a refugee camp may be enough for a religious relief agency to fail the test, while CRS, receiving over $175 million per year in surplus food, is not touched by this establishment question.

Three factors are relevant in whether or not government aid to religious institutions is indirect enough to pass the secular effect test. First, the Court would decide whether the benefited institution is "pervasively religious."[46] A parochial school in the United States was denied government assistance in 1975 because of its "predominantly religious character."[47] Numerous relief agencies that receive government assistance have been criticized because no clear boundary exists between the definition of their religious and their secular functions. World Vision, for instance, was severely scrutinized by private parties and by government officials on precisely this point both during its initial efforts to register with AID in 1962 and again during a general reregistration of all aided private voluntary organizations in 1977. Criticism centered on World Vision's lack of what the courts have called the "severability" of religious and secular functions within an organization. In 1962, World Vision was initially turned down because the State Department's Advisory Committee on Voluntary Foreign Aid ruled that World Vision's primary purpose was "other than in these fields" of relief and development.[48] They failed to demonstrate a primary "secular purpose"; in the terms of the Supreme Court's language they were "pervasively religious." World Vision then took the technical step of establishing a separately incorporated relief and development arm; this body was accepted for registration within a few months.

The issue of "severability" of secular and religious functions mentioned here in relation to the registration of World Vision is a second and closely related factor in deciding whether aid is direct enough to fail the primary effect test.[49] Courts have held that it is easier to separate religious from secular functions in colleges and universities than in parochial schools.[50] Some agencies have made bona fide efforts to separate elements of direct religious witness from aspects of their mission funded by the government. Other instances are more complicated. When a Catholic priest who works for the secular relief arm of the U.S. Catholic Conference distributes government surplus food from a Catholic church, does such government assistance directly aid the religious mission of the Catholic church? Would the verdict change if the priest were or were not wearing clerical garb?

Throughout the history of government aid to religious welfare agencies, many have said that the government aid does directly aid the mission of the church, including those Protestants who pressed the issue on Indian reservations before World War I. Many others, arguing the greater good of the refugees, consider such caviling demeaning. Others adopt the more cynical view that "what people don't know won't hurt them," and that religious identification with the government poses no problem if the public cannot explicitly make the connection. Tribe has argued that when the aid to religion is indirect (as in the case of food, medicine, or transportation), the public is less likely to perceive any symbolic identification of religion with government.[51] Therefore, to some the perception of severability may be more important than actual severability, which in any case is the more difficult of the two alternatives.

The entanglement test

James Madison warned in his *Memorial and Remonstrance* of 1785 that protection of religious freedom required that the issue "never become entangled . . . in precedents." In its *Walz* decision of 1970 the Supreme Court gave continued support to tax exemption for churches, stating that taxation would lead to "excessive entanglement" between church and state. The Supreme Court's 1971 *Lemon* decision took up the theme and formulated the test of entanglement between church and state. The test has two parts. The Court stated that a given statute may neither foster excessive *administrative* entanglement, nor may it have the potential for *political* entanglement, defined as the creation of division along religious lines in the public or in the legislature. The entanglement test rests upon Madison's view that "both religion and government can best work to achieve their lofty aims if each is left free of the other within its respective sphere."[52] It is when the work of religious relief and refugee agencies abroad is measured against this rationale that the most difficult establishment issues are joined.

Administrative Entanglement. The courts have viewed administrative entanglement from at least two perspectives: excessive government surveillance of religious institutions, and government efforts at resolving religious disputes.[53] No such specific test as "administrative entanglement" existed when the government began formalizing relationships with religious voluntary agencies during World War II. Problematic areas of religious practice were already then clearly identified by governmental and religious groups. The government did not finance worship, religious teaching, or evangelism, but neither could it hinder or discourage religious practice on the part of relief societies serving refugees.

Proponents of the entanglement standards of the Court should be as prepared to criticize their usefulness overseas as to criticize any apparent transgressions of them. The Supreme Court has in recent years acknowledged that some degree of entanglement between church and state is inevitable in domestic society; when church and state go abroad, the degree of entanglement increases. The events we have examined in postwar refugee assistance merged the spheres of religion and government in the way Madison sought to avoid. What was initially seen as an emergency wartime collaboration has grown into a permanent fixture of foreign assistance, yet millions of people have had dignity and meaning restored to their lives through this "entangling precedent." If humanitarian work is to continue on its present scale, so must the entanglement between religion and government it has entailed.

Even given explicit approval of government cooperation with religious welfare agencies, however, it is not surprising that in the 1970s the question of whether or not an institution was "pervasively religious" would arise in the courts. Separability of sacred and secular became a prominent concern as government sought to harness the beneficial aspects of religion (such as its ability to meet social welfare needs) while keeping sectarian controversies out of the public sphere. Church/state cooperation which moved in this general direction was held by the Supreme Court to be an acceptable accommodation to the complexity of modern life. The question to be answered under this view of the administrative entanglement test was this: is the entanglement in a given case "excessive"? Under *Lemon,* three aspects of the relationship between government and the religious body must here be examined:

(1) the character and purposes of the benefited organization (is it "pervasively religious"?); (2) the resulting relationship between government and religion; and (3) the nature of the aid that the state supplies.[55] These parallel the questions in the primary effect test, examining "much the same body of facts through a different lens."[56]

The first of the three questions used to examine excessive entanglement has continually dogged parochial schools in their search for federal assistance: is the institution so pervasively religious that any government supervision of the use of its funds would constitute excessive entanglement in religion? Even though the establishment clause implies a restricted definition of "religion," any effort to answer this question would require an understanding of "religion" in the agency in question.

It is unlikely that the government would want to undertake a serious move to separate religious and secular functions in religious agencies active abroad. In refugee relief the issue of the severability of religious and secular functions is more acute today than it was in the 1940s, and therefore the chances that the federal funding of these agencies refugee programs involve "excessive entanglement" are perhaps greater. Today's renewed emphasis on the theological purposes of refugee relief, whether in the realm of evangelism, migration, development, or political advocacy on behalf of refugee populations is an unmistakable component in religiously grounded organizations. Yet enforcement of the "no proselytism" clause in contracts from the Bureau of Refugee Programs would require virtually constant surveillance on the part of the U.S. government, a draconian if not impossible administrative procedure.

The second part of the test for excessive entanglement examines the nature of the relationship that results when government assists religious agencies and vice versa. If the nature of the government's contact with the agency is brief rather than sustained, then a court is less likely to find the relationship to be excessively entangled. Religious refugee agencies frequently accept direct contracts with the State Department covering activities abroad for a limited period. In this instance the religious agency becomes for a time a contractual agent of the government. When agencies accept contracts from the State Department, government involvement with a given agency understandably expands.

The final test of excessive administrative entanglement looks at the nature of the assistance provided by the state. In applying this third test a court asks whether specific types of public aid can be diverted to religious use. If it is so diverted, would the governmental surveillance necessary to prevent such diversion create excessive administrative entanglement? There are now at least four types of government assistance currently flowing to religious agencies abroad: assistance channeled through multilateral bodies, direct grants and contracts, surplus food, and surplus property. Each type of assistance now available to religious agencies working abroad can and has been diverted to religious use. Domestically the courts have not held surplus property to be on the same level as tax monies as an expression of government establishment of religion, so we may for the moment eliminate this category of assistance (and possibly food aid as well) as a potential cause of administrative entanglement. In the other types of assistance, officials face difficult choices monitoring the disbursement of funds. Religious relief organizations have always used local missionaries and religious contacts from the same or related denominations to fill staff positions. Such people are doing this work because of their desire to act on religious motivations. This strengthens the religious character of the agencies, and thereby strengthens the likelihood that government resources will be diverted to religious purposes.

We cannot simply say that the cooperation between church and state abroad as presently organized violates the establishment clause of the First Amendment. It may be that the Court has created a set of tests (admittedly designed for use in the domestic United States) that are simply not up to the complexities or realities of church and state abroad in the 1980s. A court could conceivably hold that religious freedom as protected and interpreted in the First Amendment is not among the essential protections Americans can expect from their government when they travel and work abroad.

Whatever the courts might or might not do, it is difficult to decide whether judicial intervention would help or hinder the underlying political tensions that make this area of church/state relations so extraordinarily sensitive. As we have noted, the trend in recent years has been for the courts to adopt a narrow definition of religion for establishment questions and a broad definition for free exercise questions. Yet the free exercise and establishment clauses are but different sides of the same coin, pointing to the truth that the greatest safeguard of religious freedom lies in distinguishing spheres of activity appropriate to religion and government. If religious institutions seek the protection of the free exercise clause in pursuing their mission abroad, they must also accept the burden of the establishment clause as interpreted by the courts. Much in the current practice of overseas refugee relief offends these establishment standards as they have emerged domestically since World War II. Yet the most sharply debated of all the entanglement tests, the political, has never been used as an independent test of entanglement in court. Even to address the question hypothetically involves frank appraisal of foreign affairs issues that many religious and governmental leaders prefer to avoid.

Political Entanglement. The political entanglement test has not been used by the courts as an independent test of the constitutionality of a given law. Rather, it acts as a warning signal, in the words of Justice John Harlan, for "preventing that kind and degree of government involvement in religious life that, as history teaches us, is apt to . . . strain a political system to the breaking point."[57] Religiously based refugee relief agencies may face difficulties in both the administrative and political definitions of entanglement.

The establishment clause, Justice Robert Jackson wrote in his dissent in *Everson,* "was intended not only to keep the state's hands out of religion, but to keep religion's hands off the state, and above all, to keep bitter religious controversy out of public life by denying to every denomination any advantage from getting control of public policy or the public purse."[58] Here is an ideological descendant of Thomas Jefferson, openly fretting about ecclesiastical influences on the state. The political entanglement test addresses both Jefferson's fear of church influence on the state and the fear voiced by Madison that the rights of religious minorities might be violated by state support of religion. Yet, far from considering a broad range of concrete political contacts between church and state, the test itself addresses the perception that uncontrollable problems *might* arise from some forms of church/state interaction.

The Court held in *Lemon* that "ordinary" political debate and division were to be expected in a democratic system; indeed "we could not expect otherwise, for religious values pervade the fabric of our national life." The substance of the political entanglement test lies with the Court's judgment that "political division along religious lines was one of the principal evils against which the First Amendment was intended to protect."[59] We will return to the accuracy of this assertion later, but for the time being let us accept that such a concern is of legitimate interest to a court. The test functions something like an antenna for potential problems raised by the presence of religion in political sphere. One commentator has argued that the Court's concern arose over the possibility that in a situation in which the government was providing assistance to a variety of religious groups, the religious body with the greatest size or most power could develop a position of dominance over smaller or weaker organizations, causing them financial or symbolic damage.[60]

The resulting divisions might follow religious lines, creating conflicts of the sort American society has thus far been largely spared. The Supreme Court cited the political entanglement test in a 1982 case considering the validity of a Massachusetts state law giving churches the right to veto liquor license applications for establishments within 500 feet of the church.[61] The Court struck down the Massachusetts law on the basis that it entrusted significant government authority in churches, enmeshing them in the government's political process of decision making and conferring symbolic power on church authority. When governmental and religious power were so fused, there was no means of guaranteeing that delegated power would be used "exclusively for secular, neutral and nonideological purposes."[62]

It may be argued that this potential for political division along religious lines is not relevant to the work of religious groups active abroad; that the growing participation of private secular agencies in overseas relief and development has made the issue there one of political entanglement between the public and the private voluntary sectors, but not a direct one between church and state. To some degree this is true. But many of the new secular voluntary agencies that work abroad do not have the sizable constituencies of religious voluntary societies. Some are simply creations of the government, organized to handle a particular task abroad. Such governmental creations carry no weight in electoral politics. Religious agencies do. Once religious organizations have entered the field of government-assisted foreign aid, they have proven difficult to dislodge. The White House and members of Congress understand that they represent substantial numbers of voters; State Department officials see in them a practical method of securing public support for overseas aid policies. It may be sociologically correct to say that the field of private refugee relief has been "secularized," but it would be politically naive. Such private sector power as there is in refugee relief and resettlement still rests primarily with institutions having religious affiliation.

The record of the government in handling the question of Jewish refugee assistance during World War II is a potent reminder that refugee problems—and the actions of religiously based institutions in meeting those problems—have the potential for instigating political divisions along religious lines. In *Lemon*, Chief Justice Burger wrote that "political divisiveness along religious lines was one of the principal evils against which the First Amendment was intended to protect." Lawyer and church/state scholar Edward Gaffney has pointedly asked whether the chief justice actually meant what he said in alluding to the intention of the framers of the Constitution. In Gaffney's analysis, such concern for political divisiveness along religious lines appears nowhere in the record of the debate over the religion clauses. Furthermore, he argues that if the political entanglement test were ever taken seriously, it would endanger important civil liberties, placing religiously grounded political debate at a distinct disadvantage. Adoption of the test is the equivalent of affirming a pietistic view of religion that deems all religion personal and private. According to Gaffney, the Court "can stop promulgating its quietist establishment by abandoning the political divisiveness test."[63]

During their respective terms as president, both Thomas Jefferson and James Madison approved government expenditures for religious missions to the Indians. From the earliest days of such missions, the federal government has declined to apply strict establishment standards to joint activities of religion and government beyond the borders of the United States. This has been so in part because successive administrations have used religious agencies to demonstrate the best of American standards and hopes for the world. Government officials have also recognized that support for their foreign policies within religious bodies—particularly those with active commitments abroad—was essential for the support of their foreign policy and foreign aid in general. Conversely, religious groups have at times sought to identify themselves with the power and prestige of the U.S. government for the purpose of extending their ministries overseas. Governmental support of these activities, whether in the form of political assistance, cash, property, or commodities, has become an accepted form of conducting foreign policy.

Any future establishment clause involvement of the courts may depend on whether the various forms of religious refugee relief organizations are categorized as religious institutions or welfare institutions. They frequently are both, demonstrating the contradiction inherent in the idea of a secular religious body. For many this contradiction is resolved in the idea of service; agency workers are there for the sake of others, an objective that government officials can lawfully encourage without reference to the motivation of the participants. Congress has not adequately faced the difficulty of distinguishing secular and religious elements in overseas relief today, not has it addressed the impact of international political pressures on existing standards of church/state cooperation in welfare matters.

Not surprisingly, religiously based welfare activities abroad frequently carry with them overt political and religious implications. This was reflected anew in the government's now obvious efforts at impeding rescue and resettlement efforts directed at European Jews during World War II. Once the relevant national and international political situations are clarified, it becomes more difficult to argue that government funding of the agencies can be subsumed under the Court rulings (beginning with *Bradfield*) encouraging direct aid to welfare institutions.

Undergirding the government's cooperative attitude toward religious welfare institutions is the public perception that the institutions are not primarily religious and that they serve broad secular purposes. This political fact (along with the "second-class," derivative status of refugee and relief matters in U.S. foreign policy) has in a sense bought time for the existing arrangements. Those arrangements today defy the best efforts of the Supreme Court to bring order to establishment clause questions in the United States. Each theory, from no-aid to evenhandedness, from benevolent neutrality to the *Lemon* test, could be demonstrated to be inadequate for addressing current arrangements between church and state abroad. Until the government (and specifically the Court) responds to the situation, establishment questions will continue to proliferate.

Some observers of the current situation suggest that, given the contentiousness of these church/state issues, it is perhaps best not to examine them too closely. This may be true, particularly if one's primary focus is the fate of specific refugees or the short-term political impact of their presence in one place or another. Yet if one considers the basic long-term question of religious freedom, these issues are important in their own right. Religious agencies have as much to gain in facing and clarifying this issue as the government. From their perspective, the ongoing integration of humanitarian and religious relief work into national security concerns erodes the independence of religion from government sought by the framers of the Constitution. It also erodes agreed-upon standards of humanitarian cooperation between private and public authorities. Or is it possible that the framers' view of the separation of church and state was only fully applicable in a less complicated society, one in which religion was explicitly conceived of as a private and personal matter? If this is true, then guarantees of religious freedom are also less applicable, and religious bodies active abroad are left largely unprotected by traditional understandings that have prevailed since the beginning of the republic.

15

National Security, Religious Liberty, and the Law Beyond the Water's Edge

American church/state traditions do not always travel well. When church groups expressed interest in aiding the approximately 3 million Afghan refugees who fled to Pakistan beginning in 1979, they discovered that Pakistan, itself in the process of reestablishing Islamic law, was distinctly uninterested in importing Christian agencies; Pakistan sought a legal system in which religion and the state were fully identified with each other. A compromise was reached on the refugee assistance question under which a consortium of agencies was allowed to distribute assistance, much of it furnished by the U.S. government. Observers close to this situation note that the strong U.S. desire for a presence among the Afghan refugees helped establish a compromise that neutralized any "religious" identification of the relief in order to avoid offending the Pakistanis.

"We can't separate God from Caesar," said Abdullah Khan, commissioner of refugees in Pakistan's North-West Frontier Province. "That's something you think you can do." An attempt in this setting to apply domestic U.S. church/state standards—insisting, say, that Pakistan institute pluralistic religious freedom— would be out of the question. As Ambassador Robert Spiers said in 1983, "Our personal views of human rights may be a little too esoteric in this part of the world . . . publicly, as a representative of the United States, I don't go around lecturing people on the way we do things at home."[1] Spiers's acknowledgment that U.S. law has no standing in Pakistan is undeniable. But do our laws, specifically the guarantees of the religion clauses and related civil liberties, apply to dealings between U.S. officials and U.S. citizens abroad?

While Americans routinely export their domestic political controversies, it is less clear that they are willing to use domestic legal standards to solve disputes involving Americans abroad. Our initial suggestion was that U.S. law, in this case church/state law in the context of refugee assistance, functions at best as an echo of domestic ideals rather than as a binding legal norm. John Mansfield has similarly argued that the Constitution itself embodies an overall philosophy, which includes the extension of political and religious tolerance and respect for the ways of others; these broad traces of political philosophy follow Americans in their travels.[2] The extension of U.S. standards of religious freedom overseas—even in the limited case under examination here, the contacts between U.S. citizens and the refugee programs and policies of the U.S. government—clearly depends on far more than the application of existing domestic tests of religious liberty. Individuals may use the federal government for the enforcement of personal prejudices. Local political disputes abroad may be a stronger determinant of U.S. policies than domestic guarantees of civil liberties to individual U.S. citizens. The political and cultural exigencies of foreign settings may require closer ties between American religious and political authorities than sanctioned under domestic law; refugees may be judged on their nationality or their political usefulness to the United States.

Finally, the majority of instances that have directly involved church/state disputes have been settled administratively rather than in the courts. For the Displaced Persons Commission in the late 1940s, the law served administrative ends, providing a means of getting a job done rather than an impartial standard of final justice. More recently, when religious agencies debated whether the refusal of the government to register them for federal assistance turned on religious discrimination, political and administrative adjustments precluded any formal showdown in the courts. Yet as religious agencies seek to establish the independence of their international missions from government priorities in the post-Vietnam era, they may be increasingly forced to turn to the courts as a last resort in assurring their freedom of action abroad. When State Department orthodoxy states that "the Constitution stops at the water's edge," American citizens may interpret this to mean that beyond administrative compromises they have limited remedies in cases of conflict with government programs or personnel abroad.

Despite these limitations, the role of U.S. civil liberties abroad—their "extraterritorial" application, in legal terminology—is of ongoing significance in humanitarian actions such as refugee assistance and famine relief.[3] Without some commitment to a common search for legal and moral standards, American voluntarism faces possible extinction, the victim of centrifugal forces that undermine its independence and its ideals. The central fact that this examination of extraterritoriality must confront is the greatly expanded powers of the executive branch in foreign affairs since World War II. The use of national security rationales in foreign policy has become commonplace. In this setting religious freedom and the related commitment of government and of private citizens to humanitarian assistance abroad is in a painfully weak legal position.

If far-reaching claims of governmental authority abroad are extended to cover all areas, they may mean both everything and nothing. Sovereignty in conducting foreign affairs is expressed in a cluster of related expressions, including "national security," "the national interest," and "compelling state (or governmental) interest." Since World War II, the United States has extended its national security interests to all the continents. Overseas, the transfer of gifts, trade, maintenance of private property, and certain civil liberties of U.S. citizens have all been halted during peacetime in the postwar period in the name of national security. Justice Harry Blackmun has in an opinion wondered about the infinite expansion of such powers. "I have never been able fully to appreciate just what a 'compelling state interest' is," he stated. "If it means . . . 'incapable of being overcome' upon any balancing process, then, of course, the test merely announces an inevitable result, and the test is no test at all."[4]

Church agencies active abroad have attempted to fight the encroachment of security concerns into their humanitarian work with refugees since the early days of the cold war. When the Mutual Security Act of 1951 linked government ocean freight reimbursements to mutual security concerns rather than to the earlier rationale of "economic assistance," seven Christian and Jewish agencies protested. Lutheran World Relief passed a resolution asking that the "humanitarian concern . . . of the American people be reflected explicitly in the policies of our government" and that such concerns be kept separate from the government's security concerns.[5] This was accomplished by an amendment altering the technical language of the bill, but the long-term success of the agencies in separating humanitarian from security assistance has been limited.

Nowhere in the field of refugee policy is the interplay between domestic and international issues, or between conflicting moral and legal standards, better illustrated than in the government's 1985–86 prosecution of church workers for their participation in the sanctuary movement to aid Central Americans fleeing conflict at home. Few developments have brought the plight of helpless refugees home to Americans more directly than this bold effort of local congregations to compensate for the perceived deficiencies in U.S. Central American and refugee policy by interposing the protection of the church between individuals and the state. The sanctuary trials, directed chiefly against citizens in the United States protesting the Reagan administration's foreign policy, epitomized pressures facing U.S. citizens who work with international refugees. The defendants' case—which sought to pit the rights of the refugees and the religious freedom of the defendants against the right of the president to pursue the "national interest" in his foreign policy—was essentially denied access to the courts.

This aborted confrontation was emblematic of the limited role the courts have been willing to assume in foreign policy-related issues. The judge did not want to hear a case about the existing and unresolved conflicts between religious and governmental authorities over an appropriate American response today to the world's refugee problem; he only wanted to know if immigration statutes had been broken. The very intensity of the sanctuary conflict stands in stark contrast to the cooperative church/state tradition in refugee assistance that appeared during the Second World War. We will return again to its significance in advancing common understandings of the role of U.S. law, specifically guarantees of civil liberties, in the pursuit of foreign policy and of building shared commitments to humanitarian assistance today. The sanctuary prosecutions should not be viewed as an isolated flashpoint. They help locate the political wall of separation between church and state: namely, religious institutions and values are allotted a role quite separate from the public exercise of authority and power.

Though the U.S. government prudently stops short of calling certain actions of U.S. religious groups abroad treasonous, the tension today between some religious groups and the government is intense. Some government workers question whether private U.S. relief agencies that take policy positions opposed to governmental refugee policy should be allowed to work overseas; by taking such visibly political positions, goes the argument, such groups violate the terms of their nonprofit status and undermine consensus on U.S. foreign policy.

Such disputes have become common since the 1970s. Religiously based agencies' attempts to assert the independence of their activities from government priorities have run against the grain of the built-in bias toward complementary public/

private programs in refugee aid established during World War II. In other instances, observers have noted that ties between the government and religious groups appear to be much closer than would be permitted under domestic law. In such cases a symbiotic relationship between church and state would seem to be the problem. In both instances, any attempt to address the conflict in the courts would raise a prior question: in the political cauldron of private/public cooperation in refugee assistance abroad, do the classic protections of U.S. church/state law in any way extend beyond the shores of the United States?

Despite the weight that constitutionally assured U.S. civil liberties may carry overseas in relations between U.S. civilians and U.S. government personnel, courts that have heard cases involving U.S. citizens abroad have in recent years shown a distinct reluctance to engage problems that have a markedly political component. This raises difficulties for resolving any conflict that pits religious freedom issues against other international priorities of the United States. The courts have established certain precedents for the maintenance overseas of domestic civil rights in relationships between U.S. citizens and representatives of the U.S. government. The exercise of those rights (including the free exercise of religion) are not likely under current circumstances to outweigh other broadly constructed justifications for governmental policy decisions overseas such as the "national interest" or "national security."

Access to the courts may emerge as a central issue in church/state conflicts in coming years. This chapter will examine two approaches to this matter. First, the application of U.S. law abroad, extraterritoriality, will be examined here in the light of the previous involvement of domestic courts in the civil liberties of U.S. citizens abroad. When Americans reside in the territory of other sovereign nations, the United States is not for the most part in a position to guarantee rights assured under U.S. law and custom. Yet presumably U.S. officials are still bound by constitutional considerations, including those established in the First Amendment religion clauses, in their dealings with U.S. citizens. Domestic church/state law and the social principles it embodies nevertheless frequently take a back seat to local and international political pressures. It is this limited application that is of interest to us here.

Second, we must ask whether legal remedy is likely to be available in the courts when Americans working abroad believe their religious freedom has been infringed. In 1983, John C. Bennett argued that the greatest church/state conflicts for the rest of the century are likely to shift to the field of foreign policy.[6] Since this involves not only Americans working for religious groups abroad but also citizens protesting foreign policy at home, we must ask whether U.S. courts are likely to consider themselves competent to address such conflicts between religious and secular authority. In the course of this inquiry we will examine some of the recent court decisions that bear on this critical question. Although these decisions indicate that the courts have sought to maintain a constitutional framework for relations between U.S. citizens and U.S. authorities abroad, it will also become clear that the courts have little interest in presiding over conflicts of ultimate authority. The so-called political question doctrine continues to be used to excuse the courts from involvement in sensitive matters that touch on international politics. We will also examine the government's approach to the prosecution of church workers involved in the trials surrounding the sanctuary movement aiding refugees from Central

America. When applied to church/state conflicts, both of these approaches suggest that religious groups must exercise extreme caution in searching for means of protecting religious freedom.

Political conflict between church and state abroad reaches the public eye only occasionally; unlike controversies over prayer in the public schools or the right of students to hold religious meetings in public buildings, most of it takes place beyond the reach (or interest) of many newspaper or television journalists. One of the reasons for this is the very complexity of the issues. This would be true enough if our inquiry focused only on the domestic arrangements that have emerged since 1975 between religious welfare agencies and federal, state, county, and local instrumentalities charged with resettling refugees in the United States. Fewer domestic welfare efforts have been the source of greater friction between religion and government, whether we consider the way that agencies have allocated government resettlement assistance or specific political conflicts such as arose in Florida and in the court system following the arrival of Cuban and Haitian asylum seekers in the early 1980s.

The Constitution and U.S. Citizens Abroad

State Department officials are frequently reluctant to defend guarantees of U.S. civil liberties overseas. A standard State Department attitude already mentioned is the view that the role of the Constitution "stops at the water's edge." This view in no way undercuts American traditions of public participation in the questions of diplomacy and international relations, goes the argument, as long as such participation takes place within the United States. Overseas, the State Department cannot guarantee Americans that conditions there will correspond to domestic standards and assurances of civil liberties, particularly those guaranteed in the Bill of Rights. When asked to elaborate on current factors in their contacts with Americans abroad, State Department officials often point out that the post–World War II social and political conditions are further beyond the control of America and the Western powers than was the case before the war.

In the age of colonization, nations could impose their legal systems on other states and apply police force as deemed necessary. The system of treaties of extraterritoriality was to some degree part of this mentality. In the current era of independent nation-states, Western governments find it almost impossible to exert such direct influence on the domestic policies of countries in which their nationals work, and must often resort to more subtle political tactics.

The foreign affairs power of the United States is vested directly in the president. The president's power to act in defense of U.S. interests abroad is bounded only by limited congressional oversight and international legal understandings of national sovereignty. In this century presidents have sent troops all over the globe without waiting for the approval of Congress; for some time the Central Intelligence Agency was able to mount its covert war against Nicaragua's Sandinista government without explicit congressional approval. Despite congressional concern about such actions, the Supreme Court has argued that the president's power over external affairs predates the Constitution itself, and that such power is inherent in the very notion of sovereignty. This includes "a degree of discretion and freedom from statutory restriction which would not be admissible were domestic affairs alone involved."[7]

In conflicts between presidential foreign policy objectives and the rights of U.S. citizens, the courts, when they have become involved, have sided most often with the president. A recent example of such conflict arose in the settlement of claims against Iran after President Jimmy Carter negotiated the release of the American hostages in 1979. In reaching the agreement, President Carter agreed to suspend all claims then being litigated against Iran by U.S. citizens. A corporation, Dames and Moore, objected to the need to relitigate their claim against Iran in a special claims tribunal and challenged the president in court. They argued that his suspension of claims in U.S. courts went beyond his constitutional powers. The Supreme Court disagreed, pointing out that a settlement in favor of Dames and Moore would have removed a critical bargaining chip in the president's dealings with the Iranians.[8]

Here indeed was a case in which the complexity of the international political matters at stake did not deter court involvement, presumably because the issues touched on matters of the national interest. The Court, however, sided with the president's right to pursue the national interest rather than with the rights of individual citizens. Even if it is politically prudent then to agree with the State Department's contention that the protections of the Constitution stop at the water's edge, it leaves certain very difficult questions unanswered.

"Neither the Constitution nor the laws passed in pursuance of it have any force in foreign territory," said the Supreme Court in 1936, "*unless in respect of our own citizens*" [emphasis added]. This assertion is fundamental to any claim of the extraterritorial privileges of American citizenship. However, it should be noted that subsequent commentators have called the Court's judgment in this case "exotic."[9] "Any force" is a vague expression. It might be interpreted as meaning "*complete force*" or simply "*some* force." More recent court rulings argue the restrictive case, namely that *some* laws will be in *some* force, and that enforcement will be strongly dependent on the government's assessment of the national interest in any given case.

A year after issuing the judgment just quoted the Supreme Court reviewed the extension to the states of protections in force under the Constitution, noting that this process had begun with those protections "implicit in the concept of ordered liberty."[10] This "first order" of protected rights include those addressed in the First, Fourth, and Sixth Amendments, and most of those in the Fifth Amendment. If we consider these rights fundamental to our understanding of ordered liberty, we might also expect that they would be the first to be guarded in overseas contacts between citizens and the U.S. government. This has indeed been true in some cases. The Sixth Amendment, for example, guarantees the right to trial by jury. The wife of an Air Force employee stationed in England was convicted by a court-martial of murdering her husband. The Supreme Court in 1957 granted her the right to a trial by jury. The majority opinion stated that "no agreement with a foreign nation can confer power on the Congress, or any other branch of government, which is free from the restrictions of the Constitution."[11] Further, in 1960 the Court held in a separate case that civilian employees of the military abroad were entitled to jury trial for relatively small offenses.

Such rights for citizens living abroad have not always been affirmed in U.S.

territories; trial by jury has been denied in Puerto Rico, the Philippines, and the Mariana Islands.[12] In another Supreme Court decision a U.S. citizen who had killed a Japanese in Japan was denied a U.S. trial and turned over to Japanese authorities. The record of the courts in guaranteeing Bill of Rights protections for citizens abroad is equivocal on this point.[13]

A war or its immediate aftermath can influence the force of U.S. law abroad. Church-based refugee workers in Germany after World War II came under the jurisdiction of the U.S. military command which developed its own version of extending domestic civil liberties abroad. In a 1952 case, *Madsden* v. *Kinsella,* the Supreme Court allowed court-martial jurisdiction over U.S. military and civilians in enemy territory occupied and governed by the U.S. military.[14] Non-U.S. citizens who were "enemy aliens, resident, captured and imprisoned abroad" could not demand access to the U.S. courts.[15] Such limitations affected the application of the Sixth Amendment in Germany after World War II, but since the United States is not at present governing any country by military occupation these strictures are not applicable.

We have noted that the courts have frequently sided with the president in cases in which issues of national security collided with the constitutional rights of U.S. citizens overseas. This was not the case in a 1978 ruling in which the court held that constitutional rights of American citizens overseas should prevail over trade restrictions on technological and scientific exchanges of information.[16] One commentator has noted that "the decision implies that the first amendment provides businesses with at least *some* constitutional rights . . . giving content [to these rights] will be up to future courts."[17]

The Right to Travel

Perhaps the most basic constitutionally protected right at stake when Americans go abroad is the right to travel freely, a right which domestically has been unconditionally guaranteed by the Supreme Court at least since 1969. This domestic guarantee has been broadly (though not universally) extended to citizens who want to travel to nations that are not hostile or at war with the United States. "Liberty in the fifth amendment means the freedom to go where we want" concluded a study of the history of passports.[18] Even so, the right to travel abroad is not guaranteed even in peacetime. Restrictions have been imposed for political reasons, despite a 1958 Supreme Court decision that argued that the Fifth Amendment secured the right to international travel.[19]

Travel to North Korea, Vietnam, and Cuba—three Soviet allies that have at different times been embroiled in disputes with the United States—is currently restricted. The Supreme Court has upheld the right of the secretary of state to impose such restrictions.[20] Furthermore, the same ruling holds that there is no First Amendment guarantee of an "unrestrained right to gather information" in Cuba, a little noted assessment with wide-ranging implications for church-based activities in politically troubled regions.[21]

Other nations such as Iraq have excluded American citizens in recent years; other exclude specific Americans. Jews, for instance, are not legally permitted to visit certain Arab countries. The State Department has in the past acquiesced to such limitations. It will be recalled that at first the U.S. government did little to protect American Jews when they were harassed in Russia early in the century; only a vigorous campaign of public criticism eventually moved the State Department and Congress to intervene. In the mid-1950s Americans indicating to the Passport Office their intentions to travel to the Middle East were advised to carry with them "a baptismal certificate or a letter from a pastor."[22] Jewish employees were banned from the American air base at Dhahran, Saudi Arabia, in 1956, a practice defended by Secretary of State John Foster Dulles as necessary for the maintenance of U.S. political advantage in the region.

The most notorious passport case of recent years involved the Court's 1981 support for the State Department's revocation of the passport of former CIA agent Phillip Agee. After leaving government service Agee went to Germany and began a campaign against the CIA, identifying hundreds of agents. Without prior hearing, the State Department revoked his passport. Agee claimed that the revocation interfered with the First Amendment protections of his free speech, but the Court found this claim to be without foundation. Agee lost his right to travel because the Court decided that "overriding government interests," namely safeguarding security and intelligence secrets, were more important than Agee's freedom of movement. The Court cited an earlier decision to justify this limitation: "while the Constitution protects against the invasion of individual rights, it is not a suicide pact."[23]

Governmental interference in the right to travel may stem from little more than personal prejudice. Like all human structures the passport system is only as good as the people who administer it. In the early 1950s the State Department's Passport Office was headed by Ruth Shipley, known throughout the department as the "Queen of Passports." Protestant missionary leaders recall a period early in the Eisenhower presidency in which Shipley simply decided that there were too many missionaries working overseas. Never known for her interest in consulting with the rest of the State Department, she began cutting back approvals for missionary passports. This situation was soon put to a halt administratively after public objections were made by mission leaders.

The right to travel is an excellent example of the way that conflicts between church and state may slip into the courts without directly invoking the religion clauses. While the conflicts may actually be due to the different foreign policy priorities of religious groups and government agencies, their legal resolution regularly turns on precedents less weighty than those outlining the proper relationship between church and state. Disputes arising between the overseas activities of religious groups and the government most often involve conflicts over administrative procedures or regulations and, therefore, are not likely to be decided on the basis of the religion clauses of the First Amendment. In the past, religious and governmental authorities alike have sought to move with extreme caution in order to avoid such open church/state conflict.

Political judgments within the government on travel restrictions may never reach the courts or even the press. When in 1983 a group of religious women wanted to travel to Honduras to witness for peace, some were denied visas in the United States and others were simply refused entry at the Honduran airport. In this case charges arose in Congress that the Reagan administration had been actively cooperating with Honduran authorities in denying their travel rights. In the summer of 1986 a group of U.S. church workers assisting refugees to return to their homes in El Salvador were deported by the Salvadoran government; it is not unreasonable to think that U.S. authorities were consulted in this case as well.

Judicial Control versus Judicial Acquiesence

The entire modern period under review in this book has brought a new level of attention to national security matters. Writing in the Pentagon Papers case of 1971 Justice Brennan stated that infringement of First Amendment rights once reserved for a time of war might now be extended to other situations.[24] This appears to be the case in the Court's response to travel-related disputes. As part of this ensemble of government oversight we can briefly examine three other areas: control of wills and bequests, tax provisions, and the control of the classification of nonprofit organizations for tax exempt purposes. In each of these areas the U.S. courts have accepted jurisdiction, based on interpretation of documents executed in the United States.

Since the 1930s court decisions have increasingly taken into account the political climate abroad in determining how overseas bequests are disposed. When religious institutions in nations considered hostile to the United States are the beneficiaries in a U.S. will, the courts have invoked the judicial doctrine of *cy pres* ("as near as practicable") in order to subordinate church interests to the paramount interests of the state. Officials in the State Department have on occasion supplied administrative assistance to the courts in such cases. By the 1930s, for instance, U.S. courts had begun to restrict religious bequests to churches in Germany. A World War II era bequest to missionary work in China was redirected to Taiwan when the will was finally settled in 1957. At the height of the cold war tensions of 1950, a New Jersey superior court withheld funds designated for a Catholic orphanage in Hungary. Control of the church in Hungary, according to the State Department, was then in the hands of the government. "Statements by diplomatic officers of iron curtain countries that funds distributed would be used for the purpose intended by the testator have been received reservedly and have been ignored," said the court. The church at both ends loses in this decision, which places church-related movements of funds under the political control of government. At least one analyst of such questions holds that the ideals of voluntary foreign aid should be reexamined in the light of contemporary political conditions; "state courts," notes Neill Alford, "are becoming increasingly sensitive to the national interest in their decisions involving voluntary foreign aid."[25]

One interpretation of this comment is that government is justified in extending controls over U.S. charities directed overseas. Economist Joseph Schumpeter argued that there are few better ways of understanding the way a government regulates societal functions than through an examination of its tax code. The nonprofit, tax exempt status of churches and related institutions is fiercely guarded today as an integral part of the traditional separation of church and state. Much church/state jurisprudence turns on questions of dollars and cents, and most of this concerns the state's taxing power. As noted at the beginning of this discussion the tax exempt status of religious bodies constitutes a form of extraterritoriality. Church/state specialists—a group generally disposed to the preservation of religious freedom— have in recent years detected efforts on the part of government officials to narrow the scope of tax exempt privileges accorded religious bodies. The control of extraterritorial activities of religiously based charities through the tax code is one method the government could use to control activities it considers politically suspect.

In 1984 actions widely denounced as a government effort to "defund the left," the Office of Management and Budget issued a set of revised guidelines for the use of federal funds by nonprofit organizations. The guidelines demanded a separation of government and private funds so exhaustive as to severely impair the workings of many such agencies. The alternative to compliance was the loss of tax exemption. The new guidelines were eventually revised, but many religious agencies active abroad were alarmed at the implications of the action.

In one relevant court case a state Supreme Court sided with a church agency in its efforts to retain tax exemption. The Pennsylvania Supreme Court held that a mission's extraterritorial activities were the legitimate basis of its tax exempt status. Tax assessors had attempted to tax the mission's extensive training facilities in the state on the grounds that the mission provided no local benefits and therefore deserved no tax exemption. The Supreme Court reversed this decision: "Charity begins at home, but it does not end there," said the ruling. "Benevolence knows no geographical boundary and the Legislature of Pennsylvania has imposed none."[26] Thus the extraterritorial activities of the mission determined its tax exempt status. Such reasoning is, however, double-edged: it could presumably be applied in the other direction to address the political involvements of religious agencies abroad.

Despite these examples, any response to the question of whether U.S. law extends beyond the water's edge in regulating contact between U.S. citizens and the U.S. government would have to be severely qualified. According to Article VI, Section 2, of the Constitution, treaties between the government and other nations have the status of the law of the land. Regulatory agreements and business contracts that bind nations and corporations internationally are followed as closely as possible; contracts between the government and private agencies concerning overseas activities fall under U.S. law if they are signed within U.S. territory; wills and bequests directed to overseas beneficiaries are administered under U.S. law. Yet in the field of civil liberties, restrictions are commonplace and extraterritorial application of U.S. law has been much more dependent on local and international political conditions. To complicate matters even more, courts have recently come to rely on another doctrine that has served to remove them even further from difficult conflicts between citizens and the U.S. government in international issues.

The Political Question Doctrine

Often the exercise of power precedes the rule of law. This was the case during the period of European and American colonial expansion; it is true also in wartime. Under U.S. law, this power proceeds from the exercise of national sovereignty through the person of the president. "The President . . . is the sole organ of the federal government in the field of international relations" said the Supreme Court in 1936.[27] This view is not a twentieth-century accretion, but a doctrine that the Supreme Court has recognized throughout the life of the republic. In the 1831 case involving the right of the president to remove the Cherokee Indians from land legally deeded to them, Chief Justice John Marshall argued that "in the exercise of sovereign right, the sovereign is sole arbiter of his own justice. The penalty of wrong is war and subjugation."[28] Therefore, representatives of the president have been accorded considerable flexibility in pursuing the president's objectives, including at times freedom from domestic juridical standards.

Little modification can be expected from the courts in such matters if they pursue a comparatively recent approach known as the political question doctrine. This doctrine holds that the courts have no authority to enter into political disputes committed by the Constitution to the legislative and executive branches. The doctrine is beginning to play a crucial role in matters concerning international affairs.[29]

Justice Lewis Powell formulated three questions that would help determine whether the political question doctrine is applicable in a given case. (1) Does the issue involve resolution of questions committed by the Constitution to a coordinate branch of government? (2) Would resolution of the question demand that a court move beyond areas of judicial expertise? (3) Do prudential considerations counsel against judicial intervention? If the answer is yes to any one of the three, the court is justified under this doctrine in withdrawing from the case.[30] In such instances court withdrawal amounts to a decision to let the government's action stand.

In 1983 Temistocles Ramirez, a U.S. citizen, protested the expropriation of several thousand acres of his property in Honduras for use as a military training site by the Honduran and U.S. armies. The court did not rule on whether the expropriation of land was legal or illegal. Rather, it applied the political question test and answered all three questions affirmatively. First, it held that judges have no say over the conduct of foreign policy; that is the job of the executive and Congress. The district court then held that answering Ramirez's complaint would involve "sensitive and confidential communications" between the president and a foreign power, material that is "not judicially discoverable." Finally, the court held that it is only prudent for the judiciary to avoid litigation that challenges the wisdom and propriety of the president's conduct as commander in chief of our armed forces. The court refused to pass judgment on Ramirez's claim and Ramirez appealed the decision.

The nine justices on the bench of the court of appeals in the District of Columbia were sharply divided over the case, but reversed the district court's decision in 1984 by a narrow margin of 5 to 4. Freedom from unwarranted judicial supervision, said the court, "cannot give the Executive *carte blanche* to trample the most fundamental liberty and property rights of this country's citizenry. . . . Affirmance of this dismissal on the ground that plaintiff's claims are political questions or an improper challenge to foreign affairs powers would mean that virtually *anything* done by United States officials to United States citizens on foreign soil is nonjudiciable. This is not the law." The court found a "long line of cases" that permit court rulings against unlawful actions of the executive branch in matters of foreign affairs. The doctrine of the separation of powers within the U.S. government may in some cases carry more weight than the right of citizens to access to the courts over issues involving foreign affairs, but "the prudential balance may shift decidedly when United States citizens assert constitutional violations by United States officials."[31]

Calling the majority opinion "extraordinary," the minority opinion, authored by then Circuit Judge Antonin Scalia, stated that the decision to reverse "reflects a willingness to extend judicial power into areas where we do not know, and have no way of finding out, what serious harm we may be doing." He argued that the majority was working with "an inflated notion of the function of this court, which produces stirring rhetoric but poor constitutional law . . . it is small wonder that concepts such as equitable restraint on the basis of interference with military and foreign affairs . . . have little meaning [to this court]."[32] Rather than press an appeal to the Supreme Court, government lawyers sought an out-of-court settlement with Ramirez.

In a 1986 decision a federal circuit court in Philadelphia ruled that Americans United for Separation of Church and State had no standing to sue the federal government to block appointment of a permanent ambassador to the Vatican. This matter is a delicate one that has periodically ignited interreligious controversy in the modern era ever since Franklin Roosevelt appointed Myron Taylor as his personal representative to the pope in 1939. The court hinted that should Americans United appeal they might encounter the political question doctrine at the next bend of the road. According to the circuit court diplomatic recognition is a "judicially unreviewable political decision."[33]

We have clearly not heard the last of the political question doctrine in determining the role of the courts in protecting U.S. citizens overseas. It cuts deeply into any effort to extend U.S. domestic civil liberties abroad to U.S. citizens via the courts, particularly in cases that directly implicate treaty provisions or the foreign policy and national security of the United States. The combined force of the executive branch's national security concerns and a reliance by the judiciary on the political question doctrine might be enough to undermine any broad extraterritorial structuring of civil rights for Americans in their contacts with foreign policy programs and personnel. Such a trend would give enormous freedom to the U.S. government to subjugate individual rights to the pursuit of national security.

In church/state terms, the political question doctrine announces again the government's intention of maintaining its claim of sovereignty in foreign affairs, any and all claims of religious freedom notwithstanding. This intention has become clearer in the post-Vietnam years as certain religious agencies have aggressively challenged the government's exercise of such claims. Although church groups have succeeded in maintaining some humanitarian efforts beyond the field of governmental interests (the Mennonite Central Committee, for example, was allowed to continue shipments of school kits to Cambodia in 1982–83 despite the fact that Cambodia was off limits for U.S. trade under the Trading With the Enemy Act), the range of such activities may be distinctly limited.[34]

The desire to avoid a court battle between religious freedom and national security may make it next to impossible for a foreign affairs-related church/state conflict as such to ever reach the courts. To avoid such a battle, the political question doctrine is not the only means the government has at hand. The best example to date of the government's efforts to postpone a court battle between the ultimate sovereignties of religion and the state at the international level is the sanctuary movement to aid the cause of Central American refugees. In this instance, the government itself brought the matter to the courts. There was no need to use the political question doctrine: instead the government's lawyers argued to disallow any testimony based upon religious belief or U.S. foreign policy. The court agreed.

Sanctuary: Politicizing Refugee Concerns

As religious institutions and believers struggle to understand the universal implications of their callings in the late twentieth century, the issues increasingly traverse national boundaries. The contemporary movements of refugees are an all too real demonstration of the ways that international political disputes generate extraterritorial problems. The sanctuary movement for Central American refugees shows how church/state issues that have their roots abroad or in U.S. foreign policy decisions may quickly have an impact on domestic politics and jurisprudence. The sanctuary trials may prove to be the best contemporary illustration of the obstacles blocking constitutional guarantees of religious freedom abroad, particularly when that freedom is exercised to compensate for the perceived inability of the government to incorporate humanitarian concerns into its working definition of the national interest. These trials are a sobering demonstration of the boundaries placed on religious freedom by contemporary U.S. foreign policy.

By 1981, the Central American refugee problem had come into sharp focus in the press. Most church agencies with ties to field work in Central America knew that in addition to the task of caring for residents of camps throughout the region, there was a larger and politically even more explosive issue at hand: what would the U.S. government do about Central Americans who fled their homeland, traveled through Mexico, and eventually reached the United States? There was little question that among the flow of Hispanics entering the country's southern borders were bona fide refugees, including Guatemalans, Nicaraguans, and Salvadorans, fleeing persecution and death at the hands of combatants in El Salvador's civil war. Many church leaders argued strongly that the Central Americans should be granted asylum and given the same protections granted refugees from other countries.

The INS took a different point of view. Because the State Department was then certifying every six months that human rights conditions in El Salvador were "improving," the INS could not, on the basis of its own internal regulations, certify that Salvadoran refugees had well-founded fears of persecution in El Salvador. At best these new asylum seekers were to be classified as economic migrants; at worst they were to be deported, shipped home through special contractual relations between the State and Justice departments and the Intergovernmental Committee for Migration. In the short run many were detained. The UNHCR investigated the detention facilities operated by the INS in September 1981; the resulting analysis carefully couched support for the Salvadoran refugees in mildly critical descriptions of U.S. policy. That policy, resulting in the "apparent failure" of the government to grant asylum, "would appear to represent a negation of . . . responsibilities" assumed by the United States in its acceptance of international standards for the treatment of refugees.[35]

Seizing on the extraordinary gap between the Reagan administration's views on the Salvadoran and Guatemalan refugees and the information supplied to them by regional and U.S. church workers in Central America and other sources, a group of church leaders gathering in early 1982 (including workers from Church World Service, the U.S. Catholic Conference, and other church agencies assisting refugees) saw an opportunity to dramatize a political conflict, secure rights for the refugees, and assert the right of the church to speak the truth, all at once: the churches would revive the biblical and medieval concept of providing sanctuary.

The initial goal was eminently practical and concrete: to save refugees who had reached the United States from potential deportation. Supporters of the movement sought to counter what they viewed as mistaken governmental actions. The government issued low deportation figures; sanctuary supporters and church agencies cited alternative, higher statistics.[36]

Participants in the movement incorporated an almost inexhaustible combination of theological and political motivations. Some believed sanctuary for the refugees would incarnate "a place of life-giving mystery . . . where it is clear that we worship and recognize in action a law higher than that of government or commerce."[37] The Reverend John Fife, whose church in Tucson was the first to declare sanctuary, said, "I'm looking for the whole community gathered to put our souls to work in discovering just what the symbol [of sanctuary] can mean and how it can explode into all kinds of creative pilgrimages."[38] (To anyone who has spent a lifetime crafting careful political compromises with government officials on refugee matters, this is bound to sound a bit loose.) As an "exploding symbol," sanctuary has meant many things, including sending observers to Central American refugee camps, declaring the earth a sanctuary from nuclear armaments, serving as a "congregational equivalent of baptism," stopping the slaughter of victims by death squads, ending an "acquisitive system based on maximization of profit," and halting military pacification programs in Guatemala.[39]

Jim Corbett, the Quaker rancher/philosopher credited with starting the movement, has described this ecumenical combination of motivations and political ends as "covenant ecumenism"—namely, a theology of the biblical imperatives of *shalom* and justice in which the church finds its meaning only as it stands in "protective community with the poor." As solidarity with the movement began to appear in the United States Corbett predicted that it would help "maintain some aboveground 'space' for . . . [the] post-Constantinian church." This new basis for ecumenism, heralded in church circles by at least a decade of discussion of what the church might look like once finally freed from the ancient alliance established with the third-century emperor Constantine, was truly international. It would encompass Jews, Christians, and nonbelievers alike; it required only a commitment to justice and the poor and a willingness to "co-create the human aspect of *shalom,* or peace. . . . The decision for sanctuary therefore functions as a pivot point for turning away from conquest," which was identified with the function of the modern superpower.[40]

Tensions then developed between those who believed that churches should call attention to the plight of the Central American refugees to compel U.S. officials to enforce refugee law, and those who believed that the occasion provided a way to attack Central American policies of the Reagan administration. Those holding the first perspective were content to stand on the side of the oppressed and support their cause under the law. Those holding the second view argued that there was no apolitical humanitarian position; all was political and the movement therefore had to address the root causes of refugee movements rather than the symptoms. Both perspectives took a provocative stance toward the administration, and both inevitably brought the politics of Central America into the limelight.[41] Movement leaders were, in an expression Bryan Hehir has used in assessing church/state relations today, intent on translating political debate into "concrete tactical issues."[42] This meant bringing the confrontation before the public and hoping that attention would elicit public sympathy for the refugees themselves, forcing the INS and other government agencies to alter their policies toward Central Americans, and ultimately toward Central America itself.

Corbett realized, however, that the key to the issue lay not with the number of refugees aided by the movement, nor even with its initial levels of public support, but on how well the controversy, which was at root a struggle between spiritual and political principalities, fared in the courts:

> Will the government, through the courts, permit juries to learn about sanctuary issues? That remains to be seen; yet the verdict will, in any case, still be up to the jury rather than the state. And, if the courts should prevent juries from learning the truth about sanctuary cases or about their responsibility and power to act in the defense of human rights, the public from which juries are drawn will eventually learn from church, press, and other sources. . . . The church-led opposition to our government's violation of human rights in Central America is based primarily on personal knowledge rather than reports, which cuts right through the webs of deception spun by politicians and cold warriors.[43]

The answer to the question of whether the government would allow juries to learn about the religious free exercise and foreign policy issues involved in sanctuary was no.

Immediate complications arose, even before arrests were made, which blurred the ultimate significance of the trial in matters of church/state relations in foreign policy. The direct provocations from sanctuary workers—parading undocumented illegal aliens in highly publicized cross-country "pilgrimages" and the like—drew forth the same and worse from the INS: government informers were planted in Bible classes and worship services, and tape recordings were made. This apparent violation of civil liberties in a house of worship was enough to discredit the INS's handling of the situation in the eyes of most observers, but it was only the beginning.

The Justice Department began arresting individual participants in the sanctuary movement in early 1984, and the question of religious free exercise arose in an early pretrial hearing when defendant Jack Elder submitted a motion to dismiss the charges on the basis of his right of religious free exercise. The judge then held that "there is arguably a basis in Catholicism to demonstrate the activity charged in the indictment could fall within the religious beliefs of a seriously committed and practicing Catholic. This court rules they can." The judge, however, eventually threw out the motion to dismiss by supporting the government's view that the upholding of the nation's immigration laws constituted a governmental interest that overrode the individual's right to religious free exercise.[44] Later in the year Elder and Stacey Lynn Merkt were indicted on new charges; both were convicted and given minimal sentences. But again the defense was not allowed to present testimony based on U.S. refugee law or on the religious beliefs of the defendants.

The largest of the trials, initially involving sixteen defendants, began with indictments handed down by the U.S. attorney in January 1985 in Phoenix. Each of the sixteen was charged with conspiracy; additional charges were also leveled at them and at seventy-four Central Americans and "unindicted co-conspirators." Many refugee advocates saw a court case that pitted religious freedom against Central American policy as tailor-made for an era of media coverage. But once again, the federal judge threw out any defense arguments based on international law, U.S. Central American policy or religious freedom. He wanted it limited to the question of whether immigration statutes had been violated by the defendants.

Religious motivation, international law, and humanitarian standards were not allowed to play a role in the sanctuary trials; in some sense they were classed as "imponderables" best avoided in the search for a clean ruling. As we have noted throughout this chapter, the courts have held that the Constitution confers no higher obligation on the president than conducting foreign policy in the national interest of the United States. It was highly unlikely, seen from this perspective, that the courts would use the sanctuary trials to restrict the president's freedom in a matter as closely tied to the politics of foreign policy as refugee concerns. Had testimony on religious motivation been allowed, a far more likely result would have been cold case law formally restricting the scope of religious freedom of individuals at home or abroad in situations bearing on the conduct of U.S. foreign policy. In May 1986 the remaining sanctuary defendants at the Tucson trial were each convicted on at least one count; they were given suspended sentences and paroled once the defendants agreed not to participate or publicly identify themselves with the sanctuary movement during their period of parole.

Issues became imponderable during the trials not just because they were difficult to solve, but because they were banned from the public record of the court. The strategy of the judges in banning such matters essentially confirmed the INS and State Department's commitments to prevail with their interpretations of their foreign policy and refugee mandates. Their attitude toward humanitarian standards, for instance, was incremental rather than absolute. In this view the government's approach to humanitarian standards would be to strengthen them bit by bit; one could not expect a full, complete humanitarianism to appear overnight. This incremental view has been shared by most leaders of refugee relief agencies, both religious and secular, since the beginning of modern cooperative efforts between private and public agencies.

Corbett and others in the sanctuary movement wanted to use international and humanitarian law in an absolute way. They traced the legal rationale for sanctuary not in U.S. refugee policy but in commitments to international justice expressed in the Nuremberg Military Tribunals after World War II:

> The essence of the Charter [of the Military Tribunal] is that individuals have international duties that transcend the national obligations of obedience imposed by the individual state.
>
> International law operates as a restriction and limitation on the sovereignty of nations. It may also limit the obligations which individuals owe to their states, and create for them international obligations which are binding on them to the extent that they must be carried out even if to do so violates a positive law or directive of state.[45]

It was precisely this kind of defense that the courts refused to entertain. There was, in essence, to be no open-ended "post-Constantinian space" for religious freedom in the service of higher international standards. Those standards, like international law, only existed at the sufferance of the United States and its allies, and they would be permitted to stand and develop only in concert with the interests of the state.

Any survey of humanitarian law, for instance, must acknowledge that the protections it offers in refugee-related situations are limited at the very best. Beyond the UN's 1951 Refugee Convention and 1967 Protocol on Refugees, most other humanitarian standards—certainly those most often cited by sanctuary leaders—are applicable only by inference. They may be used to bolster an argument, yet there is no fixed definition of humanitarianism in customary international law. The UN standards of refugee care, which are defined much more closely, are today violated with impunity around the world for lack of enforcement mechanisms. The UNHCR officials recognize that whatever power they exercise internationally is largely dependent on the financial and political support of the U.S. government. In virtually all instances a pragmatic relationship between such large UN assistance agencies and their patron governments provides the substance of whatever "enforceability" exists for humanitarian law. This pragmatic view of the law, namely, that it serves to codify existing practice and move states incrementally closer to a view that practicing humanitarianism is in their self-interest, acknowledges the realities of political pressures and tragic developments.

Thus the sanctuary cases of the 1980s bring us back to the fundamental problem of civil liberties and extraterritoriality: the exercise of power still routinely precedes the rule of law. It is this unhappy state of international affairs that fuels much of the frustrated rage behind the sanctuary movement. Accompanying the widespread use of absolutist humanitarian arguments in sanctuary circles are outbursts against the "absolute evil" of the Immigration and Naturalization Service, the State Department, and other arms of government. There is undeniably much to dislike in the functioning of a modern superpower. Those private citizens whose goal is to assist as many refugees as possible must see that the entire system of aid— UN agencies, governments, churches and voluntary agencies, and others—has been since World War II, is, and will probably remain dependent on the goodwill of the U.S. government. The goal of total humanitarian transcendence of the evils of the modern state is a meaningless option.

Extraterritorial Prospects and Extralegal Solutions

However political limitations affect the application of the U.S. Constitution abroad, religiously motivated Americans today carry the realities of their citizenship with them whenever they carry their missions abroad. As the Apostle Paul carried the privileges of his Roman citizenship abroad in the service of the Gospel, so Americans have traditionally included the freedom to pursue religious mandates overseas as a protected and treasured component of their citizenship, a freedom which grew in part from respect for Roman power. Yet religious bodies of various creeds have always reserved a certain independence from government, first in building the inner life of the church and more recently in such matters as internationally organized relief and refugee work. This independence frequently has been taken for granted as a component of U.S. citizenship; John Mansfield has argued that placing demands of conformity to national policies on religiously motivated Americans abroad is justifiable only under "foreign policy considerations of the gravest sort."[46] Similarly, Judge John Noonan has written that when a citizen faces conflicts between the law and the individual, "the law cannot be the sole measure of his or her conscience."[47]

The lack of consensus among different religious groups today, and between different political wings of individual churches and denominations, clearly contributes to the political polarization evident in such developments as the sanctuary movement. Such lack of consensus places severe strains on the protection of the exercise of civil rights in relation to foreign policy issues, since any given government must constantly be in search of a workable consensus in foreign relations. In many ways it is a different world from that in which the government and religious groups began their joint efforts on behalf of refugees of World War II. Many of the participants in the sanctuary movement have difficulty accepting the notion that religious refugee agencies can honestly cooperate with federal authorities and still claim to have the best interests of the refugees at heart. Under such circumstances, we may ask whether there is a healthy future for religious freedom domestically, let alone a future for the application of U.S. church/state law in the overseas dealings of federal officials and private U.S. citizens and organizations.

Citizenship in a democracy is not simply a legal warrant of privilege, but a way of participating in and belonging to a society, touching a basic human need to take pride in one's own civilization. Writing in 1938, Swiss theologian Karl Barth surveyed the mounting horror of Nazi Germany; just a few years earlier he had been principal author of the Barmen Declaration announcing the freedom of the Confession Church of Germany from Nazi coercion. He nonetheless voiced the fundamental hope for free collaboration between religion and government in creating a just state: "Can we ask God for [a just state] which we are not at the same moment determined and prepared to bring about, so far as it lies within the bounds of our possibility? Can we pray that the state shall preserve us, and that it may continue to do so as a just State, or that it will again become a just State, and not at the same time pledge ourselves personally, both in thought and action, in order that this may happen?"[48] These sentiments not only capture the fervor that generated the tradition of church/state cooperation abroad half a century ago; they remain strong today within many U.S. religious communities active overseas.

Given the precarious state of the protections of the civil liberties of U.S. citizens abroad in their dealings with the U.S. government, Barth's words are critical today in the extension of humanitarian standards and religious liberty abroad. In seeking stability and incremental growth of such freedoms, we are left with the conclusion that the humanitarian tradition functions best when it functions extralegally. Humanitarianism is not ultimately guaranteed by religious truth or in the existence of humanitarian law, though the tradition would not have emerged without either factor as counterweight to "reasons of state" arguments by government officials. In the first and last instance, it is dependent on the altruistic instincts of persons who work at every point in the system, whether it be private or public. The notion that the courts, by weighing adversarial arguments, will vindicate the religious freedom of church workers to perform the functions of the Immigration and Naturalization Service and thereby demonstrate that the Kingdom of God has prevailed over the principalities and powers is political, legal, and theological nonsense. Reliance on the extralegal goodwill found in the network of private and public humanitarian workers and on public support for assisting Central Americans will in the long run form the basis of humanitarian refugee efforts far more securely than conventions or court verdicts predicated on overt, public confrontation.

Karl Barth referred to the personal pledge of commitment by the citizen to making his or her government the best it might be; governments are more likely to emphasize the duty of their citizens to cooperate in the achievement of commonly held goals. Both perspectives are central to the healthy functioning of American democracy, but neither is likely to be the result of a court case. In this practical sense our examination of the protection of the civil liberties of religious workers abroad must in the end set aside the significance of court decisions. Their significance emerges only when goodwill between governmental and private officials has evaporated to the point that a confrontation is necessary. By that stage, as the sanctuary movement defendants discovered, religious freedom will already have become a moot point. Although the evidence of secure legal protections of religious liberty abroad may be hard to come by, it would be even harder to find a government official willing to eliminate the maintenance of religious freedom from his or her list of responsibilities toward U.S. citizens abroad, or a church official who believes that a religious mission abroad can be conducted fully independent of the influence of the United States or its government.

Given the political drifting apart, the restricted freedoms, the increasing emphasis on national security issues, and the shrinking public commitment to refugee causes in recent years, where can we expect this experiment in church/state cooperation in humanitarian concerns to go in the coming years?

16

Humanitarian Renewal

The growing engagement of church and state abroad since the 1930s has followed the domestic growth of the welfare state at home. The shared interests of political and religious leaders are self-evident: hospitals, assistance to the poor and the homeless, food and shelter, and more. The tradition of church/state separation has been modified to include vast tracts of common ground. The transfer of this arrangement to the international arena after World War II has been essential for refugee assistance and any number of other cooperative humanitarian projects. This modern cooperative trend abroad took the mantle of earlier cooperative efforts that were far less structured but no less intertwined. Church and state have always relied on each other beyond the national border; protection of the one has often gone hand in hand with legitimacy for the other. Domestic church/state law has played a secondary role, often honored in the breach and routinely the victim of short-term political ends.

The "peace without victory" that followed World War II has become the dominant political reality of the postwar era; the continuing Soviet-American rivalry has generated nuclear competition, crippled the United Nations, polarized the postcolonial nations, and hobbled the ability of U.S. leaders to achieve consensus in foreign policy.[1] It has also been the major producer of refugee flows since the war. These refugees, along with millions of other inhabitants of this modern no-man's-land, have grown dependent on a cooperative venture between the collective political and moral authorities of the West.

As religious institutions seek a legitimate role within an increasingly diverse private sector, there is no shortage of criticism of ensuing church/state ties. Voices from the left and the right warn that this partnership is dangerously diluting the moral authority of religious leaders and institutions. Strict separationists may read the entire history set forth in this book as evidence that cooperation between church and state has only left religiously based relief agencies in a hopelessly compromised position. Yet the size of the humanitarian task suggests that private and public resources alike are required, from the United States and elsewhere. Therefore there is an ongoing need for compromise and willingness on the part of all parties to search for common means and shared ends. The language of humanitarianism at times has covered a multitude of sins, but refugee work has never proceeded without it.

Aside from immediate and direct concern for refugees, all private and governmental humanitarianism must address the fragmentation and proliferation of special interests that have fractured the consensus between church and state of the 1940s and 1950s. The history since then suggests that religious organizations cannot be readily molded into utilitarian instruments of social policy; democratic government, if it is serious about religious freedom, must somehow accommodate both the particular and the transcendent in its work with religious bodies. For their part, religious groups must be willing to accept the reality of political compromise as a constant factor. Eschatologies that attempt to force political change without adequate regard for the rights of contending views may prove to be more and more distant from the political center that has maintained the American democratic tradition. Unless they can demonstrate concern for the future of all international voluntary activity, specific groups or factions may find themselves uncomfortably isolated from evolving public opinion. And without consensus, the future of voluntarism itself, including independent religious mission, will be imperiled.

The history we have examined demonstrates that religious bodies have remained prime movers behind the halting efforts of the United States to take active responsibility for refugees. In this sense the 800,000 Southeast Asians resettled in the United States since the Vietnam War owe a debt of gratitude to the Jewish activists of the 1930s and 1940s who pioneered modern efforts to organize global resettlement. In the postwar era, the political philosophy of complementarity (or its Catholic counterpart, subsidiarity) was exported along with refugee work. This view can now be found in virtually all sectors of Protestant, Catholic, and Jewish communities working with refugees overseas. Yet the independence of church and state has consistently appeared as a central ingredient in American understandings of the functions of our church/state law. As we have seen, this essentially Protestant virtue is not shared by all Protestants or by other religious communities in the United States. Distinctions between private and public roles, and between religious and secular voluntarism, have often collapsed in the complex social and political settings of refugee camps and the mass exodus of populations across borders. We have also encountered the ideological dimensions and political uses of refugee movements (Zionism, the use of refugee problems to criticize the Vietnam War effort, and the sanctuary movement), and occasional decisions of individuals and breakaway groups to establish their own independent refugee assistance programs. Realism demands that each of these developments be placed upon the larger, global stage on which policymakers must accommodate a variety of often contradictory demands.

The history of modern U.S. refugee work continues a search for common purposes between religious and secular authorities beyond our borders. An obvious case in point in the late 1930s was Franklin Roosevelt's almost mythic characterizations of the "seekers of light" and the "seekers of peace" searching out a happy convergence of their respective ends. But caution is necessary. "It was understood that there was to be no search for an absolute policy identity between the U.S. Government and the voluntary agencies in this effort," said a State Department official charged with arranging the first contracts between religious agencies and the government in 1952. Government officials understand that refugee work, even when conceived of as a defense of human rights, will be pursued with the national interest in mind. Those foreign policy concerns often come from powerful members and coalitions within Congress that determine the use of government funds. In the words of Hans Morgenthau, the defense of human rights "cannot be consistently applied in foreign policy because it can and must come in conflict with other interests that may be more important in a particular instance."[2] To date, it has served the interests of the government to encourage and support the work of a wide range of religious and secular agencies committed to refugee concerns.

Religious groups have retained power because of the wide constituencies they represent. They and other voluntary institutions will no doubt continue to be offered a complementary role to state priorities overseas. While this opportunity carries certain restrictions—for example, a willingness to focus on shared humanitarian goals rather than on open political confrontation with governments—a variety of diplomatic and other options have remained part of religious freedom as practiced for centuries in the Western democratic tradition.

Complementarity is a necessary virtue in church/state humanitarian ventures, but it is not always a sufficient one. Particular refugee populations are not always of equal interest to leaders in government and religion, such as Chilean refugees after the fall of Allende's government in 1973 or Salvadoran refugees in camps in Honduras in the 1980s. Political and personal conflicts will continue to arise, and may intensify in coming years. In such cases of open conflict between religious and governmental perspectives, the establishment and free exercise questions appear again. "We must be particularly wary that the degree of support from government for our programs and services does not diminish or compromise our ability to advocate change and carry out a prophetic ministry," a group of Protestant refugee officials stated in 1981. "Church agencies who engage in direct services with the use of government funds should fund their advocacy work from private sources."[3]

The task that lies ahead must be the strengthening of humanitarian structures in a way that both preserves their independence and assures donor governments that the funded activities will demonstrate the best ideals of Western democracy in action. In the contemporary political climate the temptation exists to replace humanitarian goals with ideological or moralistic crusades. Religion and cries for religious liberty can be a volatile fuel cast on the fires of ideological conflict between East and West, a "secret weapon" held in reserve by the state for moments of flagging enthusiasm. Conversely, religiously inspired calls for political action and justice can still marshal powerful opposition to governmental efforts, as the sanctuary movement amply demonstrates. Neither of these options holds much promise for the future of international humanitarianism.

The tradition of religiously grounded voluntarism in the United States, with its long-standing dialectic of complementarity and independence, offers some valuable lessons to policymakers searching for a means of preserving the integrity of humanitarian efforts in the midst of modern nationalism. A realistic approach to the refugee problem would minimally require a humanitarianism that keeps the best interests of the greatest number of refugees at the heart of its goals, is duly informed of and responsive to the interests of governments, and is committed to preserving humanitarian structures that can transcend short-term political limits. A much easier option would be the continued acceleration of conflict over refugee matters. As the United States has moved generally to the right since the late 1970s, refugee advocates in religious organizations have moved to the left. Given the centrifugal force that has been consistently wearing down existing structures of cooperation, and the growth of refugee problems in regions and nations that often do not already contain structures of refugee assistance, the option of intensified conflict is also the most likely.

Religious Humanitarianism and the Court

One of the primary purposes of the religion clauses of the First Amendment, in the view of their authors and in the view of the modern court system, has been to maintain the independence of religious and governmental institutions. This has not been an easy task in the second half of the twentieth century; indeed, U.S. refugee policy has encouraged religious bodies to build structures that conform to federal and intergovernmental priorities. This much of our story is clear. Even limiting our inquiry to issues that arise when religious workers find themselves in conflict with U.S. programs and policies abroad, we have seen that the protections of civil liberties, particularly of church/state law, are, for a host of reasons, routinely unenforceable. Domestic church/state law has been enforced overseas in a very weak way if at all; occasionally it has been used to serve short-term administrative and political ends. Cooperation between church and state abroad sets the stage for a conflict between ultimate claims to sovereignty. Just as religious freedom is at the heart of religious practice, the protection of sovereignty in the exercise of foreign policy and in the determination of compelling state interests is at the heart of governmental obligations.

At issue for religious groups is the independence of their international missions from control by a government that, according to Hans Morgenthau, pursues a policy of universalistic nationalism. For government officials, American citizens who travel abroad to compensate for or "correct" official policies are infuriating. Government authorities charged with administering foreign policy have employed travel and commercial restrictions, infiltrations and wiretaps of religious meetings, administrative and tax controls, contractual limitations, and the like to shape the activities of religiously affiliated private citizens. These powers have been exercised routinely since the 1940s without the prosecution of a single public official. When confrontations between private and public authorities abroad do come to a head, individual civil liberties are generally the losers.

It was not the post-Vietnam religious left that first discovered the potent force of national security arguments in the conduct of foreign affairs. We may recall John Quincy Adams's comment on the destructive character of the federal government's war power in a democracy. That power, said Adams, "is tremendous; it is strictly constitutional; but it breaks down every barrier so anxiously erected for the protection of liberty, property and of life." Religious freedom is granted no special exception in this setting, as missionaries attempting to prevent the forced relocation of the Cherokee tribes from Georgia discovered in the 1830s. The notion that national governments are primarily in the business of conducting good works and acts of mercy, and therefore likely to side with religious believers eager to see those works performed on behalf of refugees, is erroneous. "Nations are neither charities nor purveyors of moral philosophies, and they do a great deal of damage when they pretend to be either," according to Richard J. Barnet.[4]

Law, particularly as it pertains to foreign policy, has been used by successive administrations to accomplish certain ends; it was and it remains a pragmatic tool. The struggle to pass workable refugee and immigration statutes has been no exception. Under the administration of the Displaced Persons Act of 1948, the voluntary agencies were themselves in various stages of readiness to use the laws administratively; this readiness amounted to the ability to act efficiently by learning what rules existed in a politically charged atmosphere. Jews and Catholics were much better prepared in this regard than the Protestants. In recent years some Protestant and Catholic groups have worked to use refugee law as a means of limiting government actions. This was the case domestically in efforts to halt INS and Coast Guard actions against Haitian asylum seekers and in the defense of the sanctuary workers in the 1980s.

This has also been the case abroad, as agencies and their representatives have sought to force INS agents to adhere to guidelines for selecting refugees to be resettled from Southeast Asia. Though some of these efforts have effectively redirected government policies, they are often based on assumptions that officials charged with responsibility would willingly place themselves under moral constraints, or that the existence of relevant international laws mandates compliance. These are at best simplistic and inaccurate assumptions, growing from moralistic interpretations of the function of law and politics. It can be taken as a matter of pride that American society still encompasses levels of freedom that permit private organizations to undertake such challenges in public forums and in the courts, yet more bitter struggles over the responses of religious believers to foreign policy initiatives surely lie ahead.

In the course of this research, we found no government official or executive of a private religious agency eager to test the applicability of church/state law abroad in a U.S. court. Why is this so? It may be that American standards of religious liberty simply do not hold the central position abroad that they hold in the panoply of civil liberties at home. In a debate on the relation between human rights and foreign policy in 1983, Patricia Derian, assistant secretary of state for human rights and humanitarian affairs under Jimmy Carter, was queried by Ernest Lefever about the role of religious freedom in the Carter administration's human rights policy. According to Lefever, Derian responded with a remarkable question of her own: "Since when does religious freedom have anything to do with human rights?"[5] However Derian might today wish to qualify her comment, there is clearly a world of difference between the attitudes of some government officials and traditional understandings of protected civil liberties. Religious freedom today often is treated as a conservative obsession, certainly a secondary consideration for political activists on the left. The confrontations over Central American refugee policy may be changing this dated view by calling attention to the broad limitations that may be imposed on the activities of any private citizen abroad. The sanctuary cases and other recent court actions (such as the *Ramirez* case involving government appropriation of private property owned abroad) demonstrate that in international matters, religious freedom and other civil liberties of American citizens are closely intertwined, if only by the unwillingness of the courts to place absolute guarantees of individual rights on a plane above that of governmental obligations.

If the courts consider that jurisprudence concerning foreign policy must today be conducted as if in wartime, open confrontation with the government in the courts over public policy issues is not likely to produce new extraterritorial protections of religious freedom. The old maxim that "hard cases make bad law" could find no more fitting application than in such confrontations between the moral and political authorities of the republic. Pitting America's "great gift to civilization," religious freedom, against the foreign affairs power of the federal government could well produce case law that would gravely distort traditional and extralegal protections of religion. For this reason, those who believe the sanctuary movement can use the Central American refugee problem to "prove" in the courts that U.S. foreign policy is immoral and should yield before a higher moral standard are mistaken. Should the matter reach this level of confrontation between religious freedom and national security, the courts can only decide in favor of the president's fundamental power to pursue the national interest, and new case law explicitly limiting the role of religious freedom abroad will be on the books for future use.

Any effort that requires the courts to render judgments on church/state relations as experienced through the political dimensions of refugee problems would doubtless call forth the use of some version of the political question doctrine. The courts have discovered that the federal government is not interested in their historical judgments on the rightness or wrongness of particular policies. There was no political question doctrine at the time of the Cherokee removal cases, and the Court took up the issue, siding with the Indians and the missionaries and against the government's removal policies. Through his suggestion that Chief Justice John Marshall could enforce his own Indian policies, Andrew Jackson may be said to have fathered the modern doctrine. The Court's ruling on Cherokee removal was simply ignored. Then as now, the exercise of power preceded the rule of law. Faced with such roadblocks in establishing extraterritorial assurances of the freedom of religion from governmental interference and control, we can return somewhat chastened to the most frequently used method of bringing resolution to church/state conflict abroad, the constant search for administrative compromise between religious and governmental representatives beyond the court system. This administrative approach is a pragmatic one, and represents the efforts of private and public officials to meet conflicting demands of various parties in an equitable fashion.

In making assistance available to a wide variety of religious and other private organizations active overseas, the government's policy might be described as the pursuit of evenhandedness. Yet no standards for measuring such evenhandedness have proven functional. Quotalike standards are generally irrelevant to the immediate needs of particular refugee situations abroad. Religious participation in refugee assistance is increasingly diverse; since the 1970s Mormons, Buddhists, and Unificationists have all entered U.S. refugee work, often with governmental or intergovernmental subsidies. Despite the willingness of religious and governmental bodies to look for areas of overlapping concern, it is clear in the history of refugee work and related tasks that different religious bodies enter the field for different reasons, and that each has central motives they would like protected from governmental interference. Evangelicals are keen to preserve evangelistic activity from government control; Jews have focused on the right to assist fellow Jews in emigration and related concerns as a key aspect of their religious freedom. Others may

count the freedom to pursue prophetic ministries on behalf of the poor and oppressed as their central freedom. Traditional freedoms in these areas provide a
valuable base wherein the voluntary community grounds its perpetual claims of
individual duty and independence from government. The danger exists that in not
mutually supporting key elements of each other's concerns, or by failing to impose
boundaries on their own missions with a view toward the wider community of
voluntarism, individual groups may fall to governmental pressures of one form or
another.

Given the limited guarantees of extraterritoriality, the religious freedom and
other civil liberties of religious workers abroad can best be preserved only by
judicious efforts that demonstrate the truth that impartial humanitarian assistance
to refugees is in the national interest and consistent with the best traditions of U.S.
foreign policy. This is not a call for passive acquiescence to government priorities.
The voluntary sector has successfully challenged the legitimacy of various government policy choices from its earliest days of cooperation with the government
abroad; we need only recall the efforts of church workers and others to prevent the
U.S. military authorities in Germany from prematurely closing the displaced persons camps in the American Zone, or the subsequent work of religious leaders to
encourage Congress to extend the benefits of the Displaced Persons Act in 1953, in
order to remember that religious authorities are called to "speak truth to power."
When they have sought the role of militant political factions, they have been less
successful in accomplishing humanitarian goals.

If religious freedom overseas is politically identified with the right to differ
from U.S. foreign policy, the establishment of religion abroad is the obverse,
namely the building of religious institutions that function as part and parcel of U.S.
foreign policy. Neither of these stereotypes fully (or even accurately) describes the
phenomena at hand. Yet as we have examined the establishment of religion primarily as a matter of government funding, it has been with the Supreme Court's
understanding that such funding may have recognizable political and administrative
side effects.

An inquiry into the relevant legal questions produces disquieting conclusions.
Not only is it evident that extraterritorial protections of religion are thin at best, and
that religious freedom is best protected by administrative compromises and a search
for consensus among all the agencies, but also that the bulk of domestic law on
establishment issues could hardly begin to be applied abroad without the immediate
appearance of violations of the spirit if not the letter of the law. Government is
forbidden to give assistance to churches, yet many of the refugee relief agencies are
classified for tax purposes as churches by the IRS. The effort to create separately
incorporated relief arms to prevent government funds from going directly to
churches has been only marginally successful in separating secular from religious
ministries, and the lines dividing them are obscure and on occasion, contentious.
Though tax dollars cannot be spent to further pervasively religious institutions,
surplus food and property, trusts, and treaty funds have all been channeled to
religious agencies deemed less than pervasively religious. The government is forbidden to aid the religious activities of groups organized by churches for relief, but
there is no single administrative method for preventing such aid. Excessive administrative and political entanglement between religious and governmental agencies is

prohibited under modern interpretations of the establishment clause, but such entanglement is a commonplace in the oversight federal agencies require over private groups in refugee work.

Because church/state contacts abroad lack the full context of domestic settings—long-term congregational communities, the protection of governments from the local to the national, the humdrum routines of everyday life in an established democracy—they generate situations that would be considered abnormal at home. Religious institutions have hardly been independent of government in their overseas activities. This "exception" to the domestic efforts at separating religious and governmental institutions has been consistent, predating the republic and approved by such ardent separationists as Madison and Jefferson. The predominant policy in contemporary refugee care has followed these early leads in shaping a cooperative effort.

The levels of government assistance to private agencies, direct and indirect, have continued to increase since World War II. During the war the government regulated private fund raising and established a system of registration that made fund raising and overseas shipping difficult for agencies not approved by the government. In 1947 the government began offering ocean freight reimbursements to agencies shipping relief materials abroad. During the period of the Displaced Persons Act agencies began distributing government surplus food and property and were offered loans to help pay the transportation costs of refugees traveling inside the United States (intergovernmental arrangements paid for the resettlement costs between Europe and the United States). In 1952 the government began signing contracts with U.S. religious agencies for services in overseas refugee assistance; in 1961 agencies began receiving per capita fees for initial resettlement costs of refugees once in the United States. In 1974 the government initiated development grants designed to help agencies expand their overseas capacities. Despite the reservations of various agencies concerning particular programs, the postwar pattern of expanding government assistance is consistent.

Simply accepting assistance from the U.S. government does not make a religious agency a puppet of U.S. foreign policy. The State Department and other funding agencies within the government have readily acknowledged that private agencies have their own priorities whether assistance is available or not. The independence of religious agencies from governmental institutions today appears to be a healthy reality only in situations of relative social tranquillity. The unsettled world of refugee politics faces severely restricting pressures in the coming years, of which Central American concerns are only one obvious example. The long-term problem of the increased migration that the United States can expect from Latin American refugees and immigrants remains a major question, despite new amnesty legislation passed in 1986. The prospect of refugees fleeing civil turmoil in other nations allied with the United States—the Philippines, for instance, or South Africa—is not outside of the realm of possibility. The longest and most complex resettlement effort of modern times, that of Jews to Israel, remains politically unsettled, despite massive financial assistance from the United States and the injection of Jewish resettlement issues into the highest levels of political negotiations between the United States and the Soviet Union. Any structural change in the relations between church and state abroad is quite likely to depend on the political climate for addressing refugee problems rather than on more effective enforcement of U.S. church/state law.

Humanitarianism in Search of International Order

The tradition of cooperation between church and state abroad falls into a no-man's-land where theories of a wall of separation simply fail adequately to define the realities of international political life. In the past, deviations from strict church/state separation theories have been explained by an appeal to common sense grounded in the national interest and in shared human commitments. This search for shared responsibilities between church and state can be seen in the history of such long-standing institutions as legislative and military chaplaincies, welfare and hospital programs, or proclamations of national days of prayer and thanksgiving.

On the subject of national proclamations of days of thanksgiving, James Madison wrote that such actions "imply a religious agency [behind governmental actions], making no part of the trust delegated to political rulers." He believed it was "difficult to frame such a religious Proclamation . . . without referring to them in terms that have some bearing on party questions."[6] His observation that in proclaiming a day of thanksgiving the government is assuming a function belonging primarily to religion may also be applied to the care of refugees and other humanitarian problems of today. One may disagree with the theological or legal underpinnings of state-sponsored religious charity and relief, but it is hard to deny that political recourse to the symbols and substance of Judeo-Christian religion has many times helped recall Americans to fundamental duties and ideals. It is precisely such governmental use of religion that distresses both religious internationalists and supporters of expansive interpretations of the establishment clause. The climate created by governmental use of religion puts religion under a canopy of statist authoritarianism. This inevitably limits the scope of religious freedom.

In the search for consensus in structuring international refugee work, the American tradition of securing the independence of religion from governmental control may provide a valuable intellectual and policy tool for building humanitarian structures of assistance that take seriously the notion that humanitarian aid should continue as a primarily human (rather than a primarily political) obligation the people of the world owe to their fellow creatures in distress. Humanitarian work is not an ultimate goal; it is not the first step on a crusade to take control of the world. It is an intermediate, often thankless task, but one that most religious traditions and humanistic teachings value for its own sake. It deserves independent recognition and standing, and has substantially attained such a footing in the democratic West.

That standing may be cumulatively strengthened or weakened. Its future lies with the ability of religious and other voluntary agencies to gauge correctly the functional boundaries of a humanitarian "space" that will provide the greatest good for the greatest number, and on their ability to arrive at a measured and realistic internationalism that does not set about blazing the path to a utopia. There is no doubt that governments will continue to take an active interest in refugee problems. But the growing disintegration of voluntarism into partisanship and opposition to governmental policies toward refugees is an ominous development. One hears echoes of the sober judgment of Alasdair MacIntyre in *After Virtue*, who argued that "modern politics cannot be a matter of genuine moral consensus. And it is not. Modern politics is civil war carried on by other means."[7] The next steps in the organization of international humanitarian assistance will be steps backward or forward. Any moves by government to play one end of the voluntary community against another would be a step backward; so also would be an "us first" trend among voluntary agencies that takes no account of the significance of particular agencies in the larger picture of relations between private groups and the government. Forward motion can only consist of continued efforts towards consensus and moderation in the voluntary community, which might elicit from government officials a new respect for the independence of an international humanitarian "space."

One option that must be discarded as an overall strategy for religious humanitarianism (even though individual groups will continue to pursue it) is the proposed return to a pre-Constantinian church, in which ties to state power were neither sought or accepted. This enthusiasm for a "post-Constantinian" church, which in effect is a romantic call for a return to the pre-Constantinian reality, has gained currency with the development of liberation theology and its spread in the 1970s and 1980s as the obvious (and for some, only) orthodoxy in a world dominated by potentially terminal superpower conflicts.

Such a radical realignment separating the forces of religion and government would cut directly across the pragmatic cooperation that U.S. religious agencies have developed with the U.S. government since World War II. For those frustrated with compromise as a constant factor in the relations between religious bodies and temporal powers, the "preferential option for the poor" suggests that the conversion called for in the Bible will inevitably turn religious believers toward the poor, changing the orientation toward power that has been common in the church since Constantine. Other religious leaders have justified their closeness to state power on the grounds that it has extended their ability to perform acts of justice and mercy. Cooperation in refugee assistance draws directly on this latter approach, and will continue to do so in the future.

This struggle is not a modern one, except in its reemergence within modern democratic forms of governance. It was familiar at the time of the American Revolution; in his *Memorial and Remonstrance* of 1785, James Madison called attention to the ambivalence of eighteenth-century religious leaders to the pre-Constantinian independence of the church:

> Enquire of the teachers of Christianity for the ages in which it appeared in its greatest lustre; those in every sect point to the ages prior to its incorporation with Civil policy. Propose a restoration of this primitive State in which its Teachers depended on the voluntary rewards of their flocks, many of them predict its downfall. On which side ought their testimony to have greatest weight, when for or when against their interest?[8]

There can be no general "restoration of this primitive state" in a democracy, let alone under current international political conditions. As Roger Mehl has noted, primitive Christians had no sense whatsoever of their political involvement in what Madison here calls "Civil policy." For them, the only "political" questions revolved around their submission to established authorities. Democratic citizenship requires active participation in the affairs of governance, both directly and through elected representatives; this spirit is foreign to the pre-Constantinian church.[9]

From the 1920s onward the leaders of the mainline Protestant establishment cast themselves primarily as defenders of international ideals rather than as defenders of the established order. The Protestant leaders who accepted and developed a prophetic role for the churches in the modern age believed fervently that the inequities of the Versailles Treaty ought not to be repeated; for them the true significance of the war would lie in its transformation of the international order.

In their goals for a new postwar international order, Catholic and Jewish leaders were on the whole less adventurous than their Protestant brethren. The Catholic church, by virtue of its size and moral authority, was promoted during World War II as "the logical religious organization with which governments can cooperate in reconstruction of the social order." The Catholic church retained its authority by continuing to condemn "the erroneous concept of an absolutely autonomous sovereignty" for the modern nation-state.[10] Jews frequently were willing to assent to the principle of an international organization, but their priorities relating to the Jews of Europe and the establishment of a Jewish homeland prevailed in the 1930s and 1940s. In the midst of their own struggles, liberal American Jewish leaders found time to speak to postwar concerns common across America, including the global extension of democracy, the creation of an international organization, and an international police force. As with American Catholics, American Jews were more conservative than Protestant liberals in their expectations for postwar political order.

Refugee agencies have taken an advocacy stance from their earliest days, but in recent years many seem to have lost the art of incorporating advocacy into a broader cooperative effort. The notion that independence from government priorities inevitably led church refugee agencies to an adversarial stance toward government became widespread. As agencies have moved from pastoral and material relief to a broader philosophical commitment to internationalism, ties to U.S. policies have predictably weakened. "As more governments put restrictive policies in place, impose visas, tighten selection procedure and refuse asylum, the gospel calls us to be defenders of the defenseless and take up the cause of the exile as never before," said church leaders attending a 1981 World Council of Churches conference on the topic. "Pastoral care is not enough. TO BE INVOLVED IN REFUGEE WORK IN THE 1980'S MEANS ALSO TO BE INVOLVED IN ADVOCACY."[11]

Increasingly, this has meant for church groups a renewed attention to the root causes of refugee problems, namely their political sources. In the case of the Palestinians, this effort has pitted Protestants and Catholics against Jews, causing further deterioration of interreligious cooperation in refugee concerns. Too often religious workers believe that they are free to ignore the impact of global political pressures in the current climate of "peace without victory." This is simply not the case. As several examples in this book attest, the U.S. government can move against religious workers or agencies it perceives to be acting in ways hostile to the national interest. Humanitarian freedom, much like religious freedom, has never been unqualified; under current conditions, religious workers overseas should measure their actions against the future of U.S. voluntarism at least as seriously as they measure their refugee activities by the needs and political ends of refugee populations. Without the ongoing consent of U.S. authorities, the cooperative structure that now exists internationally would cease to be.

Today it is common to find Christian relief and development agencies emphasizing biblical themes that implicitly or explicitly transcend nationalism. These themes include the concept of the church as a pilgrim people, the "wandering people of God"; the unity of the household of God in a global fellowship. It has also been suggested that refugees provide the best model for Christians to understand their relationship to the rest of the world. Paul McCleary, former director of Church World Service, wrote that the agency "finds itself under some limitations in fulfilling its . . . ongoing relationships with church bodies around the world. These limitations are created by the U.S. Government." Over against the limitations are "the theological values stemming from our Judeo-Christian heritage of the universality of the church."[12] This debate is approaching its limits under current governmental provisions, and religious and other voluntary societies (having failed to secure the independence of their overseas humanitarian efforts from governmental policies) often seek alliance with international bodies against the policies of the nation-state.

Religious believers, by virtue of their commitment to a transcendent vision of the future, must regard all temporal orders and institutions as transitional and provisional. The postwar climate of "peace without victory" has consistently eroded the best temporal efforts by governments and by private voluntarism. Governments have retrenched their commitments to international organizations; religious and other voluntary societies have sought to distance themselves from anticommunist partisanship. For the United States, the consistent goal in this struggle surrounding refugee assistance is continued expansion of U.S. efforts to bring international peace and order and preservation of the central commitments of a humane foreign policy.

The difficulties that religious voluntarism faces in international refugee care are paralleled in the U.S. experience with the World Court. Fear of a binding, external authority over U.S. policy was enough to block U.S. participation in the early days of the World Court during the Harding administration. When the matter of the World Court arose again in 1934, President Roosevelt was forced to tell the Senate that acceptance of the World court's jurisdiction would not jeopardize U.S. sovereignty. Once again, the World Court was rejected by Americans fearful that the country would be contaminated by placing its interests under international control. Similarly, administrations are not about to cede actual political control of refugee problems to private citizens or to supranational bodies, be they religiously or multilaterally rooted.

In discussing the background of the U.S. decision to enter the United Nations, Eric Hula makes several observations that should be kept in mind when looking at the efforts to establish international law and international institutions:

> The scheme of the future world body had to satisfy both American internationalists, who were pleading for an organization approximating world government, and American isolationists, who were still opposed to an international organization, even one no stronger than the defunct League of Nations. The only solution to the dilemma was a scheme of supranational government in the operation of which the United States and the other great powers of the day would be assured a leading role without being subject themselves to its coercive powers.[13]

This is the context in which refugee assistance takes place, and within which religious agencies must find their own authentic role. Armed with a theology of ultimate ends and purpose, religious believers still face political constraints that were alive in 1945—or 1495, for that matter. This leaves very little place for the strong forms of religious universalism that were envisaged at the end of World War II.

The current structuring of U.S. international refugee assistance was inspired by a profound sense of duty that had parallel roots in the national interest and in the religious commitments of Americans. "In its most fundamental sense, the foreign policy of our country rests on a belief in human dignity and freedom and concerns itself therefore with the complete well-being of people everywhere," wrote leaders of the American Council of Voluntary Agencies for Foreign Service in 1958. "This belief has been carried out in the public sector in many overseas programs of aid and cooperation which are part and parcel of our whole foreign policy. In this concept, biblical in origin, the voluntary sector of American overseas activity finds its common ground with the public sector."[14] This sense of religious duty was in fact far more ancient than the structures of U.S. polity.

Madison acknowledged in his *Memorial and Remonstrance* that religious duty falls into the category of ultimate duty, antedating the civil authority:

> This duty is precedent, both in order of time and in degree of obligation, to the claims of Civil Society. Before any man can be considered as a member of Civil Society, he must be considered as a subject of the Governor of the Universe: and if a member of Civil Society, who enters into any subordinate Association, must always do it with a reservation of his duty to the General Authority; much more must every man who becomes a member of any particular Civil Society, do it with a saving of his allegiance to the Universal Sovereign. We maintain therefore that in matters of Religion, no man's right is abridged by the institution of Civil Society and that Religion is wholly exempt from its cognizance.[15]

Embedded here is the balance required in classic American definitions of religious freedom, namely the preservation of religious freedom depends on the government's willingness to respect independent claims of religious obligation. Such religious freedom in turn cannot be further guaranteed without the efforts at separating religion and government implied in the establishment clause.

We may return to a source of much Protestant thinking on international affairs, the Oxford Conference on Church, State and Society of 1937, to address the dilemma modern cooperation in refugee affairs poses to this American tradition of church/state relations. Religious internationalism as such has in recent decades proven unpalatable as a corrective or alternative to government intervention in humanitarian fields once regarded as the sole province of the church. Its expansion has been allowed in concert with, but not in advance of, the extension of democracy. Protestant leaders assembled in Oxford in 1937 argued that rather than press for ultimate solutions, their role in the modern world was to seek "middle axioms" that promoted religious values and religious freedom while at the same time addressed overlapping concerns of individual communities and the state.

The language, structure, and ideals of humanitarian assistance to refugees quite properly fall within the Oxford definition of a middle axiom. No other framework for the legal, political, and historical problems of church and state abroad that has arisen in postwar refugee assistance is capable of maintaining and strengthening the cooperative structures between private and governmental bodies that, for all their failings, have brought hope to millions of victims of political and religious persecution around the world.

Middle Axioms of Humanitarian Renewal

Three essential factors define the moral content of the international humanitarian ethic. First, humanitarian aid must focus on the needs of the victims themselves; this is an ideal at the heart of humanitarian practice that distinguishes it from the broader purposes of states. Its "apolitical" or "nonpolitical" substance is determined by two other strictures: such aid must be politically neutral, and it must not discriminate in the distribution of assistance. This commonsense definition finds expression in the few existing attempts to define international humanitarian law.[16]

Self-interest, whether on the part of government or a private agency, inevitably clouds humanitarian practice. This is equally true in matters of religious freedom. The traditional American response to the problem of religiously motivated self-interest has been to insist on the independence of religious and governmental activities. This insistence relies on the tacit assumption that the spiritual and material dimensions of life will continue to advance in tandem, albeit at arm's length. The "harmony of interests" is at no time perfect or complete.[17] When religious and governmental institutions actively cooperate internationally, some means must be found to buffer humanitarian cooperation against broader political and religious pressures.

Efforts in this regard have met with real but limited success. Both religious and governmental institutions routinely ignore various aspects of the humanitarian ethic just set forth. The unhappy result has been the encroachment of adversarial politics rather than the strengthening of humanitarian cooperation. Today, the adjective "humanitarian" is used as a cover both for unpalatable national security goals and for partisan ends of highly politicized private efforts.

In the late 1960s and the 1970s, Hubert Humphrey and others championed the idea that U.S. relief and development assistance should be further separated from the State Department. Humphrey's idea was based on the perception that the best interests of the United States would be served by an independent humanitarian operation free of the political constraints of the State Department. His plan involved establishing a government-funded, privately administered endowment that would finance the bulk of overseas development and relief. Conservatives and others interested in downplaying foreign aid fought it on the grounds that it was a giveaway that served no clear national purpose. The multibillion dollar endowment such an effort presupposed was another sticking point in Congress. Nevertheless, Humphrey realized that the national interests could be damaged should humanitarian and development aid become even more entwined with the pursuit of national security.

A similar plan on a much smaller scale, the Inter-American Development Institute, functioned in the area of Latin American development aid for more than a decade. Endowed by Congress with $25 million in the late 1960s, the institute had an independent board of directors and sponsored innovative, nonpartisan development in the region. In 1984, however, President Reagan relieved the executive director and a majority of the board of their responsibilities, replacing them with political appointees. Without the base of public support available to religious agencies the institute's independent status was more vulnerable to short-term political pressures. This would not be the case if the Congress established an endowment that worked primarily with religious agencies and other voluntary societies with large constituencies. The failure of the institute and of Humphrey's effort demonstrate, however, that government has not been interested in placing its foreign aid under the administration of an independent authority.

John Quincy Adams said it was not for America to impose its principles of government on mankind, but to practice them in such a way that others were naturally attracted to them. Consensus around a broadly shared humanitarian ethic is one of the most attractive principles Americans (and Europeans as well) have brought to international political life. This ethic cannot be guaranteed by law, it must be demonstrated in practice. Barring the administration of foreign assistance by a totally independent government-funded endowment—a most unlikely development—new means of securing the shared practice of a humanitarian ethic must be sought by all parties. Humanitarianism must be protected in ways that assure governmental and private donors that it will demonstrate the best ideals of Western democracy in action.

The function of establishing independent humanitarian standards in refugee relief could, for instance, be delegated to the Advisory Committee on Voluntary Foreign Aid, the successor to Roosevelt's War Relief Control Board. From its inception this body has been charged with tying together private and public relief assistance abroad. But the committee's purposes and functions have over the years been severely constricted. Established by executive order, it initially had an independent existence and reported directly to the president. Today it is a part of a subdivision within the State Department, a setting unlikely to generate adequate consensus on humanitarian efforts abroad. To perform this function the Advisory Committee would have to regain its original function and prominence. It would also have to draw more of its membership from professionals in the field and from representatives of private voluntary organizations.

The "middle axioms" of a new humanitarian realism necessarily return to the core of the ethic stated earlier: the needs of victims, political neutrality, and nondiscrimination. To be credible, middle axioms have to take into account the postwar history of private and public efforts abroad, noting in particular the need for complementarity of private and national goals. Joint efforts to secure the independence of humanitarian assistance from foreign policy should be given prominence as an expression of the moral content of foreign policy.

The following axioms are suggested by the history examined in this book. They are applicable to the entire range of private voluntary activity that has evolved in the postwar period.

For the sake of suffering victims of natural or political disasters, humanitarian realism requires simultaneous attention to what is morally good and politically useful. It is impossible to describe the humanitarian "space" explored in this book in apolitical terms. While its aspirations for independence are real, so are its boundaries, even though they shift with the political circumstances. Attention to these political boundaries, be they imposed by the United Nations, the United States, or other sovereign governments, will assure that private voluntarism (and in particular, its religious expressions) is not seduced by moralistic interpretations of its task.

Humanitarianism as defined here is not a rubberband that can be stretched to cover every circumstance of need, nor may it be strictly identified with national security. It is a coherent set of moral responsibilities that must remain identified with national purpose, both public and private. Private officials with distance from official state responsibilities are often in an excellent position to recall the primary focus on human need required to generate joint private/public activities. Without consensus on what is morally good, the entire enterprise disintegrates into a series of special interest situations or political mopping-up exercises. The resettlement of hundreds of thousands of Southeast Asians in the 1970s and 1980s is an outstanding example of how moral and political ends found consensus in international refugee service. Humanitarianism is particularly vulnerable to the ravages of faction; this vulnerability has received far too little attention from humanitarian workers in the post-Vietnam world.

The law offers only weak and fragmentary protection for international humanitarian work. While encouraging the growth of legal support for humanitarian and religious independence, participants must place the greatest emphasis on building extralegal means of accomplishing given tasks as they arise. Whether we look at domestic church/state law, the protection of the civil liberties of citizens abroad, international humanitarian law, or international refugee conventions, we see that the United States has played a dual role. It focused the political will needed for their creation, yet it has accepted the role of law in international affairs only in settings it believed were prudential and expedient. Domestic traditions of religious liberty, for instance, including prohibitions against the establishment of religion, have been carried into international humanitarian cooperation when possible, but not with any strict force of law.

Therefore, legalistic defenses of humanitarian actions or religious freedom abroad are much less important to the actual provision of refugee assistance than attention to the extralegal elements that make any assistance operation work. At a minimum these include administrative coordination, professional commitment to announced goals, successful working relationships between private and public authorities, the ability to report back conditions and progress abroad to constituents, and a firm grounding in the substance of the humanitarian ethic itself. It is at this level, that of moral substance, that it draws its greatest strength. That substance can only be understood in the concrete response to the humanitarian problem in question. This means attention to the personal relationships functioning at all levels of the system.

This is quite different from an absolutist stance that tries to use humanitarian law as a *rappel à l'ordre,* an adversarial tool for setting errant governments aright.[18] The public rhetoric of many church agencies today reflects this approach. The problem here is that humanitarianism in its various forms of food aid, refugee assistance, and the like has never been a tail that wagged the dog. This stance should be evaluated not by the effects of its public attack on government morality but by its effects on private working relationships within the humanitarian world.

All parties must commit themselves to address the content of humanitarianism with integrity. This includes joint attention to broad humanitarian goals which exist beyond the framework of given private or public agencies. Whether the "three faiths" consensus of the 1940s and 1950s could (or should) be revived, its lessons in cooperative approaches to humanitarianism remain solid. Many participants from that era recall that even then the existing consensus was often thin, punctuated by one dispute after another. The strategy of Jewish refugee advocates of the 1930s and 1940s (later adopted by Roosevelt) of seeking the support of Protestant and Catholic leaders in pressing their cause to the government offered a lead in cooperative engagement of the issue by combined religious leaders. It concentrated on the needs of the refugees and sought wide religious and governmental participation in the problem.

When both Oxfam and World Vision can sign a newspaper ad protesting Reagan administration definitions of humanitariansim in Central America, it is evident that cooperative efforts among voluntary agencies today still follow mutual humanitarian concerns as well as common political positions.[19] Far more often, however, cooperative efforts to address refugee and related concerns—particularly in the approaches relief agencies make to the Congress—follow a political rather than theological or humanitarian line. Particular agencies lobby for their own special interest populations among the world's refugees while interest in cooperative efforts, common standards, and the "big picture" of refugee problems declines.

The American Council of Voluntary Agencies served many of these needs, though even there the function of the ACVA was limited to coordination of efforts and information sharing. Rather than replace ACVA with a strengthened agency, the voluntary sector opted in 1984 for a compromise organization, InterAction, which has encountered serious difficulties. Catholic Relief Services, the backbone of the ACVA era, withdrew from InterAction in the summer of 1986, arguing that InterAction was no longer meeting its needs. Fragmentation rather than renewed cooperation in tackling humanitarian problems from a broad perspective has become the order of the day. It is doubtful that this pattern is in the long-term interests of the refugees or others who benefit from the services of these agencies.

Preserving the nonpolitical nature of humanitarianism requires that the needs of victims take precedence over the desire to achieve political or social change through the assistance process. This is a stumbling block for both private and public groups involved with refugees. Refugees are vulnerable from nearly every point of view; they may be exploited by any combination of superpower politics, armed insurgencies, opposition politicians at home, religious crusades, unsympathetic citizens of the country in which they seek asylum, and more. Most people with political or administrative responsibility for deflecting or channeling these pressures on refugee populations have ready justifications for their actions toward the refugees. Most of the explanations given by any group of such authorities in a refugee setting are contradictory; often they are tied to preexisting political positions on the conflict which produced the refugees themselves.

The UNHCR has set a valuable example for preserving humanitarian standards of assistance in settings where various parties have been eager to make political use of the refugee population. So have the State Department and other voluntary agencies, but standards in this field have taken a dramatic turn for the worse in the 1980s. The Reagan administration, for example, has armed refugee populations in Honduras and Pakistan, and encouraged them to attack their oppressors in Nicaragua and Afghanistan. Certain voluntary agencies have shown a marked preference for aiding Salvadoran refugees in Honduras or Hmong refugees in Thailand. When things reach this state, when refugee assistance simply becomes a means of carrying out political agendas by other means, a return to humanitarian basics is in order. Disputes between public and private authorities on this level should be the subject of continual dialogue in a setting somewhat removed from the day-to-day operation of the programs themselves.

Humanitarian practice has not replaced specific religious goals and motivations; it coexists with them. Whenever possible, governmental authorities should provide broad latitude for worship, social ministries, evangelism, and religious education. Similarly, religious agencies pursuing humanitarian ends must adapt their practices to pluralistic settings and sensibilities. As argued earlier, any effort to apply a strict separatist approach to church/state relations abroad would destroy a humanitarian coalition that actually represents the interests of a plurality of groups in the United States. Emphasis on good working relationships becomes essential, and religious agencies in particular must appropriate the lessons of past cooperative successes.

Experience has shown that while religious organizations are capable of developing forms of service that downplay religious distinctions, individuals retain the religious motivations that led them into service in the first place, and their activities often take explicitly religious forms overseas. This factor cannot be eliminated, nor should any forced homogenization along these lines be a policy objective in government. New revivals in Christian circles in the last ten years have sent increasing waves of Americans into overseas service.

Religious agencies in many cases have learned to work alongside those who do not share their faith. Relatively newer agencies such as World Vision have encountered settings hostile to their evangelical faith or where their willingness to trust officials backfired. The protocol for relief workers of one faith assisting refugees of another is still unclear. Religious workers have on occasion invoked UN guarantees of religious freedom to support their own evangelism in refugee camps. Ultimate suppression of such witness would lead to an unpalatable (and, given the essential goodwill of most relief officials, probably unintended) homogenization that would be dispiriting for the entire enterprise. Creating room for middle axioms of shared goals among various groups appears to be a more viable approach to the presence of religious organizations within broader international efforts.

The use of government assistance by private groups will continue and probably expand. Therefore new attention should be corporately directed toward finding ways of effectively sheltering private-public humanitarian cooperation from the vastly greater political power of the state. We have seen that the government has interests in overseeing all aspects of the operation that it funds. Taxpayers could not ask for less. Is there any set of effective safeguards that would meet the need for governmental oversight and humanitarian independence at the same time?

The inability of private humanitarian leaders to generate serious national debate over the Reagan administration's use of the term "humanitarian" for its aid to Nicaraguan contras demonstrated that there is at present no final "court of appeal" in humanitarian matters. Voluntary agencies ran newspaper ads protesting this development, but they were no match for the State Department and the Pentagon in mobilizing their policies of choice. One alternative is an independent presidentially appointed standing committee on humanitarian concerns. Including public officials and private citizens, such a commission could set internal national standards for humanitarian practice and consensus while avoiding charges of unjustified internationalism. By definition the purpose of such a commission would be to determine independent humanitarian standards that demonstrated the concrete relationship between humanitarian practice and the national interest.

Forms of private voluntarism that are either exclusively bound to the will of the state or are routinely hostile to the state both raise potentially fatal difficulties for the entire humanitarian enterprise. The implications of humanitarianism inevitably transcend the state, since they extend to all victims of natural or political disasters. Institutional arrangements must be kept open to transformations that will strengthen the ability of all parties to serve persons in need. Any ideological hardening, either toward or away from the interests of the state is in the long run counterproductive for the humanitarian enterprise. A humanitarianism totally identified with the national interests of the United States will not long retain the essential political neutrality; this has been the case, for instance, in the Christian Broadcasting Network's Operation Blessing, which has been closely tied to U.S. efforts to aid the contra rebels fighting the Sandinista government of Nicaragua. And when private agencies take the responsibility of compensating for the perceived inhumanity, belligerency, or illegitimacy of U.S. policies, their stance is usually based on criteria irrelevant to the three central tenets of humanitariansim. While compelling moral arguments can be advanced to support such choices, these moral imperatives should not be identified with the values essential to large-scale cooperative efforts.

As the logic of American democratic pluralism erodes a privileged place for religious institutions and belief, the battle for fundamental authority rages on, with religious agencies, sensing the possibility that they are being marginalized, looking either to an increasingly desperate struggle with the state or to greater reliance upon it. In refugee work abroad, the possibility of alternative approaches to state policies—religiously based or other—is in decline, while programs that complement state policies are increasingly urged.

Elihu Root said that a civilization can be judged by the treatment it accords the alien on its shores, a statement as true today as in the ancient Hebrew scriptures. Perhaps this is all the justification we need for a new effort in humanitarianism, one that isolates it somewhat from the flow of nationalistic politics and preserves its integrity from the rough and tumble political surroundings. New efforts will fail, however, if they are perceived as an abandonment of the nation-state. The goal must be to preserve the best ideals of the nation-state in the midst of political transformations we cannot ourselves adequately gauge. In this sense humanitarianism that combines the forces of religion and government cannot be moralistic or idealistic; it cannot be controlled by a particular church, much less by a particular government. It must be controlled by the common search for shared ends that lead us away from no-man's-land and back toward the home for which we all long.

Notes

Chapter 1

1. Quoted in Victor Ferkiss, "Foreign Aid: Moral and Political Aspects," in Kenneth Thompson, ed., *Moral Dimensions of American Foreign Policy* (New Brunswick, N.J.: Transaction Press, 1984), p. 237; Hans J. Morgenthau, "Human Rights and Foreign Policy," in Thompson, *Moral Dimensions,* p. 345.

2. See the First Geneva Convention of 1949, Articles 12 and 18; Fourth Geneva Convention of 1949, Articles 59–63, in *United Nations Treaty Series,* 75, p. 1; Additional Protocol II, Article 18 (2).

3. Hans J. Morgenthau and Kenneth W. Thompson, *Politics Among Nations* (New York: Alfred A. Knopf, 1985), p. 349.

4. Interview with Pierce Gerety, Jr., UNHCR legal officer, Geneva, August 1983.

5. Interview with Anglican church official, Juba, Sudan, August 1983.

6. U.S. embassy officials in Honduras in early 1982 were concerned that a voluntary agency sympathetic to the Miskito Indian refugees from Nicaragua be placed in charge of the relief operation in eastern Honduras. Both Secretary of State Alexander Haig and UN Representative Jeane Kirkpatrick had called public attention to the Miskito Indians as an example of vicious Sandinista attacks on the Indians. The agency chosen, the World Relief Commission of the National Association of Evangelicals, had no staff with refugee experience in Honduras. Knowledgeable observers have charged that the selection of an agency to administer the Miskito Indian camp was strongly influenced by the desire of the U.S. embassy to maintain a dominant role in that work, and by the strong antipathy of high embassy officials toward other applicants among the voluntary agencies. The choice appeared to fit the embassy's desire for an agency that would avoid a critical stance toward U.S. policy in the region and maintain the Miskito situation in the public eye as an example of Soviet-inspired political miscalculation and violation of human rights. In the case of World Relief, their appointment (which came indirectly through the United Nations after preferences were clarified at the UN High Commissioner for Refugees headquarters by officials of the U.S. Mission, Geneva) involved a significant reorientation of World Relief services in Honduras. In this case the embassy's calculation of a quiescent World Relief operation was not entirely well placed. See Chapter 8.

7. Eileen Egan and Elizabeth C. Reiss, *Transfigured Night: The CRALOG Experience* (New York: Livingston Publishing Company, 1964), p. 14.

8. William Shawcross, *The Quality of Mercy: Cambodia, Holocaust and Modern Conscience* (New York: Simon and Schuster, 1984).

9. Morgenthau, quoted in Roger L. Shinn, "Realism and Ethics in Political Philosophy," in Kenneth Thompson and Robert J. Myers, eds., *Truth and Tragedy: A Tribute to Hans J. Morgenthau* (New Brunswick, N.J.: Transaction Press, 1984), p. 97.

Chapter 2

1. J. Moss Ives, *The Ark and the Dove* (London: Longmans, Green, 1936), p. 400.

2. Merle Curti, *American Philanthropy Abroad: A History* (New Brunswick, N.J.: Rutgers University Press, 1963), p. 10.

3. R. Pierce Beaver, "Church and State Relations in the Missions to the Native Americans" (n.p., n.d. [circa 1967]), pp. 1–2.

4. Chester James Antieau, Arthur T. Downey, and Edward C. Roberts, *Freedom from Federal Establishment: Formation and Early History of the First Amendment Religion Clauses* (Milwaukee: Bruce Publishing Company, 1964), p. 201.

5. Beaver, "Church and State Relations," p. 2.

6. Ibid., p. 3.

7. *Samuel A. Worcester* v. *State of Georgia* (1832).

8. Ibid., at 521.

9. "The Indian Problem and the Catholic Church," *Catholic World* 48, 284 (February 1889): 577–84.

10. *Report of the Commissioner of Indian Affairs of 1892,* p. 182. Cited in Fredrick Mitchell and James W. Skelton, "The Church-State Conflicts in Early Indian Education," *History of Education Quarterly* 6 (Spring 1966): 179.

11. *12th Annual Report, Executive Committee of the Indian Rights Association,* Missionary Council of the Protestant Episcopal Church (1894), p. 9.

12. Harry J. Sievers, "The Catholic Indian School Issue and the Presidential Election of 1892," *Catholic Historical Review* 38, 2 (July 1952): 140.

13. Francis Paul Prucha, *The Churches and the Indian Schools 1888–1912* (Lincoln: University of Nebraska Press, 1979), p. 31.

14. *Reuben Quick Bear* v. *Leupp,* 210 U.S. 50 (1908). For further discussion of this case see Chapter 14.

15. See "Catholics and the Indian Schools," *The Outlook* (Oct. 5, 1912), pp. 234–35.

16. See discussion in Bernard J. Coughlin, *Church and State in Social Welfare* (New York: Columbia University Press, 1965), p. 44.

17. *Bradfield* v. *Roberts,* 175 U.S. 291 (1899).

18. For this and following quotations see Coughlin, *Church and State in Social Welfare,* p. 45.

19. For useful background material on overseas relief at the turn of the century see Curti, *American Philanthropy Abroad,* pp. 199–223.

20. Richmond Mayo-Smith and Thomas A. Ingram, "Migration," *Encyclopedia Britannica* (1911), 18: 427–33; Caldwell Lipsett, "Coolie," 7: 77–78.

21. Paul Johnson, *Modern Times: The World from the Twenties to the Eighties* (New York: Harper & Row, 1983), p. 158.

22. Michael R. Marrus, *The Unwanted: European Refugees in the Twentieth Century* (New York: Oxford University Press, 1985), pp. 82–84.

23. Richard M. Linkh, *American Catholicism and European Immigrants (1900–1924)* (Staten Island: Center for Migration Studies, 1975), chaps. 5–7.

24. Curti, *American Philanthropy Abroad,* p. 299.

25. Quoted in Nathan Schachner, *The Price of Liberty* (New York: American Book-Stratford Press, 1948), p. 7.

26. Ibid., pp. 24–25.

27. In 1895 the American minister at St. Petersburg wrote to a Russian official, in reference to the First Amendment's protection of religious freedom, "Thus, you see my Government is prohibited in the most positive manner possible by the very law of its existence from even attempting to put any form of limitation upon any of its citizens by reason of his religious belief. How, then, can we permit this to be done by others? To say that they can thereby be discriminated against by foreign governments, and are only safe-guarded against their own, would be a remarkable position for us to occupy." Cited in John Mansfield, "The Religion Clauses of the First Amendment and Foreign Relations," *De Paul Law Review* 36 (1986), n. 169. The words of the American official in this case amount to a strong statement of the case for extraterritorial application of U.S. law, particularly concerning religious freedom. It is not a position that successive U.S. governments have defended.

28. Schachner, *The Price of Liberty,* p. 42.

29. "Jewish War Relief Work," in Samson D. Oppenheim, ed., *American Jewish Year-book 5678 1917–1918* (Philadelphia: Jewish Publication Society of America, 1917), p. 196.

30. Ibid., p. 214.

31. Ibid., p. 220.

32. Cited in correspondence between the author and Eileen Egan, July 24, 1985.

33. John F. Piper, Jr., *The American Churches in World War I* (Athens: Ohio University Press, 1985), p. 81. World War I appears to be the first time questions were raised about the government's participation in building houses of worship for those involved in the war effort. In the United States, the War Department proposed building multidenominational worship centers at its hastily constructed munitions production centers, known as "ordnance reservations." While Protestant leaders had been glad to accept preference in national fund-raising efforts, this plan for government-funded worship centers seemed to many to be a violation of the separation of church and state. Apparently an unofficial, political Protestant establishment was acceptable, but not the multidenominational worship centers. Protestant chapels were eventually built on the reservations with private funds. See Piper, pp. 142–44.

34. Ibid., p. 79

35. Ibid., p. 82

36. Registration files of the American Friends Service Committee, Office of Private and Voluntary Cooperation, Agency for International Development, Washington, D.C. See evaluation form of the National Information Bureau.

37. Curti, *American Philanthropy Abroad,* pp. 255–56.

38. Ibid., p. 251.

Chapter 3

1. For a full account see Clarence E. Pickett, *For More Than Bread* (Boston: Little, Brown, 1953).

2. Charles E. Strickland, "American Aid to Germany, 1919 to 1921," *Wisconsin Magazine of History* (Summer 1962): 256–70.

3. Ibid.

4. Senator Vernon Kellogg, quoted in Curti, *American Philanthropy Abroad,* p. 272.

5. Ibid., p. 276.

6. Herbert Hoover, *Addresses on the American Road, 1948–1950* (Stanford, Calif.: Stanford University Press, 1951), pp. 64–65.

7. See Curti, *American Philanthropy Abroad,* pp. 279–93.

8. Notable exceptions include the Presiding Bishop's Fund for World Relief of the Episcopal church (1938) and the Brethren Service Committee (1933), patterned after the Anabaptist, nonviolent style of the AFSC and the Mennonite Central Committee.

9. John Lankford, "Protestant Stewardship and Benevolence, 1900–1941: A Study in Religious Philanthropy." Ph.D. dissertation, U. of Wisconsin, 1962.

10. Ibid., p. 115.

11. Marrus, *The Unwanted,* p. 125.

12. For a valuable study of the complexities of this situation see John P. Fox, "Weimar Germany and the Ostjuden, 1918–1923," in Anna Bramwell, ed., *Refugees in the Age of Total War: Europe and the Middle East* (London: Unwin Hyman, 1988).

13. Haim Genizi, *American Apathy: The Plight of Christian Refugees from Nazism* (Ramat-Gan, Israel: Bar-Ilan University Press, 1983), p. 59.

14. Henry Feingold, *The Politics of Rescue* (New York: Holocaust Publications, 1970), p. 16.

15. Genizi, *American Apathy,* p. 60.

16. Ibid., p. 62.

17. See for instance Curti, *American Philanthropy Abroad,* pp. 361–390; Marrus, *The Unwanted,* pp. 161–164.

18. Genizi, *American Apathy,* pp. 72–73.

19. Ibid., p. 61.

20. Curti, *American Philanthropy Abroad,* p. 392.

21. Pickett, *For More Than Bread,* p. 118.

22. Ibid., p. 153.

23. Curti, *American Philanthropy Abroad,* p. 395.

24. Journalist Dorothy Thompson is generally credited as the most effective private lobbyist for refugee causes in the 1930s. She published an article in the spring 1938 issue of *Foreign Affairs* entitled "Refugees, a World Problem." She later testified before Congress that this article gave President Roosevelt the impetus to call the Evian Conference. Such a move was not without political risk during the Depression. Refugee supporters—notably Rabbi Stephen Wise and Dorothy Thompson—were delighted with Roosevelt's call for a conference. Jews in particular, including New York's Governor Herbert Lehman, flooded Roosevelt's office with congratulations on his decision. Many other Americans opposed further extension of immigration quotas, and were prepared to say so publicly. See Feingold, *The Politics of Rescue,* p. 23, n. 7.

25. Feingold, *The Politics of Rescue,* p. 25.

26. Ibid., p. 33.

27. Genizi, *American Apathy,* p. 76.

28. Arthur D. Morse, *While Six Million Died: A Chronicle of American Apathy* (New York: Hart, 1968), p. 237.

29. Feingold, *The Politics of Rescue,* p. 85, emphasis added.

30. Ibid., p. 83.

31. The full text is available in the Franklin D. Roosevelt Library, Hyde Park, N.Y. A lengthy excerpt appears in Cyrus Adler's memoir *I Have Considered the Days* (Philadelphia: Jewish Publication Society of America, 1945), pp. xv–xvii.

Chapter 4

1. Curti, *American Philanthropy Abroad,* p. 479.

2. Quoted in Ernest Barker, *Church, State and Education* (Ann Arbor, University of Michigan Press, 1957), p. 168.

3. The Non-Sectarian Committee for German Refugee Children joined leaders in support of the Wagner-Rogers Bill, which allowed 20,000 nonquota refugee children of all faiths to enter the United States. Protestant and Catholic supporters quoted Jesus' admonition "Suffer little children to come unto me." But despite such strong religious support, which included a heart-rending recitation of Psalm 46 ("God is our refuge and strength, a

very present help in trouble") by Rabbi Stephen Wise before Congress, the bill did not pass. Testimony such as the following carried the day in Congress:

> These refugees have a heritage of hate. They could never become loyal Americans. Let us not be maudlin in our sympathies, as charity begins at home. We must protect our own children. No society, no state can successfully assume the tremendous responsibility of fostering thousands of motherless, embittered, persecuted children of undesirable foreigners and expect to convert these embattled souls into loyal, loving American citizens.

Such were the sentiments with which private and public refugee advocates contended. Isolationist sentiment carried directly into Americans' response to abandoned children. See Susan Forbes and Patricia Weiss Fagan, "Unaccompanied Refugee Children: The Evolution of U.S. Policies—1939–1984," Washington, D.C., Refugee Policy Group, August 1984, p. 6.

4. Papers in A. A. Berle Collection, Box 64, "Neutrality" folder, Roosevelt Library, Hyde Park, N.Y.

5. Pickett, *For More Than Bread,* pp. 169–71, 182.

6. Feingold, *The Politics of Rescue,* p. 26.

7. Memorandum to Secretary of State Hull from A. A. Berle et al., in Berle Collection, Box 64.

8. *Commonweal,* June 14, 1940, pp. 157–58.

9. Public outcry from Protestants over the appointment of Myron Taylor as Roosevelt's envoy to the Vatican was only one of the indications that religious divisions were thrown into high relief when power in Washington was at stake. Despite the concern, the resulting pragmatic contacts with the Vatican never met Roosevelt's expectations of full cooperation. Taylor's appointment to the Holy See was directly tied to Catholic participation in solving the refugee problem. However, Pope Pius XII was unwilling to believe early accounts of mass extermination. Furthermore, there were millions of Catholics in Axis-dominated territories. Even after Stephen Wise reported to Taylor in the fall of 1943 that Nazis were deporting Jews from Rome, and the news was forwarded to the Vatican, no official Catholic action was taken. See Feingold, *The Politics of Rescue,* p. 185.

10. Harold J. Seymour, *Design for Giving: The Story of the National War Fund, Inc., 1943–1947* (New York: Harper & Brothers, 1947), pp. vii, 3.

11. Ibid., p. 94; see also Appendix A, Certificate of Incorporation of National War Fund, Inc., pp. 140–41.

12. Ibid., p. 8. The United Service Organization (USO), which received more assistance than any other agency that participated in the fund, met the special need of "rest and relaxation" for U.S. armed forces abroad. While the entertainment industry has given us the comic, song and dance revue image of the USO, it is worth noting that the organization itself emerged from a federation of six national agencies, of which five (the YMCA, the YWCA, the National Catholic Community Service, the National Jewish Welfare Board, and the Salvation Army) were religiously inspired.

13. Ibid., p. 9. The question of Jewish activity abroad began with the fact that Jewish fund raising was conducted separately from other appeals and was primarily spent on Jewish recipients abroad, fulfilling passionate injunctions to observe primary responsibility for the community of faith. Furthermore, European Jews constituted a disproportionate segment of the refugee population, and much Jewish giving focused on Zionist solutions involving massive resettlement to Palestine. With the War Fund's emphasis on nondiscrimination, this was sure to cause difficulties. The government's fear of a backlash against charity associated with the cause of Jewish refugees is evident from the fact that no Jewish presence whatsoever is visible in the names of the twenty-three instrumentalities listed as War Fund agencies, despite the fact that Jewish agencies did indeed benefit from the fund through subcontracting and cooperative arrangements.

In the structuring of agency cooperation smaller Protestant and Jewish agencies did not fare well. The War Fund insisted, for the purpose of distributing funds raised nationally, that three agencies, the American Christian Refugee Committee (Federal Council of Churches), the Unitarian Service Committee, and the International Rescue and Relief Committee (an independent organization founded in 1933 to aid Jewish refugees, and today known as the International Rescue Committee) were governmentally amalgamated into the "Refugee Relief Trustees." Similarly, services to prisoners of the new War Relief Services of the National Catholic Welfare Conference and of the YMCA were consolidated into "War Prisoners Aid, Inc." The essential questions in the minds of administrators of the day did not stem from the finely tuned church/state theories of Madison or Jefferson. Their thoughts were on winning a war, and on uniting the American people on the most direct route to that end. If the Catholic church received a larger benefit than Protestants or Jews, it was because the Catholic church had offered the most developed system for moving relief abroad.

14. Seymour, *Design for Giving,* p. 9.

15. Telephone interview, Edward M. O'Connor, member, Displaced Persons Commission, 1948–1952, New York, August 1985.

16. This discussion is from "Progress Report to the Board of Trustees," November 1943 ("printed but not for publication"), National Catholic Welfare Conference, New York pp. 1, 2, 10.

17. Telephone interview, Edward M. O'Connor, New York, December 1984.

18. Within this context, registered agencies were nonetheless active in humanitarian assistance in Europe and the Far East, which included the provision of food, shelter, and clothing to 4 million refugees in China through the National War Fund's amalgamated wartime agency, United China Relief. (When intelligence officials determined that United China Relief had been infiltrated by Russians, the government acted on its supervisory authority and reorganized the agency.) Even though this was one of the major relief efforts of the war, no more than 15 percent of governmental resources going abroad through voluntary agencies ever reached the Far East in a given year; 85 percent was concentrated in Europe, with less than 1 percent going to Latin America and Africa combined. See Seymour, *Design for Giving,* p. 81; also see chart, "Private Voluntary Assistance Overseas, 1945–57," n.d., in the archive of the American Council of Voluntary Agencies in Foreign Service, Rutgers University Archives, New Brunswick, N.J.

19. Feingold, *The Politics of Rescue,* p. 135. The depressing story of the State Department's refusal to act on reports of persecution, murder, and refugee needs in German territories has been extensively studied. For a more complete treatment of this period see Feingold; also, David S. Wyman, *The Abandonment of the Jews: America and the Holocaust, 1941–1945* (New York: Pantheon, 1984); and Breckinridge Long, *The War Diary of Breckinridge Long,* Fred L. Israel, ed. (Lincoln: University of Nebraska Press, 1966).

20. Feingold, *The Politics of Rescue,* p. 206.

21. Ibid., p. 221.

22. Personal interview with Elizabeth Clark Reiss, former acting director, American Council of Voluntary Agencies for Foreign Service, New York, February 1983.

23. Elizabeth Clark Reiss, *The American Council of Voluntary Agencies for Foreign Service: Four Monographs* (New York: American Council of Voluntary Agencies for Foreign Service, 1985), pp. 1–15.

24. Ibid., p. 12.

25. See chart in Curti, *American Philanthropy Abroad,* pp. 506–7.

26. Feingold, *The Politics of Rescue,* p. 241.

27. Ibid., p. 260.

28. See Ruth Gruber, *Haven: The Unknown Story of 1000 World War II Refugees* (New York: Coward-McCann, 1983).

29. Feingold, *The Politics of Rescue,* p. 283.

30. Ibid., pp. 292–93.

31. Wyman, *The Abandonment of the Jews*, pp. 288–307.

32. Maurice R. Davie, "Refugee Aid," in Harry Schneiderman and Morris Fine, eds., *The American Jewish Yearbook* (Philadelphia: Jewish Publication Society of America, 1947–8), 49:215.

33. Jane Perry Clark Carey, "The Admission and Integration of Refugees in the United States," *Journal of International Affairs* 7, 1 (1953): 66–74.

34. Davie, "Refugee Aid," p. 213.

35. Quoted in *A Memo to America: The DP Story: The Final Report of the United States Displaced Persons Commission* (Washington, D.C.: Government Printing Office, 1952), p. 9.

36. *Department of State Bulletin* 8 (January 16, 1943): 37.

Chapter 5

1. Curti, *American Philanthropy Abroad*, pp. 488–89.

2. Earl G. Harrison et al., "The Problem of the Displaced Persons," Survey Committee on Displaced Persons, American Council of Voluntary Agencies for Foreign Service, June 1946, p. 65.

3. "Report to Board of Trustees, War Relief Service-N.C.W.C." ("printed but not for publication"), August 1, 1943–September 30, 1944, p. 17. Hereafter these reports are cited as "Report to Board of Trustees."

4. "The Problem of the Displaced Persons," p. 66.

5. Reiss, *The American Council of Voluntary Agencies*, "Committee on Refugee and Migration Affairs," p. 14.

6. "The Problem of the Displaced Persons," p. 35.

7. "Report to Board of Trustees," October 1, 1944–September 30, 1945, p. 35.

8. Julius A. Elias, "Relations Between Voluntary Agencies and International Organizations," *Journal of International Affairs* 7, 1 (1953): 30–34.

9. Egan and Reiss, *Transfigured Night*, p. 17.

10. Arthur C. Ringland, "The Organization of Voluntary Foreign Aid, 1939–1953," *Department of State Bulletin* 30 (March 15, 1954): 386.

11. Reiss, "The Organization," pp. 65–75.

12. Ringland, "The Organization of Voluntary Foreign Aid," p. 386.

13. Speech given by Eileen Egan at the Carnegie Council on Ethics and International Affairs, New York, October 30, 1985.

14. Curti, *American Philanthropy Abroad*, p. 504.

15. Ibid., pp. 491–502.

16. "Report to Board of Trustees," October 1, 1944–September 30, 1945, p. 26.

17. "Report to Board of Trustees," October 1, 1945–September 30, 1946, pp. 4, 9.

18. Ibid., p. 2.

19. Philip S. Bernstein, "Displaced Persons," in Schneiderman and Fine, eds., *American Jewish Yearbook*, 49:524.

20. David A. Baldwin, *Foreign Aid and American Foreign Policy* (New York: Praeger, 1966), p. 20.

21. Curti, *American Philanthropy Abroad*, p. 492.

22. Baldwin, *Foreign Aid*, p. 21.

23. Herbert Hoover, *Addresses on the American Road, 1945–48* (New York: D. Van Nostrand, 1949), pp. 22–23.

24. Louise W. Holborn, *Refugees: A Problem of Our Time* (Metuchen, N.J.: Scarecrow Press, 1975), pp. 26–28.

25. *A Memo to America*, p. 13.

26. Mark R. Elliot, *Pawns of Yalta: Soviet Refugees and America's Role in Their Repatriation* (Chicago: University of Illinois Press, 1982).

27. Davie, "Refugee Aid," pp. 212–22.

28. Transcript on file, Archives of the American Council of Voluntary Agencies, Rutgers University, New Brunswick, N.J.

29. *A Memo to America,* pp. 13, 14.

30. Anita J. Prazmowska, "Polish Refugees as Military Potential: The Polish Objectives of the Polish Government in Exile, 1939–1945," in Bramwell, *Refugees in the Age of Total War.*

31. Carey, "The Admission and Integration of Refugees in the United States," p. 68.

32. "Post-War Catholic Relief: An Interview with Bishop Edward E. Swanstrom," *Newsletter on the Church and State Abroad,* New York, Carnegie Council on Ethics and International Affairs, no. 4, May 1984, p. 5.

33. *A Memo to America,* pp. vi, vii.

34. Ibid., p. 58.

35. Ibid., p. 91.

36. Nathan Schachner, "Church, State and Education," in Schneiderman and Fine, eds., *American Jewish Yearbook,* 49:42–43.

37. P.L. 84, passed by joint resolution of Congress, May 31, 1947. For discussion see Reiss, *The American Council of Voluntary Agencies,* "Committee on Material Resources," pp. 35–45.

38. The first such legislation appeared in Section 416 of the Agricultural Act of 1949, followed by P.L. 480, known as Food for Peace. See ibid., pp. 60–69, 82–93.

39. In particular, Jewish officials both in and outside the IRO objected to the inclusion of many ethnic Germans on the lists of displaced persons going to the United States. Struggles over this were protracted, continuing into the 1980s with the deportation proceedings pressed by the Justice Department's Office of Special Investigations against Nazi "collaborators" who entered the country during the postwar era.

40. Barent Landstreet to Herbert C. Lytle, November 16, 1948, in the files of the National Council of Churches of Christ in the United States, Presbyterian Historical Society, Philadelphia.

41. Sue Stille to Wayland Zwayer, September 19, 1950; Sue Stille et al. to Edgar Chandler, September 19, 1950, ibid.

42. Barent Landstreet to Herbert C. Lytle, August 2, 1948, ibid.

43. It took an "assurance," filed by one of the registered resettlement agencies with the Displaced Persons Commission in Washington, to start an applicant in the pipeline. An assurance was a document from an individual sponsor pledging to provide suitable housing and employment for a refugee or refugee family. When the Displaced Persons Act was amended, a clause was added stating that the sponsor certified that the refugees involved would not become "public charges," returning to the restrictive language of earlier immigration legislation. Once verified, word of the assurance was forwarded to the U.S. government's assurance office in Frankfort and to relevant state authorities in the United States. Agencies were permitted to issue "blanket assurances" for entire groups of refugees. In resettlement centers run by the IRO, representatives of the Displaced Persons Commission analyzed cases and selected recommended candidates for resettlement. State Department consular officers, Public Health Service doctors, and army officers completed the U.S. government teams at the centers. Once a person was selected through the method appropriate to his or her assurance, the IRO began a certification and identification process as required under the act. Once this was successfully completed, commission authorities issued a preliminary statement of eligibility. The case then went to the Army Counterintelligence Corps, which was authorized to make over twenty different investigations into the applicant's past political affiliations. Members of Communist or Nazi parties were automatically excluded. After screening, the commission ruled on the final determination of the case. Judgments were made on the basis of the cumulative file, which by then might include entries

from the Department of State, the CIA, the Army Counterintelligence Corps, the FBI, and the IRO. If the ruling was favorable, the case was sent to the local consul for consideration for a visa. Only if this last commission ruling was favorable did the refugee actually receive a "call forward notice"; the only hurdle that remained was a health inspection. After a successful examination and interviews with the INS and consular officials, the refugee was placed on a ship for America chartered by the IRO. The entire process could take from three to twelve months. While the individual elements of the process have varied over the years, the establishment of resettlement pipelines based on U.S. voluntary agency assurances remains in effect in a variety of refugee settings today, most notably in Southeast Asia.

One problem that emerged under the 1948 act concerned the movement of displaced persons from the port of entry in the United States to their inland destinations; the agencies did not have funds for this final stage of a refugee's journey. The 1950 act amendments created a loan fund for inland transport, to be administered through the agencies. Abroad, the amendments removed authority for administration of the "expellees" program from the State Department, which had been dragging its feet on issuing visas. As with the loan fund amendment, voluntary agency lobbying had been a critical factor in the change. Even the normally diplomatic Displaced Persons Commission found it hard to refrain from commenting on unpleasant incidents that the INS created in its processing of resettlement cases. The INS agents sometimes turned back applicants who had been moved along the pipeline as far as the docks in Bremerhaven, causing "the whole humanitarian operation to lose in quality." Such failures were blamed directly on the overseas staff of INS: "Honesty requires us to record a Commission belief that the overseas staff of the [INS] failed to carry out the same spirit of cooperation and the same sympathetic understanding of the basic purposes and aim of the Act as that Service exhibited in Washington" (*A Memo to America*, p. 151). At least one of the voluntary agencies specifically accused the INS of discrimination. This pattern of INS antipathy for refugees awaiting resettlement would be repeated in similar circumstances in Southeast Asia in the 1970s and 1980s, with Washington officials hurriedly blaming incompetent field personnel. See *A Memo to America*, pp. 72–76, 150, 151.

44. Ibid., p. 154.

45. Ibid., p. 157.

46. Ibid., p. 159.

47. Ibid., p. 169.

48. Ibid., p. 176.

49. Some of the political danger for religious and governmental agencies in the refugee field in this era have only emerged recently. One area concerns former facist authorities who had served Hitler during the war in Eastern European nations, and who became refugees after the consolidation of Soviet political control. For discussion see "Vatican Is Reported to Have Furnished Aid to Fleeing Nazis," *New York Times,* Jan. 26, 1984, and William Bole, "Newly Public Documents Shed Light on Allegations Vatican Aided Nazis," *National Catholic Reporter,* May 16, 1986.

50. In the files of the National Council of Churches of Christ, Presbyterian Historical Society, Philadelphia.

51. Benny Morris, "The Initial Absorption of the Palestinian Refugees in the Arab Host Countries, 1948–49," in Bramwell, *Refugees in the Age of Total War.*

52. See for instance *Khalaf et al.* v. *Regan.* October 6, 1983. U.S. District Court for the District of Columbia. Civil Action Number 83–29-63. Extreme church/state separatists have also sought to bar diplomatic relations with Israel on the grounds that the American government was constitutionally barred from relations with a "theocracy."

53. In 1950 and 1951 Israel's supporters requested $150 million in economic aid. The administration had earmarked $125 million for the entire region, including the Arab states and Iran; out of that total $23.5 million would go to Israel and an equal amount to all the Arab states. A separate request for $50 million had been submitted by the administration for

Palestinian refugees. This imbalance, particularly considering that Israelis were resettling and rehabilitating their refugees while UNRWA was merely conducting a feeding and holding operation with little help from Arab governments, infuriated Jews and their supporters.

In House committee hearings, Clarence Pickett of the AFSC and representatives of the National Council of Churches and the Catholic church argued the opposite view, namely that an equal appropriation both to Israel and to all the Arab states combined did not do justice to the difficulty that Arabs faced in resettling and caring for the Palestinians. They openly favored an increase in aid to the Arab states; Pickett further argued that Israel's request for $150 million for resettling Jews would "uproot" millions of people from their homes.

I. L. Kenan, Israel's effective chief lobbyist in Washington, approached Congressman Jacob Javits (R-N.Y.) with a compromise recommendation that proposed $73.5 million for Israel: this included the administration's original $23.5 request and an additional $50 million for refugees, matching the request already submitted for the Palestinians. Debate was heated. Opponents claimed that many of the Jews moving to Israel were immigrants, not refugees, and that the United States was under no obligation to finance such migrations. Judaism was a religion, they argued, not the basis for a nation, and the separatism inherent in Zionism was the root cause of the refugee problem in the region. Supporters of Israel included many prominent Christians who argued for strengthening the inherent ties between Jews and Christians; others argued that Israel would be a democratic and military ally in a region where the United States needed reliable friends. In the end the House approved the $73.5 million total.

In the Senate there were protracted efforts to reduce the $50 million in refugee appropriations to Palestinians and Israelis. Missionary forces opposed increased support for Israel. Eventually both houses of Congress agreed to a compromise solution: the Israelis and the Palestinians would receive $50 million each for refugee aid (no effort was made to solve any lingering problems of what constituted refugee status); Israel's initial appropriation of $23.5 million in economic assistance was reduced to $15 million.

The battle for the heart and mind of Congress on these and related issues continued (Kenan himself proposed shortly after this round of debate that Israel build forty-eight new coastal towns and name them after the forty-eight states as a means of securing American sympathy). The State Department's sympathy for Arab perspectives was entrenched, but Israel won considerable support for its refugee programs by going directly to Congress. See I. L. Kenan, *Israel's Defense Line* (Buffalo: Prometheus Books, 1981), pp. 66–81.

Chapter 6

1. See Section 117(c), Economic Cooperation Act of 1948.

2. Memorandum from Elizabeth C. Reiss to Leon O. Marion, American Council of Voluntary Agencies for Foreign Service, May 3, 1982, in the files of the American Council of Voluntary Agencies, Rutgers University Archives, New Brunswick, N.J. For complete wording of the law see P.L. 165, 82d Congress, H.R. 5113.

3. Gilburt D. Loescher and John Scanlan, "The Politics of Rescue: U.S. Policy towards East European Refugees, 1945–56," in Bramwell, *Refugees in the Age of Total War.* See also Gilburt Loescher and John Scanlan, *Calculated Kindness* (Glencoe, Ill.: Free Press, 1986).

4. "Working Paper on the Responsibility of the American Churches for Displaced Persons," n.d., circa 1949, Church World Service, National Council of Churches of Christ, Presbyterian Historical Society, Philadelphia.

5. Telephone interview with Lawrence Dawson, Philadelphia, July 1985. The early pattern of Lutheran conservatism in cooperative church/state ties continued through the 1960s; see pp. 97, 202.

6. Carey, "The Admission and Integration of Refugees in the United States," p. 68.

7. Elias, "Relations Between Voluntary Agencies and International Organizations," p. 33.

8. Prazmowska, "Polish Refugees as Military Potential," in Bramwell, *Refugees in the Age of Total War.*

9. Loescher and Scanlan, "The Politics of Rescue," in Bramwell, *Refugees in the Age of Total War.*

10. Personal interview with Elizabeth C. Reiss, New York, October 1984.

11. Pickett, *For More Than Bread,* p. 405.

12. Personal interview with Elizabeth C. Reiss, October 1984.

13. Quoted in Dean Acheson, *Present at the Creation* (New York: Norton, 1969), p. 231.

14. "Convention Relating to the Status of Refugees of 28 July 1951." In *Collection of International Instruments Concerning Refugees* (Geneva: United Nations High Commissioner for Refugees, 1979), pp. 3–30.

15. Personal inverview with James M. Read, New York, November 1983.

16. Telephone interview with Lawrence Dawson, Philadelphia, July 1985. Religious and other voluntary agencies active in refugee resettlement have since built close working relationships with ICM and ICMC. Yet despite their role in transporting refugees around the globe, both agencies remain virtually unknown outside professional refugee circles. Both receive the bulk of their funding from participating Western governments. In recent years, some agencies have charged that ICM has cooperated in political decisions far removed from humanitarian goals; a case in point has been ICM's willingness to handle the deportation of Salvadorans and Guatemalans who had fled their homelands to the United States but failed to qualify as refugees under INS application of the Refugee Act of 1980. See the discussion of the sanctuary movement, Chapter 15.

17. Oscar Handlin, *A Continuing Task: The American Jewish Joint Distribution Committee* (New York: Random House, 1964), p. 103.

18. Lucy Dawidowicz, "The United States, Israel and the Middle East," in Morris Fine and Jacob Sloan, eds., *American Jewish Yearbook* (1957), 58:208–10.

19. Ibid., p. 216.

20. The UNRWA predated the UNHCR, but the unique circumstances of the Palestinians required special attention. Unlike the UNHCR, UNRWA was given no legal protection function; its work was limited to health, feeding, and education programs. A similar special refugee organization beyond the UNHCR mandate, the United Nations Border Relief Operation (UNBRO), was created in 1983 to supervise assistance to Cambodian and Vietnamese refugee camps along the Thai-Cambodian border.

21. Roland Elliott correspondence with Church World Service officials, December 12, 1957, National Council of Churches of Christ, Presbyterian Historical Society, Philadelphia.

22. Chicago *Daily News,* November 26, 1956.

23. Reiss, *The American Council of Voluntary Agencies for Foreign Services,* "ACVAFS: Committee on Migration and Refugee Affairs," pp. 73–74.

24. This discussion was drawn from the registration and membership files of the American Council of Voluntary Agencies, Rutgers University Archives, New Brunswick, N.J.

25. "Post-War Catholic Relief: An Interview with Bishop Edward E. Swanstrom," p. 5.

26. See Franklin Graham and Jeanette Lockerbie, *Bob Pierce: This One Thing I Do* (Waco, Tex.: Word Books, 1983).

27. "Proselytizing with Food Aid," *Christian Century* 75 (June 18, 1958): 707.

28. See Pieter DeJong, "Migration in Biblical Perspective," and J.J. Norris, "A Roman Catholic Viewpoint," in "In A Strange Land," Report of a World Conference on Problems of International Migration and the Responsibility of the Churches, Leysin, Switzerland, June 11–16, 1961. Geneva: World Council of Churches, 1961.

29. The ICA documentation is in the files of the American Council of Voluntary Agencies, Rutgers University Archives, New Brunswick, N.J.

30. Personal interview with Francis B. Sayre, Vineyard Haven, Mass., August 1984.

31. Ibid.

32. Reiss, *American Council of Voluntary Agencies,* p. 81.

33. George La Noue, "Church-State Relations in the Federal Policy Process," Ph.D. dissertation, Yale University, 1966, p. 206.

34. Ibid., pp. 215, 220.

35. *Abington Township School District* v. *Schempp,* 374 U.S. 203 (1963).

36. La Noue, "Church-State Relations," pp. 258, 260.

37. Ibid., p. 268.

38. See internal National Council of Churches memoranda on this study process and debate, Archive on Church and State Abroad, Carnegie Council on Ethics and International Affairs, New York.

39. La Noue, "Church-State Relations," p. 268.

40. *McCollum* v. *Board of Education,* 333 U.S. 203 (1948).

41. Robert T. Miller and Ronald B. Flowers, *Toward Benevolent Neutrality: Church, State, and the Supreme Court,* rev. ed. (Waco, Tex.: Markham Press Fund, 1982), p. 322.

42. *Engel* v. *Vitale,* 370 U.S. 421 (1962); *Abington Township School District* v. *Schempp,* 374 U.S. 203 (1963).

Chapter 7

1. U.S. Congress, Senate, S. Rept. 748, 89th Cong., 1st Sess., 1965, pp. 7–8.

2. David M. Reimers, *Still the Golden Door: The Third World Comes to America* (New York: Columbia University Press, 1985), pp. 160–61.

3. Memo from Elfan Rees, June 1, 1950, on World Council of Churches suggestions for the UNHCR mandate, in the files of the National Council of Churches of Christ, Presbyterian Historical Society, Philadelphia.

4. "Report on Vietnamese Refugees and Displaced Persons, by a Delegation from the American Council of Voluntary Agencies for Foreign Service," New York, October 1965, p. 1.

5. Victor Marchetti and John D. Marks, *The CIA and the Cult of Intelligence* (New York: Dell, 1980), p. 127.

6. Gary MacEoin, "The European Church and the War," in Thomas Quigley, ed., *American Catholics and Vietnam* (Grand Rapids, Mich.: William B. Eerdmans, 1968), p. 159.

7. "Report on Vietnamese Refugees and Displaced Persons," American Council of Voluntary Agencies.

8. See James W. Douglass, "Catholicism, Power, and Vietnamese Suffering," in Quigley, *American Catholics and Vietnam,* pp. 102, 110.

9. James H. Forest, "No Longer Alone," in Quigley, *American Catholics and Vietnam,* p. 148.

10. Robert W. Miller, "The Role and Contribution of the Foreign Voluntary Agencies in South Vietnam," M.A. thesis, Graduate School of Public and International Affairs, 1972, University of Pittsburgh, p. 64.

11. Ibid., p. 65.

12. Ibid., p. 21.

13. Ibid., pp. 52–53.

14. Ibid., p. 18.

15. Ibid., p. 17.

16. Ibid., p. 73.

17. Ibid., p. 104.

18. Ibid., p. 105.

19. David Butler, *The Fall of Saigon* (New York: Simon and Schuster, 1985), p. 439.

20. Reimers, *Still the Golden Door*, p. 173.

21. See D. Hostetter and M. McIntyre, "The Politics of Charity," *Christian Century* 91, 31 (September 18, 1974).

22. Daniel J. Elazar, "The Rediscovered Polity: Selections from the Literature of Jewish Public Affairs, 1967–1968," in Morris Fine and Milton Himmelfarb, eds., *American Jewish Yearbook* (1969), 70:172.

23. Ibid., pp. 178, 183.

24. Telephone interview with Lawrence Dawson, Philadelphia, July 1985.

25. William D. Korey, "The Struggle Over Jackson-Mills-Vanik," in Fine and Himmelfarb, *American Jewish Yearbook* (1974), 75:202.

26. William W. Orbach, *The American Movement to Aid Soviet Jews* (Amherst: University of Massachusetts Press, 1979), p. 159.

27. Ibid., p. 158.

28. Joseph Edelman, "Soviet Jews in the United States: A Profile," in Fine and Himmelfarb, eds., *American Jewish Yearbook* (1977), 78:162.

29. Ibid., p. 163.

30. Misha Louvish, "Israel," in Fine and Himmelfarb, eds., *American Jewish Yearbook* (1978), 79:479.

31. Reimers, *Still the Golden Door*, pp. 185–86.

32. Personal interview with Cyrus Vance, New York, May 1983.

33. Shawcross, *The Quality of Mercy*, p. 184.

34. Ibid. For Mrs. Carter's role in Cambodia, see pp. 187–90. The figure of $60 million was provided by Frank Kichne, a YMCA official active in the Cambodia Crisis Committee.

35. For a critical study see David S. North, Lawrence S. Lewin, and Jennifer R. Wagner, *Kaleidoscope: The Resettlement of Refugees in the United States by Voluntary Agencies* (Washington, D.C.: New TransCentury Foundation, Lewin and Associates, and National Opinion Research Center, February 1982).

Chapter 8

1. Personal interview with John Negroponte, U.S. ambassador to Honduras, Tegucigalpa, October 1982.

2. Raymond Bonner, "Miskito Indians Are Focus of Debate," *New York Times*, August 13, 1982, p. 27.

3. General Accounting Office, "Central American Refugees: Regional Conditions and Prospects and Potential Impact on the United States," GAO/NSIAD-84–106, Washington, D.C.: General Accounting Office, July 20, 1984, p. 6.

4. Personal interview with Marian Chambers, staff member, House Foreign Affairs Committee, Washington, D.C., March 1982.

5. Personal interview with John Contier, Honduras director, Catholic Relief Services, Tegucigalpa, November 1982.

6. William Baumann, "Report on La Virtud Refugee Camp, March 15–28, 1982" (Philadelphia: American Friends Service Committee, 1982), p. 1.

7. Ibid., p. 4.

8. For a report of two such murders see "A Report on the Refugee Relief Program of World Vision in Honduras," Monrovia, Calif: World Vision, December 17, 1981.

9. A number of U.S. religious missions were active in the region. Conservative evangelical missions had flooded Central America since World War II, and Catholic officials openly expressed their alarm. The largest staff belonged to the World Gospel Mission, an independent Protestant group with fifty missionaries in Honduras alone—more than the

number of Honduran-born Catholic priests active in 1982. In the relief community, Catholics and mainline Protestants often cast a wary eye on their evangelical counterparts. More liberal church leaders, themselves often drawn to analyses and practices derived from liberation theology, predictably expected evangelicals to seek close ties with U.S. officials in the region. They also found the conservative emphasis on evangelism—direct written or verbal witness to the gospel of Christ—inappropriate under the current circumstances. It was obvious to them that social and political conditions in Central America, not the salvation of individuals, were the appropriate focus of North American mission efforts in the 1980s.

10. This discussion was drawn from personal interview with John Contier, Catholic Relief Services Director in Honduras, Tegucigalpa, November 1982.

11. "Report and Recommendations to the United Nations High Commissioner for Refugees Regarding the Protection of Refugees and the Coordination of Material Assistance by the UNHCR in Honduras," Toronto: Interchurch Committee for Refugees, September, 1982, pp. 5–6.

12. See documentation in "Ad Hoc Assessment Visit to Central America, Lutheran World Federation, 28th September–9th October 1983" (Geneva: Lutheran World Federation), p. 1.

13. "Report and Recommendations to the United Nations High Commissioner," pp. 2–3.

14. Report of trip to Honduran refugee border camps, Robert Brauer, special counsel to Congressman Ronald V. Dellums (D-Calif.), November 1981, p. 5. In Archive on Church and State Abroad, Carnegie Council on Ethics and International Affairs, New York.

15. Ibid., p. 7.

16. Ibid., pp. 12–13.

17. Interview given by Robert Brauer to Linda Griffin Kean, Washington, D.C., May 26, 1983.

18. The UNHCR had little enthusiasm for an operational role in the situation. To accept it was a departure from its standard role that had been established in a variety of countries over the previous thirty years. The UNHCR officials hoped to resign from this operational role within three months, and with that prospect in mind began direct negotiations with Oxfam. Oxford Famine Relief (Oxfam for short) had begun in Oxford, England, during World War II by Christians eager to act on the social dimensions of the Gospel by providing relief to victims of the war. In recent years its base of support had broadened to include a constituency highly attuned to human rights issues. Perhaps anticipating official resistance to such a vocal agency as coordinator, Oxfam officials suggested that the agency "be introduced gradually and discreetly into Honduras under [the] UNHCR umbrella." The U.S. coordinator for refugees reacted extremely negatively when UNHCR officials raised the possibility of bringing Oxfam to Honduras. Furthermore, the U.S. ambassador to Honduras had previously worked in the American embassy in Cambodia in the early 1970s. There, he had encountered Oxfam as a blockade-running agency that brought food and medical supplies into Cambodia against the will of the U.S. government. He was not about to have an old nemesis active in Honduras if he could avoid it, and he certainly could. The United States vetoed the choice of Oxfam through officials at UNHCR's Geneva headquarters. See UNHCR cable traffic, Geneva-Tegucigalpa, March 1982, in the Archive on Church and State Abroad, Carnegie Council on Ethics and International Affairs, New York.

19. UNHCR cable traffic, Geneva-Tegucigalpa, May 1, 1982, Archive on Church and State Abroad, Carnegie Council on Ethics and International Affairs, New York.

20. Baumann, "Report on La Virtud Refugee Camp." See especially the attached appendix.

21. "Report and Recommendations to the United Nations High Commissioner for Refugees," p. 23.

22. Brauer interview, April 1983.

23. "Report and Recommendations to the High Commissioner for Refugees."

24. Ibid.

25. "Update on the Salvadoran Refugees in Honduras," Washington, D.C.: Washington Office on Latin America, March 1983, pp. 1–2.

26. Oldrich Hasselman and Catherine Bertrand, "Mission Report: Honduras (June 1983)," Geneva: UNHCR, June 30, 1983, p. 5.

27. Martin Barber and Meyer Brownstone, "Report and Recommendations to the United Nations High Commissioner for Refugees Regarding the Protection of Refugees in Honduras and the Promotion of Durable Solutions," London: British Refugee Council, September 9, 1983.

28. Ibid., p. 7.

29. Ibid., p. 8.

30. Ibid., p. 11.

31. Report by Julia Cameron submitted to the International Council of Voluntary Agencies (ICVA) Consultation on Refugees and Displaced Persons in Central America and Mexico, January 23–26, 1984, Nyon, Switzerland. Geneva: ICVA.

32. Linda Shelley, Mennonite Central Committee, to Joseph McLean, U.S. Embassy, Tegucigalpa, January 4, 1984. In Archive on Church and State Abroad, Carnegie Council on Ethics and International Affairs, New York.

33. Interview with John Negroponte, U.S. Ambassador to Honduras, Tegucigalpa, November 1982.

Chapter 9

1. Personal interview with Hal Barber, executive vice-president, World Vision, Monrovia, Calif., July 1983.

2. Jane Hamilton-Merritt, "The Poisoning of the Hmong." The *Bangkok Post,* March 7, 1982. See also by the same author, "The Challenge of Yellow Rain: Where Are We Now?" *Bangkok Post,* July 4, 1982.

3. Lester A. Sobel, ed., *Refugees: A World Report* (New York: Facts on File, 1979), p. 9.

4. Vang Pao to George Bush, March 6, 1981, Lao Family Community, Inc., Santa Ana, Calif.

5. Vang Pao to George Bush, March 16, 1981, ibid.

6. World Vision, Bangkok, letter drafted to the *Bangkok Post* (n.d., circa March 1982) and memo to Watt Santatiwat, February 22, 1982 on yellow rain. All World Vision documentation and related material is in the Archive on Church and State Abroad, Carnegie Council on Ethics and International Affairs, New York.

7. Ibid.

8. C. J. Mirocha, March 30, 1982, "Testimony to the House Foreign Affairs Committee on Illegal Chemical Warfare in Asia," p. 9. Transcript in Archive on Church and State Abroad, Carnegie Council on Ethics and International Affairs, New York.

9. Dr. Richard C. Harruff, "Statement Before the Subcommittee on Asian and Pacific Affairs, House Foreign Affairs Committee," March 30, 1982. New York: Freedom House, p. 4.

10. Dr. Milton Amayun, "Yellow Rain in Laos," April 21, 1982, report to the Subcommittee on Asian and Pacific Affairs. Draft in Archive on Church and State Abroad, Carnegie Council on Ethics and International Affairs, New York.

11. Ibid.

12. Personal interview with Phillip Passmore, acting director, World Vision Foundation of Thailand, Bangkok, July 1983.

13. Don Scott, "Ban Vinai Trip and Yellow Rain Issue, May 11–14, 1982." World

Vision International, Archive on Church and State Abroad, Carnegie Council on Ethics and International Affairs, New York.

14. Draft, Phillip Passmore to Ed McWilliams, U.S. Embassy, n.d. World Vision International, ibid.

15. Dr. Tony Atkins to Janet Lim, UNHCR, May 28, 1982, ibid.

16. "Visit by U.S. Ambassador Douglas to Ban Vinai," memo, D. Millham to P. Passmore, June 3, 1982.

17. "Yellow Rain," memo, Philip J. Hunt to Harold Henderson, June 21, 1982, World Vision International, Archive on Church and State Abroad, Carnegie Council on Ethics and International Affairs, New York.

18. Ibid.

19. Ibid.

20. Jacques L. F. G. Terlin, Chef de Mission, UNHCR, Thailand, to Mr. Wattanapong Santatiwat, World Vision Foundation of Thailand, July 15, 1982, ibid.

21. Alexander M. Haig, Jr., "Chemical Warfare in Southeast Asia and Afghanistan," *Special Report* no. 98 to Congress. Washington, D.C.: Department of State, March 22, 1982.

22. Amos R. Townsend, Testimony before the Senate Foreign Relations Committee, Subcommittee on Arms Control, February 24, 1983. Transcript in Archive on Church and State Abroad, Carnegie Council on Ethics and International Affairs, New York.

23. Ibid.

Chapter 10

1. Curti, *American Philanthropy Abroad,* p. 298, n. 87. Curti cites this early (1940) reference to the Falasha issue in Cyrus Adler's autobiography. It does not appear in later editions.

2. Leon Wieseltier, "Brothers and Keepers," *New Republic,* February 11, 1985; Roberta Fahn Reisman, "The Falashas," n.p., February 1982, p. 1.

3. Damas Deng, "Root Causes of the Refugee Phenomenon in Africa," paper presented at Seminar on Refugees, Khartoum, Sudan, September 11–14, 1982.

4. Personal interviews with U.S. Embassy officials, Khartoum, January–August 1983.

5. "The Falasha Jews of Ethiopia," New York: Council of Jewish Federation and Welfare Funds, January 1976.

6. Reisman, "The Falashas," p. 2.

7. Charles T. Powers, "Ethiopian Jews: Exodus of a Tribe," *Los Angeles Times,* July 7, 1985.

8. Reisman, "The Falashas," p. 4.

9. "OAU Convention of 10 September 1969 governing the specific aspects of refugee problems in Africa," in *Collection of International Instruments Concerning Refugees,* 2d ed. (Geneva: UNHCR, 1979), pp. 193–200.

10. "Exodus for a Twice-Lost Tribe," *New York Times,* March 3, 1984.

11. Powers, "Ethiopian Jews."

12. "Airlift to Israel Is Reported Taking Thousands of Jews From Ethiopia," *New York Times,* December 11, 1984.

13. "L' 'epopee heroique' des falachas," *Le Monde Diplomatique,* February 1985, p. 6.

14. "Disclosure of Secret Airlift Opens Rift at Israeli Agency," *New York Times,* January 5, 1985.

15. "Peres Vows Israel Will Finish Rescue," *New York Times,* January 8, 1985.

16. Charles T. Powers, "A New Life in Israel for Ethiopians," *Los Angeles Times,* July 8, 1985; "Sudan Blames Ethiopia for the Airlift to Israel," *New York Times,* January 8, 1985.

17. "Ethiopian Jews Said to Resettle on West Bank," *New York Times,* January 18, 1985.

18. "Sudan Lets U.S. Fly 800 Ethiopia Jews to Israeli Refuge," *New York Times,* March 24, 1985.

19. "Exodus from Ethiopia," *Economist,* January 12, 1985.

Chapter 11

1. Personal interview with Reverend Billy Harrell, World Gospel Missions, Tegucigalpa, November 1982.

2. "An Edited Transcript of a Conference on Ethical Issues and Moral Principles in U.S. Refugee Policy," transcript, Washington, D.C.: United States Coordinator for Refugee Affairs. This March 24–25, 1983, conference was cosponsored by the Office of the U.S. Coordinator for Refugee Affairs and the Religious Advisory Committee.

3. Ibid., p. 27.

4. Ibid., p. 28.

5. Amos Perlmutter, *Israel: The Partitioned State: A Political History Since 1900* (New York: Charles Scribner's Sons, 1985), pp. 290–93.

6. "State of World Need in the '80s," Wheaton, Ill.: World Relief Commission of the National Association of Evangelicals, n.d.

7. Edited transcript of "a Conference on Ethical Issues," p. 8.

8. Maimonides, *Laws of Gifts to the Poor,* VIII, 10, quoted in Wieseltier, "Brothers and Keepers."

9. Handlin, *A Continuing Task,* pp. 12–13.

10. See Wieseltier, "Brothers and Keepers." *Bitzu'ism* was often practiced in the name of *chesed.* During World II, 400 Orthodox rabbis arrived in Washington three days before Yom Kippur to call for the rescue of European Jews. Vice-President Henry Wallace had an opportunity to feel the power of Jewish leadership approaching in the name of a divine covenant:

> Early in the afternoon, the rabbis, conspicuous with their beards and long black coats, praying aloud, marched in a dignified procession from Union Station to the Capitol. They were met there by Vice-President Henry A. Wallace and a score of congressmen. Some rabbis sobbed audibly as their petition was read in Hebrew and English, then handed to Wallace. It called for a rescue agency and for the nations to open their gates to the stricken Jews. "The Vice-President," reported *Time* magazine, "squirmed through a diplomatically minimum answer."

Rather than face the rabbis, President Roosevelt "slipped away" to perform an unnecessary function at a nearby airfield. Cited in Wyman, *The Abandonment of the Jews,* p. 152.

11. Quoted in Handlin, *A Continuing Task,* p. 79.

12. For the political significance of these terms see "The Behind the Scenes Story Regarding the Aliyah of the Ethiopian Jews," confidential memorandum to the Board of Directors and Friends of the American Association for Ethiopian Jews from Howard M. Lenhoff, President, AAEJ, n.d. [1982], p. 2. In the Archive on Church and State Abroad, Carnegie Council on Ethics and International Affairs, New York.

13. James G. McDonald, *My Mission in Israel* (New York: Simon and Schuster, 1951), p. 273.

14. Daniel Elazar and Stuart Cohen, *The Jewish Polity* (Philadelphia: Temple University Press, 1984), p. 10–11.

15. For an explanation of this phenomenon see Arthur Hertzberg, "The New Religious Right in Israel," in Robert J. Myers, ed., *The Annals of the American Academy of Political and Social Science* (Beverly Hills, Calif.: Sage Publications, January 1986), 483:84–92.

16. Telephone interview with Lawrence Dawson, Philadelphia, May 1985.

17. Reinhold Niebuhr, *Beyond Tragedy* (New York: Charles Scribner's Sons, 1937), p. 123.

18. Reinhold Niebuhr, *Faith and History* (New York: Charles Scribner's Sons, 1949), p. 185.

19. J. H. Oldham. *The Oxford Conference (Official Report)* (New York: Willett, Clark & Company, 1937), p. 231.

20. The arrival of the war temporarily limited further development of a critical Protestant distance from the state. Two of the Americans attending Oxford would themselves encourage stronger coordination between religious and governmental activities abroad in the coming years. Charles P. Taft agreed in 1942 to serve as one of three commissioners on Roosevelt's War Relief Control Board, which took over the process of registering private relief groups with the State Department. John Foster Dulles, a New York lawyer long active in the Federal Council of Churches, organized the critical campaign among Protestants to register support in the U.S. Senate for the new United Nations. These were men accustomed to the pressures of public life. They realized that sacrifices were required from all segments of society, particularly religious groups, if the West was to survive international pressures. They both eventually achieved positions where they could encourage the wartime complementarity of religious and governmental bodies in refugee work.

21. Oldham, *The Oxford Conference,* p. 71.

22. Ibid., p. 66.

23. Ibid., p. 64.

24. Ibid., p. 66.

25. John C. Bennett, "Church and State in the United States." In *Reformed Faith and Politics,* ed. Ronald Stone (Lanham, Md.: University Press of America, 1983).

26. Paul Ramsey, quoted in Richard John Neuhaus, "Let the Church Be the Church," *Center Journal* (Washington, Ethics and Public Policy Center), Fall 1983, p. 39.

27. Reg Reimer, paper delivered at January 1977 Christian Ministries Seminar, Bangkok, p. 2. In the Archive on Church and State Abroad, Carnegie Council on Ethics and International Affairs, New York.

28. Ibid., p. 1.

29. Ibid., p. 3.

30. Robin Shell, "Working in Political Front Border Camps," Christian Ministries Seminar, December, 1981. Archive on Church and State Abroad, Carnegie Council on Ethics and International Affairs, New York.

31. Drawn from material from April 1980 Christian Ministries Seminar, Bangkok. Archive on Church and State Abroad, Carnegie Council on Ethics and International Affairs, New York.

32. Ron Hill, "Statement on Freedom of Conscience and Religion for Indochinese Refugees in Thailand," Thailand Baptist Mission, Addressed with cover letter to UNHCR, Bangkok, September 15, 1980. Archive on Church and State Abroad, Carnegie Council on Ethics and International Affairs, New York.

33. Ibid.

34. Leo XIII, *Rerum Novarum,* 1891.

35. Peter Brown, *Augustine of Hippo* (Berkeley and Los Angeles: University of California Press, 1969), pp. 313–29.

36. J. Milton Yinger, *Religion in the Struggle for Power* (Durham, N.C.: Duke University Press, 1946), pp. 191–92.

37. Quoted by Roger Mahoney, "There Your Heart Will Be: A Pastoral Reflection on the American Economy," *Catholicism and Crisis,* July 1984.

38. Walter J. Ong, S.J., *American Catholic Crossroads* (New York: Macmillan, 1959), pp. 23–32.

39. Pope Pius XI, "Reconstructing the Social Order [*Quadragessimo Anno*]," in *Five Great Encyclicals* (New York: Paulist Press, 1939), pp. 125–68.

40. Rev. Francis X. Clarke, S.J., "The Purpose of the Missions, a Study of Mission

Documents of the Holy See, 1909–1946," *Missionary Union of the Clergy Bulletin* (June 1948).

41. Pope Paul VI, *On Evangelization in the Modern World* [*Evangelii Nuntiandi*], (Washington, D.C.: U.S. Catholic Conference, 1976), pp. 28, 22.

42. *Christus Dominus* 18, *Gaudium et Spes* 84, cited in letter from Agostino Cardinal Casaroli to Cardinal Bernard Gantin (on behalf of Pope John Paul II), "The Refugee Problem Is Still Grave," *L'Osservatore Romano*, September 10, 1984.

43. Edwin S. Gaustad, ed., *A Documentary History of Religion in America* (Grand Rapids, Mich.: William B. Eerdmans, 1983), 2: 475–76.

44. Casaroli, "The Refugee Problem Is Still Grave."

45. "Key Sections from Vatican Document on Liberation Theology," *New York Times,* April 6, 1986.

Chapter 12

1. *Welch* v. *Kennedy*, 319 F. Supp. 945 (D.D.C. 1970).

2. Personal interview with William Snyder, executive director, Mennonite Central Committee, Akron, Pa., April 1983.

3. "U.S. Seeking a Curb on Testimony Citing Religion in Sanctuary Case," *New York Times,* January 27, 1985.

4. *Reynolds* v. *United States*, 98 U.S. 145 (1878).

5. See *Davis* v. *Beason*, 133 U.S. 333 (1890); and *Church of Jesus Christ of Latter-Day Saints* v. *United States*, 136 U.S. 1 (1890).

6. *Cantwell* v. *Connecticut*, 310 U.S. 296 (1940).

7. *Minersville School District* v. *Gobitis*, 310 U.S. 586 (1940).

8. Ibid.

9. *West Virginia State Board of Education* v. *Barnette*, 319 U.S. 624 (1943).

10. *Murdock* v. *Pennsylvania*, 319 U.S. 105 (1943); *Jones* v. *Opelika I*, 316 U.S. 584 (1942).

11. *Murdock* v. *Pennsylvania*, 319 U.S. 105 (1943).

12. Nevertheless, the Supreme Court has been straightforward in its support of government authority over individual rights in the foreign affairs arena. See *Zemel* v. *Rusk*, 381 U.S. 1 (1965); also *Haig* v. *Agee*, 453 U.S. 278 (1981). John Mansfield of the Harvard Law School offers the following caveat on the matter of travel restrictions that might be imposed by the government on American religious workers active abroad: "The right to spread a religious message is so close to the heart of what the free exercise clause was intended to protect that only foreign policy considerations of the gravest sort could justify prohibiting the evangelists from setting out on their mission, and that an idea of citizenship that requires conformity to national policy in the absence of such considerations would be in conflict with the first amendment." See Mansfield, "The Religion Clauses of the First Amendment and Foreign Relations," p. 66.

13. Mansfield, "The Religion Clauses of the First Amendment and Foreign Relations," pp. 51–59.

14. See *Buckley* v. *Valeo*, 424 U.S. 1 (1976).

15. See *United States* v. *Washington Post*, 446 F.2d 1327, 1329 (1971).

16. See *Wisconsin* v. *Yoder*, 406 U.S. 205 (1972), for "compelling state interests."

17. Note: "Revocation of Tax-Exempt Status," in *Brigham Young University Law Review* (1981): 9; L. Henkin, *Foreign Affairs and the Constitution* (New York: Columbia University Press, 1972).

18. Chief Justice Warren Burger, writing for the Court, recently stated that "it is 'obvious and unarguable' that no governmental interest is more compelling than the security of the Nation. Protection of the foreign policy of the United States is a governmental interest

of great importance, since foreign policy and national security cannot be neatly compartmentalized." See John Jenkins, "The Free Exercise Clause and Religiously Based Voluntary Agencies," n. 160, unpublished paper in the Archive on Church and State Abroad, Carnegie Council on Ethics and International Affairs, New York.

19. Compare the use of the test in *Wisconsin* v. *Yoder*, 406 U.S. 205 (1972), and in *Thomas* v. *Review Board of the Indiana Employment Security Division*, 49 L.W. 4341 (1981).

20. Two employees of the Domestic and Foreign Missionary Society of the Protestant Episcopal Church, both Puerto Rican nationalists, were convicted in 1983 of political activities carried out as part of their work for the society. Church officials protested the conviction, but it was not overturned.

21. Members of Congress made such charges against the Reagan administration when a group of religious women were refused entry into Honduras for the purpose of conducting prayer vigils for peace in the region. Similar charges arose when a group of U.S. religious workers accompanying displaced refugees as they returned to their homes in El Salvador were deported in the summer of 1986.

22. One instance of a governmental attack on religious mission abroad concerned the 1980 actions of the State Department toward the Voice of Hope radio station, operated in southern Lebanon as an evangelistic ministry by High Adventure Ministries, Inc., of California. High Adventure's Lebanon station broadcasts largely religious material such as Bible studies, sermons, and religious music. The Carter administration, eager to downplay regional conflicts between Lebanese, Israelis, and Palestinian refugees, became concerned that the Voice of Hope was making its microphones available to Major Saad Haddad, leader of the independent Christian Phalangist militia and a strong ally of the Israelis in their efforts to control Palestinian Liberation Organization (PLO) terrorism. When efforts to mediate the dispute with High Adventure were unsuccessful, the Carter administration, rather than pursue the matter in the courts, directed the Internal Revenue Service (IRS) to investigate the financial records of the California agency.

The IRS began its investigation on the basis that High Adventure's broadcasting of Major Haddad's talks constituted political activity forbidden to agencies registered under the Internal Revenue Code as "religious, charitable or educational" institutions. Efforts by the court system at defining these terms have been tortuous. High Adventure fought the move in the tax courts, requesting a declaratory judgment concerning its tax exemption. The tax courts eventually held that since High Adventure had not exhausted all administrative remedies available, the tax court lacked jurisdiction. This move ended the possibility of an unpleasant showdown between the government and the radio station. Even though the government was not ultimately successful in this instance, it is clear that if it wishes to intervene, there are ways to do so that can limit the freedom of all tax exempt religious agencies through use of the tax system and by limiting conditions for obtaining tax exempt status. See *High Adventure Ministries* v. *Commissioner of Internal Revenue*. U.S. Tax Court. Docket no. 4585-82 "X" "Petition for Declaratory Judgement (Exempt Organization)." April 20, 1982; *High Adventure Ministries* v. *Commissioner of Internal Revenue*, on Appeal from the Decisions of the U.S. Tax Court, Brief for Appellant, Brief for Appellee, U.S. Court of Appeals, Ninth Circuit, No. 83-7245, 1983.

23. "Standard Provisions for Grant Agreements," Washington, D.C.: Department of State, Bureau for Refugee Programs, March 1981.

24. *Welch* v. *Kennedy*, 319 F. Supp. 945 (D.D.C. 1970).

25. See *Lemon* v. *Kurtzman*, 403 U.S. 602 (1971).

26. See *Green* v. *Connally*, 330 F. Supp. 1150 (U.S. District Court, District of Columbia, June 30, 1971); *Christian Echoes National Ministry, Inc.* v. *United States*, 404 Fed. 2d. 1066 (U.S. Ct. of Appeals, 10th Cir., Dec. 30, 1968); *U.S. Catholic Conference* v. *National Abortion Rights Mobilization* (S. Ct. Docket 87-416; Cert. filed Sept. 11, 1987); *Bob Jones University* v. *United States*, 461 U.S. 574 (1983).

27. See Dean Kelley, *Why Churches Should Not Pay Taxes* (New York: Harper & Row, 1977).

28. See *Bob Jones University* v. *United States*, 461 U.S. 574 (1983).

29. See *United States* v. *Lee*, 455 U.S. 252, 257-8 (1982).

30. For such a debate see the response to "Office of Management and Budget, Circular A-122: Cost Principles for Nonprofit Organizations; Lobbying and Related Activities," *Federal Register* 48, 214 (November 3, 1983). This effort attempted to force nonprofit organizations to separate all aspects of their political and lobbying efforts from the rest of their programs. Private agencies argued that enforcement (which was seen as a means for targeting left-wing organizations) would put many nonprofit organizations out of business. See Sharon Ferguson, "Federal Lobbying Rules and OMB's 'Son of A-122'," Washington, D.C.: OMB Watch, July 13, 1983; and "Summary of the 'Son of OMB-122 Circular,' " Washington, D.C.: OMB Watch, n.d.

31. National Security Directive 68 (1950).

32. *New York Times* v. *United States*, 403 U.S. 713 (1971). When the government sought to block publication of classified Pentagon documents on the Vietnam War, the *New York Times* took them to court. Excerpts were eventually published.

33. Sharon Worthing, "Government Surveillance of Religious Organizations," *Journal of Church and State* 23, 3 (Autumn 1981): 551–63.

34. Ibid., pp. 557, 558.

35. Internal memorandum on the question of registering Compassion International, an evangelical private voluntary organization, Advisory Committee on Voluntary Foreign Aid, U.S. Agency for International Development, June 6, 1978, in the registration files of Compassion International, AID, Office of Private and Voluntary Cooperation, Roslyn, Va.

36. *Hunt* v. *McNair*, 413 U.S. 734 (1973).

37. Quoted in *Wolman* v. *Walter*, 45 L.W. 4861 (1977).

Chapter 13

1. La Noue, "Church-State Relations in the Federal Policy Process," p. 208. See also Chapter 6 of this book.

2. Ibid., p. 298.

3. *Abington Township School District* v. *Schempp*, 374 U.S. 203 (1963).

4. This quote and the following account and quotes are drawn from interviews with officials of the U.S. embassy, the office of the Sudanese Commissioner for Refugees, the United Nations High Commissioner for Refugees, the Southern Sudan Refugee Assistance Project, the Sudan Council of Churches, and the Anyanya guerilla movement, Khartoum and Juba, August 1983.

5. Personal interview with CRS official, New York, February 1984.

6. Edward Marasciulo, "The Roman Catholic Church in Voluntary Foreign Aid," paper delivered at Senior Seminar in Foreign Policy, Department of State, 1974–75, pp. 1, 2.

7. Quoted in Os Guinness, "Beware the Boa: The Constricting of Christian Discipleship in the Modern World," 1978, p. 13, in the Archive on Church and State Abroad, Carnegie Council on Ethics and International Affairs, New York.

8. Herbert Titus, quoted in debate in *Transformation* 2, 3 (July/September 1985): 11–12.

9. See registration files, World Concern, AID, Office of Private and Voluntary Cooperation, Roslyn, Va. This file may be contrasted with those of the Community Consortium for Self-Help, a Jewish umbrella organization, and the relief efforts of the Salesians, a Catholic order.

10. Curti, *American Philanthropy Abroad*, pp. 241–44, 376.

11. Wyman, *Abandonment of the Jews*, p. 213.

12. On the whole such an assessment is historically accurate. However, the missionary and tithe collections in numerous small Protestant bodies have kept pace with and in some cases exceeded the high per capita contributions to international voluntarism within the Jewish community.

13. Handlin, *A Continuing Task,* pp. 89, 90.

14. Ibid., p. 111.

15. Orbach, *The American Movement to Aid Soviet Jews,* p. 11.

16. U.S. Senate, 96th Congress, Judiciary Committee, Subcommittee on Immigration and Refugees, "Hearings on Refugee Resettlement Issues," September 1979.

17. "Report to the Congress: International Assistance to Refugees in Africa Can Be Improved," GAO/ID-83-2, Washington, D.C.: General Accounting Office, December 29, 1983.

18. Personal interview with UNHCR financial officer, Geneva, October 1984.

19. "The Problem of the Displaced Persons," American Council of Voluntary Agencies for Foreign Service, New York, 1946, p. 65.

20. For these and the preceding figures, see La Noue, "Church-State Relations in the Federal Policy Progress," pp. 176–79. Whatever the total postwar cumulative figures may be, government funding of refugee and relief activity in the 1950s provided a continual cycle of growth for those religious agencies that had been "in the business" since the war. For the wartime agencies that began the program of privately adminstered refugee relief, the most substantial government aid began to flow through the agricultural surplus programs. In 1953, the year before passage of the Food for Peace legislation, Washington-based State Department figures show voluntary agencies handled just over $22 million of government food and freight subsidies. By FY 1958, $154 million in surplus goods and ocean freight subsidies went through the agencies. Of the twenty-four registered agencies listed in an International Cooperation Administration accounting in 1958, eleven had religious ties; the rest were largely ethnically based or had their origins in religious efforts, such as CARE. More than $134 million of the $154 million was distributed to and through the eleven religiously affiliated agencies. Catholic Relief Services alone accounted for $95 million of the total. Commerce Department figures for 1958 (prepared from data collected from voluntary agencies) indicate that private contributions for the same year to Protestant, Catholic, and Jewish activities overseas totaled $206 million.

21. Reiss, *The American Council of Voluntary Agencies for Foreign Service: Four Monographs,* "Migration and Refugee Affairs," p. 86.

22. Ibid., pp. 80–92.

23. Inspector General, "Audit of Cooperative Agreement 1037-220019 between the Bureau for Refugee Programs and the Lutheran Immigration and Refugee Service," Washington, D.C.: Inspector General, January 17–April 29, 1983, p. 5.

24. General Accounting Office, "Oversight of State Department's Refugee Reception and Placement Program," GAO/NSIAD-83-85, Washington, D.C.: General Accounting Office, September 30, 1983.

Chapter 14

1. Max Warren, *Caesar The Beloved Enemy* (London: SCM Press Ltd., 1955).

2. La Noue, "Church-State Relations in the Federal Policy Process," pp. 349–403.

3. Antieau, Downey, and Roberts, *Freedom from Federal Establishment,* p. 207.

4. See *Lemon* v. *Kurtzman,* 403 U.S. 602 (1971).

5. Antieau, Downey, and Roberts, *Freedom from Federal Establishment,* p. 66.

6. John F. Wilson, *Public Religion in American Culture* (Philadelphia: Temple University Press, 1979), p. 3.

7. Beaver, "Church and State Relations in Missions to the Native Americans," p. 1.

8. For the record of Kirkland's dealings with the Congress, see W. Pilkington, ed., *The Journals of Samuel Kirkland* (Clinton, N.Y.: Hamilton College), 1980.

9. See *The Federalist Papers,* no. 10 (Alexander Hamilton, John Jay, and James Madison).

10. *Reuben Quick Bear* v. *Leupp,* 210 U.S. 50 (1908); *Bradfield* v. *Roberts* 175 U.S. 291 (1899); see Chapter 2 for further discussion.

11. In the 1890s the secretary of the interior approached appropriation battles in Congress over church-run Indian schools with a frankly pragmatic appeal, that the issue at hand was one of keeping the schools open for the least amount of money. The church agencies accurately pointed to the fact that they could run the schools at less expense than the government. For discussion of this see *Reuben Quick Bear* v. *Leupp,* 210 U.S. 50 (1908).

12. Rennard Strickland and Charles F. Wilkenson, eds., *Felix S. Cohen's Handbook of Federal Indian Law* (Charlottesville, Va.: Michie, 1982), p. 547.

13. Prucha, *The Churches and the Indian Schools 1888–1912,* p. 154.

14. See *Valley Forge Christian College* v. *Americans United for Separation of Church and State,* 50 L.W. 4103 (1982).

15. See Coughlin, *Church and State in Social Welfare,* p. 45.

16. Worthing. "Government Surveillance of Religious Organizations," p. 352.

17. See *United States* v. *Seeger,* 380 U.S. 163 (1965); Laurence Tribe, *American Constitutional Law* (New York: Foundation Press, 1978), pp. 812–55.

18. *Fowler* v. *Rhode Island,* 345 U.S. 67, cited in Tribe, *American Constitutional Law,* p. 829.

19. Tribe, *American Constitutional Law,* p. 831.

20. Worthing, "Government Surveillance of Religious Organizations," p. 321.

21. Norman Cousins, '*We Hold These Truths* . . . ' (New York: Harper & Row, 1960).

22. "Neither a state nor the Federal Government can set up a church. Neither can pass laws which aid one religion, aid all religions, or prefer one religion over another. Neither can force nor influence a person to go to or remain away from church against his will or force him to profess a belief or disbelief in any religion. No person can be punished for entertaining or professing beliefs or disbeliefs, for church attendance or non-attendance. No tax in any amount, large or small, can be levied to support any religious activities or institutions, whatever they may be called, or whatever form they may adopt to teach or practice religion. Neither a state nor the Federal Government can, openly or secretly, participate in the affairs of any religious organizations or groups and *vice versa.* In the words of Jefferson, the clause against establishment of religion by law was intended to erect "a wall of separation between church and State." *Everson* v. *Board of Education,* 330 U.S. 1, 15-16 (1947).

23. *Cochran* v. *Louisiana State Board of Education,* 281 U.S. 370 (1930).

24. Foreign Assistance Act of 1961 (P.L. 87–95, 75 Stat. 424 [1961]).

25. *Everson* v. *Board of Education,* 330 U.S. 1 (1947).

26. Ibid.

27. John C. Bennett, "Church and State in the United States," in Ronald H. Stone, ed., *Reformed Faith and Politics* (Washington, D.C.: University Press of America, 1983), p. 126.

28. *Everson* v. *Board of Education,* 330 U.S. 1 (1947).

29. *Zorach* v. *Clauson,* 343 U.S. 306 (1952).

30. *Torcaso* v. *Watkins,* 367 U.S. 495 (1961).

31. Ibid.

32. *A Memo to America,* p. 349.

33. *Mueller* v. *Allen,* 103 S.Ct. 3062 (1983).

34. *Mueller* v. *Allen,* 103 S.Ct. 3070 (1983).

35. The distribution of government surplus property has been another area that has generated controversy over the role of evenhandedness and proportionality in governmental dealings with religious institutions. It will continue to be donated to parties that apply for it, probably without explicit policies covering donations to religious groups. From 1944 to 1963, the Seventh Day Adventists and the Assemblies of God, two evangelical churches sponsoring various domestic and foreign service programs, received government surplus far in excess of the ratio of their membership to the population of the country at large, while the majority of Protestants showed little interest in surplus property. The Catholic church received 98 percent of all surplus property donated by the government to religious bodies from 1960 to 1963. As far as overseas ministries of the churches are concerned, the Catholic church, through Catholic Relief Services (along with CARE), has become the principal private distributor of surplus food under P.L. 480 (Food for Peace Program). A former administrator of CRS went so far as to say that "without the surplus food program, CRS would be left with very little" (Personal interview, former CRS administrator, New York, February 1983). Since the program involves no tax expenditure, there is no need to evaluate its evenhandedness toward religious groups. Yet as George La Noue has said, "When the government selects certain of the churches' institutions or activities to support, it not only increases the prestige of that sector of the church, but the size of its budget as well. This shift, of course, alters the internal politics of any organization and affects the church's overall policies and image." See La Noue, "Church-State Relations in the Federal Policy Process," pp. 386, 393.

36. *Walz* v. *Tax Commission of the City of New York,* 397 U.S. 664 (1970), at 669.

37. Emphasis in original, quoted in *Abington Township School District* v. *Schempp,* 374 U.S. 203 (1963).

38. See *Walz* v. *Tax Commission of the City of New York,* 397 U.S. 664 (1970).

39. Ibid.

40. See *Lemon* v. *Kurtzman,* 403 U.S. 602 (1971); *Epperson* v. *Arkansas,* 393 U.S. 97, 107 (1968); *Abington Township School District* v. *Schempp,* 374 U.S. 203, 222 (1963); Miller and Flowers, *Toward Benevolent Neutrality,* p. 302; C. Ronald Ellington, "The Principle of Nondivisiveness and the Constitutionality of Public Aid to Parochial Schools," *Georgia Law Review* 5 (1971): 429, 439.

41. Tribe, *American Constitutional Law,* p. 835.

42. P.L. 87-195, 75 Stat. 424 (1961). See Tribe, *American Constitutional Law,* pp. 865–66 (tracing purpose and effect tests to Madison, political entanglement test to Jefferson, and administrative entanglement test to Williams); and J. Curry, "James Madison and the Burger Court: Converging Views of Church-State Separation," *Indiana Law Journal* 56 (1981): 615 (tracing political entanglement test to Madison).

43. See Miller and Flowers, *Toward Benevolent Neutrality,* p. 302; J. Nowak, R. Rotunda, and J. Young, *Handbook on Constitutional Law* (St. Paul, Minn.: West Publishing, 1986), p. 1031; *Lynch* v. *Donnelly,* 52 U.S.L.W. 4317, 4320 (U.S. Mar. 5, 1984); *Mueller* v. *Allen,* 103 S. Ct. 3062, 3067 (1983); *Larkin* v. *Grendel's Den, Inc.,* 103 S. Ct. 505, 510 (1982); *Lemon* v. *Kurtzman,* 403 U.S. 602, 612 (1971).

44. See *Meek* v. *Pittenger,* 421 U.S. 349, 373 n. 1 (1975); Brennan, J., concurring in part and dissenting in part, quoting *Committee for Public Education & Religious Liberty* v. *Nyquist,* 413 U.S. 756, 783 n. 39 (1973).

45. See *Walz* v. *Tax Commission of the City of New York,* 397 U.S. 664, 674 (1970).

46. See Miller and Flowers, *Toward Benevolent Neutrality,* p. 302; *Meek* v. *Pittenger,* 421 U.S. 349, 363 (1975) (unconstitutional primary effect of advancing religion found because of "predominantly religious character" of benefited parochial schools); *Hunt* v. *McNair,* 413 U.S. 734, 743 (1973): "Aid normally may be thought to have a primary effect of advancing religion when it flows to an institution in which religion is so pervasive that a substantial portion of its functions are subsumed in the religious mission or when it funds a specifically religious activity in an otherwise substantially secular setting."

47. *Meek* v. *Pittenger,* 421 U.S. 349, 363 (1975).

48. McCahon to World Vision International, April 6, 1962, in World Vision registration file, AID, Office of Private and Voluntary Cooperation.

49. See Miller and Flowers, *Toward Benevolent Neutrality,* p. 302; Tribe, *American Constitutional Law,* pp. 840–42; Denise Cote, "Establishment Clause Analysis of Legislative and Administrative Aid to Religion," *Columbia Law Review* 74 (1974): 1175, 1179, 1183–84. *Roemer* v. *Board of Public Works of Maryland,* 426 U.S. 736, 755 (1976) (plurality opinion); *Hunt* v. *McNair,* 413 U.S. 734, 743 (1973).

50. See *Roemer* v. *Board of Public Works of Maryland,* 426 U.S. 736 (1976).

51. See Tribe, *American Constitutional Law,* p. 843–44.

52. See use of this logic in *Illinois ex rel. McCollum* v. *Board of Education,* 333 U.S. 203, 212 (1948); *Larkin* v. *Grendel's Den, Inc.,* 103 S. Ct. 505, 512 (1982); *Lemon* v. *Kurtzman,* 403 U.S. 602, 614 (1971); Tribe, *American Constitutional Law,* p. 866.

53. Tribe, *American Constitutional Law,* pp. 869–70.

54. See *Larkin* v. *Grendel's Den, Inc.,* 103 S. Ct. 505, 510 (1982); *Roemer* v. *Board of Public Works,* 426 U.S. 736, 745–46 (1976); *Committee for Public Education & Religious Liberty* v. *Nyquist,* 413 U.S. 756, 760-61 & n. 5 (1973); *Lemon* v. *Kurtzman,* 403 U.S. 602, 614 (1971); *Walz* v. *Tax Commission of the City of New York,* 397 U.S. 664, 676 (1970).

55. *Roemer* v. *Board of Public Works,* 426 U.S. 736, 748 (1976); *Lemon* v. *Kurtzman,* 403 U.S. 602, 614 (1971); Nowak, Rotunda, and Young, *Handbook on Constitutional Law,* p. 1031.

56. Tribe, *American Constitutional Law,* p. 865.

57. The Court has never invalidated a statute solely because it violated the political entanglement test. See *Lynch* v. *Donnelly,* 52 U.S.L.W. 4317, 4323 (U.S. Mar. 5, 1984) (O'Connor, J., concurring); *Decker* v. *O'Donnell,* 661 F.2d 598, 616 n. 34 (7th Cir. 1980); Harlan in *Walz* v. *Tax Commission of the City of New York,* 397 U.S. 664 (concurring).

58. *Everson* v. *Board of Education,* 330 U.S. 1, 26–27 (1947).

59. *Lemon* v. *Kurtzman,* 403 U.S. 602, 622–23 (1971).

60. See Scheidemantle, "Political Entanglement as an Independent Test of Constitutionality Under the Establishment Clause," *Fordham Law Review* 52 (1984).

61. *Larkin* v. *Grendel's Den, Inc.,* 103 S.Ct. 505 (1982).

62. See *Abington Township School District* v. *Schempp,* 374 U.S. 203, 222 (1963); *Committee for Public Education & Religious Liberty* v. *Nyquist,* 413 U.S. 780 (1973).

63. Edward Gaffney "Political Divisiveness Along Religious Lines." *St. Louis Law Journal* 25 (1980): 205–36.

Chapter 15

1. Quotations from Richard Reeves, "Journey to Pakistan," *New Yorker,* October 1, 1984, p. 67.

2. Mansfield, "Religion Clauses of the First Amendment and Foreign Relations."

3. Extraterritoriality may refer to many different phenomena arising from the limits of national legal systems. Ambassadors are generally exempted from the jurisdiction of the legal system of the country in which they serve; they are granted extraterritorial privileges and their embassies are considered extraterritorial, or beyond the legal system of the host country. In a unique situation, the Vatican negotiated extraterritorial status within from Italy in the Lateran Treaties of 1929. Vatican officials argued that the supreme pontiff could not be the subject of any earthly government and required an independent jurisdiction. It was this extraterritoriality that permitted the State of Vatican City to give refuge to people whose freedom and very lives were in jeopardy under fascist and Nazi regimes. Poles and other Eastern Europeans, leftists, communist politicians, and Jews, including the grand rabbi of Rome, were protected by the extraterritorial status of the 108-acre Vatican State.

Some strong interpretations of extraterritoriality have placed the church itself beyond the sovereignty of the state in which it is found. The extraterritorial status of the Vatican State was, for instance, extended to some houses of international religious communities which were technically outside the walls of Vatican City. Hunted people were given refuge in these houses during the war years. A limited version of this independence has been granted to religious institutions in the United States. Dean Kelly has, for instance, argued that the tax-exempt status of the churches in the United States represents a limited but real achievement of extraterritoriality from the U.S. government's fundamental power to tax. See Kelley, *Why Churches Should Not Pay Taxes.*

Extraterritoriality can refer (as in the cases just cited) to the freedom of an institution or diplomatic mission to function under different standards of legality than those normally applicable in the territory in which it operates. It can also refer to the operation of a nation's laws outside the territory of the nation itself; it is this sense that applies directly to our discussion of church/state relations abroad. Before World War II, treaties of extraterritoriality in this second sense between the United States and other nations were common. Such treaties generally included provisions for the operation of U.S. law within the diplomatic compound. This extraterritoriality often extended to legal jurisdiction over private U.S. citizens, including missionaries, but since the 1940s the formal scope of extraterritoriality has focused primarily on overseas military bases and the operation of courts martial. In several cases U.S. courts have indicated that provisions of the Constitution do apply overseas, but most such cases concern the application of commercial regulations.

4. *Illinois Election Board* v. *Socialist Workers Party,* 440 U.S. 178 (1978).

5. Elizabeth C. Reiss to Leon O. Marion, May 3, 1982. Archive of the American Council of Voluntary Agency for Foreign Service, Rutgers University.

6. Bennett, "Church and State in the United States."

7. *United States* v. *Curtiss-Wright Export Corp.,* 299 U.S. 301, 319 (1936).

8. *Dames and Moore* v. *Regan,* 453 U.S. 654 (1981) (in the area of foreign affairs, congressional silence does not imply congressional disapproval of presidential action).

9. *United States* v. *Curtiss-Wright,* 299 U.S. 301 (1936); correspondence between the author and John Mansfield, Harvard Law School, July 1985.

10. *Palko* v. *Connecticut,* 302 U.S. 319, 325 (1937).

11. *Reid* v. *Covert,* 354 U.S. 1, 16 (1957).

12. Mansfield, "Religion Clauses of the First Amendment and Foreign Relations," p. 46.

13. See *Wilson* v. *Girard,* 354 U.S. 524 (1957), cited in ibid.

14. See *Reid* v. *Covert,* 354 U.S. 1 (1957) (requiring jury trial for serviceman's wife accused of murder committed abroad); *Kinsella* v. *United States ex rel. Singleton,* 361 U.S. 234 (1960) (requiring civilian trial for serviceman's dependent accused of noncapital offense committed abroad); *McElroy* v. *Guagliardo,* 361 U.S. 281 (1960) (overseas civilian employees of armed forces entitled to civilian trial by jury for even relatively small offenses); *O'Callahan* v. *Parker,* 395 U.S. 258 (1969) (member of U.S. Army could not be tried by court-martial for a nonservice-connected crime); *Relford* v. *Commandant,* 401 U.S. 355 (1971) (upholding court-martial of soldier accused of kidnapping and rape on a military reservation).

15. *Johnson* v. *Eisentrager,* 339 U.S. 763 (1950) (holding that "enemy aliens, resident, captured, and imprisoned abroad" cannot demand access to U.S. courts).

16. *United States* v. *Elder, Inc.,* 579 F.2d. 516 (1978).

17. Thomas C. Self, "International Trade Export Restrictions," *Howard International Law Journal* 20 (1979): 201

18. Note: "Passports and Freedom of Travel," *Georgetown Law Review* 41 (1952): 63, 71–72, for a discussion of the constitutional history of the right to travel.

19. *Kent* v. *Dulles,* 357 U.S. 116 (1958).

20. *Zemel* v. *Rusk,* 381 U.S. 1 (1965).

21. Ibid., at 16–17.

22. Lucy Dawidowicz, "The United States, Israel, and the Middle East," in Fine and Sloan, eds., *American Jewish Yearbook* (1957), 58: 218.

23. See *Haig* v. *Agee,* 453 U.S. at 310 (1981), citing *Kennedy* v. *Mendoza-Martinez,* 372 U.S. 144, 160 (1963).

24. *New York Times* v. *U.S.,* 403 U.S. 713, 726 (1971).

25. Neill H. Alford, "Voluntary Foreign Aid and American Foreign Aid: The Element of State Control," *Virginia Law Review* 46 (1960): 477.

26. Ibid.

27. *United States* v. *Curtiss-Wright Export Corp.,* 299 U.S. 301, 320 (1936)

28. *Worcester* v. *State of Georgia* (1831).

29. The political question doctrine received new attention during the Vietnam war, as individuals sought to limit the war effort in the courts. See discussion in John F. and Rosemary Bannan, *Law, Morality and Vietnam: The Peace Militants and the Courts* (Bloomington, Ind.: Indiana University Press, 1974), pp. 199–205; also Stephen Wexler, "The Political Question Doctrine: A Decision Not to Decide" and Kai Nielsen, "The 'Political Question' Doctrine," in *Ethics* 79,1 (1968): 70–76, 77–79.

30. Cited in prosecutor's submission, *Temistocles Ramirez de Arellano et al.* v. *Weinberger et al.,* U.S. Court of Appeals for the District of Columbia, slip op. 83–1950 (Civil Action no. 83-02002) (1984).

31. Ibid.

32. Ibid., Scalia dissent, p. 33.

33. *Americans United for Separation of Church and State* v. *Reagan,* 786 F.2d. 201 (3d. cir. 1986). Cited in Mansfield, "Religious Clauses of the First Amendment and Foreign Relations," n. 10.

34. The field of export regulations has also been of increasing interest to the private voluntary community in recent years. Church World Service, Oxfam America, and other shipments of relief and development goods to Nicaragua and Vietnam have been blocked. See J. Spragens and J. Charney, *Embargo: Implications of the U.S. Humanitarian Embargo in Vietnam and Kampuchea* (Boston: Oxfam, 1985); also Pierre Bergeron, *Export-Import Controls: Their Nature and Accountability* (New York: Church World Service, 1980).

35. "Treatment of Salvadoran Refugees in the United States," Geneva: UNHCR, September 1981.

36. See Church World Service's *Refugee and Human Rights Newsletter* 5, 3 (Fall 1981).

37. *Seeking Safe Haven: A Congregational Guide to Helping Central American Refugees in the United States* (New York and Philadelphia: Interreligious Task Force on El Salvador and Central America, Lutheran Immigration and Refugee Service, Church World Service, and the American Friends Service Committee, 1983), p. 64.

38. *New York Times,* April 6, 1986.

39. Ignatius Bau, *This Ground Is Holy* (New York: Paulist Press, 1985), pp. 29–37; Philip Wheaton, quoted in *Religion and Society Report* (New York: Center on Religion and Society, 1985), p. 4.

40. Jim Corbett, "The Covenant as Sanctuary," *Crosscurrents* 34, 4 (1984/5): 401.

41. Bau, *This Ground Is Holy,* pp. 29–37, for excellent discussion of this division in the movement.

42. Bryan Hehir, "Church and State: Implications for Ministry and Mission," paper delivered to the American Missiological Society, Fort Worth, Texas (1981), p. 21.

43. Corbett, "Covenant as Sanctuary," p. 402.

44. Bau, *This Ground Is Holy,* p. 81.

45. Corbett, "Covenant as Sanctuary," pp. 401–2.

46. Mansfield, "Religious Clauses of the First Amendment and Foreign Relations," p. 66.

47. Quoted in introduction to Bau, *This Ground Is Holy,* p. xii.

48. Karl Barth, *Community, State and Church* (Garden City, N.Y.: Anchor Books, 1960), p. 145.

Chapter 16

1. Concern about "peace without victory" was not limited to religious and political conservatives. See John Haynes Holmes, "If Russia Wins" (July 30, 1941), in H. Fey and M. Frakes, eds., *The Christian Century Reader* (New York: Association Press, 1962), pp. 240–44.

2. Telephone interview with Lawrence Dawson, Philadelphia, February 1986, in the Archive on Church and State Abroad, Carnegie Council on Ethics and International Affairs, New York; Morgenthau, in Morgenthau and Thompson, *Politics Among Nations*, p. 277.

3. "Report of the World Council of Churches Consultation on Refugee Resettlement," Geneva: World Council of Churches, May 8–11, 1981.

4. Richard J. Barnet, "What Is the National Interest?" in Thompson and Myers, *Truth and Tragedy: A Tribute to Hans J. Morgenthau.*

5. Reported by Ernest Lefever after a debate with Patricia Derian held at the Franklin Porter Graham Conference on Human Rights, University of North Carolina at Chapel Hill, October 6, 1983.

6. Quoted in E. Fleet, ed., "Madison's 'Detached Memoranda,' " in *William and Mary Quarterly* 3 (Oct. 1946): 560.

7. Alasdair MacIntyre, *After Virtue* (South Bend: Notre Dame Press, 1981), p. 236.

8. Cited in R. T. Miller and R. B. Flowers, *Toward Benevolent Neutrality, Church, State and the Supreme Court* (Waco, Tx: Markham Press, 1982), p. 691.

9. Roger Mehl, *The Sociology of Protestantism* (Philadelphia: Westminster Press, 1970), p. 266.

10. Michael O'Shaughnessy, *Peace and Reconstruction: A Catholic Layman's Approach* (New York: Harper and Brothers, 1943), p. 11; Pope Pius XII, Christmas Message of 1948.

11. "Report of the World Council of Churches," 1981, p. 10.

12. McCleary introduction to Pierre Bergeron, *Import-Export Controls: Their Nature and Accountability* (New York: Church World Service, 1980), p. 1.

13. Eric Hula, "Fifty Years of International Government: Reflections of the League of Nations and the United Nations," in Thompson and Myers, *Truth and Tragedy*, p. 183.

14. Statement issued by the American Council of Voluntary Agencies for Foreign Service, September 1958, p. 4.

15. The full *Memorial and Remonstrance* may be found in R. Miller and R. Flowers, *Toward Benevolent Neutrality*, pp. 689–93.

16. First Geneva Convention of 1949, Articles 12 and 18, in *United Nations Treaty Series* 75: 1; on nondiscrimination see Protocol II, Article 18, text in *American Journal of International Law* 72 (1978): 457.

17. For a masterful discussion of the importance of theories of an international "harmony of interests" before World War II, see E. H. Carr, *The Twenty Years' Crisis, 1919–1939* (London: Macmillan, 1984), pp. 41–62, 80–85.

18. This discussion applies to the political role of religious voluntary agencies in their understanding of their relationship to public authority. Clearly, the work of immigration and asylum attorneys charged with the defense of individuals requires public use of international and national laws in defense of their clients. Humanitarian agencies per se cannot afford to assume the role of political factions without doing damage to contemporary understandings of the humanitarian ethic.

19. These agencies and six others published a full page protest in the *New York Times* on April 7, 1986, against U.S. policies abroad.

Selected
Bibliography

Magazine, Newspaper and Journal Articles

A[11]. A[frica]. C[ouncil]. [of] C[hurches]. Bulletin, 11, 4 (1981). Special Issue "Evangelism/ Refugees and the Churches." Nairobi, Kenya: Communications Unit of the All Africa Conference of Churches. See the following articles: "Refugees and the Churches," "Human Rights and Refugees in Africa," "Urban Refugee Sufferers in Africa," "Evangelisation for Francophone Africa," "The Gospel, An Education for Development," "On a Dynamic Pedagogy for an In-Depth Integrated Christian Education."

"Administration Lags on Refugee Aid." *Christian Century* 77, 36 (January 13, 1960).

Alford, Neill H., Jr. "Voluntary Foreign Aid and American Foreign Aid: The Element of State Control." *Virginia Law Review* 46, 477 (1960).

Asher, Robert E. "Multilateral Versus Bilateral Aid: An Old Controversy Revisited." *International Organization* 16 (Autumn 1962).

Askin, Steve. "Nazi Aid Claims: Vatican Says Little." *National Catholic Reporter* 20, 16 (February 10, 1984).

———. "Relief Agency 'Not Doing All It Can'." *National Catholic Reporter* 18,9 (December 25, 1981).

Austin, Charles. "More Churches Join in Offering Sanctuary for Latin Refugees." *New York Times.* September 16, 1983.

Barnet, Richard J. "The Search for National Security." *New Yorker.* April 27, 1981.

Bates, M. Searle. "Religious Liberty—Church and State." *Occasional Bulletin.* New York: Missionary Research Library. 10 (July 15, 1959).

Belair, Felix, Jr. "U.S. to Press Taiwan Food Aid Despite Protestant Withdrawal." *New York Times.* May 10, 1962.

Benjamin, Walter W. "Separation of Church and State: Myth & Reality." *Journal of Church and State* 11 (1969).

———. "Editorial Notes [re: church and state]." *Christianity & Crisis* 8,1 (February 2, 1948).

Blumenthal, Ralph. "Catholic Relief Services Involved in Dispute Over Spending of Ethiopia Aid." *New York Times.* August 7, 1985.

———. "U.S. Jews Ask Papal Inquiry into Reports of Aid to Nazis." *New York Times.* January 27, 1984.

———. "Vatican Is Reported to Have Furnished Aid to Fleeing Nazis." *New York Times.* January 26, 1984.

Bogdanich, Walt, Christopher Jensen, and Joe Frolik. "In the Name of Charity." [*Cleveland*] *Plain Dealer*. November 21–27, 1982.

Bole, William. "Shift in Overseas Aid Agencies' Focus May Expose Them to Unaccustomed Heat." *Week in Religion*. New York: Religious News Service. January 25, 1984.

———. "Newly Public Documents Shed Light on Allegations Vatican Aided Nazis." *National Catholic Reporter* (May 16, 1986).

Bonner, Raymond. "Miskito Indians Are Focus of Debate." *New York Times*. August 13, 1982.

Brady, Edward J. "Some Refugees Are Welcomed and Others Turned Away. Who Should Decide Their Plight?" *America* 145,13 (October 31, 1981).

Briggs, Kenneth A. "Diplomatic Ties with the Vatican: For U.S., an Old and Divisive Question." *New York Times*. December 12, 1983.

Campbell, Colin. "Refugees Moving Back to Cambodia." *New York Times*. October 13, 1982.

Carey, Jane Perry Clark. "The Admission and Integration of Refugees in the United States." *Journal of International Affairs* 7,1 (1953).

Carollo, Virginia A. "An Emerging Profession—the Voluntary Sector in World Development." *Personnel* 47, 1 (January-February 1970).

Casaroli, Agostino Cardinal (letter in the name of the Pope [John Paul II] to Cardinal Bernardin Gantin). "The Refugee Problem Is Still Grave." *L'Osservatore Romano*. September 10, 1984.

"Catholic Relief Services' Role: Christ's Work—or the CIA's?" *National Catholic Reporter* 13,9 (December 17, 1976).

"Challenge of Abundance." *Commonweal* 62 (May 20, 1955).

Chandler, Russell. "Bible Translators: The Word for the World." *Washington Post*. July 25, 1981.

Cherne, Leo. "Thirty Days That Shook the World." *Saturday Review* 39 (December 22, 1956).

"The Churches Act in the Crisis; Our Commissions in this Crisis." *Christian Century* 73 (November 14, 1956).

"CIA and the Missionaries." *Christian Century* (September 3, 1975).

Clarke, Rev. Francis X. "The Purpose of the Missions, a Study of Mission Documents of the Holy See, 1909–1946." *Missonary Union of the Clergy Bulletin* (June 1948).

Clines, Francis X. "White House Exploring Closer Vatican Ties." *New York Times*. December 9, 1983.

Clowney, Frank Sherman III. "Extending the Constitution to Refugee Parolees." *San Diego Law Review* 15 (1977).

Cockburn, Andrew. " 'Yellow Rain' Reminds Us How War Plays on the Imagination." *Wall Street Journal*. June 9, 1983.

Comfort, Richard O. "Missionaries in Disguise." *Christian Century* 74 (November 20, 1957).

Committee for East Asia and the Pacific, Division of Overseas Ministries, National Council of the Churches of Christ in the U.S.A. "The Development of Guidelines on Missionary Involvement in Social-Justice and Human-Rights Issues." *International Bulletin of Missionary Research* 6,1 (January 1, 1982).

Corbett, Jim. "The Covenant as Sanctuary." *Crosscurrents* 34, 4 (Winter 1984–85).

Cote, Denise. "Establishment Clause Analysis of Legislative and Administrative Aid to Religion." *Columbia Law Review* 74 (1974).

Cotter, George. "Spies, Strings and Missionaries." *Christian Century* 38, 10 (March 25, 1981).

Curry, J. "James Madison and the Burger Court: Converging Views of Church-State Separation." *Indiana Law Journal* 56 (1981).

"Defense Lawyer in Trial on Aliens Assailed for Religious Arguments." *New York Times.* April 5, 1985.

Douglas, H. Eugene. "The Problem of Refugees in a Strategic Perspective." *Strategic Review* (Fall 1982).

Dulles, John Foster. "Policy for Security and Peace." *Discussions of Foreign Affairs* II, 9 [Council on Foreign Relations] (1954).

Elias, Julius A. "Relations Between Voluntary Agencies and International Organizations." *Journal of International Affairs* 7, 1 (1953).

Ellington, C. Ronald. "The Principle of Nondivisiveness and the Constitutionality of Public Aid to Parochial Schools." *Georgia Law Review* 5 (1971).

Ember, Lois R. "Yellow Rain." *Chemical & Engineering News* 62, 2 (January 9, 1984).

"Evangelization and Civilization: Protestant Missionary Motivation in the Imperialist Era (Symposium)." *International Bulletin of Missionary Research* 6, 2 (April 1982).

"Excerpts From President's Speech to National Association of Evangelicals." *New York Times.* March 9, 1983.

"Exodus for a Twice-Lost Tribe." Editorial. *New York Times.* March 3, 1984.

"Exodus from Ethiopia." *Economist* (January 12, 1985).

"Exodus from Hungary." *Christian Century* 73 (December 19, 1956).

"Foreign Aid in Vietnam." *America* 95 (April 7, 1956).

"Freedom to Be Religious Is Not Religious Freedom." *Christian Century* 73 (February 8, 1956).

Fulbright, J. W. "Foreign Aid? Yes, But with a New Approach." *New York Times Magazine.* March 21, 1965.

Gaffney, Edward McG. "Political Divisiveness Along Religious Lines." *St. Louis Law Journal* 25: 205–236 (1980).

Garinger, Louis D. "Church-State Involvement Grows." *Christian Science Monitor.* November 18, 1965.

Gianella, Donald A. "Religious Liberty, Nonestablishment, and Doctrinal Development: Part I. The Religious Liberty Guarantee." *Harvard Law Review* 80, 7 (May 1967).

———. "Religious Liberty, Nonestablishment, Doctrinal Development: Part II. The Nonestablishment Principle." *Harvard Law Review* 81, 3 (January 1968).

Gibson, John W. "The Displaced Person." *Journal of International Affairs* 7, 1 (1953).

Golden, Renny, and Michael McConnell. "Sanctuary: Choosing Sides." *Christianity & Crisis* 43, 2 (February 21, 1983).

Gwertzman, Bernard. "Haig Fears Exiles From Latin Areas May Flood the U.S." *New York Times.* February 23, 1982.

———. "Panel Suggests Combined Agency for U.S. Economic and Arms Aid." *New York Times.* November 22, 1983.

Hamilton-Merritt, Jane. "America's Refugee Mess." *Reader's Digest.* June, 1985. See also Lutheran Immigration and Refugee Service's "Fact Sheet in Response to Reader's Digest Article." New York: LIRS, May 1985.

———. "The Challenge of Yellow Rain: Where Are We Now?" *Bangkok Post.* July 4, 1982.

———. "The Poisoning of the Hmong." *Bangkok Post.* March 7, 1982.

Handlin, Oscar. "Democracy Needs the Open Door: Immigration and America's Future." *Commentary* 3 (January 1947).

Handy, Robert T. "The American Religious Depression, 1925–35." *Church History* 29, 1 (March 1960).

Hargous, Sabine. "L'action de Vision Mondiale en Equateur." *Le Monde Diplomatique.* June 12, 1985.

Harrell-Bond, Barbara. "Humanitarianism in a Straightjacket." *African Affairs* 84, 1 (January 1985).

Hatfield, Mark O. "World Hunger is a Spiritual Problem." *World Vision* 27, 3 (March 1983).

Hehir, J. Bryan. "The Struggle in Central America: A View From the Church." *Foreign Policy* 43 (Summer 1981).

Hiatt, Fred. "Private Groups Press Contra Aid." *Washington Post*. December 10, 1984.

Hiebert, Murray, and Linda Gibson-Hiebert. "Famine in Kampuchea: Politics of a Tragedy." *Indochina Issues*. Washington, D.C.: Center for International Policy, Indochina Project. December 1979.

Holmes, John Haynes. "If Russia Wins." [July 30, 1941]. In H. Fey and M. Frakes, eds., *The Christian Century Reader*. New York: Association Press, 1962.

Hoskins, Lewis M. "Voluntary Agencies and Foundations in International Aid." *The Annals of the American Academy of Political and Social Science* 329 (May 1960).

"Hospitality for the Hungarians: Jews and Non-Jews in Hungary." *America* 96 (December 1, 1956).

Hostetter, Doug, and Michael McIntyre. "The Politics of Charity." *Christian Century* 91, 31 (September 18, 1974).

"Hungarian Refugees." *Commonweal* 65 (December 7, 1956).

Hutcheson, Richard G., Jr. "Crisis in Overseas Mission: Shall We Leave It to the Independents?" *Christian Century* 38, 9 (March 18, 1981).

Illich, Ivan. "The Seamy Side of Charity." *America* 116, 3 (January 21, 1967).

"Implications of the New Conception of 'Separation.' " *Christianity & Crisis* 8, 12 (July 5, 1948).

"Indian Church Schools: The Way Out." Editorial. *The Outlook* 82 (February 3, 1906).

"Is the Refugee Relief Act a Deliberate Fake?" Editorial. *Christian Century* 72 (February 16, 1955).

Johnson, Ernest F. "Protestant-Catholic Controversy." *Christianity & Crisis* 8, 8 (May 10, 1948).

Jorstad, Eric. "Sanctuary for Refugees: A Statement on Public Policy." *Christian Century* 101, 9 (March 14, 1984).

Karadawi, Ahmed. "Constraints on Assistance to Refugees: Some Observations from the Sudan." *World Development* 11, 6 (1983).

Karsten, Janet. "Wolf in Shepherd's Frock." *Christian Century* 93 (August 18, 1976).

Kastor, Elizabeth. "Reagan's Night for the Refugees." *Washington Post*. April 16, 1985.

Keely, Charles B. "The Development of U.S. Immigration Policy Since 1965." *Journal of International Affairs* 33 (Winter 1979).

Keller, Robert. "American Indians and Church-State Relations in the 1870s." *Christian Legal Society Quarterly* 4, 2 and 3 (1983).

Kiehne, Frank C. "Deported to Salvador." *New York Times*. February 3, 1982.

Kleiman, Robert. "Hungary: A Nation in Flight." *U.S. News & World Report* 41 (December 7, 1956).

Kurland, Philip B. "Of Church and State and the Supreme Court." *University of Chicago Law Review* 29 (Autumn 1961)

"Letters from Readers [re: yellow rain]." *Commentary* (February 1984).

Leupp, Francis E. "Indian Funds and Mission Schools." *The Outlook* 83 (June 9, 1906).

Lichtenberg, Judith. "Persecution vs. Poverty: Are the Haitians Refugees?" *Report from the Center for Philosophy & Public Policy*. College Park, Md.: University of Maryland. 2, 2 (Spring 1982).

Luray, Martin. "Refugees—Still the Paper Chase." *New Republic* 138 (February 24, 1958).

MacEoin, Gary. "U.S. Mission Efforts Threatened by CIA 'Dirty Tricks.' " *St. Anthony Messenger*. March 1975.

MacGuire, James. "Scandals in Catholic Relief." *National Review* (July 3, 1987).

McGrory, Mary. "Shultz Follows Haig's Lead in Playing the Nicaraguan Waltz." *Washington Post.* August 17, 1982.

Makinda, Samuel M. "Conflict and the Superpowers in the Horn of Africa." *Third World Quarterly* 4, 1 (January 1982).

Mann, Erica, and Eric Estorick. "Private and Governmental Aid of Refugees." *Annals of the American Academy of Political and Social Science* 203 (May 1939).

Mansfield, John H. "The Religion Clauses of the First Amendment and Foreign Relations." *De Paul Law Review* 36 (1986).

Markowitz, Arthur A. "Humanitarianism vs. Restrictionism: The United States and the Hungarian Refugees." *International Migration Review* 7 (Spring 1973).

Martin, David A. "The Refugee Act of 1980: Its Past and Future." *1982 Michigan Yearbook of International Legal Studies* (1982).

Menendez, Albert J. "Religious Lobbies." *Liberty*. March/April 1982.

"Mexican and U.S. Bishops Meet on the Pastoral Care of Immigrants." *Pastoral Care of Migrants & Refugees.* Washington, D.C.: National Conference of Catholic Bishops. 2, 1 (January 1984).

Meyers, Albert J. "Airlift From Terror—The Refugees' Story." *U.S. News & World Report* 49 (July 25, 1960).

Miller, Darrow. "Principles of Cooperation." *Symbiosis* [monthly publication of Food for the Hungry, Scottsdale, Ariz.]. August 1986.

"Millions on the Run." *Newsweek*. December 12, 1955.

Mitchell, Fredric, and James W. Skelton. "The Church-State Conflicts in Early Indian Education." *History of Education Quarterly* 6 (Spring 1966).

"Mr. Justice Reed's Dissent in the Religious Instruction Decision of the Supreme Court." *Christianity & Crisis* 8, 5 (March 29, 1948).

Neuhaus, Richard J. "Relief v. Liberation: Another Misplaced Debate." *Worldview* 17, 10 (October 1974).

———. "Let the Church Be the Church." *Center Journal* (Ethics and Public Policy Center) 31 (Fall 1983).

"New Permanent Foreign Aid." *Business Week*. April 30, 1955.

"Nicaraguans Block $5.1 Million in U.S. Aid." *Philadelphia Inquirer*. August 4, 1982.

Nichols, Bruce. "Rubberband Humanitarianism." *Ethics and International Affairs* 1 (1987).

Niebuhr, Reinhold. "Editorial Notes." *Christianity & Crisis* 8, 5 (March 29, 1948).

Nielsen, Kai. "The 'Political Question' Doctrine." *Ethics* 79, 1 (1968).

Nietschmann, Bernard. "Nicaraguan Indians' Struggle." *New York Times*. January 1, 1984.

"No CIA Involvement." *Christian Century* 99, 23 (July 7–14, 1982).

"No Federal Assistance to Protestant Institutions." *Christian Century* 76 (April 8, 1959).

Nordland, Ron. "Refugees 'Doomed' by the Letter of the Law." *Philadelphia Inquirer*. September 9, 1982.

———. "Savagery at Sea: No End to a Refugee Nightmare." *Philadelphia Inquirer*. March 30, 1982.

Oberdorfer, Don. "Nicaragua Bars U.S. Aid to Private Groups." *Washington Post*. August 4, 1982.

The Other Side 19, 3 (March 1983). Philadelphia: Jubilee, Inc. [Issue devoted to survey of the work of private relief and development agencies].

Owens, Ralph C., Jr. "Relief and Development Work Is No Part of the Great Commission." *Evangelical Missions Quarterly*. January 1982.

Panaritis, Andrea. "Yellow Rain: A Vanishing Trail?" *Indochina Issues* 47 (June 1984).

Pardo, Paul. "Beneficiaries of Vatican Wartime Rescue." Letter to the editor. *New York Times*. February 5, 1984.

Peterson, Wilfred H. "The Thwarted Opportunity for Judicial Activism in Church-State

Relations: Separation and Accommodation in Precarious Balance." *Journal of Church and State* 22, 3 (Autumn 1980).

Pfeffer, Leo. "The Church an Instrument of National Policy?" *Christian Century* 72 (September 21, 1955).

Phillips, Cabell. "That Phoney Refugee Law." *Harper's* 210 (April 1955).

Plowman, Edward E. "Conversing with the CIA." *Christianity Today* 20 (October 10, 1975).

"The Politics of Food [Mennonite Central Committee shipments to Vietnam]." [Lancaster, Penn.] *Intelligencer Journal.* May 28, 1981.

Pope John Paul II. "Migrants and Refugees in the Plan of Evangelization." *Pastoral Care of Migrants and Refugees* 2, 1 (January 1984).

Pope Pius XI. "Reconstructing the Social Order [*Quadragessimo Anno*]." In *Five Great Encyclicals.* New York: Paulist Press, 1939.

"Postwar Catholic Relief: An Interview with Bishop Edward E. Swanstrom." *Newsletter on Church and State Abroad* 4. New York: Council on Religion and International Affairs, May 1984.

Powers, Charles T. "Ethiopian Jews: Exodus of a Tribe." *Los Angeles Times.* July 7, 1985.

———. "A New Life In Israel for Ethiopians." *Los Angeles Times.* July 8, 1985

"Preserve Perspective in Philanthropy!" *Christian Century* 73 (December 5, 1956).

"President Submits New Legislation on Refugee Aid Programs." Washington, D.C.: *Department of State Bulletin* 45, August 7, 1961.

"Proselytizing with Food Aid." *Christian Century* 75 (June 18, 1958).

Rashke, Richard. "CIA Funded, Manipulated Missionaries." *National Catholic Reporter* 11, 36 (August 1, 1975).

"Reagan on Nicaragua Draws Missioners' Ire." *National Catholic Reporter* 44 (May 20, 1983).

Reddig, William. "Agency Mirrors U.S. Global Aims." *National Catholic Reporter* 39 (January 13, 1978). See also "CIA short of 'covers' "; "AID says 'Spies gone' "; and "Editorials: Who should CRS serve?"

Rees, Elfan. "The Refugee Problem: Joint Responsibility." *Annals of the American Academy of Political and Social Science* 329 (May 1, 1960).

"The Refugees Are Coming!" Editorial. *New York Times.* June 24, 1983.

"Refugees Are 'Moral Obligation' for World: Interview with the Rev. Emmett Curran." *U.S. News & World Report* 87 (August 6, 1979).

"Religious Garb in Indian Schools." Editorial. *The Independent* 72 (February 15, 1912).

"Rescue by Sea? [on the future of the Falasha operation]" *Economist.* January 12, 1985.

Riding, Alan. "Refugees Resisting Move in Honduras." *New York Times.* March 4, 1982.

Ringland, Arthur C. "The Organization of Voluntary Foreign Aid, 1939–1953." *Department of State Bulletin* 30 (March 15, 1954).

Robinson, Julian, Jeanne Guillemin and Matthew Meselson. "Yellow Rain: The Story Collapses." *Foreign Policy* 68 (Fall 1987).

Rockwell, Hays, and Linda Rockwell. "Haves Helping Have-Nots." *New York Times.* November 6, 1983.

Roper, Elmo. "The Americans and the Hungarian Story." *Saturday Review* 40 (May 11, 1957).

Samuel, Vinay, and Charles Corwin. "Assistance Programs Require Partnership." *Evangelical Missions Quarterly* 15, 2 (April 1979).

Samuels, Gertrude. "People in Search of Identity." *New York Times Magazine.* September 23, 1956.

Santoli, Al. "The New Indochina War." *New Republic.* May 30, 1983.

Sayre, Francis B., Jr. "The World Refugee Year." *Christian Century* 76 (June 10, 1959).

Schanberg, Sydney. "Memory is the Answer." *New York Times*. April 23, 1985.

Scheidemantle, David R. Note. "Political Entanglement as an Independent Test of Constitutionality Under the Establishment Clause." *Fordham Law Review* 52 (May 1984).

Schwartz, Leo. "Summary Analysis of the AJDC Program in the U.S. Zone of Occupation, Germany." *Menorah Journal* 35 (Spring 1947).

Seagrave, Sterling. "Yellow Rain's Year: 'Like Laughing at Guernica.' " *Asian Wall Street Journal*. September 21, 1982.

Self, Thomas C. "International Trade Export Regulations." *Howard International Law Journal* 20 (1979).

Shaughnessy, Daniel E., Thomas Nagel, Norge M. Jerome, and Michael F. Brewer. "Plowshares into Swords: The Political Uses of Food." *Report from the Center for Philosophy & Public Policy* 2, 4 (Fall 1982). College Park, MD: University of Maryland.

Shenefield, John H. "Extraterritorial Application of United States Antitrust Laws: Economic Imperialism or Correcting the Evil at the Source?" *Wirtschaft und Recht* 35 (February 3, 1983).

Shenk, Wilbert R. "The Missionary and Politics: Henry Venn's Guidelines." *Journal of Church and State* 24, 3 (1982).

Shipler, David K. "For Palestinian Refugees, Acute Difficulties and Few Solutions." *New York Times*. July 16, 1982.

Sievers, Harry I. "The Catholic Indian School Issue and the Presidential Election of 1892." *The Catholic Historical Review* 38, 2 (July 1952).

" 'Slightly Ridiculous': Question of Communist Affiliation." *Commonweal* 65 (March 22, 1957).

Smock, Audrey. "The Politics of Relief [in the Nigerian civil war, 1968–69]." *Africa Report* (January 1970).

Solarz, Stephen J. " 'Yellow Rain': The Holes in a Bee-Excrement Hypothesis." Letter to the editor. *New York Times*. December 14, 1983.

Solberg, Mary. "Human Rights and U.S. Central America Policy." *The Lutheran* 21, 12 (June 15, 1983).

———. "Reflections on a Tour" [Central American refugees]. *Christianity and Crisis* 42, 19 (November 5, 1982).

Somerville, Frank P. L. "Bible Group Turns Freighter Into Mission Vessel." *Religious News Service*. January 6, 1984.

Southerland, Daniel. "U.S. Blocks Private Shipment of Wheat to Vietnam." *Christian Science Monitor*. May 13, 1981.

"Spies in the Sacristy." *America* 133 (August 16, 1975).

Spring, Beth. "Are Military Chaplains Illegal?" *Christianity Today* 27, 4 (February 18, 1983).

Srole, Leo. "Why the DP's Can't Wait: Proposing an International Plan of Rescue." *Commentary* 3 (January 1947).

Stam, John. "Missions and U.S. Foreign Policy—A Case Study From the 1920's." *Evangelical Mission Quarterly* 15, 3 (July 1979).

"The State, the Church and the Indian." Editorial. *The Outlook* 79 (February 11, 1905).

Stevenson, A. Russell. "Relief and Rehabilitation as a Part of the Missionary Task." *Occasional Bulletin* 7 (February 27, 1956). New York: Missionary Research Library.

Strachan, R. Kenneth. "New Emphasis in Missions." *Occasional Bulletin* 5 (November 12, 1954). New York: Missionary Research Library.

Strickland, Charles E. "American Aid to Germany, 1919 to 1921." *Wisconsin Magazine of History* (Summer 1962).

Suhrke, Astri. "A New Look at America's Refugee Policy." *Indochina Issues* 10 (September, 1980). Washington, D.C.: Center for International Policy.

Swartzendruber, J. Fred. " 'Yellow Rain': Unanswered Questions." *Indochina Issues* 23 (January 1982). Washington, D.C.: Center for International Policy.

Taubman, Philip. "Private Groups in U.S. Aiding Managua's Foes." *New York Times.* July 15, 1984.

Teitelbaum, Michael S. "Right Versus Right: Immigration and Refugee Policy in the United States." *Foreign Affairs* 59, 1 (Fall 1980).

Teltsch, Kathleen. "New Jewish Philanthropy Aiming at Nonsectarian Aid for All Poor." *New York Times.* August 13, 1985.

Thompson, Dorothy. "Refugees, a World Problem." *Foreign Affairs* (Spring 1938).

"Tibetan Refugees Helped by Church World Service." *Christian Century* 76 (April 22, 1959).

Tillman, Robert B. "Churches' Aid to Refugees Unique." *Christian Century* 72 (June 8, 1955).

"The Treatment of the Nicaraguan Indians by the Sandinista Government." *Freedom at Issue* 66 (May/June 1982). New York: Freedom House.

"Vatican Denies It Helped Nazis." *New York Times.* February 5, 1984.

Viviano, Frank. "CIA Church Group in Honduras." *Guardian.* August 26, 1981.

———. "Honduras: The Politics of Charity." *Lucha* 5 (November 1981).

Wade, Nicholas. "The Embarrassment of 'Yellow Rain'." *New York Times.* November 28, 1983.

Wain, Barry. "Scholar Discusses Life in Kampuchea Today." *Asian Wall Street Journal.* July 22–23, 1983.

———. "Vietnam's Unwanted Citizens Await Their Fate." *Bangkok Post.* September 2, 1980.

———. "Yellow Rain Continues to Drive Hmong from Laos." *Asian Wall Street Journal.* July 25, 1983.

Warren, George L. "The Escapee Program." *Journal of International Affairs* 7, 1 (1953).

———. "Meeting the Challenge of Moving Hungarian Refugees." *Department of State Bulletin* 36 (May 6, 1957).

Wexler, Stephen. "The Political Question Doctrine: A Decision Not to Decide." *Ethics* 79, 1 (1968).

"What Hope for the Escapees?" *America* 93 (May 14, 1955).

Whelan, Charles M. " 'Church' in the International Revenue Code: The Definitional Problems." *Fordham Law Review* 45 (1977).

"When the Church Goes to the State." *Christian Century* 73 (February 15, 1956).

"Why Poles but Not Salvadorans?" Editorial. *New York Times.* May 31, 1983.

Wieseltier, Leon. "Brothers and Keepers." *New Republic* 192, 6 (February 11, 1985).

Winkler, Elizabeth. "Voluntary Agencies and Government Policy." *International Migration Review* 15, 1–2 (Spring-Summer 1981). Barry N. Stein and Sylvano M. Tomasi, eds. New York: Center for Migration Studies.

Woodward, Kenneth L., with Eloise Salholz. "Missionarries on the Line." *Newsweek.* March 8, 1982. See also response in "Letters." *Newsweek.* March 22, 1982.

"World Refugee Year Began July 1." *Christian Century* 76 (July 29, 1959).

Worthing, Sharon L. "Government Surveillance of Religious Organizations." *Journal of Church and State* 23, 3 (Autumn 1981).

———. "The Internal Revenue Service as a Monitor of Church Institutions: The Excessive Entanglement Problem." *Fordham Law Review* 45 (1977).

———. " 'Religion' and 'Religious Institutions' Under the First Amendment." *Pepperdine Law Review* 7, 2 (1980).

———. "The State Takes over a Church." *Annals of the American Academy of Political and Social Science* 446 (November 1979).

Wright, Robert G. "Voluntary Agencies and the Resettlement of Refugees." *International Migration Review* 15, 1–2 (Spring-Summer 1981). Barry N. Stein and Sylvano M. Tomasi, eds. New York: Center for Migration Studies.

Books

Acheson, Dean. *Present at the Creation*. New York: Norton, 1969.

Adler, Cyrus. *I Have Considered the Days*. Philadelphia: Jewish Publication Society, 1940.

Antieau, Chester A., Arthur T. Downey, and Deward C. Roberts. *Freedom From Federal Establishment: Formations and Early History of the First Amendment Religion Clauses*. Milwaukee: Bruce Publishing, 1964.

Baldwin, David A. *Foreign Aid and American Foreign Poilcy: A Documentary Analysis*. New York: Praeger, 1966.

Banfield, Edward C. *American Foreign Aid Doctrines*. Washington, D.C.: American Enterprise Institute for Public Policy Research, 1963.

Bannan, John F., and Rosemary Bannan. *Law, Morality and Vietnam: The Peace Militants and the Courts*. Bloomington, Ind.: Indiana University Press, 1974.

Barker, Ernest. *Church, State and Education*. Ann Arbor: Michigan University Press, 1957.

Barth, Karl. *Community, State and Church*. Garden City, N.Y.: Anchor Books, 1960.

Bau, Ignatius. *This Ground is Holy*. New York: Paulist Press, 1985.

Bauer, Yehuda. *My Brother's Keeper: A History of the American Jewish Joint Distribution Committee 1929–1939*. Philadelphia: The Jewish Publication Society of America, 1974.

Beaver, R. Pierce. *Church, State and the American Indians*. St. Louis: Concordia, 1966.

Bennett, John C. "Church and State in the United States." In *Reformed Faith and Politics*. Ronald H. Stone, ed. Lanham, Md.: University Press of America, 1983.

Blanshard, Paul. *God and Man in Washington*. Boston: Beacon Press, 1960.

Bolling, Landrum, with Craig Smith. *Private Foreign Aid: U.S. Philanthropy and Development*. Boulder, Colo.: Westview Press, 1982.

Bramwell, Anna, ed. *Refugees in the Age of Total War: Europe and the Middle East*. London: Unwin Hyman, 1988.

Brewer, Kathleen, and Patrick A. Taran. *Manual for Refugee Sponsorship*. New York: Church World Service, Immigration and Refugee Program, 1982.

Brown, Peter. *Augustine of Hippo*. Los Angeles: University of California, 1969.

Brown, Peter, and Douglas MacLean, eds. *Human Rights and U.S. Foreign Policy*. Lexington, Mass.: Lexington Books, 1979.

Cogswell, James G. *No Place Left to Call Home*. New York: Friendship Press, 1983.

Coughlin, Bernard J. *Church and State in Social Welfare*. New York: Columbia University Press, 1965.

Cressey, George B. "Mission to Everywhere: The Religious Agencies." In *The Art of Overseasmanship*. Harlan Cleveland and Gerald J. Mangone, eds. Syracuse, N.Y.: Syracuse University Press, 1957.

Curti, Merle. *American Philanthropy Abroad: A History*. New Brunswick, N.J.: Rutgers University Press, 1963.

Dawidowicz, Lucy S. *The War Against the Jews, 1933–1945*. New York: Holt, Rinehart and Winston, 1975.

Dayton, Edward R., and Samuel Wilson, eds. *The Refugees Among Us: Unreached Peoples '83*. Monrovia, Calif.: MARC, 1983.

Egan, Eileen, and Elizabeth Clark Reiss. *Transfigured Night: The CRALOG Experience*. New York: Livingston Publishing Company, 1964.

Elazar, Daniel, and Stuart Cohen. *The Jewish Polity*. Philadelphia: Temple University Press, 1984.

Elliott, Mark R. *Pawns of Yalta: Soviet Refugees and America's Role in Their Repatriation*. Chicago: University of Illinois Press, 1982.

Feingold, Henry. *The Politics of Rescue*. New York: Holocaust Publications, 1970.

Fine, Morris, and Milton Himmelfarb, eds. *American Jewish Yearbook 1969*. [Vol. 70] Philadelphia: Jewish Publication Society, 1970.

———. *American Jewish Yearbook 1974*. [Vol. 75] Philadelphia: Jewish Publication Society, 1975.

———. *American Jewish Yearbook 1977*. [Vol 78] Philadelphia: Jewish Publication Society, 1978.

———. *American Jewish Yearbook 1978*. [Vol. 79] Philadelphia: Jewish Publication Society, 1979.

Fine, Morris, and Jacob Sloan, eds. *American Jewish Yearbook 1957*. [Vol. 58] Philadelphia: Jewish Publication Society, 1958.

Five Great Encyclicals [Pope Leo XIII and Pope Pius XI]. New York: Paulist Press, 1939.

Forsythe, David O. *Humanitarian Politics: The International Committee of the Red Cross*. Baltimore: Johns Hopkins University Press, 1977.

Gaustad, Edwin S., ed. *A Documentary History of Religion in America* [2 vols.] Grand Rapids: William B. Eerdmans, 1983.

Genizi, Haim. *American Apathy: The Flight of Christian Refugees from Nazism*. Ramat-Gan, Israel: Bar-Ilan University Press, 1983.

Graham, Franklin, and Jeanette Lockerbie. *Bob Pierce: This One Thing I Do*. Waco: Word, 1983.

Grahl-Madsen, Atle. *Territorial Asylum*. Dobbs Ferry, N.Y.: Oceana Publications, 1980.

Gruber, Ruth. *Haven: The Unknown Story of 1000 World War II Refugees*. New York: Coward McCann, 1983.

Handlin, Oscar. *A Continuing Task: The American Jewish Joint Distribution Committee, 1914–1964*. New York: Random House, 1964.

Harrell-Bond, Barbara. *Imposing Aid: Emergency Assistance to Refugees*. Oxford: Oxford University Press, 1986.

Henkin, Louis. *Foreign Affairs and the Constitution*. New York: Columbia University Press, 1972.

Hirschmann, Ira A. *Life Line to a Promised Land*. New York: Vanguard, 1946.

Holborn, Louise. *Refugees: A Problem in Our Time*. [2 vols.] Metuchen, N.J.: Scarecrow Press, 1975.

Hoover, Herbert. *Addresses on the American Road, 1941–1945*. Stanford: Stanford University Press, 1946.

———. *Addresses on the American Road, 1945–48*. New York: Van Nostrand, 1949.

———. *Addresses on the American Road, 1948–50*. Stanford: Stanford University Press, 1951.

Israel, Fred L., ed. *The War Diary of Breckinridge Long*. Lincoln: University of Nebraska Press, 1966.

Ives, J. Moss. *The Ark and the Dove*. London: Longmans, Green, 1936.

Johnson, Paul. *Modern Times: The World from the Twenties to the Eighties*. New York: Harper and Row, 1983.

Keely, Charles B. 1981. *Global Refugee Policy: The Case of a Development-Oriented Strategy*. New York: The Population Council, Inc.

Kelley, Dean M., ed. *Government Intervention in Religious Affairs*. New York: Pilgrim Press, 1982.

———. *Why Churches Should Not Pay Taxes*. New York: Harper and Row, 1977.

Kenan, I.L. *Israel's Defense Line*. Buffalo, N.Y.: Prometheus Books, 1981.

Kessler, David. *The Falashas: The Forgotten Jews of Ethiopia*. New York: Holmes and Meier, 1982.

Kurland, Philip B. *Religion and the Law: Of Church and State and the Supreme Court*. Chicago: Aldine, 1962.

Linkh, Richard M. *American Catholicism and European Immigrants (1900–1924).* Staten Island: Center for Migration Studies, 1975.

Lissner, Jorgen. *The Politics of Altruism: A Study of the Political Behavior of Voluntary Development Agencies.* Geneva: Lutheran World Federation, 1977.

Loescher, Gilburt D., and John Scanlan. *Calculated Kindness.* Glencoe, Ill.: Free Press, 1986.

Luce, Don, and John Sommer. *Vietnam: The Unheard Voices.* Ithaca: Cornell University Press, 1969.

Macalister-Smith, Peter. *International Humanitarian Assistance: Disaster Relief Actions in International Law and Organization.* Dordrecht, The Netherlands: M. Nijhoff, 1985.

MacEoin, Gary, and Nivita Riley. *No Promised Land: American Refugee Policies and the Rule of Law.* Boston: Oxfam America, 1982.

Marchetti, Victor, and John S. Marks. *The CIA and the Cult of Intelligence.* New York: Dell, 1980.

Maritain, Jacques (trans. Doris C. Anson). *Christianity and Democracy.* New York: Scribner's, 1947.

Marrus, Michael. *The Unwanted: European Refugees in the Twentieth Century.* New York: Oxford, 1985.

McDonald, James G. *My Mission in Israel.* New York: Simon and Schuster, 1951.

Mehl, Roger. *The Sociology of Protestantism.* Philadelphia: Westminster Press, 1970.

Melander, Goran, and Peter Nobel, eds. *African Refugees and the Law.* Upsala: Scandanavian Institute of African Studies, 1978.

Miller, Robert T., and Ronald B. Flowers. *Toward Benevolent Neutrality: Church, State, and the Supreme Court.* Waco, Tx.: Markham Press Fund, 1982.

Morgenthau, Hans J., and Kenneth W. Thompson. *Politics Among Nations.* New York: Knopf, 1985.

Morse, Arthur D. *While Six Million Died: A Chronicle of American Apathy.* New York: Hart, 1968.

Neuhaus, Richard John. *Christian Faith and Public Policy.* Minneapolis: Augsburg, 1977.

———. *The Naked Public Square.* Grand Rapids, Mich.: Eerdmans, 1984.

Niebuhr, Reinhold. *Beyond Tragedy.* New York: Scribner's, 1937.

———. *Faith and History.* New York: Scribner's, 1949.

Nowak, J., R. Rotunda, and J. Young. *Handbook on Constitutional Law.* St. Paul, Minn.: West Publishing, 1986.

Oldham, J.H. *The Oxford Conference.* [Official Report] New York: Willett, Clark, 1937.

Ong, Walter J. *American Catholic Crossroads.* New York: Macmillan, 1959.

Oppenheim, Samson D., ed. *American Jewish Yearbook 5678 1917–1918.* Philadelphia: Jewish Publication Society of America, 1917.

Orbach, William W. *The American Movement to Aid Soviet Jews.* Amherst: University of Massachusetts Press, 1979.

O'Shaughnessy, Michael. *Peace and Reconstruction: A Catholic Layman's Approach.* New York: Harper, 1943.

Perlmutter, Amos. *Israel: The Partitioned State: A Political History Since 1900.* New York: Scribner's, 1985.

Pickett, Clarence. *For More Than Bread.* Boston: Little, Brown, 1953.

Pilkington, Walter, ed. *The Journals of Samuel Kirkland.* Clinton, N.Y.: Hamilton College Press, 1980.

Piper, John F., Jr. *The American Churches in World War I.* Athens, Ohio: Ohio University Press, 1985.

Pope Paul VI. *On Evangelization in the Modern World.* [*Evangelii Nuntiandi*] Washington, D.C.: United States Catholic Conference, 1976.

Proudfoot, Malcolm J. *European Refugees: 1939–52*. Evanston, Ill.: Northwestern University Press, 1956.

Prucha, Francis Paul. *The Churches and the Indian Schools, 1888–1912*. Lincoln: University of Nebraska Press, 1979.

Quigley, Thomas, ed. *American Catholics and Vietnam*. Grand Rapids, Mich.: Eerdmans, 1968.

Reimers, David M. *Still the Golden Door: The Third World Comes to America*. New York: Columbia University Press, 1985.

Reiss, Elizabeth Clark. *The American Council of Voluntary Agencies for Foreign Service: Four Monographs*. New York: American Council of Voluntary Agencies, 1986.

Salamon, Lester, and Alan J. Abramson. *The Federal Budget and the Nonprofit Sector*. Washington, D.C.: The Urban Institute Press, 1982.

Schachner, Nathan. *The Price of Liberty*. New York: American Book-Stratford Press, 1948.

Schmidt, Elizabeth, Jane Blewett, and Peter Henriot. *Religious Private Voluntary Organizations and the Question of Government Funding* (final report). Ossining, N.Y.: Orbis Books, 1981.

Schneiderman, Harry, and Morris Fine, eds. *The American Jewish Yearbook 1947*. Philadelphia: Jewish Publication Society, 1948.

Seymour, Harold J. *Design for Giving: The Story of the National War Fund, Inc., 1943–47*. New York: Harper and Brothers, 1947.

Shawcross, William. *The Quality of Mercy: Cambodia, Holocaust and Modern Conscience*. New York: Simon and Schuster, 1984.

Snyder, Harold E. "People to People: The Voluntary Agencies," in *The Art of Overseasmanship*. Harlan Cleveland and Gerald J. Mangone, eds. Syracuse, N.Y.: Syracuse University Press, 1957.

Spragens, Joel, and J. Charney. *Embargo: Implications of the U.S. Humanitarian Embargo in Vietnam and Kampuchea*. Boston: Oxfam, 1985.

Thompson, Kenneth, ed. *Moral Dimensions of American Foreign Policy*. New Brunswick, N.J.: Transaction Press, 1984.

——— and Myers, Robert J., eds. *Truth and Tragedy: A Tribute to Hans J. Morgenthau*. New Brunswick, N.J.: Transaction Press, 1984.

Tribe, Laurence. "Rights of Religious Autonomy." In *American Constitutional Law*. New York: Foundation Press, 1978.

Tripp, Rosemary E., ed. *World Refugee Survey 1987*. New York: U.S. Committee for Refugees, 1987. This is an annual publication.

Warren, Max A.C. *Caesar the Beloved Enemy: Three Studies in the Relation of Church and State*. The Reincker Lectures at Virginia Theological Seminary, Alexandria, February 1955. London: SCM Press, n.d.

———. "The Concept of Partnership," in *Partnership: The Study of an Idea*. Chicago: SCM Bookclub, 1956.

Weber, Paul J., and Dennis A. Gilbert. "Religious Tax Exemptions: The Case-Knife Approach;" "Aid to Religion: Who Gets What;" "Distinction Without Merit;" and "Conclusion." In *Private Churches and Public Money: Church-Government Fiscal Relations*. Westport, Conn.: Greenwood Press, 1981.

Wilson, John F. *Public Religion and American Culture*. Philadelphia: Temple University Press, 1979.

Wyman, David S. *The Abandonment of the Jews: America and the Holocaust 1941–45*. New York: Pantheon, 1984.

Yinger, J. Milton. *Religion in the Struggle for Power*. Durham: Duke University Press, 1946.

Zucker, Norman L., and Naomi Flink Zucker. *The Guarded Gate: The Reality of American Refugee Policy*. New York: Harcourt Brace Jovanovich, 1987.

Dissertations, Reports, Pamphlets, Working Papers, and Unpublished Materials

"Accountability with Independence: Toward a Balance in Government/Independent Sector Partnerships." Washington, D.C.: Task Force on Organizational and Financial Relationships with Government, Independent Sector, May 11, 1983.

"Ad Hoc Assessment Visit to Central America, Lutheran World Federation, 28th September–9th October, 1983." Geneva: Lutheran World Federation, 1983.

Ahern, Trish, and Mary Risacher. "Report on a Visit to the Salvadoran Refugee Camps of Colomoncagua and Mesa Grande in Honduras, March 13–27, 1983." Washington, D.C.: Washington Office of Latin America, April 15, 1983.

"Alleged Violations of Human Rights in Kampuchea and Laos." Bangkok: Asian Lawyers Legal Committee, June 4–11, 1982.

Amayun, Dr. Milton B. "Yellow Rain in Laos." Report to the U.S. House of Representatives, Subcommittee on Pacific and Asian Affairs. April 21, 1982. Draft in Archive on Church and State Abroad, Carnegie Council, New York.

"Anchor of Hope: The Ministry of Refugee Resettlement." New York: Presiding Bishop's Fund for World Relief, 1979.

Arrupe, Pedro (Superior-General of the Society of Jesus). "The Refugee Crisis in Africa: Opportunity and Challenge for the Church." Rome: Society of Jesus, 1981.

"Assistance to African Refugees by Voluntary Organizations in the Years 1974–1978." Geneva: International Council of Voluntary Agencies, April 1979.

Barber, Martin, and Meyer Brownstone. "Report and Recommendations to the United Nations High Commissioner for Refugees Regarding the Protection of Refugees in Honduras and the Promotion of Durable Solutions." London: British Refugee Council, September 9, 1983.

"The Basel Letter." In "Liberation, Development, Evangelism: Must We Choose in Mission?" Fifth Annual Working Consultation on the Future of the Missionary Enterprise. Ventnor, N.J.: Overseas Study Center, May 2–5, 1978. From the September 1976 meeting sponsored by the World Evangelical Fellowship, Theological Commission, entitled "Church and Nationhood," held at St. Chrischona, near Basel, Switzerland. Cited from *Emerging Models for Mission*. Bronkema, Frederick H., and Pat VanHeel Gaughan, eds. New York: IDOC/North America, 1978.

Batz, Reuben C. "Five Year Report of Lutheran World Federation Service to Refugees." Geneva: Lutheran World Federation, July 1952.

Bauman, William. "Report of American Friends Service Committee/National Council of Churches Observer Team of Visits to Salvadoran and Guatemalan Refugee Camps in Honduras—April 12th to the 25th, 1982." Portland, Ore.: American Friends Service Committee, May 10, 1982.

———. "Report on La Virtud Refugee Camp, March 15–28, 1982." Philadelphia: American Friends Service Committee.

Beaver, Pierce. "Church and State Relations in Missions to the Native Americans." n.d. [1967?].

Bergeron, Pierre. *Import-Export Controls: Their Nature and Accountability*. New York: Church World Service, 1980.

Berryman, Angela. "Central American Refugees: A Survey of the Current Situation." Philadelphia: American Friends Service Committee, January 1982.

"A Biblical Theology of Development for World Concern." Seattle: World Concern, n.d. [ca. 1982].

Bradley, Mark. "Report on La Virtud Camp, March 15–28, 1982." Philadelphia: American Friends Service Committee.

Brauer, Robert. "Report on a Trip to Honduran Refugee Camps." New York: Archive on

Church and State Abroad, Carnegie Council on Ethics and International Affairs, November 1981.

Brook, Benjamin N. "Voluntary Foreign Aid: Voluntary Agency Relationship to the United States Government." M.S. thesis, New York School of Social Work, Columbia University, 1949.

"Christian Conduct and Intelligence Agencies." Pamphlet Number 4. Elkhart, Ind.: [Mennonite] Council of International Ministries. April 1978.

"Christian Conduct in Situations of Conflict." Pamphlet Number 1. Elkart, Ind.: [Mennonite] Council of International Ministries. n.d.

Christian Ministries Seminars. Collection of documents from quarterly seminars of Christian relief agencies in Thailand, 1976–1983. In the Archive on Church and State Abroad, Carnegie Council on Ethics and International Affairs, New York.

"Church Leaders Consultation on African Refugees: A Challenge to the Churches." Report of conference held October 26–30, 1981, in Arusha, Tanzania, sponsored by the All Africa Conference of Churches, Lutheran World Federation, World Council of Churches. Geneva: World Council of Churches, 1981.

"The Church of Christ in Thailand and the World Council of Churches: Joint Relief Programme for Displaced Persons in Thailand, October 1979 to December 1981." Bangkok: Church of Christ in Thailand, January 1982.

"Church World Service, Inc. and Use of Government Resources." Legal memorandum from Charles H. Tuttle to H. Leroy Brininger, National Council of Churches, September 25, 1965.

"The Churches and the World Refugee Crisis." Geneva: Refugee Service of the Commission on Inter-Church Aid Refugee and World Service, World Council of Churches, 1981.

"The Church's Refugees: A New Look." Report of a conference convened September 29, 1952. New York: National Council of Churches, Migration Services, Department of Church World Service, n.d. [ca. 1952–53].

"Comments by Father V. Cosmao on the Theological Principles of Co-Financing." Brussels: Cooperation Internationale pour la Development Socio-Economique, October 15, 1980.

Darrow, Robert M. "Catholic Political Power: A Study of the American Catholic Church Activity on Behalf of Franco During the Spanish Civil War (1936–39)." Ph.D. dissertation, Columbia University, 1953.

Davie, Maurice. "What Shall We Do About Immigration?" Public Affairs Pamphlet 115. New York: Public Affairs Committee, March 1946.

——— and Samuel Koenig. "The Refugees are Now Americans." Public Affairs Pamphlet 111. New York: Public Affairs Committee, December 1945.

"Defining Development." In "Food for the Hungry Development Manual." Scottsdale, Ariz.: Food for the Hungry, Inc., n.d.

Deng, Damas. "Root Causes of the Refugee Problem in Africa." Delivered at the Khartoum Seminar on Refugees, sponsored by the Office of the Commissioner of Refugees, Government of Sudan, September 1982.

"D[isplaced] P[erson]'s Are People! Background, Current Program, and Future Plans of the Committee on Displaced Persons of Church World Service." New York: National Council of Churches, n.d. [1948].

"Displaced Persons: Whose Responsibility?" [pamphlet] New York: War Relief Services—National Catholic Welfare Conference, n.d. [ca. 1947–48].

Douglas, James, and Peter Wright. "English Charities, Part I: Legal Definition, Taxation and Regulation." PONPO Working Paper 15. New Haven, Conn.: Program on Non-Profit Organizations, Institution for Social and Policy Studies, Yale University, n.d.

Ebersole, Luke E. "Church Lobbying With Special Reference to Federal Legislation." Ph.D. dissertation, University of Pennsylvania, 1962.

Ellman, Ira M. "Driven from the Tribunal: Judicial Resolution of Internal Church Disputes." PONPO Working Paper 44. New Haven, Conn.: Program on Non-Profit Organizations, Institution for Social and Policy Studies, Yale University, September 1981.

Escape to Freedom. [booklet on the U.S. Escapee Program] Washington, D.C.: Foreign Operations Administration, n.d. [1954].

"Ethical Issues and Moral Principles in U.S. Refugee Policy." Edited transcript of conference proceedings. Washington, DC: Meridian House International, March 24–25, 1983. Sponsored by the U.S. Coordinator for Refugee Affairs (U.S. Department of State) and the [State Department] Religious Advisory Committee [on Refugee Issues].

"Evangelism and Social Responsibility: An Evangelical Commitment." Lausanne Occasional Paper 21. Consultation on the Relationship Between Evangelism and Social Responsibility, Grand Rapids, Mich., June 19–25, 1982. Lausanne: Lausanne Committee for World Evangelization and the World Evangelical Fellowship, 1982.

"Face to Face: Introduction to the People and History of Cuba." In "LIRS Manual for Sponsors of Refugees." New York: Lutheran Immigration and Refugee Service, Lutheran Council in the USA, 1980.

"The Falasha Jews of Ethiopia." New York: Council of Jewish Federations and Welfare Funds, January 1976.

Florin, Dr. Hans W. "Government Aid and Mission Operations: Occasional Paper No. 6." New York: World Council of Churches, May 1963.

Forbes, Susan S., and Patricia Weiss Fagan. "Unaccompanied Refugee Children: The Evolution of U.S. Policies—1939–1984." Washington, D.C.: Refugee Policy Group, August 1984.

"F[oreign] O[perations] A[dministration] and U.S. Voluntary Agencies." [includes chapter on U.S. Escapee Program.] Washington, D.C.: Foreign Operations Administration, 1955.

Forsythe, David P. "Humanizing American Foreign Policy: Non-Profit Lobbying and Human Rights." PONPO Working Paper 12. New Haven, Conn.: Program on Non-Profit Organizations, Institution for Social and Policy Studies, Yale University, n.d.

Friedman, Ray. "The Role of Non-Profit Organizations in Foreign Aid: A Literature Survey." PONPO Working Paper 32. New Haven, Conn.: Program on Non-Profit Organizations, Institution for Social and Policy Studies, Yale University, December 1980.

Gallagher, Dennis, Susan Forbes, and Patricia Weiss Fagan. "Of Special Humanitarian Concern: U.S. Refugee Admissions Since Passage of the Refugee Act." Washington, D.C.: Refugee Policy Group, September 1985.

"Government Funding." Report of the Consultation held at Aurora Conference Centre, Toronto, Canada, February 8–10, 1983. Geneva: World Council of Churches, 1983.

Hancock, Robert L. "Statement of Religious Concerns: Summer Institute of Linguistics." Washington, D.C.: Summer Institute of Linguistics, January 10, 1981.

Harrison, Earl G., et al. "The Problem of the Displaced Persons." Report of the Survey Committee on Displaced Persons of the American Council of Voluntary Agencies for Foreign Service. New York: American Council of Voluntary Agencies, June 1946.

Harruff, Dr. Richard C. "Statement Before the Subcommittee on Asian and Pacific Affairs, House Foreign Affairs Committee," New York: Freedom House, March 30, 1982.

Hehir, Bryan. "Church and State: Implications for Ministry and Mission." Unpublished paper delivered to the American Missiological Society, Ft. Worth, Texas, 1981.

"Humanitarian Operations Arising out of Developments in Kampuchea." Bangkok: United Nations Border Relief Operation, September 3, 1982.

"ICVA [International Council of Voluntary Agencies] Consultation on Central America and Mexico." Documents of the consultation. Geneva: ICVA, 23–26 January 1984.

"The Immigration of European Displaced Persons to the United States." New York: Citizens Committee for Displaced Persons, Spring 1946.

"The Impact of Government Funding on the Management of Voluntary Agencies." New York: Greater New York Fund/United Way, n.d. [ca. 1978].

"In a Strange Land." Report of a World Conference on Problems of International Migration and the Responsibility of the Churches. Geneva: Division of Inter-Church Aid and Service to Refugees, World Council of Churches, June 11–16, 1961.

"The International Refugee Organization." Washington, D.C.: Office of Public Affairs, Department of State, March 1947.

Joblove, Leonard. "Special Treatment of Churches Under the Internal Revenue Code." PONPO Working Paper 21. New Haven, Conn.: Program on Non-Profit Organizations, Institution for Social And Policy Studies, Yale University, June 1980.

Karadawi, Ahmed (Assistant Commissioner for Refugees, Sudan). "Relationship Between Government and Non-Governmental Organizations in Refugee Work in the Sudan." Khartoum, Sudan: Seminar on Refugees, September 11–14, 1982.

Knight, Doris Jean Holden. "Church World Service: The Power of the Humanitarian Ideal." M.A. thesis, Creighton University, 1984.

La Noue, George R. "Church-State Relations in the Federal Policy Process." Ph.D. dissertation, Yale University, 1966.

Lankford, John E. "Protestant Stewardship and Benevolence, 1900–1941: A Study in Religious Philanthropy." Ph.D. dissertation, University of Wisconsin, 1962.

Lefever, Ernest W. "Protestants and U.S. Foreign Policy, 1925–1954." Ph.D. dissertation, Yale, 1954.

Lewis, James Ford. "The Unitarian Service Committee." Ph.D. dissertation, University of California, 1952.

Livezey, Lowell W. "Nongovernmental Organizations and the Ideas of Human Rights." Monograph, Woodrow Wilson School of Public and International Affairs, Princeton University, 1988.

Luhan, J. Michael. "Is the Nicaraguan Government Committing Atrocities against its Miskito Indians?" New York: Council on Hemispheric Affairs, March 5, 1982.

"Memorial to the Council of the United Nations Relief and Rehabilitation Administration from the American Council of Voluntary Agencies for Foreign Service." New York: AVCA, October 25, 1943. In the ACVA Archive, Rutgers University.

Miller, Harold F. "The Voluntary Agency as an Actor in International Affairs: A Study of a Voluntary Agency Collectivity." M.A. thesis, University of Pittsburgh, 1972.

Miller, Robert W. "The Role and Contribution of the Foreign Voluntary Agencies in South Vietnam." M.A. thesis, University of Pittsburgh, 1972.

Mirocha, C.J. "Testimony to the House Foreign Affairs Committee on Illegal Chemical Warfare in Asia." Unpublished transcript, March 30, 1982. In the Archive on Church and State Abroad, Carnegie Council on Ethics and International Affairs, New York.

Muodathir, Abdel Rahim. "Asylum and Sanctuary in Islam." Khartoum, Sudan: Office of the Commissioner for Refugees, September 1982.

"The Nature of the Church and Its Relationship with Government, A Statement with Public Policy Recommendations on Church-State Issues Adopted by the Lutheran Council in the U.S.A." Adopted May 16, 1979, Minneapolis, at 1979 annual meeting.

Newsletter on Church and State Abroad. New York: Carnegie Council on Ethics and International Affairs, 1982–.

Nichols, Bruce. "Favour In the Wilderness: Sanctuary Politics and the Shaping of American Refugee Policy." *Refugee Issues: British Refugee Council/Queen Elizabeth House Working Papers on Refugees* 2, 4 (August 1986).

Nietschmann, Bernard. "Statement before the Organization of American States Inter-American Commission on Human Rights, on the Situation of the Indians in Nicaragua, Presented by Bernard Nietschmann, October 3, 1983." Washington, D.C.: Indian Law Resource Center, October 6, 1983.

"1982 Report: Where Your Dollars Go." New York: [Episcopal] Presiding Bishop's Fund for World Relief, 1982.

North, David S., Lawrence S. Lewin, and Jennifer R. Wagner. *Kaleidoscope: The Resettlement of Refugees in the United States by Voluntary Agencies.* Washington, D.C.: New TransCentury Foundation, Lewin and Associates, and National Opinion Research Center, January 1982.

O'Connor, Edward M. "The United States and Displaced Persons—Current Policies and Programs." Speech to the National Conference of Social Work, Atlantic City, N.J., April 25, 1950.

"On the Role of Joint Voluntary Agency Representatives." New York: Committee on Migration and Refugee Affairs, American Council of Voluntary Agencies for Foreign Service, September 15, 1982.

"Organizing Principles." In "Food for the Hungry Corps Manual." Scottsdale, Ariz.: Food for the Hungry, Inc., October 7, 1982.

"Outline of the Organization and Work of the President's Committee for Hungarian Refugee Relief in Assisting in Resettlement of Hungarian Refugees." January 7, 1957. Archive on Church and State Abroad, Carnegie Council on Ethics and International Affairs, New York.

Pao, Vang. "Biological-Chemical Warfare in Laos." Santa Ana, Calif.: Laos Family Community, March 16, 1981.

"Philosophy of Development." Working Draft 1. Seattle: World Concern, June 1982.

Pifer, Alan. "The Non-Governmental Organizations at Bay." In "1966 Annual Report." New York: Carnegie Corporation of New York, 1966.

"A Policy Statement of the National Council of the Churches of Christ in the United States of America: Church-State Issues for Social and Health Services in the U.S.A.: Adopted by the General Board, February 22, 1967." New York: National Council of Churches, 1967.

"Political Responsibility: Choices for the 1980's." Statement of the Administrative Board of the USCC, October 26, 1979. Washington, D.C.: United States Catholic Conference, 1979.

"The Politics of Church Aid: Report of the Lutheran World Federation Consultation on Church Agencies' Fundraising, Education and Advocacy; Aarhus, Denmark, April 25–29, 1977." Geneva: Lutheran World Federation, Department of Studies, 1977.

"Preparatory Papers for the National Study Conference on Church and State, February 4–7, 1964, Aurora, Illinois." New York: National Council of Churches, Department of Religious Liberty, 1964.

"Private Organizations in Post-War Relief." Organizational memorandum for the American Council of Voluntary Agencies for the Foreign Service, December 30, 1942. In the Archive of the American Council, Rutgers University.

"Protection of Asylum Seekers in Western Countries." Report and Recommendations of the World Council of Churches Consultation, May 15–18, 1984, Niagara Falls, Ontario, Canada. New York: Church World Service, July 1984.

"Questions and Answers Concerning American Voluntary Agencies and Their Programs Overseas (for use in the IBM RAMAC Electronic Brain at the American National Exhibition in Moscow—presented at Executive Committee meeting May 15, 1959)." New York: American Council of Voluntary Agencies for Foreign Service, May 15, 1959.

"Refugees: A Global Concern." Geneva: World Council of Churches, Programme Unit on Justice & Service, Commission on Inter-Church Aid Refugee and World Service, June 1977.

Reisman, Roberta Fahn. "The Falashas." n.p., February 1982. In the Archive on Church and State Abroad, Carnegie Council on Ethics and International Affairs, New York.

"Report and Recommendations to the United Nations High Commissioner for Refugees

Regarding the Protection of Refugees and the Coordination of Material Assistance by the UNHCR in Honduras." Toronto: Interchurch Committee for Refugees, September 1982.

"Report of the Executive Secretary of Sudanaid [states view that Catholic Relief Services is too closely tied to U.S. Government]." Harare, Zimbabwe: Fourth Anglophone Africa CARITAS Zonal Meeting, September 19–25, 1982.

"Report of the National Study Conference on Church and State held at Columbus, Ohio, February 4–7, 1964." New York: National Council of Churches, Department of Religious Liberty, 1964.

"Report of the World Council of Churches Consultation on Refugee Resettlement, May 8–11, 1981." Geneva: World Council of Churches [1981].

"A Report on the Refugee Relief Program of World Vision in Honduras." Monrovia, Calif.: World Vision International, December 17, 1981. For a critical response to this report see also de Espinosa, Naomi [then director of CEDEN, Honduras] "A Response to 'A Report on the Refugee Relief Program. . .' " (February 22, 1982) in the Archive on Church and State Abroad, Carnegie Council on Ethics and International Affairs, New York.

"Report on Vietnamese Refugees and Displaced Persons." New York, American Council of Voluntary Agencies for Foreign Service, October, 1965.

"Report to the Board of Trustees, War Relief Services—N.C.W.C. [National Catholic Welfare Conference], New York: N.C.W.C., August 1, 1943—September 30, 1944. Also reports from periods October 1, 1944—September 30, 1945; October 1, 1945—September 30, 1946; October 1, 1946—September 30, 1947; and Annual Report, 1948.

"Revised Report of the Special Committee on NCC Use of Government Resources [internal directive establishing guidelines for NCC use of government resources]." New York: National Council of Churches, June 2, 1967.

Rose-Ackerman, Susan. "Do Government Grants to Charity Reduce Private Donations?" PONPO Working Paper 13. New Haven, Conn.: Program on Non-Profit Organizations, Institute for Social and Policy Studies, Yale University, March 1980.

Santa Fe, Committee of. "A New Inter-American Policy for the Eighties." Washington, D.C.: Council for Inter-American Security, 1980.

Scholz, Dieter B., S.J. "The Jesuit Refugee Service." Rome: Curia Praepositi Generalis, Societatis Iesu (Society of Jesus), n.d.

Seeking Safe Haven: A Congregational Guide to Helping Central American Refugees in the United States. Published jointly by American Friends Service Committee, Philadelphia; Church World Service, New York; Inter-Religious Task Force on El Salvador and Central America, New York; and Lutheran Immigration and Refugee Service, New York, 1983.

Sommer, John G. "U.S. Voluntary Aid to the Third World: What Is its Future?" Development Paper 20. Washington, D.C.: Overseas Development Council, December 1975.

Sparks, Donald T. "The Influence of Official Protestant Church Groups on the Formulation and Conduct of American Foreign Policy, 1940–1950." Ph.D. dissertation, University of Chicago, 1954.

"State of World Need in the '80s: Touching a Needy World in Jesus' Name." Wheaton, Ill.: World Relief Commission of the National Association of Evangelicals, n.d. [ca. 1981].

"Statement of the United States Catholic Conference on Central America." Washington, D.C.: U.S. Catholic Conference, November 19, 1981.

"Statement on Freedom of Conscience and Religion for Indochinese Refugees in Thailand." With cover letter from Ron Hill, Thailand Baptist Mission, addressed to the UNHCR, Bangkok, dated September 15, 1980. In the Archive on Church and State Abroad, Carnegie Council on Ethics and International Affairs, New York.

"A Statement on Immigration Policies: Undocumented Persons." Adopted at May 12–13,

1981 annual meeting of the Lutheran Council in the USA. New York: Lutheran Council in the USA. 1981.

"Study Document of Principles on the Issue of Undocumented Aliens." Released after November 1978 conferencce of the Lutheran Immigration and Refugee Service; adopted by LIRS standing committee September 1980. New York: Lutheran Immigration and Refugee Service, February 1981.

Sullivan, Robert Richard. "The Politics of Altruism: A Study of the Partnership between the United States Government and American Voluntary Relief Agencies for the Donations Abroad of Surplus Agricultural Commodities, 1949–1967." Ph.D. dissertation, Johns Hopkins University, 1968.

Taran, Patrick A. "Salvadoran Refugees: Haven Denied in the United States." New York: National Council of Churches, Division of Overseas Ministries, Immigration and Refugee Program, November 1981.

———, ed. "Summary Report: Witness to Immigration: NCCC Consultation on Immigrants, Refugees & Migrants." January 28–30, 1982, Washington, D.C. New York: National Council of the Churches of Christ in the U.S.A., Church World Service, Immigration and Refugee Program, June 1982.

Theological Reflections on Refugees. New York: Church World Service, n.d. [ca. 1981].

Toms, Robert L. "What Is a Church? The Dilemma of the Parachurch." Monograph 1, Center for Law & Religious Freedom. Oak Park, Ill.: Christian Legal Society, n.d.

TR-axis: A Newsletter on Taxation and Religion 1, 1 (July–August 1981). New York: National Conference of Christians and Jews.

Vishniak, Marc. *The Legal Status of Stateless Persons.* Pamphlet 6, Jews and the Post-War World Series. New York: American Jewish Committee, 1945.

Wiley, Thomas. "American Christianity, the Jewish State, and the Arab-Israeli Conflict." Occasional Paper Series. Washington, D.C.: Center for Contemporary Arab Studies, Georgetown University, 1983.

Selected Government and United Nations Publications

Agency for International Development (U.S. Department of State)

Advisory Committee on Voluntary Foreign Aid. *Here's How: Handbook for Use by U.S. Voluntary Agencies Registered with A.I.D.'s Advisory Committee on Voluntary Foreign Aid.* Washington, D.C.: Agency for International Development, February 1970.

Indigenous PVOs: Issues for AID Discussion. Washington, D.C.: Agency for International Development, Office of Private and Voluntary Cooperation, New TransCentury Foundation, March 1983.

"Religious Organizations and the United States Aid Program." AID Policy Determination no. 10, July 16, 1962.

Wilhelm, Marion. "Voluntary Foreign Aid: 25 Years of Partnership." In *War on Hunger.* Washington, D.C.: Agency for International Development, Office of Public Affairs, May 1971.

Bureau of Public Affairs (U.S. Department of State)

"Communist Interference in El Salvador." In *Special Report No. 80.* Washington, D.C.: Bureau of Public Affairs, Department of State, February 23, 1981.

Haig, Alexander M., Jr. "Chemical Warfare in Southeast Asia and Afghanistan." In *Special Report No. 98.* Washington, D.C.: Department of State, March 22, 1982.

Purcell, James N., Jr. "Refugees: Overseas Aid and Domestic Admissions." In *Current Policy No. 571.* Washington, D.C.: Department of State, Bureau of Public Affairs, March 30, 1984. Address given by James N. Purcell, Jr., Director of the Bureau for Refugee Programs, before the 7th annual National Legal Conference on Immigration and Refugee Policy, Center for Migration Studies, Washington, D.C., March 30, 1984.

Clark, William P. *Memorandum: Refugee Policy and Refugee Processing in Indochina.* National Security Decision, Directive no. 93. Washington, D.C.: White House, May 13, 1983.

Commerce Department, International Trade Administration. Case no. A 566924. Mennonite Central Committee application for shipment of school supplies to Kampuchea. August 4, 1981.

Commission on Security and Economic Assistance [The Carlucci Commission]. "A Report to the Secretary of State." Washington, D.C.: Commission on Security and Economic Assistance, November 1983.

Coordinator for Refugee Affairs (U.S. Department of State)

"An Edited Transcript of a Conference on Ethical Issues and Moral Principles in U.S. Refugee Policy." Washington, D.C.: Meridian House International, March 23–24, 1983.

"A Summary of the Conference on Ethical Issues and Moral Principles in U.S. Refugee Policy." Washington, D.C.: Meridian House International, March 23–24, 1983.

Federal Register

"Registration of Agencies for Voluntary Foreign Aid." 22, 209 (October 26, 1957).

"Registration of Agencies for Voluntary Foreign Aid." 28, 23 (March 16, 1963).

"Registration of Agencies for Voluntary Foreign Aid." 46, 235 (December 8, 1981).

"Registration of Agencies for Voluntary Foreign Aid." 48, 15 (January 21, 1983).

General Accounting Office

"Central American Refugees: Regional Conditions and Prospects and Potential Impact on the United States." GAO/NSIAD 84-106. Washington, D.C., July 20, 1984.

"Channelling Foreign Aid Through Private and Voluntary Organizations." GAO/ID 76-58. Washington, D.C., May 5, 1976.

"International Assistance to Refugees in Africa Can Be Improved." GAO/ID 83-2. Washington, D.C., December 29, 1982.

"Oversight of State Department's Refugee Reception and Placement Program." GAO/NSIAD 83-35. Washington, D.C., September 30, 1983.

"Private Sector Involvement In the Agency for International Development's Programs." GAO/ID 82-47. Washington, D.C., August 16, 1982.

"U.S. Exports Subject to National Security Controls." Letter Report GAO/NSIAD 84-137. Washington, D.C., June 15, 1984.

Inspector General. "Audit Report: Audit of Cooperative Agreement 1037-220019 between the Bureau for Refugee Programs and the Lutheran Immigration Refugee Service." Washington, D.C.: U.S. Inspector General, April 1983.

International Refugee Organization. *The Facts About Refugees.* Geneva: International Refugee Organization, 1948.

A Memo to America: The DP Story: The Final Report of the United States Displaced Persons Commission. Washington, D.C.: Government Printing Office, 1952.

Reagan, Ronald W. "Executive Order 1233, United States Intelligence Activities." Washington, D.C.: Office of the Press Secretary, December 4, 1981.

Select Commission on Immigration and Refugee Policy. *U.S. Immigration and the National Interest. Staff Report* [and nine appendix volumes]. Washington, D.C., April 30, 1981.

State Department

Brennan, Dennis and Christian Holmes. "Cambodian Border Relief." Bangkok: Embassy of the United States, December 7, 1979.

Bureau of Refugee Programs. "Migration and Refugee Assistance, Fiscal Year 1983." Washington, D.C., 1982.

Bureau of Refugee Programs. "Standard Provisions for Grant Agreements." Washington, D.C., March 1981.

Lange, John D., Jr. "Private Foreign Aid From Europe and North America, A Case Study." Seventeenth Session, Senior Seminar in Foreign Policy. Washington, D.C., April 30, 1975.

Marasciulo, Edward. "The Roman Catholic Church in Voluntary Foreign Aid." Seventeenth Session, Senior Seminar in Foreign Policy. Washington, D.C., 1974–75.

Treasury Department. Sommerfield, Stanley L. (Acting Director, Office of Foreign Assets Control, Department of the Treasury). Speech on Treasury regulations affecting trade with certain foreign countries (untitled). Washington, D.C.: U.S. Department of the Treasury, Office of Foreign Assets Control, April 25, 1974.

United Nations General Assembly. "Chemical and Bacteriological (Biological) Weapons: Report of the Secretary-General." A/37/259. New York: United Nations, December 1, 1982.

United Nations High Commissioner for Refugees
Collection of International Instruments Concerning Refugees. Geneva: 1979.
"Final Act of the United Nations Conference of Plenipotentiaries on the Status of Refugees and Stateless Persons and Text of the 1951 Convention Relating to the Status of Refugees (Convention and Protocol Relating to the Status of Refugees)." HCR/INF/29/Rev. 2. New York: United Nations, 1968.
Handbook for Emergencies. Geneva: December 1982.
Handbook on Procedures and Criteria for Determining Refugee Status. Geneva: September 1979.
Hasselman, Oldrich, and Catherine Bertrand. "Mission Report: Honduras (June 1983)." Geneva, June 30, 1983.
"Refugees, Victims of Xenophobia: A Roundtable Discussion Organized by the United Nations High Commissioner for Refugees." Geneva: United Nations High Commissioner for Refugees, 1984.
"United Nations Resolutions and Decisions Relating to the Office of the United Nations High Commissioner for Refugees." HCR/INF/48/Rev. 2. Geneva: United Nations High Commissioner for Refugees, October 1975.

U.S. Congress, Committees on the Judiciary of the House of Representatives and the Senate, "U.S. Immigration and the National Interest." 97th Cong., 1st Sess., August 1981.

U.S. Congress, House of Representatives, Committee on Foreign Affairs
"Domestic and Foreign Policy Implications of U.S. Immigration and Refugee Resettlement Policy." 97th Cong., October 5, 1981; March 16, 1982.
"Overseas Programs of Private Nonprofit American Organizations: Report No. 3 on Winning the Cold War: The U.S. Ideological Offensive." Subcommittee on International Organizations and Movements. 89th Cong., 1st Sess., May 25, 1965.

U.S. Congress, House of Representatives, Committee on the Judiciary, "Extension of Indochina Refugee Assistance Program." Subcommittee on Immigration, Citizenship and International Law. 95th Cong., 1st Sess., September 23 and 27, 1977.

U.S. Congress, Joint Hearings, Senate Subcommittee on Immigration and Refugee Policy and House Subcommittee on Immigration, Refugees and Internationaal Law, on the Final Report of the Select Commission on Immigration and Refugee Policy. 97th Cong., 1st Sess., May 5–7, 1981.

U.S. Congress, Senate, Committee on the Judiciary
"Hearings on Refugee Resettlement Issues." Subcommittee on Immigration and Refugees. 96th Cong., September 1979.
"Humanitarian Problems of Southeast Asia, 1977–78." 95th Cong., 2d Sess., March 1978.

"Immigration Emergency Powers." Subcommittee on Immigration and Refugee Policy. 97th Cong., 2nd Sess., September 30, 1982.

"Immigration Reform and Control." 98th Cong., 1st Sess., April 21, 1983.

U.S. Immigration Law and Policy: 1952–1979. Prepared by the Congressional Research Service, Library of Congress. 96th Cong., 1st Sess. Washington, D.C.: Government Printing Office, May 1979.

"Selected Readings on U.S. Immigration Policy and Law." 96th Cong., 2nd Sess., October 1980.

"World Refugee Crisis: The International Community's Response." 96th Cong., 1st Sess., August 1979.

U.S. Congress, Senate, Select Committee to Study Government Operations. "The Domestic Impact of Foreign Clandestine Operations: The CIA and Academic Institutions, the Media, and Religious Institutions." *Foreign and Military Intelligence, Book 1,* April 26, 1976.

Legal Cases

Abington Township School District v. *Schempp.* 374 U.S. 203 (1963).

Americans United for Separation of Church and State v. *Reagan.* 786 F.2nd 201 (3rd Circuit) (1986).

Bob Jones University v. *United States.* 461 U.S. 574 (1983).

Buckley v. *Valeo.* 424 U.S. 1 (1976).

Bradfield v. *Roberts.* 175 U.S. 291 (1899).

Cantwell v. *Connecticut.* 310 U.S. 296 (1940).

[Vaughn V.] Chapman [and Mildred E. Chapman] v. *IRS.* Docket No. 6024-65 (1967).

Cherokee Nation v. *State of Georgia.* 30 U.S. 1 (1831).

Christian Echoes National Ministry v. *United States.* 470 F.2nd 849 (1972).

Church of Jesus Christ of Latter Day Saints v. *United States.* 136 U.S. 1 (1890)

Cochran v. *Louisiana State Board of Education.* 281 U.S. 370 (1930).

Committee for Public Education & Religious Liberty v. *Nyquist.* 413 U.S. 756 (1973).

Dames and Moore v. *Regan.* 453 U.S. 654 (1981).

Davis v. *Beason.* 133 U.S. 333 (1890).

Engel v. *Vitale.* 370 U.S. 421 (1962).

Epperson v. *Arkansas.* 393 U.S. 97 (1968).

Everson v. *Board of Education.* 330 U.S. 1 (1947).

Flast et al. v. *Cohen.* 392 U.S. 83 (1968)

Fowler v. *Rhode Island.* 345 U.S. 67 (1953).

Haig v. *Agee.* 435 U.S. 278 (1981).

High Adventure Ministries, Inc. v. *Commissioner of Internal Revenue.* United States Tax Court. Docket No. 4585-82 "X" "Petition for Declaratory Judgment (Exempt Organization)." April 20, 1982.

High Adventure Ministries, Inc. v. *Commissioner of Internal Revenue.* On Appeal From the Decision of the United States Tax Court/Brief for Appellant. U.S. Court of Appeals, Ninth Circuit, No. 83-7245.

High Adventure Ministries, Inc. v. *Commissioner of Internal Revenue.* On Appeal From the Decision of the United States Tax Court/Brief for Appellee. U.S. Court of Appeals, Ninth Circuit, No. 83-7245.

Hunt v. *McNair.* 413 U.S. 734 (1973).

Illinois Election Board v. *Socialist Workers Party.* 440 U.S. 178 (1978).

INS v. *Stevic.* No. 82-973. June 5, 1984.

Johnson v. *Eisentrager* 339 U.S. 763 (1950).

Kent v. *Dulles.* 357 U.S. 116 (1958).
Kinsella v. *U.S. ex rel. Singleton.* 361 U.S. 234 (1960).
Larkin v. *Grendel's Den, Inc.* 103 S.Ct. 505 (1982).
Lemon v. *Kurtzman.* 403 U.S. 602 (1971).
Lynch v. *Donnelly.* 52 U.S.L.W. 4317 (1984).
Madsden v. *Kinsella.* 343 U.S. 341 (1952).
McCollum v. *Board of Education.* 333 U.S. 203 (1948).
McElroy v. *Guagliardo.* 361 U.S. 281 (1960).
Meek v. *Pittenger.* 421 U.S. 349 (1975).
Minersville School District v. *Gobitis.* 310 U.S. 586 (1940).
Mueller v. *Allen.* 103 S.Ct. 3062 (1983)
Murdock v. *Pennsylvania.* 319 U.S. 105 (1943).
New York Times v. *United States.* 403 U.S. 713 (1971).
O'Callahan v. *Parker* 395 U.S. 258 (1969).
Palko v. *Connecticut.* 302 U.S. 319 (1937).
[Reuben] Quick Bear v. *Leupp.* 210 U.S. 50 (1908).
[Temistocles] Ramirez [de Arellano et al.] v. *Weinberger et al.* (Court of Appeals for D.C., slip op. 83-1950, Civil Action no. 83-02002) (1984).
Regan, Secretary of the Treasury, et al. v. *Wald et al.* [*Regan* v. *Wald*]. No. 83-436. June 28, 1984.
Reid v. *Covert.* 354 U.S. 1 (1957).
Relford v. *Commandant* 401 U.S. 355 (1971).
Reynolds v. *United States.* 98 U.S. 145 (1878).
Roemer v. *Board of Public Works of Maryland.* 426 U.S. 736 (1976).
Thomas v. *Review Board of the Indiana Employment Security Division.* 49 L.W. 434. (1981)
Torcaso v. *Watkins.* 367 U.S. 495 (1961).
United States v. *Curtiss-Wright Export Corp.* 299 U.S. 301 (1936)
United States v. *Elder.* 579 F.2nd 516 (1978).
United States v. *Lee.* 255 U.S. 252 (1982).
United States v. *Pink.* 315 U.S. 203 (1942).
United States v. *Seeger.* 380 U.S. 163 (1965).
United States v. *Washington Post.* 446 F.2nd 1327 (1971).
Valley Forge Christian College v. *Americans United for Separation of Church and State.* 50 L.W. 4103 (1982).
Walz v. *Tax Commission of the City of New York.* 397 U.S. 664 (1970).
Welch v. *Kennedy.* 319 F.Supp. 945, D.D.C. (1970).
West Virginia State Board of Education v. *Barnett.* 319 U.S. 624 (1943).
Wilson v. *Girard.* 354 U.S. 524 (1957).
Wisconsin v. *Yoder.* 406 U.S. 205 (1972).
Wolman v. *Walter.* 45 L.W. 4861 (1977).
Worcester v. *State of Georgia.* 8 Pet. 515 (1832).
Zemel v. *Rusk.* 381 U.S. 1 (1965).
Zorach v. *Clausen.* 343 U.S. 306 (1952).

Archives

Research materials for this book, including many that do not appear in the bibliography, are currently housed at the Archive on Church and State Abroad at the Carnegie Council on Ethics and International Affairs, New York. The archives of many agencies are either not fully cataloged or not open to the public. In some instances, governmental and private agencies were responsive to requests for specific information. The following archives were fully accessible:

American Council of Voluntary Agencies for Foreign Service, Rutgers University, New Brunswick, New Jersey

American Friends Service Committee, Philadelphia, Pennsylvania

Church World Service, National Council of Churches of Christ, in the Presbyterian Historical Society, Philadelphia, Pennsylvania

Day Mission Library, Yale Divinity School, New Haven, Connecticut

Lutheran Archives, Lutheran Council in the U.S.A., New York, New York

National Archives, Washington, D.C.

Registration Files, Office of Private and Voluntary Cooperation, Agency for International Development, Roslyn, Virginia

Franklin D. Roosevelt Library, Hyde Park, New York

Index